SCARCE AND VALUABLE

ECONOMICAL TRACTS.

A

SELECT COLLECTION

OF

SCARCE AND VALUABLE

ECONOMICAL TRACTS,

FROM THE ORIGINALS OF

DEFOE, ELKING, FRANKLIN, TURGOT, ANDERSON, SCHOM-
BERG, TOWNSEND, BURKE, BELL, AND OTHERS.

WITH A PREFACE, NOTES, AND INDEX.

CL Reprints

CL Press | Fraser Institute

CL Press

Published by CL PRESS

A Project of the Fraser Institute

1770 Burrard Street, 4th Floor

Vancouver, BC V6J 3G7 Canada

www.clpress.net

A Select Collection of Scarce and

Valuable Economical Tracts

By J.R. McCulloch

A Select Collection of Scarce and Valuable Economical Tracts
was originally published in 1859 by Lord Overstone.

First printed: February 2024

Cover image: Cover illustration titled "Gutenberg's Press" by Dave Grey, licensed under a Creative Commons Attribution-NoDerivs 2.0 Generic license.

ISBN: 978-1-957698-11-3

Cover design by John Stephens

Foreword by CL Press, 2024

The present volume was edited by a man with a calling to expound and promote the teachings of political economy. John Ramsay McCulloch (1789–1864) understood the truths and conclusions of political economy to run along classical-liberal lines, in the tradition of Adam Smith. For more than 40 years McCulloch promoted use of the word *liberal* in its original political sense, which is to say its Smithian sense.

Part of McCulloch's calling was to recover the early developments of liberal political economy. He avidly collected books, especially on economic topics. His collection of 8,000 books was perhaps the best collection of the kind of his time.

McCulloch was again a proselytizer, laboring to republish the old literature he found "scarce and valuable." The present volume reprints one of six volumes compiled by McCulloch, volumes consisting of writings from the 17th, 18th, and early 19th centuries. McCulloch wanted people to know of such works, some going back more than 200 years before his own time, works that helped to develop political economy. Financial assistance from Lord Overstone helped McCulloch to edit and publish the six volumes:

1. **Early English Tracts on Commerce** (1856) –& CL Press 2024
2. *Scarce and Valuable Tracts on Money* (1856)
3. *Scarce and Valuable Tracts on Paper Currency and Banking* (1857)
4. *Scarce and Valuable Tracts on the National Debt and the Sinking Fund* (1857)
5. **Scarce and Valuable Tracts on Commerce** (1859) –& CL Press 2024
6. **Scarce and Valuable Economical Tracts** (1859) –& CL Press 2024

The bolded titles are now reprinted by CL Press.

All six of the volumes were republished in 1995 by the publisher Pickering & Chatto, titled *Classical Writings on Economics*, Volumes 1–6. The first volume contains a new general introduction by Denis Patrick O'Brien, who had earlier published *J. R. McCulloch: A Study in*

Classical Economics (1970). O'Brien also edited McCulloch's collected works and Overstone's correspondence.

O'Brien's 1995 general introduction helps with the authorship of the items. We now list the contents of three volumes newly reprinted by CL Press. In the following listing we modernize spellings and abridge the titles for the sake of conciseness:

Early English Tracts on Commerce (1856)

Contents:

1. A DISCOURSE OF TRADE (1621) by **Thomas Mun**
2. A DISCOURSE OF FOREIGN TRADE (1641) by **Lewes Roberts**
3. ENGLAND'S TREASURE BY FOREIGN TRADE (1664) by **Thomas Mun**
4. ENGLAND'S INTEREST AND IMPROVEMENT (1673) by **Samuel Fortrey**
5. ENGLAND'S GREATEST HAPPINESS; OR, A DIALOGUE BETWEEN *CONTENT* AND *COMPLAINT* (1677), *authorship unknown*
6. *BRITANNIA LANGUENS*, OR A DISCOURSE OF TRADE (1680) by *authorship unknown, possibly* **William Petty**
7. DISCOURSE UPON TRADE (1691) by **Dudley North** (the first part perhaps written by **Roger North**)
8. CONSIDERATIONS ON THE EAST-INDIA TRADE (1701), by (probably) **Henry Martyn**

Scarce and Valuable Tracts on Commerce (1859)

Contents:

1. OBSERVATIONS TOUCHING TRADE AND COMMERCE WITH OTHER NATIONS (*circa* 1610) perhaps by **Walter Raleigh**, perhaps by **John Keymore**
2. NAVIGATION AND COMMERCE, THEIR ORIGINAL AND PROGRESS (1674) by **John Evelyn**
3. EXTRACTS FROM A PLAN OF THE ENGLISH COMMERCE (1730) by **Daniel Defoe**

4. An Essay on the Causes of the Decline of the Foreign Trade (1744) perhaps by **Matthew Decker**, perhaps by a **Mr. Richardson**

5. Brief Essay on the Advantages and Disadvantages to France and Great Britain with Regard to Trade (1750) by **Josiah Tucker**
   —Appended: A Letter on the State of France in 1765 by **Tobias Smollett**

6. Proposals for Redressing and Amending the Trade of the Republic (1751) by **Prince William of Orange**

7. A Vindication of the Commerce and the Arts (1758) by **William Temple**

8. New and Old Principles of Trade Compared (1788) perhaps by **William Vaughan**

Scarce and Valuable Economical Tracts (1859)

Contents:

1. An Apology for the Builder (1685) by (probably) **Nicholas Barbon**

2. Giving Alms No Charity, and Employing the Poor a Grievance to the Nation (1704) by **Daniel Defoe**

3. A View of Greenland Trade and Whale-Fishery (1722) by **Henry Elking**

4. An Apology for the Business of Pawn-Broking (1744), *authorship unknown but perhaps* **Thomas Wise**

5. Extracts on Population, Commerce, Etc. (1751–74) by **Benjamin Franklin**

6. Reflections on the Formation and Distribution of Wealth (French 1767; English trans. 1793) by **Anne Robert Jacques Turgot**

7. Extract from an Inquiry into the Corn Laws (1777) by **James Anderson**

8. A Treatise on the Maritime Laws of Rhodes (1776) by **Alexander C. Schomberg**

9. A DISSERTATION ON THE POOR LAWS (1776) by Joseph Townsend
10. THOUGHTS AND DETAILS ON SCARCITY (written 1795, pub. 1800) by Edmund Burke
11. AN INQUIRY INTO THE PROHIBITION OF THE USE OF GRAIN IN THE DISTILLERIES (1808) by Archibald Bell

In her entry on McCulloch in the *Oxford Dictionary of National Biography*, Phyllis Deane wrote: "It is now apparent that for most of the half-century preceding his death [in 1864] this hard-working, largely self-educated Scot did more than any other economist of this day to introduce the new science of political economy to an interested public." The volumes now reprinted by CL Press show the enduring value of McCulloch's service to those interested in the history of economic thought and the historical arc of liberalism.

₊ This Volume, printed by LORD OVERSTONE for distribution among his friends, has been edited by J. R. MᶜCULLOCH, Esq.

[TWO HUNDRED COPIES PRINTED.]

With Lord Overstone's compliments

PREFACE.

THIS volume of miscellaneous Tracts, being the last of the series reprinted by Lord Overstone, contains the following articles; viz.

1. An Apology for the Builder; or a Discourse shewing the Cause and Effects of the Increase of Building. 1685.

2. Giving Alms no Charity, and Employing the Poor a Grievance to the Nation. Addressed to the Parliament of England. 1704.

3. A View of the Greenland Trade and Whale-Fishery, with the National and Private Advantages thereof. 1722.

4. An Apology for the Business of Pawn-Broking. By a Pawn-Broker. 1744.

5. Extracts from the Works of Dr. Franklin, on Population, Commerce, &c.

6. Reflections on the Formation and Distribution of Wealth. By M. Turgot. 1793.

7. Extract from an Inquiry into the Nature of the Corn Laws; with a View to the New Corn-Bill proposed for Scotland. 1777.

8. A Treatise on the Maritime Laws of Rhodes. By Alexander C. Schomberg, M.A. 1776.

9. A Dissertation on the Poor Laws. By a Well-Wisher to Mankind. 1776.

10. Thoughts and Details on Scarcity, presented to Mr. Pitt, in November, 1795. By the Right Hon. Edmund Burke. 1800.

11. An Inquiry into the Policy and Justice of the Prohibition of the Use of Grain in the Distilleries, &c. By Archibald Bell, Esq., Advocate. 1808.

1. The first of the above-mentioned tracts, the "Apology for the Builder," published in 1685, is a well-written and well-reasoned publication. The magnitude and increase of London early became subjects of complaint. The older inhabitants of the city regarded the new buildings with an evil eye, as tending, by increasing competition, to lower their profits and the value of their houses; the country gentlemen feared lest the drain for the town should depopulate the country, raise wages, and lower rents; and divines and moralists lamented that what they called the simplicity and virtues of a country life should be exchanged for the corruption and vices of the city. And hence in the reign of Elizabeth, and at other periods, various restraints were imposed on building in the latter. But it is almost needless to add, that these had but little effect; and the author of the pamphlet now laid before the reader shows that it was fortunate that such was the case. The country is not the Eden nor the town the Tartarus that writers unacquainted with the one and the other would have us to suppose. On the whole their virtues and their vices are pretty nearly balanced. And it is farther obvious that the existence of great towns, that is, of considerable portions of the

population congregated together, and practising the arts is necessary to national progress. Without them there would be no market for the surplus produce of the country; and its population, deprived of the advantages resulting from the division of labour, would be thinly dispersed over its surface, and immersed in poverty and barbarism. These results are very well exhibited in this tract.

The more " easy government of the people" is one of the beneficial consequences which its author ascribes to the growth of cities. But this is an erroneous inference, its influence being quite the other way. Men seldom entertain a just sense of their own importance, or acquire a knowledge of their rights, or are able to assert and vindicate them with courage and success, till they have been collected into towns. An agricultural population, scattered over an extensive country, and without any point of reunion, rarely opposes any very vigorous resistance to arbitrary and oppressive measures. But such is not the case with the inhabitants of towns; they are actuated by the same spirit, and derive courage from their numbers and union : the bold animate the timid ; the resolute confirm the wavering ; the redress of an injury done to one citizen becomes the business of all ; they take their measures in common, and prosecute them with a vigour and resolution that generally make the boldest minister pause in an unpopular career.* The most superficial as well as the

---

* For some further illustrations of this topic, see " Miller's Historical View of the English Government," iv., pp. 102—137.

most profound reader of history, must acknowledge the
truth of this statement.   The number and magnitude of
their towns, coupled with their trade and advantageous
situation, gave the people of the Low Countries courage
to undertake and means to carry on their long and desperate struggle with the Spanish monarchy when in the
zenith of its power—a struggle which, by securing the
independence of the Seven United Provinces, contributed
more, perhaps, than anything else to consolidate and promote the great principles of civil and religious liberty.

2. The tract entitled "Giving Alms no Charity,"
published in 1704, is one of the scarcest, as well as most
celebrated of the minor works of the author of Robinson
Crusoe.   It was written in opposition to a Bill introduced
into Parliament by Sir Humphrey Mackworth, to autho-
rize the levy of a parochial rate for the carrying
on of manufactures in workhouses, at which the inmates in these establishments were to be employed.
Though highly instrumental in stopping the progress of
the Bill, and often referred to, this tract, from its extreme
rarity, has been seen by few of the economists of this
century.   And this circumstance, and the attention that
is still given to the project, have procured for it a place
in this collection.

It would be easy to show that, except in very peculiar
cases, the adoption of Mackworth's, or of any similar
scheme, would unavoidably lead to mismanagement, job-
bing, and abuse.   But Defoe did not rest his opposition
to it on these grounds.   He attacked its principle, and
contended that it was founded on an entirely erroneous

theory. " For every skein of worsted the poor children in a workhouse spin, there must (said he) be a skein the less spun by some poor family or person that spun it before." And hence he concluded that, by adopting the scheme, Parliament would merely change the seats of employment and pauperism ; taking, as he expresses it, " the bread out of the mouths of the poor of one part of the country, to put it into the mouths of the poor of another part."

But though plausible, and stated with much ingenuity, these arguments are not so conclusive as many have supposed. The occupiers of workhouses and prisons have to be supported, whether they are employed or kept in idleness. And such being the case, and supposing it were practicable to employ them so that the produce of their labour should sell for more than the cost of the material on which it is exerted, would it be prudent to refuse to avail ourselves of their services? Whatever they produce while in confinement is so much added to the public wealth, and the sums required for their support may be in so far reduced. It is no good reason for refusing to profit by their labour to allege, with Defoe, that so much less labour must be performed elsewhere. The fact is quite otherwise. Labour is not a constant quantity. On the contrary, the demand for its produce and, therefore, for itself is altogether illimitable. Occasionally there may be an excess of one or of a few things ; but it is impossible, seeing the endless cravings of the human mind, that there should ever be a surplus of the various products of art and industry; or that if workpeople be thrown out of one business or employment, there should not be an equivalent demand for them in others.

Nec Crœsi fortuna unquam nec Persica regna
Sufficient animo——

Defoe has repeated the identical sophism which is always in the mouths of those who are opposed to every improvement. It might have been, and no doubt was, objected to Arkwright's inventions, that for every skein of yarn spun by a spinning-frame a skein the less would be spun by the common hand-wheel. And if that had been held to be a reason why the former should not be introduced, the cotton manufacture, which supplies from 1,250,000 to 1,500,000 persons in the United Kingdom with subsistence and the means of rising to distinction, would never have had any footing amongst us.

But it is needless to insist upon what is now so generally admitted and so very obvious. In matters of this sort the author of Robinson Crusoe was quite as prejudiced and purblind as the mass of those around him. He had not read, or if he had read, he at all events had not profited by the reasonings by which Sir Dudley North and the author of the tract on the East India Trade,* have conclusively shewn the advantage of new and cheaper markets and of new and improved methods of production.

But notwithstanding he erred in objecting to the principle of Mackworth's project, and not to the abuses inseparable from every attempt to carry it into practice, Defoe's tract is extremely valuable. His observations on the condition of the poor and the causes of poverty, and

* In the volume of Early English Tracts on Commerce, reprinted in 1856 for the Political Economy Club.

on the proper methods of bestowing charity, are alike able and discriminating. They evince sound good sense, free from all affectation of sentiment or philanthropy; and are but little less applicable at present than at the period when they were written.

3. The "View of the Greenland Trade and Whale-Fishery," is valuable from its being the only original work in the language, on the subject of which it treats.* At present, indeed, the interest that formerly attached to the whale fishery, has greatly declined. But, for a lengthened period it was considered of first rate importance; and was fostered and promoted by the aid of high bounties and other encouragements. Hence it is not a little surprising, that with the exception of this solitary and little known tract, we have no separate work on its rise and progress. It was prosecuted by the Dutch with greater vigour and success than by any other people; and at page 83, the reader will find an account of the number of ships sent from Holland to the fishery, from 1675 to 1721, with the number of whales caught, and their produce in oil. The scarcity of fish, which have been all but exterminated in some seas where they were formerly found in the greatest abundance, has been the main cause of the decline of the fishery.

4. The fourth article in this volume, the "Apology for Pawn-Broking," published in 1744, is an able, and, in

* Preface to Scoresby's Account of the Arctic Regions.

most respects, a conclusive tract. We have elsewhere observed, in regard to this subject, that the practice of pledging or pawning goods, in order to raise loans, always exists in civilised societies, and is, on the whole, productive of considerable advantage. But it may, at the same time, be easily perverted and abused. By far the largest portion of the bonâ fide borrowers of money on pawn, consist of the lowest and most indigent classes; and were the lenders not subjected to efficient regulations, they might take advantage of the necessities of the borrowers, (as, indeed, is frequently done, despite every precaution), to inflict on them the most grievous extortion. And, besides those whose wants compel them to have recourse to pawnbrokers, they are resorted to by others who wish to get rid of the property they have unlawfully acquired. Not only, therefore, are they instrumental in relieving the necessities of the poor, but they may also without either intending or even knowing it, become the most efficient allies of thieves and swindlers, by affording them safe and convenient outlets for the disposal of their ill gotten gains. Hence the policy of giving legislative protection to a business so liable to abuse, has been doubted by many. But though it were suppressed by law, it would always really exist. An individual possessed of property, which he may neither be able nor willing to dispose of, may be reduced to the greatest difficulties; and in such case, what can be more convenient or advantageous for him than to get a loan upon a deposit of such property, under condition that if he repay the loan, and the interest upon it, within a certain period, the property will be returned? It is said, indeed, that the facilities of raising money in this way foster habits of imprudence; that the first resort for aid to a pawnbroker almost always leads to a second; and that it is impossible so to regulate the business as to prevent the ignorant and the necessitous from being plundered. That this statement, though exaggerated, is in some degree true, none can deny. On the other hand, however, the capacity of obtaining supplies on the deposit of goods, by affording the means of meeting pressing exigencies, tends to prevent crime, and to promote the security of property; and it would seem as if the desire to redeem property in pawn would be a powerful motive to industry and economy. It is further, too, to be borne in mind, that it is not possible, do what you will, to prevent those who are poor and uninstructed from borrowing; and that they will in all cases obtain loans at a great sacrifice, and be liable to be imposed upon. But the fair presumption is, that there is less chance of improper advantages being taken of them by licensed pawnbrokers, than by private and irresponsible individuals. Although, however, the business had all the inconveniences, without any portion whatever of the good which really belongs to it, it would be to no purpose to attempt its suppression. Those who have property will not submit to the extremity of want, without endeavouring, at all hazards, to raise money upon it. Any attempt to put down pawnbroking would merely drive respectable persons from the trade, and throw it entirely into the hands of those who have neither property nor character to lose. And hence the object of the legislature should not be to abolish what must always exist, but to endeavour, in as far as possible, to free it from abuse, by enacting such regulations as may appear to be best calculated to protect the ignorant and the unwary from becoming the prey of swindlers, and to facilitate the discovery of stolen property. And this is the view of the subject taken in the tract now reprinted.*

5. It is needless to draw the reader's attention to the "Extracts from the works of Dr. Franklin, on Population, Commerce, &c." They are characterised by all his sagacity and good sense, expressed in his plain, perspicuous style. Many of his views display great ingenuity; and he skilfully developes some of the leading principles of commercial freedom. The bringing together of those scattered portions of his works, and giving them a place in this volume, have, no doubt, considerably increased its value.

6. We have reprinted the "Reflections on the Formation and Distribution of Wealth," of the justly celebrated, M. Turgot, partly because the work is little known in this country, but principally because it gives within a short compass a well-condensed epitome of the theory of the Economists. This tract was originally published in 1767, nine years before the publication of the Wealth of Nations. But there do not seem to be any good grounds for regarding it, as some have done, as the "germ" of the latter. In addition to it, Smith had before him the lucubrations of Quesnay,

---

* "Commercial Dictionary," Art. Pawn-Brokers.

the founder of the theory, with those of Dupont, the elder Mirabeau, the Abbé Baudeau, Letrosne, and other zealous apostles of the new doctrines. And Smith has himself stated that he was in the habit of teaching in Glasgow so early as 1753 those liberal and enlarged views with respect to the intercourse between nations that form so important a part of the Wealth of Nations. But though they did not originate his views, the writings of Turgot and other leading Economists undoubtedly gave a decided bias to the reasonings of Smith. He stoutly resisted their conclusions in regard to the unproductiveness of manufactures and commerce ; but, in compliance with their theory, he so far swerved from the sound principles of his own system, as to admit that there are other tests than the rate of profit which they respectively yield by which to estimate the productiveness of the various branches of industry. Hence we doubt whether Smith was really indebted for much that was valuable to the Economists. He did not profit to so great an extent as he might have done by the precision of their definitions, and the scientific manner in which they usually conducted their investigations. And his masterly exposition of the advantages of industrial freedom, and of the injurious operation of the protective system, owes nothing to their labours. Nevertheless, their system is both liberal and ingenious. And despite the fundamental errors which it involves, Smith was justified in saying that when it appeared "it was the nearest approximation to the truth that had been published upon the subject of Political Economy." (Wealth of Nations, p. 307).

Besides the tract on the Formation of Wealth,

Turgot published a number of memoirs, letters, and pamphlets, mostly on subjects connected with public economy. He was not, however, a mere theorist. On the contrary he was engaged for a considerable period in the public service; and his experience and the observations which he made in conducting the affairs intrusted to his superintendence, furnished the materials for some of his most valuable publications. In 1761 he became Intendant of Limoges, a situation in which he distinguished himself by his efforts to improve the provincial administration, by providing, in as far as practicable, for the more equal assessment of the taxes, commuting or abolishing the charge of compulsory labour (*corvées*) on account of the high roads, and so forth. After being for a short while Minister of Marine, he was finally chosen in 1774, by Louis XVI, to fill the important place of Comptroller-General of Finance. Much was expected of him in this position, and these expectations were not disappointed. He established the freedom of the internal corn trade throughout the kingdom; abolished the system of compulsory labour; and began to introduce sundry reforms of a searching and efficient character into the various departments connected with the assessment, collection and disposal of the public revenue. But these measures, though indispensable, gave rise to a vast deal of opposition; and the outcry against them raised by the nobility, clergy, and others, who profited, or supposed that they profited, by the abuses which Turgot had determined to suppress, was so very violent that it speedily drove him from power. It is but fair to Louis XVI, to state that he approved generally of the proceedings of his minister; and had he possessed sufficient firmness and decision of character to give him an effectual support, it is possible that such improvements would have been effected in the administration as might have gone far to avert the Revo-lution. But Louis was totally unequal to the crisis. And the dismissal of Turgot having put an end to all hopes of anything like an adequate reform being brought about by constitutional means, nothing was left to obstruct, or turn aside, the tremendous catastrophe which soon after precipitated the throne, the aristocracy, the clergy, and the entire system of government, into the abyss of ruin.

7. The publication, in 1777, of the " Inquiry into the Nature of the Corn Laws," marks an interesting æra in the history of Economical Science. This will be evident when we mention that the extract from it given in this volume embodies the earliest explanation that is any-where to be met with of the real nature and origin of rent—a discovery of which it would be difficult to exag-gerate the importance. And it is to be observed that its author (Dr. Anderson) did not stumble upon it as it were by chance, and without being aware of its value. On the contrary, nothing can be more complete and satis-factory than his analysis of the circumstances in which rent originates, and which occasion its increase and dimi-nution; and he did not fail to recur to the subject in subsequent publications. But despite their being essential to a right understanding of the principles of political economy, and of the constitution of society, Anderson's profound and original speculations do not appear to have attracted any attention from his contemporaries. Though published nearly at the same time as the Wealth of Nations, Smith, to whom they might have been of in-

finite service, did not profit by them in revising any subsequent edition of his great work. And so completely were they forgotten, that when, in 1815, Malthus and Sir Edward West published their tracts exhibiting the nature and progress of rent, they were universally believed to be the original discoverers of the laws by which it is governed. And perhaps their originality cannot be justly impeached. But whether this be so or not, those who read the extract in this volume will be satisfied that the true theory of rent had been quite as well and satisfactorily explained by Anderson in 1777, as it was by them in 1815.*

8. The Treatise of Schomberg on the "Maritime Laws of Rhodes" is both interesting and learned. Antiquity is unanimous in commending the wisdom of the Rhodian laws with respect to navigation. Previously to their promulgation, this important subject appears either to have been neglected, or at best regulated only by the ill-digested, and often conflicting municipal ordinances of different states. The regulations of the Rhodians with respect to average contributions, and other difficult nautical questions, were so much esteemed, that

---

* Anderson was a native of Hermandston, in Mid-Lothian, where he first saw the light in 1740. Having been long engaged in the business of farming in the neighbourhood of Aberdeen, the University of that city conferred on him, in 1780, the honorary degree of LL.D. Anderson left Aberdeenshire in 1783, and resided for some time in the vicinity of Edinburgh, where he projected and edited the "Bee," a weekly publication. In 1797 he removed to London, and there he edited "Recreations in Agriculture, Natural History, Arts, &c." In vol. v., pp. 401—405, he gave a new and lucid exposition of the theory of rent. He died in 1808.

they were adopted into the legislation of Rome. And having thence been transferred into the statute-books of this and other commercial countries, they continue, even at present, to be of the highest authority.*

We may further, perhaps, be allowed to mention, that the reputation of Rhodes as a learned and polished city, was nowise inferior to her celebrity as a first-rate emporium. Towards the termination of the republic, and during the early ages of the empire, the noble and aspiring youth of Rome resorted in great numbers to her hospitable shores to study science and philosophy. In this respect, indeed, she was preferred by many even to Athens. Among others, Cicero and Pompey studied at Rhodes. Julius Cæsar was taken by pirates when on his way thither; and Tiberius resided on the island for about seven years. The tract now reprinted, illustrates these and other circumstances, and may, therefore, be expected to attract the reader's attention.

9. The next tract in this volume, "The Dissertation on the Poor Laws," published in 1786, is the work of the Rev. Mr. Townsend, author of the "Travels in Spain."† It is extremely well-written. And though we dissent entirely from his views in regard to the impolicy of a public provision for the support of the poor, it must be admitted that he has set some of the principal objections to such provision in the clearest light, and has, also, exposed many of the abuses with which the administra-

---

* For proofs of this statement see "Schomberg's Tract *passim*."

† A work of the highest order of merit, and the best that had been published on the interesting country of which it treats, previously to its invasion by the French.

tion of the poor laws was formerly infected. But the
tract is chiefly remarkable for its elucidation of the theory
of population. The statements given in it, in reference
to the island of Juan Fernandez, afford as perfect an
illustration as can well be imagined of the balance between
population and food, and of their influence on each other.
They are not so much a foreshadowing of Malthus' theory,
as the theory itself. And only required to have been
presented in a more detailed and systematic manner to
have anticipated the Essay on Population.

10. We come next to the "Thoughts and Details on
Scarcity," of the Right Hon. Edmund Burke. It appears from the preface to this tract, that it had been
presented in manuscript to Mr. Pitt in 1795, shortly
before the death of its illustrious author, but it was not
printed till 1800. And nothing could be more oppor-
tune than its appearance at a period when the country
was afflicted by scarcity. Mr. Burke protests, with his
usual ability and energy, and with even more than his usual
eloquence, against all attempts to interfere at such a crisis,
with the prices of corn, or the wages of labour; and he
shows that though the pressure of scarcities may be
alleviated, it is not possible by any scheme of charity, to
exempt the labouring classes from the privations, calami-
ties, and sufferings inseparable from such visitations. His
observations on the shutting up of the distilleries, and on
the consumption of ardent spirits, are highly deserving of
attention, especially at the present moment, when so much
crude sophistry is afloat upon the subject. His exposure of
the worthlessness of the project, which had been repeatedly
brought forward, for warehousing corn in plentiful years

at the public expense to serve as a resource in years of scarcity is, also, most satisfactory. It were idle, indeed, to imagine that such a scheme, even if it were approved of, could be established on such a scale as to be of any practical importance in making good the deficiency of a really bad harvest. But on whatever scale it might be tried, the abuse and waste it would inevitably occasion would be so great, and so obvious, that it hardly required the splendid eloquence of Burke to make the scheme be rejected by the Parliament and the public.

Being printed in the various editions of Burke's works, the appearance of this tract in this place may, perhaps, be considered superfluous. But its extraordinary merit is more than enough to justify its republication. It is certainly one of the best pamphlets of its class in the language, if it be not the very best. And the possessors of this volume will be glad to have so brilliant a gem, detached from the mass of other matter in which it is usually buried.

11. The last tract in this collection, " An Inquiry into the Policy and Justice of the Prohibition of the use of Grain in the Distilleries," appeared in 1808, from the pen of Archibald Bell, Esq., Sheriff of Ayr. It owed its origin to the measure that was then under discussion, for preventing distillation from corn; the impolicy of which had already been denounced by Burke, and is here fully established. It may be supposed, perhaps, that there is but little risk of any such prohibition being enacted in future. This, however, is by no means clear. And though it were, the tract is to be understood in a wider sense, or as being an able and energetic protest against

those ill-advised and quackish measures, by which it is attempted to stave off some immediate evil, or to gain some temporary advantage by trenching on those great principles, all tampering with which is sure to be productive of ruinous results.

This terminates the collection of Tracts, reprinted by Lord Overstone. It will, perhaps, be generally admitted, that the volumes are both interesting and valuable. But the defects of the collection, whatever they may be, are entirely to be set down to the account of the Editor, and not of the Noble Lord who has defrayed the expense of the publication. He made no stipulations of any kind. I ventured to suggest to his Lordship that the reprinting of a selection of the rarest and best tracts connected with our trade, finance, paper currency, &c., would be desirable; and having approved of the suggestion, he left me to carry it out as I thought best. But for this munificence on the part of my noble friend, not one of these volumes would have appeared. And though a better collection may be easily imagined, yet, such as it is, it will hardly be disputed that it will assist in preserving some valuable and little known works; and that it makes a desirable addition to the historical and political literature of the empire.

J. R. M.

London, December 1859.

CONTENTS.

AN

APOLOGY

FOR THE

BUILDER:

OR A

DISCOURSE

SHEWING THE

CAUSE AND EFFECTS

OF THE

INCREASE

OF

Building.

LONDON, Printed for *Cave Pullen*, at the *Angel* in St. *Pauls*-Church-yard, 1685.

AN
APOLOGY
BUILDER.

TO write of architecture and its several parts, of *situation*, *platforms* of building, and the quality of *materials*, with their *dimensions* and *ornaments* : To discourse of the several orders of columns, of the *Tuscan*, *Dorick*, *Ionick*, *Corinthian*, and *Composit*, with the proper inrichments of their capitals, *Freeze* and *Cornish*, were to transcribe a folio from *Vitruvius* and others; and but mispend the readers and writers time, since we live in an age and country, where all the arts belonging to architecture are so well known and practised : And yet at the same *time* and *place* to write an apology for the artist may seem a greater trifling. In a time when since the *Grecian* greatness their arts were never better performed. In a place where buildings are generally so well finish'd, that almost every house is a little book of architecture; and as the ancient artists made *Athens* and the rest of their cities famous by their buildings, and still preserve the memory of the places by the ruins of their excellent arts : So the artists of this age have already made the city of *London* the metropolis of *Europe*, and if it be compared for the number of good houses, for its many and

3   large

large piazzas, for its richness of inhabitants, it must be allowed the largest, best built, and richest city in the world. But such is the misfortune of greatness to be envied. The citizens, nay the whole nation is astonished at the flourishing condition of this metropolis, to see every year a new town added to the old one; and like men affrighted are troubled with misapprehensions, and easily imposed on by the false suggestions of those that envy her grandeur, and are angry with the builders for making her so great.

The citizens are afraid that the building of new houses will lessen the rent and trade of the old ones, and fancy the inhabitants will remove on a sudden like rats that they say run away from old houses before they tumble.

The country gentleman is troubled at the new buildings for fear they should draw away their inhabitants, and depopulate the country, and they want tenants for their land. And both agree that the increase of building is prejudicial to the government, and use for argument a *simile* from those that have the rickets, fansying the city to be the head of the nation; and that it will grow too big for the body.

This is the charge that is laid on the builders: Therefore the design of this discourse is to answer these aspersions, to remove these fears and false conceptions, by confuting these popular errors, and shewing that the builder ought to be encouraged in all nations as the chief promoter of their welfare.

This is done by shewing the *cause* of the increase of building, and the *effects;* as they relate to the *city*, to the *country*, and to the *government*.

Of the Cause.

THE cause of the increase of building is from the *natural increase of mankind*, that there are more born than die. From the first blessing of the creation, *increase and multiply*, joined to the good government of a gracious king.

There are three things that man by nature is under a necessity to take care of, to provide *food* for himself, *clothes* and a *house*. For the *first*; all the rest of creation as well as man is under that necessity to take care of: For life cannot be maintained without *food*.

The *second* belongs only to man, and it is a question by some, whether it is required of him by nature, or custom, because in some countries (and those cold) men go naked.

But as to the *last*, it is most certain, that man is forced to build by nature, as all those creatures are, whose young are born so weak (like the offspring of mankind), that they require some time for strength after their birth, to follow their parents, or feed themselves. Thus the rabbit, the fox and lion make themselves burrows, kennels, and dens to bring forth, and shelter their young, but the mare, cow, sheep, &c. bring forth in the open field, because their young are able to follow them as soon as folded.

So that the natural cause of building a house is to provide a shelter for their young; and if we examine man in his natural condition without arts, his tenement differs little from the rest of nature's herd: The fox's kennel though not so large, being a lesser creature, may yet for its contrivance in its several apartments be compared with any of his cottages: Earthen walls, and covering are the manner of both their buildings, and the furniture of both their houses alike: Now as the rabbits increase, new bur-

rows

rows are made, and the boundaries of the warren are enlarged. So it is with man, as he increaseth, new houses are built, and his town made bigger.

When mankind is civilized, instructed with arts, and under good government, every man doth not dress his own *meat*, make his own *clothes*, nor *build his own house.* He enjoys property of land and goods, which he or his ancestors by their arts and industry gained. These possessions make the difference among men of rich and poor. The rich are fed, clothed, and housed by the labour of other men, but the poor by their own, and the goods made by this labour are the rents of the rich mens land (for to be well fed, well clothed, and well lodged, without labour either of body or mind, is the true definition of a rich man).

Now as men differ in estates, so they differ in their manner of living. The rich have variety of dishes, several suits of clothes, and larger houses: and as their riches increase, so doth their wants, as Sir *William Temple* hath observed, men are better distinguished by what they want, than by what they injoy. And the chief business of trade is the making and selling all sorts of commodities to supply their occasions. For there are more hands imployed to provide things necessary to make up the several distinctions of men; things that promote the ease, pleasure and pomp of life, than to supply the first natural necessities from hunger, cold, and a house only to shelter their young. Now the trader takes care from time to time to provide a sufficient quantity of all sorts of goods for mans occasions, which he finds out by the market: That is, by the quick selling of the commodities, that are made ready to be sold. And as there are butchers, brewers and cooks, drapers, mercers and taylors, and a hundred more, that furnish him with food and clothes; so there are bricklayers, carpenters, playsterers, and many more traders, that build houses for him, and they make

6

houses

houses of the first, second, and third rate of building in proportion to the increase of the several degrees of men, which they find out by the market, that is by letting of houses already built: so that if it were thoroughly believed, that mankind doth naturally increase; this miracle of the great increase of houses would cease, it is therefore necessary to shew that man doth naturally increase.

This may be sufficiently proved by Sacred History, that the world was first peopled by the increase from *Adam* and *Eve*, and after the Deluge repeopled by *Noah* and his sons *Shem, Ham,* and *Japhet.* That the *Jews* began from the single stock of *Abraham* by *Isaac*, and so from *Jacob ;* and when *Moses* numbered them, which was not long distance of time (being computed to be about two hundred and sixty years from *Jacob*) they were above six hundred thousand fighting men, reckoning only from twenty years old and upward, besides women and children. And when numbered by *David,* which was about four hundred and fifty years after, they were grown a very great nation, being thirteen hundred thousand fighting men of *Judah* and *Israel.*

But the late Lord Chief Justice *Hale* in his Discourse on this subject was not contented to relye wholly on arguments from authority of Holy Writ, and therefore takes other topicks to confirm the relation of *Moses* concerning the beginning of the world, and the peopling of it by a natural increase.

I. *From the novity of History,* That no authentick history is older than four thousand years, and none so old as *Moses* of the beginning of the world.

II. *From the Chronological Account of Times.* That the *Assyrian, Egyptian,* and *Grecian* accounts are to be found out in what year of the world they began.

III. *From the beginning of the ancient Kingdoms,* That

Rome

Rome was built by *Romulus* in the seventh *Olympiad*, the *Assyrian* monarchy began by *Cyrus* in 55 *Olympiad*, and the *Grecian* by *Alexander* in 111.

IV. *From the first invention of Arts,* That the times of the first invention of husbandry and making of wine are as well known, as the later inventions of gun-powder and printing.

V. *From the beginning of Religions,* That the time of the inauguration of the heathen deities are known; as when that *Jupiter, Bacchus, Ceres* and *Æsculapius,* and the rest of them were but men of great renown, and for their *good deeds* after their death worshipped; as well as when *Moses,* our *Saviour,* and *Mahomet* were born.

VI. *From the decays of Humane Nature;* but how far that may be true, I leave to further inquiry.

VII. *From the beginning of the Patres familias,* or the first planters of the continents and islands of the world; that *Helen* gave denomination to the *Grecians* called *Hellenista, Pelasigus* to the *Pelasgi, Latinus* to the *Latins,* and the place called *Latium, Italus* to the *Italians,* and *Italy* is as much to be believed, as that the *English* gave name to *New England* in *America,* and the names of the towns there, *London* and *New York.*

VIII. *From the gradual increase of Mankind;* That considering the time of his first procreation, which is agreed to be about 15 or 16 years, to the time he gives over, which is about sixty: It cannot be otherwise believed but that in the space of five and forty years he must produce a numerous off-spring: And it is no wonder amongst us; for a person to live to see some hundreds descended from his loyns.

Afterwards

Afterwards he comes to a particular observation of the increase of *England* by comparing the present state of it with the survey set down in the Doomsday-Book, and makes an instance in *Gloucester-Shire*, by which it appeareth, that the inhabitants of that county since that time are greatly increased. And last of all he argueth the increase of *London* from the *Bills of Mortality*.

These are the arguments of the late Lord Chief Justice *Hale*, to prove that mankind naturally increaseth, of which he discourseth at large in his book of the *Origination of Mankind*, and therein answereth all the objections to the contrary. And because these two last arguments from the survey of the *Doomsday-Book*, and *Bills of Mortality* carry with them the greatest force, for they best discover the matter of fact as to our own nation. I have therefore made it my business to make a scrutiny into the truth of them: As to the *first*, it is easie to make it appear that there are thirty times more people in *England* than there were in *William* the Conqueror's time, when the survey was taken. And as to the *latter*, I shall have occasion to discourse of at large hereafter.

And if it were necessary to use any further arguments for the proof this matter, they would plainly appear by comparing ancient histories with modern in the descriptions they give of the countries. As to the *great woods*, the many *little governments*, and the *manner of the peoples living without arts*: But not to wander over many countries, and among several historians I will only take the short description that *Cæsar* giveth of our own, to shew how it differs from what it now is.

He says, " That the inner part of *Britain* is in-
" habited by such as memory recordeth to be born in the
" island : And the maritime coast by such as came out
" of *Belgia*, either to make incursions or invasions, and
" after the war was ended they continued in the posses-
" sions they had gained, and were called by the name of

the

" the cities from whence they came." "It is true," he saith,
" The country is very populous and well inhabited, with
" houses like unto them in *Gallia:*" But that must be
understood as other countries of *Europe* were then. It
appears that in *England* there were many governments
and little colonies of people, " for he reckons four kings
" in the county of *Kent,* besides some little states." And
he says, "Most of the inland people sow no corn, but
" live on milk and flesh, clothed with skins, and having
" their faces painted with a blew color to the end they
" might seem more terrible in fight. The *Britans* towns,"
he says, " are places ditched about to make a shelter for
" themselves and cattel. And their manner of fighting
" was by making sudden excursions out of the woods,
" and then retiring into them for shelter." All which
descriptions shew the country was not so populous as
now.

For where there are great *woods,* there is not room
for pasture or corn, to feed mankind: Besides they are
a shelter for beasts of prey, which man as he increaseth
doth every where destroy, and suffers no flesh-eaters to
live but himself, except the dog and cat, which he
maketh tame for his use. The lion, wolf, and the bear
are not to be found in a populous country; and it is the
first business of all the planters in *America* to destroy
the wild beasts, and the woods, to make room for themselves to plant in.

And the reason probably of those *Roman* causeways,
that we find in *England,* was to make roads through
great woods to the several *Roman* colonies; though at
this time we find them in open champaign countries; for
had the country been so then, they would certainly have
made them straiter than we now find them.

The many *little governments* shew the infancy of a
country, for from single families government first began;
those governments were but so many families of great

men:

men: Now the large boundaries that so many *little Governments* take up in a country, make one half of the country useless: For men are afraid to plant or sow too near their enemies country for fear they should lose their harvest. Therefore the same land cannot feed so many people as when it is under but one government.

Besides *without arts, a great number of people cannot live together;* the earth by the arts of husbandry produceth ten times more food than it can naturally. And neither can there be any great cities, for the inhabitants have nothing to exchange for their food, for it is the arts of the city which are paid for the provisions of the country.

To conclude, nothing is so plain from ancient history as that *Asia* was first peopled, and (according to the description of *Moses*) began about *Babylon*: And as mankind increased, and the country filled with inhabitants; arts were invented, and they possest more ground, till they spread themselves into *Egypt*, and so over *Africa*, and from thence into *Greece*, over *Europe*, and now *Europe* being full, their swarm begins to fill *America*.

And all the ancient descriptions of the countries of *Europe*, in the times of the *Roman* greatness, are just such as are now given of *America*, and differ vastly from what they are now, in the number of cities, towns, and arts of inhabitants.

For were *America* so well peopled as *Europe* is, those great countries that are possest there by the *Spaniards*, *French*, *Dutch* and *English*, some of them bigger than their own countries in *Europe*, could not be so quietly held, and injoyed by not a hundredth part of the people of their own country.

And although the valor of the *Roman* soldiers, and their affected bravery (grown as it were a fashion, and a popular emulation) conduced much to the greatness of the *Roman* empire; yet nothing promoted its success so much, and gave it such large extent as the infancy of *Eu-*

rope

rope at that time, being thinly inhabited *with people, without arts,* and full of *little monarchies and states.* For had it not been so, *Cæsar* could never have over-run *Gallia, Belgia, Britain,* and some part of *Germany,* and kept them in subjection with only ten legions of soldiers, which was but fifty thousand men; for we have seen within these late years much greater armies in *Belgia* alone, (that is within the Seventeen Provinces,) and amongst them men not inferior either in courage or skill in war, and yet have not wholly subdued one province. And perhaps had these forces at the same time been sent into *America,* they might have extended their conquest over as much ground and over as many people as *Cæsar* did.

Nor was *England* so populous then as now it is; for had it been, *Cæsar* would never at first have ventured to invade it with two legions; and at the second time when he designed a full conquest brought over with him but five legions, that is but five and twenty thousand men.

For although some may think from the great armies we read of; neer two millions of men under *Cyrus* and *Xerxes* in *Asia;* and of vast swarms of the *Goths* and *Vandals* in *Europe,* in their invasions under King *Attila* and others, that the world was more populous than now, because we hear of no such numbers of late; yet if it be considered, it demonstrates only the *manner of their fighting,* and the *infancy of the world;* the *want of people,* and *arts,* rather than *that it was populous.*

For the Gentiles armies were made up after the manner of the *Jews,* by taking all that were able to bear armes, reckoning from about 20 years old to sixty. For when *Cæsar* had slain the army of the *Nervii,* being about 50000 men (a valiant people, one of the Seventeen Provinces); the old men and women petitioning for mercy, declared that there were not 500 men left in the whole nation, that were able to bear arms.

And if the King of *England* should reckon his army

after

after this manner; of his eight* millions of subjects (as they are computed to be) there could not be less than three millions that were able to bear armes, which would be a greater army than ever we read of; which must show that the world was *thin of people;* since the *Assyrian* empire the oldest, and therefore most populous did never raise so great a number.

And those great numbers shew that they *wanted arts;* for we read that the *Athenians* a small but learned people baffled and destroyed all the great army of *Xerxes,* reckoned by some to be seventeen hundred thousand men; and *Alexander* with a small number of skilful and valiant *Greeks* subdued the then inhabited world.

And although the *Goths* and *Vandals,* and the cold parts of the world made their invasion for want of room to live in, yet that proceeded from the *want of arts.*

For by *arts* the earth is made more fruitful, and by the invention of the *compass* and *printing,* the world is made more habitable and conversable : By the *first* the countries traffick and exchange the commodities they abound with, for those they want. The timber, pitch and tarr of the cold countries are exchanged for the wine, brandy, and spices of the hot. By the *latter* all arts are easier discovered; by traffick and arts the inhabitants of the cold countries are better fed, better clothed, and better lodged; which make them indure the extremities of their climates better than formerly; and as they increase they build new towns, inlarge their cities, and improve their own country; instead of invading and destroying their neighbours.

---

* If this statement be meant, as it appears to be, to apply to England only, it is far beyond the mark ; for in 1685, its population was certainly under *six* millions. If, however, it be understood as comprising the entire population of the British Islands, there will be little to object to in it.

But to return home: It is plain that the natural increase of mankind is the cause of the increase of the city, and that there are no more houses built every year in it, than are necessary for the growth of the inhabitants: As will somewhat appear by the number of *apprentices* made free, and *marriages* every year in the city.

By the best computation that I can learn, there are no less than ten thousand married every year in the city; which is no great number considering the number of inhabitants: And if we should allow two weddings in a parish every week one with another, (there being a hundred and thirty parishes in all) it will much exceed this proportion. Now in some parishes there is seldom less than ten in a week. And in *Dukes-place*, and St. *Katharine's*, being privileg'd places, there is ordinarily twenty or thirty in a week.

As to the number of apprentices that come every year out of their time, there are not less than nine thousand; which will not be thought too great a number, if we reckon the houses in the city, to be about fourscore thousand: And if the fourth part of this number be allowed for the gentry, or those which live without trades or professions; and the three other parts being sixty thousand, for trades or professions; and one apprentice to every house (though in some houses are three or four apprentices); and that in seven years the whole number come out of their time; then in every year a seventh part of sixty thousand (which is about nine thousand a year) will come out of their time. Now if Mr. *Graunt's* computation be right, that these houses contain eight persons, one with another, then there ought to be a thousand houses at least built every year for these nine thousand apprentices that come out of their time, and the ten thousand weddings to have room to breed in. And this proportion is only sufficient to lodg them, and not for places to trade in, for nine traders cannot live in one house. Therefore

some

some of their masters, or other traders must either die, break, or being grown too rich give over their trades to make room for some of them to have places to trade in, besides those that are furnish'd with places by the new houses.

But I find Mr. *Graunt* much mistaken in his account about the number of inhabitants in each house in the out-parts; perhaps it was from the rebuilding of the city with houses more capacious and more in number. For in this last five and twenty years : the inhabitants are now a third part more, as appeareth by the Bills of Mortality; for in the year 1660 and 1661 there died between thirteen and fourteen thousand a year, and now there dies betwixt twenty-one and twenty-two thousand a year. So that there ought to have been built above twenty-six thousand houses in these twenty-five years, which is above a thousand houses a year to lodg this increase, which are much more than have been built in the out parts, for it appears by Mr. *Morgan's* map of the city that there have not been built in this time 8000 houses, that is not 300 houses one year with another.

But this is certain, that there are no more houses built every year than are occasion for; because there are tenants for the houses, when built, and a continuance every year to build more. For the builders will do as other traders, who, when the market is over-stocked with their commodities, and no occasion for those already made, forbear to make any more, or bring them to market, till a new occasion requireth them. And when they find they cannot lett those already built, they will desist from building, and need no Act of Parliament to hinder them. So that we may as well complain that there is too much cloth and stuff made, too much corn sowed, too many sheep or oxen bred, as that there are too many houses built; too many taylors, shoo-makers, bakers and brewers, as there are too many builders.

Of

*Of the Effects of the increase of Buildings, and first as
it relateth to the City.*

NEW buildings are advantageous to a city, for they
raise the rents of the old houses. For the bigger
a town is, the more of value are the houses in it. Houses
of the same conveniency and goodness are of more value
in *Bristol, Exeter* and *Northampton,* than in the little
villages adjoyning.

Houses in the middle of a town are of more value than
those at the out-ends; and when a town happens to be
increased by addition of new buildings to the end of a
town, the old houses which were then at the end, become
nearer to the middle of the town, and so increase in
value.

Houses are of more value in *Cheapside* and *Cornhill,*
than they are in *Shoreditch, White-Chappel, Old-Street,*
or any of the out-parts: and the rents in some of these
out-parts have been within this few years considerably
advanced by the addition of new buildings that are beyond
them. As for instance, the rents of the houses in *Bishopsgate-street,* the *Minories,* &c. are raised from fifteen or
sixteen pounds *per annum,* to be now worth thirty, which
was by the increase of buildings in *Spittle-Fields, Shadwell*
and *Ratcliff-Highway.* And at the other end of the town
those houses in the *Strand* and *Charing-Cross* are worth
now fifty and threescore pounds *per annum,* which within
this thirty years were not lett for above twenty pounds
per annum; which is by the great addition of buildings
since made in St. *James's, Leicester-Fields,* and other adjoyning parts. But in those out-parts where no new
buildings have been added, as in *Old-street, Grub-street,*
and all that side of the city which does not increase,
houses continue much of the same value, as they were

twenty

twenty years ago : And the reason of this is; because houses are of value, as they stand in a place of trade, and by the addition of new buildings the place becomes to be a greater thorough-fare, by the passing and repassing of the inhabitants to these new buildings.

2. They are advantageous to the city, because they increase the trade of it : The trade of the city is either *wholesale*, or *retail*. Now the new buildings of *Blooms-berry, Leicester-Fields*, St. *James's, Spittle-Fields, &c.* are like so many new towns for the wholesale-trader to traffick in. The inhabitants of these places do eat, wear clothes, and furnish their houses, and whatsoever commoditie they use, come first from the merchants, or wholesale-trader. For the city is the great mart for goods, from whence all other places must be furnished; so that the new buildings are beneficial to the wholesale trade of the city. And it appears that they are likewise advantageous to the retail-traders, because they can afford to give more rent for their old houses, than they did formerly; for otherwise none would believe that the tenants of *Bishopsgate-street*, and the *Minories* could subsist and pay double the rent for their houses within this thirty years, had they not a better trade in those places than formerly.

Of the Effects of New Buildings as they relate to the Country.

NEW buildings are advantageous to the country;
1. By taking off the commodities of the country.

The materials of these houses, as stones, bricks, lime, iron, lead, timber, &c. are all the commodities of the country. And whatsoever the inhabitants of these new

houses

houses have occasion for, either for food, apparel, or furniture for their houses, are at first the growth of the country; and the bigger the town grows, the greater is the occasion and consumption of these commodities, and so the greater profit to the country.

II. New buildings provide an habitation and livelihood for the supernumerary and useless inhabitants of the country. The younger sons of the gentry, the children of the yeomen and peasants are by these means provided with callings, imployments, and habitations to exercise them in; which should they have continued in the country, would have been burdensome, and chargeable to their friends, for want of imployments.

For there is always inhabitants enough left in the country for the imployments of the country. For if the country wanted people, there would be a want of their commodities, for want of hands to provide them.

Now there is as much land plowed, and all sorts of grain sown, and reaped every year, as there is occasion for; and sometimes more: For the Crown in some years hath been at charge to export it. And there is as much wooll provided and made into clothes and stuffs, as the market can take off, and so for all other commodities of the country.

Nay there are more of all the country commodities every year made than formerly: There are more stuffs, more clothes sent up to *Gerard's* and *Blackwell-Hall*, as appears by the entries of those halls; and more sheep and oxen sent to *London*, and eaten, than formerly. For there are more people in the city to be fed; so that there must be more hands in the country to provide this greater quantity of commodities: And the country does increase as well as the city, as hath been already observed from the *Doomsday-Book.*

Therefore if the rents of the lands fall in the country, it must not be ascrib'd to the *new-buildings draining their*

inhabitants,

inhabitants, but to some other occasions; which probably may be from the great improvements that are made upon the land in the country, either by draining of fens; improving of land by *zanfoin*; or other profitable seeds; inclosing of grounds, or disparking and plowing of parks, by which means the markets are over stock'd and furnished at a cheaper rate than those lands can afford, who have had no advantage from improvements: Or else the market is removed at a greater distance, and the lands are forced to abate in their price for the carriage; the town perhaps is decayed, that they used to furnish, and the trade removed to some other flourishing place at a greater distance; occasioned some times by the death or removal of some great clothier or trader; or some other natural obstruction of the place; as the choaking up of some haven, and the forsaking of the sea, which is the reason of the decay of the Cinque-Ports. These or some other occasions may make some particular mens farms fall in value; but there is never a county in *England*, where the land of the whole county doth not produce a third part more in value than it did within a 100 years, and whosoever will compare these present rents, with what they were then, will find them generally increased. Therefore the new buildings of this city cannot prejudice the country, but are greatly advantageous to it.

Of the Effects of the New Buildings, as they relate to the Government.

I. NEW buildings are advantageous to the king and government. They are instrumental to the preserving and increasing of the number of the subjects; and

numbers

numbers of subjects is the strength of a prince : for houses are hives for the people to breed and swarm in, without which they cannot increase; and unless they are provided for them from time to time in proportion to their increase, they would be forced to go into the plantations and other countries for habitations; and so many times become the subjects of other princes; but at the best the country loseth the profit of feeding them; for they that live in a city are unskilful and unfit for country life; and this is the reason why so many *Scotch* citizens are wandring pedlers : and that every town in *Europe* hath a *Scotchman* for an inhabitant.

And that this will be the effects will appear plainly by examining the growth of the city of *London,* since the buildings have flourished, with its condition, when the buildings were prohibited; and we cannot make a better discovery of it than by the Bills of Mortality, for it is reasonable among such a number of mankind, such a number should die; and whether it be in such a proportion as one in three and thirty, as Mr. *Graunt* and Sir *William Petty* have observed, is not so material to this purpose; but it is a certain demonstration, that if the burials have increased, the number of citizens hath increased, though the proportion may be uncertain.

Now to begin the observation from the first Bills, that were printed, which was in the year 1606, for the space of six and seven and twenty years, we shall find very little increase in the city, for in 1606 and 1607, there died between six and seven thousand a year; and in the years 1632 and 1633 there died betwixt eight and nine thousand : Now the reason of this was the people of *England* were a little before that time under the same mistake, as they are generally now, and cried out against the builders, that the city would grow too big; and therefore in the 38 of Queen *Elizabeth* they made a law to prohibit buildings in the city of *London,* which though it was but a

　　　　　　　　　　　　probationary

probationary Act, to continue only to the next sessions of parliament (which was but a short time) yet its effects were long; for it frighted the builders, and obstructed the growth of the city; and none built for thirty years after, all King *James* his reign, without his Majesties license: But for want of houses the increase of the people went into other parts of the world; for within this space of time were those great plantations of *New England, Virginia, Mariland,* and *Burmudas* began; and that this want of houses was the occasion is plain; for they could not build in the country, because of the law against cottages. For people may get children and so increase, that had not four acres of ground to build on.

But the people of *England* at last were convinced of this popular error, and petitioned in parliament his Majestie K. *Charles* the Martyr, that he would take his restraint from the builders; and if the next period of seven and twenty years be examined, wherein there was a greater liberty of building, though in this space there was a great rebellion and civil wars, which is a great allay to the growth of the people, yet there appeareth a much greater increase of the city of *London*; for in the years 1656 and 1657, the burials were twelve and thirteen thousand.

But the flourishing condition of the city of *London* raised a new clamour against the builders, and *Oliver* the Usurper glad of any pretence to raise a tax, made use of this clamor, and laid it upon the new foundations; but though it was an heavy and unjust tax upon the builders, yet he got little by it, for the whole summ collected was but twenty thousand pounds clear of all charges, as appears by the records of the Exchequer; however it had the same ill effects to stop the builders, and growth of the city; for the people for want of houses in that time began that great and flourishing plantation of *Jamaica.*

Now if the last period since his Majesties happy res-

tauration

tauration be examined, wherein the builders have had the greatest liberty, it will appear that the inhabitants of the city have increased more than in both of the former periods, for the yearly Bills of Mortality are now betwixt two and three and twenty thousands, so that the city is since increased one third, and as much as in sixty years before.

This is sufficient to shew that a nation cannot increase without the metropolis be inlarged, and how dangerous a consequence it may be to obstruct its growth, and discourage the builders. It is to banish the people, and confine the nation to an infant estate, while the neighbouring nations grow to the full strength of manhood, and thereby to render it an easie conquest to its enemies.

For the metropolis is the heart of a nation, through which the trade and commodities of it circulate, like the blood through the heart, which by its motion giveth life and growth to the rest of the body; and if that declines, or be obstructed in its growth, the whole body falls into consumption: And it is the only symptome to know the health, and thriving of a country by the inlarging of its metropolis; for the chief city of every nation in the world that flourisheth doth increase.

And if those gentlemen that fancy the city to be the head of the nation, would but fancy it like the heart, they would never be afraid of its growing too big; for I never read of such a disease, that the heart was too big for the body. And if we are of *Machiavel's* opinion, this *simile* is the best, for he saith, that citizens make no good counsellors, for having raised their fortunes by parsimony and industry, they are usually too severe in punishing of vice, and too niggardly in rewarding of vertue.

2. It is the interest of the government, to incourage the builders; not only because they preserve and increase the subjects, but they provide an imploy for them, by which they are fed, and get their livelihood.

There

There are three great ways that the people in all governments are imployed in : In providing *food, clothes,* and *houses.* Now those ways are most serviceable to the government, that imploy most of the people; those that are imployed in feeding of them, are the fewest in number; for ten men may provide food enough for a thousand : but to cloth, and build houses for them, requireth many hands : And there is that peculiar advantage that ought to be ascribed to the builder, that he provideth the place of birth for all the other arts, as well as for man. The cloth cannot be made without houses to work it in. Now besides the vast numbers of people that are imployed in digging and making the materials, the bricks, stone, iron, lead, *&c.* all those trades that belong to the furnishing of an house, have their sole dependencies on the builders, as the upholsterers, chair-makers, *&c.*

But that which is the greatest advantage, they do not only provide a livelihood to those that belong to the building, and furnishing of houses, but for the tenants of those new houses : For the people being collected and living together in one street, they serve and trade one with another : For trade is nothing else but an exchange of one mans labour for another : as for instance, supposing an hundred men which lived at great distance before; some in *Cornwall,* others in *Yorkshire,* and so dispersed over all the countries in *England,* live together in one street; one is a baker, the other a brewer, a shoo-maker, taylor, *&c.* and so in one trade or other the whole hundred are imployed : the baker gets his living by making bread for the other ninety, and so do all the rest of them ; which while they were dispersed at distances, were useless and could not serve one another, and were ready to starve for want of a livelihood.

3. But they get not only a livelihood, but grow rich : There ariseth an emulation among them to out-live and

out-vye

out-vye one another in arts. This forceth them to be industrious, and by industry they grow rich.

4. The increasing of buildings, and inlarging of towns, preserveth the peace of a nation, by rendring the people more easily governed. First it is the builders interest of all sorts of men to preserve peace: Every man that buildeth an house, gives security to the government for his good behaviour. For war is the builders ruin. The countryman may expect to enjoy his land again, though for a time it be laid wast; the merchant may hide his goods, or remove them; but when the town is besieged, the houses are fired, the place made desolate, and nothing is left to the builder but ruins, the sad remembrance of his condition.

Besides, all cities are more inclined to peace, than the country; the citizens estates are in trade, and in goods; many of which grow useless in war, and lye in other peoples hands, and their debtors run away, and take sanctuary under the sword; and citizens being usually rich, cannot endure the hardship of war. Next, great cities are more easily governed, because they are under the eye of the Prince, as generally the metropolis is; or else under some governour, who by his rewards from the Crown, is engaged to be very watchful in preserving the peace, so that if they should grow factious, they are more easily corrected. Thus the *Ottoman* power governs his conquest by destroying villages and lesser towns, and driving the people into capital cities, which by the presence of some *Basha* are governed. Thus the King of *France* in his late conquests in *Flanders* and *Alsatia,* burnt some hundreds of villages; but *Luxembourg, Strasbourg,* and other great towns are preserved. And the bigger the city, the more advantageous to the government; for from thence they are on a sudden the better supplied with men and ammunition, to suppress any rebellion, or oppose a foreign enemy.

Lastly,

Lastly, new buildings increase his Majesties revenues, not only by the chimney-money, which makes it a growing revenue; but by the customs paid for the materials to build and furnish the houses. Besides they being the cause of the increase of the city, all the increase of the revenues from the excise and customs (since the cities increase) must be ascribed to them: which are a fourth part more than they were five and twenty years ago. And the excise is not only increased in the city, but it is so in the country; which must not be ascribed solely to the good management, but chiefly to the natural increase of the people. For if there be a third part more people in the city than there were five and twenty years ago, there must be a proportionable increase in the country to provide food and clothes for them.

To conclude, it was upon these considerations, that by the building and inlarging of a city, the people are made great, rich, and easily governed: That those ancient and famous governments, *Thebes, Athens, Sparta, Carthage,* and *Rome,* began their dominions, and inlarged them with their cities; and of late the States of *Holland* have followed these examples.

The citizens of *Amsterdam* have thrice flung down their walls to inlarge it; so that from a little fisher-town within less than 200 years it is become the third or fourth city of *Europe:* and the rest of their cities have followed their pattern; and made grafts and streets at the charge of the government; endeavouring to outvie one another by giving priviledges to incourage the builders and inhabitants. And these States have found the effects of it; for by this means they have changed their style from the Poor Distressed States, (as they wrote to Queen *Elizabeth*) to the High and Mighty States of the United Provinces.

And if the city of *London* hath made such a progress within this five and twenty years, as to have grown one third bigger, and become already the metropolis of *Europe,*

notwithstanding

notwithstanding the popular error the nation have been infected with, and the ill censures and discouragements the builders have met with; had they been for this last hundred years encouraged by the government, the city of *London* might probably have easily grown three times bigger than now it is.

And if we consider what the natural effects of so great a city must have been; to be furnished with such large provisions for war suitable to its greatness; such a vast number of ships; being situate on an island and navigable river; filled with innumerable inhabitants, of such natural courage as the *English* are; and to be so easily transported on a sudden with all things necessary for war, it would long before this time have been a terror to all *Europe;* and now would have had the opportunity, under the government of such a martial prince as now reigns, to be made the metropolis of the world; to have caused *England's* monarch to be acknowledged lord of all the navigable cities and sea-port-towns in the world; to have made an universal monarchy over the seas, an empire no less glorious, and of much more profit, than of the land; and of larger extent, than either *Cæsar's* or *Alexander's.*

FINIS.

Giving Alms no Charity,

And Employing the

POOR

A Grievance to the

NATION,

Being an

ESSAY

Upon this

Great Question,

Whether Work-houſes, Corporations, and Houſes of Correction for Employing the Poor, as now prac-tis'd in *England;* or Parish-Stocks, as propos'd in a late Pamphlet, Entituled, *A Bill for the better Relief, Imployment and Settlement of the Poor,* &c. Are not mischievous to the Nation, tending to the Destruction of our Trade, and to Encreaſe the Number and Misery of the Poor.

Addreſſed to the Parliament of England.

LONDON:

Printed, and Sold by the Booksellers of *London* and *Westminster.* MDCCIV.

GIVING ALMS NO CHARITY.

To the Knights, Citizens, and Burgesses in Parliament
Assembled.

Gentlemen,

HE that has truth and justice, and the interest of *England* in his design, can have nothing to fear from an *English* Parliament.

This makes the author of these sheets, however despicable in himself, apply to this Honourable House, without any apology for the presumption.

Truth, *Gentlemen*, however meanly dress'd, and in whatsoever bad company she happens to come, was always entertain'd at your bar; and the Commons of *England* must cease to act like themselves, or which is worse, like their ancestors, when they cease to entertain any proposal, that offers it self at their door, for the general good and advantage of the people they represent.

I willingly grant, that 'tis a crime in good manners to interrupt your more weighty councils, and disturb your debates; with empty nauseous trifles in value, or mistaken schemes, and whoever ventures to address you, ought to be well assur'd he is in the right, and that the matter suits the intent of your meeting, *viz. To dispatch the weighty affairs of the kingdom.*

And as I have premis'd this, so I freely submit to any

censure

censure this Honourable Assembly shall think I deserve, if I have broke in upon either of these particulars.

I have but one petition to make with respect to the author, and that is, that no freedom of expression, which the arguments may oblige him to, may be constru'd as a want of respect, and a breach of the due deference every *English* man owes to the representing power of the nation.

It would be hard, that while I am honestly offering to your consideration something of moment for the general good, prejudice should lay snares for the author, and private pique make him an offender for a word.

Without entering upon other parts of my character, 'tis enough to acquaint this Assembly, that I am an *English* freeholder, and have by that a title to be concern'd in the good of that community of which I am an unworthy member.

This Honourable House is the representative of all the freeholders of *England*; you are assembl'd for their good, you study their interest, you possess their hearts, and you hold the strings of the general purse.

To you they have recourse for the redress of all their wrongs, and if at any time one of their body can offer to your assistance, any fair, legal, honest and rational proposal for the publick benefit, it was never known that such a man was either rejected or discourag'd.

And on this account I crave the liberty to assure you, that the author of this seeks no reward; to him it shall always be reward enough to have been capable of serving his native country, and honour enough to have offer'd something for the publick good worthy of consideration in your Honourable Assembly.

Pauper ubique jacet, said our famous Queen *Elizabeth,* when in her progress thro' the kingdom she saw the vast throngs of the poor, flocking to see and bless her; and the thought put her Majesty upon a continu'd study how

4

to

to recover her people from that poverty, and make their labour more profitable to themselves in particular, and the nation in general.

This was easie then to propose, for that many useful manufactures were made in foreign parts, which our people bought with *English* money, and imported for their use.

The Queen, who knew the wealth and vast numbers of people which the said manufactures had brought to the neighbouring countries then under the King of *Spain*, the *Dutch* being not yet revolted, never left off endeavouring what she happily brought to pass, *viz.* the transplanting into *England* those springs of riches and people.

She saw the *Flemings* prodigiously numerous, their cities stood thicker than her peoples villages in some parts; all sorts of useful manufactures were found in their towns, and all their people were rich and busie, no beggars, no idleness, and consequently, no want was to be seen among them.

She saw the fountain of all this wealth and workman-ship, I mean the wool, was in her own hands, and *Flanders* became the seat of all these manufactures, not because it was naturally richer and more populous than other coun-tries, but because it lay near *England*, and the staple of the *English* wool which was the foundation of all their wealth, was at *Antwerp* in the heart of that country.

From hence, it may be said of *Flanders*, it was not the riches and the number of people brought the manufactures into the *Low Countries*, but it was the manufactures brought the people thither, and multitudes of people make trade, trade makes wealth, wealth builds cities, cities enrich the land round them, land enrich'd rises in value, and the value of lands enriches the Government.

Many projects were set on foot in *England* to erect the woollen manufacture here, and in some places it had found encouragement, before the days of this Queen, es-pecially as to making of cloath, but stuffs, bays, says,

serges,

serges, and such like wares were yet wholly the work of
the *Flemings.*

At last an opportunity offer'd perfectly unlook'd for,
viz. the persecution of the Protestants, and introducing
the *Spanish* inquisition into *Flanders,* with the tyranny of
the Duke *D'Alva.*

It cannot be an ungrateful observation, here to take
notice how tyranny and persecution, the one an oppression
of property, the other of conscience, always ruine trade,
impoverish nations, depopulate countries, dethrone princes,
and destroy peace.

When an *English* man reflects on it, he cannot without
infinite satisfaction look up to Heaven, and to this Honourable House, *that* as the spring, *this* as the stream *from* and
by which the felicity of this nation has obtain'd a pitch of
glory, superior to all the people in the world.

Your Councils especially, when blest from Heaven, *as
now we trust they are,* with principles of unanimity and
concord, can never fail to make trade flourish, war successful, peace certain, wealth flowing, blessings probable,
the Queen glorious, and the people happy.

Our unhappy neighbours of the *Low Countries* were
the very reverse of what we *bless our selves for in you.*

Their kings were tyrants, their governours persecutors,
their armies thieves and blood-hounds.

Their people divided, their councils confus'd, and their
miseries innumerable.

D'Alva the *Spanish* Governor, besieg'd their cities,
decimated the inhabitants, murther'd their nobility, pro-
scrib'd their princes, and executed 18,000 men by the
hand of the hang-man.

Conscience was trampl'd under foot, religion and reformation hunted like a hare upon the mountains, the inquisition threaten'd, and foreign armies introduc'd.

Property fell a sacrifice to absolute power, the countrey
was ravag'd, the towns plunder'd, the rich confiscated, the

poor

poor starv'd, trade interrupted, and the 10*th* penny demanded.

The consequence of this was, *as in all tyrannies and persecutions it is*, the people fled and scatter'd themselves in their neighbours countries, trade languish'd, manufactures went abroad, and never return'd, confusion reign'd and poverty succeeded.

The multitude that remain'd push'd to all extremities, were forc'd to obey the voice of nature, and in their own just defence to take arms against their governours.

Destruction it self has its uses in the world, the ashes of one city rebuilds another, and God Almighty, who never acts in vain, brought the wealth of *England,* and the power of *Holland* into the world from the ruine of the *Flemish liberty.*

The *Dutch* in defence of their liberty revolted, renounc'd their tyrant prince, and prosper'd by Heaven and the assistance of *England,* erected the greatest common-wealth in the world.

Innumerable observations would flow from this part of the present subject, but brevity is my study, I am not teaching; for I know who I speak to but relating and observing the connexion of Causes, and the wonderous births which *lay then* in the womb of Providence, and are since come to life.

Particularly how Heaven directed the oppression and tyranny of the poor should be the wheel to turn over the great machine of trade from *Flanders* into *England.*

And how the persecution and cruelty of the *Spaniards,* against religion should be directed by the secret over-ruling Hand, to be the foundation of a people, and a body that should in ages then to come, be one of the chief bulwarks of that very liberty and religion they sought to destroy.

In this general ruine of trade and liberty, *England* made a gain of what she never yet lost, and of what she has since encreas'd to an inconceivable magnitude.

As *D'Alva* worried the poor *Flemings*, the Queen of *England* entertain'd them, cherish'd them, invited them, encourag'd them.

Thousands of innocent people fled from all parts from the fury of this merciless man, and as *England, to her honour* has always been the sanctuary of her distress'd neighbours, so now she was so to her special and particular profit.

The Queen who saw the opportunity put into her hands which she had so long wish'd for, not only received kindly the exil'd *Flemings,* but invited over all that would come, promising them all possible encouragement, privileges and freedom of her ports and the like.

This brought over a vast multitude of *Flemings, Walloons,* and *Dutch,* who with their whole families settled at *Norwich,* at *Ipswich, Colchester, Canterbury, Exeter,* and the like. From these came the *Walloon* Church at *Canterbury,* and the *Dutch* Churches at *Norwich, Colchester,* and *Yarmouth;* from hence came the true born *English* families at those places with foreign names; as the *DeVinks* at *Norwich,* the *Rebows* at *Colchester,* the *Papilons,* &c. at *Canterbury,* families to whom this nation are much in debt for the first planting those manufactures, from which we have since rais'd the greatest trades in the world.

This wise Queen knew that number of inhabitants are the wealth and strength of a nation, she was far from that opinion, we have of late shown too much of in complaining that foreigners came to take the bread out of our mouths, and ill treating on that account the *French* Protestants who fled hither for refuge in the late persecution.

Some have said that above 50,000 of them settled here, and would have made it a grievance, tho' without doubt 'tis easie to make it appear that 500,000 more would be both useful and profitable to this nation.

Upon the setling of these forreigners, the scale of trade visibly turn'd both here and in *Flanders.*

8

The

The *Flemings* taught our women and children to spin, the youth to weave, the men entred the loom to labour instead of going abroad to seek their fortunes by the war, the several trades of *bayes* at *Colchester*, *sayes* and *perpets*, at *Sudbury*, *Ipswich*, &c. *stuffs* at *Norwich*, *serges* at *Exeter*, *silks* at *Canterbury*, and the like, began to flourish. All the counties round felt the profit, the poor were set to work, the traders gain'd wealth, and multitudes of people flock'd to the several parts where these manufactures were erected for employment, and the growth of *England*, both in trade, wealth and people since that time, as it is well known to this Honourable House; so the causes of it appear to be plainly the introducing of these manufactures, and nothing else.

Nor was the gain made here by it more visible than the loss to the *Flemings*, from hence, and not as is vainly suggested from the building the *Dutch* fort of *Lillo* on the *Scheld*, came the decay of that flourishing city of *Antwerp*. From hence it is plain the *Flemings*, an industrious nation, finding their trade ruin'd at once, turn'd their hands to other things, as making of *lace*, *linnen*, and the like, and the *Dutch* to the sea affairs and fishing.

From hence they became *poor*, thin of people, and *weak* in trade, the flux both of their wealth and trade, running wholly into *England*.

I humbly crave leave to say, this long introduction shall not be thought useless, when I shall bring it home by the process of these papers to the subject now in hand, *viz. The providing for and employing the poor.*

Since the times of *Queen Elizabeth* this nation has gone on to a prodigy of trade, of which the encrease of our customs from 400,000 crowns to two millions of pounds sterling *per ann.* is a demonstration beyond the power of argument; and that this whole encrease depends upon, and is principally occasion'd by the encrease of our

9   manufacturers

manufacturers is so plain, I shall not take up any room
here to make it out.

Having thus given an account how we came to be a
rich, flourishing and populous nation, I crave leave as concisely as I can to examine how we came to be poor again,
if it must be granted that we are so.

By poor here I humbly desire to be understood, not
that we are a poor nation in general; I should undervalue
the bounty of Heaven to *England,* and act with less understanding than most men are masters of, if I should not
own, that in general we are *as rich a nation* as any in the
world; but by poor I mean burthen'd with a crowd of
clamouring, unimploy'd, unprovided for poor people, who
make the nation uneasie, burthen the rich, clog our
parishes, and make themselves worthy of laws, and peculiar management to dispose of and direct them : How
these came to be thus is the question.

And first I humbly crave leave to lay these heads down
as fundamental maxims, which I am ready at any time to
defend and make out.

1. *There is in* England *more labour than hands to perform
   it, and consequently a want of people, not of employment.*
2. *No man in* England, *of sound limbs and senses, can be
   poor meerly for want of work.*
3. *All our work-houses, corporations and charities for employing the poor, and setting them to work, as now they
   are employ'd, or any Acts of Parliament to empower
   overseers of parishes, or parishes themselves, to employ
   the poor, except as shall be hereafter excepted, are, and
   will be publick nusances, mischiefs to the nation which
   serve to the ruin of families, and the encrease of the
   poor.*
4. *That 'tis a regulation of the poor that is wanted in*
   England, *not a setting them to work.*

If

If after these things are made out, I am enquir'd of what this regulation should be, I am no more at a loss to lay it down than I am to affirm what is above; and shall always be ready, when call'd to it, to make such a proposal to this Honourable House, as with their concurrence shall for ever put a stop to poverty and beggery, parish charges, assessments and the like, in this nation.

If such offers as these shall be slighted and rejected, I have the satisfaction of having discharg'd my duty, and the consequence must be, that complaining will be continued in our streets.

'Tis my misfortune, that while I study to make every head so concise, as becomes me in things to be brought before so honourable and august an assembly, I am oblig'd to be short upon heads that in their own nature would very well admit of particular volumes to explain them.

1. I affirm, *that in* England *there is more labour than hands to perform it.* This I prove,

1*st*. From the dearness of wages, which in *England* out goes all nations in the world; and *I know no greater demonstration in trade.* Wages, like exchanges, rise and fall as the remitters and drawers, the employers and the workmen, ballance one another.

The employers are the remitters, the work-men are the drawers, if there are more employers than work-men, the price of wages must rise, because the employer wants that work to be done more than the poor man wants to do it, if there are more work-men than employers the price of labour falls, because the poor man wants his wages more than the employer wants to have his business done.

Trade, like all nature, most obsequiously obeys the great law of cause and consequence; and this is the occasion why even all the greatest articles of trade follow, and as it were pay homage to this seemingly minute and inconsiderable thing, *the poor man's labour*.

I omit, with some pain, the many very useful thoughts

11   that

that occnr on this head, to preserve the brevity I owe to
the dignity of that assembly I am writing to. But I
cannot but note how from hence it appears, that the
glory, the strength, the riches, the trade, and all that's
valuable in a nation, as to its figure in the world, depends
upon the number of its people, be they never so mean or
poor; the consumption of manufactures encreases the
manufacturers; the number of manufacturers encreases
the consumption; provisions are consum'd to feed them,
land improv'd, and more hands employ'd to furnish provisions: All the wealth of the nation, and all the trade is
produc'd by numbers of people; but of this by the way.

The price of wages not only determines the difference
between the employer and the work-man, but it rules the
rates of every market. If wages grow high, provisions
rise in proportion, and I humbly conceive it to be a mistake in those people, who say labour in such parts of
England is cheap because provisions are cheap, but 'tis
plain, provisions are cheap there because labour is cheap,
and labour is cheaper in those parts than in others;
because being remoter from *London* there is not that
extraordinary disproportion between the work and the
number of hands; there are more hands, and consequently
labour cheaper.

'Tis plain to any observing eye, that there is an equal
plenty of provisions in several of our south and western
counties, as in *Yorkshire*, and rather a greater, and I
believe I could make it out, that a poor labouring man
may live as cheap in *Kent* or *Sussex* as in the bishoprick
of *Durham*; and yet in *Kent* a poor man shall earn 7*s.*
10*s.* 9*s.* a week, and in the north 4*s.* or perhaps less; the
difference is plain in this, that in *Kent* there is a greater
want of people, in proportion to the work there, than in
the north.

And this on the other hand makes the people of our
northern countries spread themselves so much to the south,

                                                    where

where trade, war and the sea carrying off so many, there is a greater want of hands.

And yet 'tis plain there is labour for the hands which remain in the north, or else the country would be depopulated, and the people come all away to the south to seek work; and even in *Yorkshire,* where labour is cheapest, the people can gain more by their labour than in any of the manufacturing countries of *Germany, Italy* or *France,* and live much better.

If there was one poor man in *England* more than there was work to employ, either somebody else must stand still for him, or he must be starv'd; if another man stands still for him he wants a days work, and goes to seek it, and by consequence supplants another, and this a third, and this contention brings it to this; no, says the poor man, *that is like to be put out of his work,* rather than that man shall come in I'll do it cheaper; nay, says the other, but I'll do it cheaper than you; and thus one poor man wanting but a days work would bring down the price of labour in a whole nation, for the man cannot starve, and will work for any thing rather than want it.

It may be objected here, this is contradicted by our number of beggars.

I am sorry to say I am obliged here to call begging an employment, since 'tis plain, if there is more work than hands to perform it, no man that has his *limbs* and his *senses* need to beg, and those that *have not* ought to be put into a condition not to want it.

So that begging is a meer scandal in the general, *in the able* 'tis a scandal upon their industry, and *in the impotent* 'tis a scandal upon the country.

Nay, the begging, as now practic'd, is a scandal upon our charity, and perhaps the foundation of all our present grievance.—How can it be possible that any man or woman, who being sound in body and mind, may as 'tis apparent they may, have wages for their work, should be so base, so meanly spirited, as to beg an alms for God-sake.—Truly the scandal lies on our charity: and people have such a notion in *England* of being pittiful and charitable, that they encourage vagrants, and by a mistaken zeal do more harm than good.

This is a large scene, and much might be said upon it; I shall abridge it as much as possible.—The poverty of *England* does not lye among the craving beggars but among poor families, where the children are numerous, and where death or sickness has depriv'd them of the labour of the father; these are the houses that the sons and daughters of charity, if they would order it well, should seek out and relieve; an alms ill directed may be charity to the particular person, but becomes an injury to the publick, and no charity to the nation. As for the craving poor, I am perswaded I do them no wrong when I say, that if they were incorporated they would be the richest society in the nation; and the reason why so many pretend to want work is, that they can live so well with the pretence of wanting work, they would be mad to leave it and work in earnest; and I affirm of my own knowledge, when I have wanted a man for labouring work, and offer'd 9*s per* week to strouling fellows at my door, they have frequently told me to my face, they could get more a begging, and I once set a lusty fellow in the stocks for making the experiment.

I shall, in its proper place, bring this to a method of tryal, since nothing but demonstration will affect us, 'tis an easie matter to prevent begging in *England*, and yet to maintain all our impotent poor at far less charge to the parishes than they now are oblig'd to be at.

When Queen *Elizabeth* had gain'd her point as to manufactories in *England*, she had fairly laid the foundation, she thereby found out the way how every family might live upon their own labour, like a wise princess she knew 'twould be hard to force people to work when there

was

was nothing for them to turn their hands to; but as soon as she had brought the matter to bear, and there was work for every body that had no mind to starve, then she apply'd herself to make laws to oblige the people to do this work, and to punish vagrants, and make every one live by their own labour; all her successors followed this laudable example, and from hence came all those laws against sturdy beggars, vagabonds, stroulers, &c., which had they been severely put in execution by our magistrates, 'tis presum'd these vagrant poor had not so encreas'd upon us as they have.

And it seems strange to me, from what just ground we proceed now upon other methods, and fancy that 'tis now our business to find them work, and to employ them rather than to oblige them to find themselves work and go about it.

From this mistaken notion come all our work-houses and corporations, and the same error, with submission, I presume was the birth of this bill now depending, which enables every parish to erect the woollen manufacture within it self, for the employing their own poor.

'Tis the mistake of this part of the bill only which I am enquiring into, and which I endeavour to set in a true light.

In all the parliaments since the Revolution, this matter has been before them, and I am justified in this attempt by the House of Commons having frequently appointed committees to receive proposals upon this head.

As my proposal is general, I presume to offer it to the general body of the House; if I am commanded to explain any part of it, I am ready to do any thing that may be serviceable to this great and noble design.

As the former Houses of Commons gave all possible encouragement to such as could offer, or but pretend to offer at this needful. thing, so the imperfect essays of several, whether for private or publick benefit. I do not

attempt

attempt to determine which have since been made, and which have obtain'd the powers and conditions they have desir'd, have by all their effects demonstrated the weakness of their design; and that they either understood not the disease, or know not the proper cure for it.

The imperfection of all these attempts is acknowledg'd, not only in the preamble of this new Act of Parliament, but even in the thing, in that there is yet occasion for any new law.

And having survey'd, not the necessity of a new act, but the contents of the act which has been propos'd as a remedy in this case; I cannot but offer my objections against the sufficiency of the proposal, and leave it to the consideration of this wise assembly, and of the whole nation.

I humbly hope the learned gentleman, under whose direction this law is now to proceed, and by whose order it has been printed, will not think himself personally concern'd in this case, his endeavours to promote so good a work, as the relief, employment, and settlement of the poor, merit the thanks and acknowledgment of the whole nation, and no man shall be more ready to pay his share of that debt to him than my self. But if his scheme happen to be something superficial, if he comes in among the number of those who have not search'd this wound to the bottom, if the methods propos'd are not such as will either answer his own designs or the nations, I cannot think my self oblig'd to dispense, with my duty to the publick good, to preserve a personal value for his judgment, tho' the gentleman's merit be extraordinary.

Wherefore, as in all the schemes, I have seen laid for the poor, and in this act now before your Honourable House; the general thought of the proposers runs upon the employing the poor by work-houses, corporations, houses of correction, and the like, and that I think it plain to be seen, that those proposals come vastly short of

the

the main design. These sheets are humbly laid before you, as well to make good what is alledg'd, *viz.* That all these work-houses, &c., tend to the encrease, and not the relief of the poor, as to make an humble tender of plain, but I hope, rational proposals for the more effectual cure of this grand disease.

In order to proceed to this great challenge, I humbly desire the bills already pass'd may be review'd, the practice of our corporation work-houses, and the contents of this proposed act examin'd.

In all these it will appear that the method chiefly proposed for the employment of our poor, is by setting them to work on the several manufactures before-mention'd; as *spinning, weaving,* and manufacturing our *English wool.*

All our work-houses lately erected in *England,* are in general thus employ'd, for which without enumerating particulars, I humbly appeal to the knowledge of the several members of this Honourable House in their respective towns where such corporations have been erected.

In the present Act now preparing, as printed by direction of a member of this Honourable House, it appears, *that in order to set the poor to work, it shall be lawful for the overseers of* every town, *or of one or more* towns joyn'd together to *occupy any trade, mystery, &c. And raise stocks for the carrying them on for the setting the poor at work, and for the purchasing wool, iron, hemp, flax, thread, or other materials for that purpose. Vide the Act publish'd by Sir* Humphry Mackworth.

And that charities given so and so, and not exceeding 200*l. per annum* for this purpose, shall be incorporated of course for these ends.

In order now to come to the case in hand, *it is necessary to premise,* that the thing now in debate is not the poor of this or that particular town. The House of Commons are acting like themselves, as they are the represen-

tatives

tatives of all the commons of *England*, 'tis the care of all the poor of *England* which lies before them, not of this or that particular body of the poor.

In proportion to this great work, I am to be understood that these work-houses, houses of correction, and stocks to employ the poor may be granted to lessen the poor in this or that particular part of *England*; and we are particularly told of that at *Bristol*, that it has been such a terror to the beggars that none of the strouling crew will come near the city. But all this allow'd, in general, 'twill be felt in the main, and the end will be an encrease of our poor.

1. The manufactures that these gentlemen employ the poor upon, are all such as are before exercis'd in *England*.

2. They are all such as are manag'd to a full extent, and the present accidents of war and foreign interruption of trade consider'd rather beyond the vent of them than under it.

Suppose now a work-house for employment of poor children, sets them to spinning of worsted.—For every skein of worsted these poor children spin, there must be a skein the less spun by some poor family or person that spun it before; suppose the manufacture of making bays to be erected in *Bishopsgate-street*, unless the makers of these bays can at the same time find out a trade or consumption for more bays than were made before. For every piece of bays so made in *London* there must be a piece the less made at *Colchester*.

I humbly appeal to the Honourable House of Commons what this may be call'd, and with submission, I think it is nothing at all to employing the poor, since 'tis only the transposing the manufacture from *Colchester* to *London*, and taking the bread out of the mouths of the poor of *Essex* to put it into the mouths of the poor of *Middlesex*.

If these worthy gentlemen, who show themselves so

commendably

commendably forward to relieve and employ the poor, will find out some new trade, some new market, where the goods they make shall be sold, where none of the same goods were sold before; if they will send them to any place where they shall not interfere with the rest of that manufacture, or with some other made in *England*, then indeed they will do something worthy of themselves, and may employ the poor to the same glorious advantage as Queen *Elizabeth* did, to whom this nation, as a trading country, owes its peculiar greatness.

If these gentlemen could establish a trade to *Muscovy* for *English* serges, or obtain an order from the *Czar*, that all his subjects should wear stockings who wore none before, every poor child's labour in spining and knitting those stockings, and all the wool in them would be clear gain to the nation, and the general stock would be improved by it, because all the growth of our country, and all the labour of a person who was idle before, is so much clear gain to the general stock.

If they will employ the poor in some manufacture which was not made in *England* before, or not bought with some manufacture made here before, then they offer at something extraordinary.

But to set poor people at work, on the same thing which other poor people were employ'd on before, and at the same time not encrease the consumption, is giving to one what you take away from another; enriching one poor man to starve another, putting a vagabond into an honest man's employment, and putting his diligence on the tenters to find out some other work to maintain his family.

As this is not at all profitable, so *with submission for the expression*, I cannot say 'tis honest, because 'tis transplanting and carrying the poor peoples lawful employment from the place where was their lawful settlement, and the hardship of this *our law consider'd* is intolerable. For example.

The manufacture of making bays is now establish'd at *Colchester* in *Essex,* suppose it should be attempted to be erected in *Middlesex,* as a certain worthy and wealthy gentleman near *Hackney* once propos'd, it may be suppos'd if you will grant the skill in working the same, and the wages the same, that they must be made cheaper in *Middlesex* than in *Essex,* and cheapness certainly will make the merchant buy here rather than there, and so in time all the bay making at *Colchester* dyes, and the staple for that commodity is removed to *London.*

What must the poor of *Colchester* do, there they buy a parochial settlement, those that have numerous families cannot follow the manufacture and come up to *London,* for our parochial laws impower the Church-wardens to refuse them a settlement, so that they are confin'd to their own countrey, and the bread taken out of their mouths, and all this to feed vagabonds, and to set them to work, who by their choice would be idle, and who merit the correction of the law.

There is another grievance which I shall endeavour to touch at, which every man that wishes well to the poor does not forsee, and which, with humble submission to the gentlemen that contriv'd this Act, I see no notice taken of.

There are arcanas in trade, which though they are the natural consequences of time and casual circumstances, are yet become now so essential to the publick benefit, that to alter or disorder them, would be an irreparable damage to the publick.

I shall explain my self as concisely as I can.

The manufactures of *England* are happily settled in different corners of the kingdom, from whence they are mutually convey'd by a circulation of trade to *London* by wholesale, like the blood to the heart, and from thence disperse in lesser quantities to the other parts of the kingdom by retail. For example.

Serges

Serges are made at *Exeter, Taunton,* &c. stuffs at *Norwich; bayes, sayes, shaloons,* &c. at *Colchester, Bocking, Sudbury,* and parts adjacent, fine cloath in *Somerset, Wilts, Gloucester* and *Worcestershire,* coarse cloath in *Yorkshire, Kent, Surry,* &c. druggets at *Farnham, Newbury,* &c. All these send up the gross of their quantity to *London,* and receive each others sorts in retail for their own use again. *Norwich* buys *Exeter* serges, *Exeter* buys *Norwich* stuffs, all at *London; Yorkshire* buys fine cloths, and *Gloucester* coarse, still at *London;* and the like, of a vast variety of our manufactures.

By this exchange of manufactures abundance of trading families are maintain'd by the carriage and re-carriage of goods, vast number of men and cattle are employed, and numbers of inholders, victuallers, and their dependencies subsisted.

And on this account I cannot but observe to your honours, and 'tis well worth your consideration, that the already transposing a vast woollen manufacture from several parts of *England* to *London,* is a manifest detriment to trade in general, the several woollen goods now made in *Spittlefields,* where within this few years were none at all made, has already visibly affected the several parts, where they were before made, as *Norwich, Sudbury, Farnham,* and other towns, many of whose principal tradesmen are now remov'd hither, employ their stocks here, employ the poor here, and leave the poor of those countries to shift for work.

This breach of the circulation of trade must necessarily distemper the body, and I crave leave to give an example or two.

I'll presume to give an example in trade, which perhaps the gentlemen concern'd in this bill may, without reflection upon their knowledge, be ignorant of.

The city of *Norwich,* and parts adjacent, were for some ages employ'd in the manufactures of stuffs and stockings.

The latter trade, which was once considerable, is in a manner wholly transpos'd into *London*, by the vast quantities of worsted hose wove by the frame, which is a trade within this 20 years almost wholly new.

Now as the knitting frame performs that in a day which would otherwise employ a poor woman eight or ten days, by consequence a few frames perform'd the work of many thousand poor people; and the consumption being not increased, the effect immediately appear'd; so many stockings as were made in *London* so many the fewer were demanded from *Norwich*, till in a few years the manufacture there wholly sunk, the masters there turn'd their hands to other business; and whereas the hose trade from *Norfolk* once return'd at least 5,000*s. per* week, and as some say twice that sum, 'tis not now worth naming.

'Tis in fewer years, and near our memory, that of *Spittlefields* men have fallen into another branch of the *Norwich* trade, *viz.*, making of stuffs, drugets, &c.

If any man say the people of *Norfolk* are yet full of employ, and do not work; and some have been so weak as to make that reply, avoiding the many other demonstrations which could be given, this is past answering, *viz.* That the combers of wool in *Norfolk* and *Suffolk*, who formerly had all, or ten parts in eleven of their yarn manufactur'd in the country, now comb their wool indeed, and spin the yarn in the country, but send vast quantities of it to *London* to be woven; will any man question whether this be not a loss to *Norwich*; can there be as many weavers as before? And are there not abundance of workmen and masters too remov'd to *London*?

If it be so at *Norwich, Canterbury* is yet more a melancholy instance of it, where the houses stand empty, and the people go off, and the trade dyes, because the weavers have follow'd the manufacture to *London*; and whereas there was within few years 200 broad looms at

work

work, I am well assur'd there are not 50 now employ'd in
that city.

These are the effects of transposing manufactures, and
interrupting the circulation of trade.

All methods to bring our trade to be manag'd by
fewer hands than it was before, are in themselves pernicious to *England* in general, as they lessen the employment
of the poor, unhinge their hands from the labour, and
tend to bring our hands to be superior to our employ,
which as yet they are not.

In *Dorsetshire* and *Somersetshire* there always has been
a very considerable manufacture for stockings, at *Colchester* and *Sudbury* for bayes, sayes, &c. most of the wool
these countries use is bought at *London*, and carried down
into those counties, and then the goods being manufactur'd are brought back to *London* to market; upon transposing the manufacture as before, all the poor people and
all the cattel who hitherto were employ'd in that *voiture*,
are immediately disbanded by their country, the inkeepers
on the roads must decay, so much land lye for other uses,
as the cattle employ'd, houses and tenement on the roads,
and all their dependencies sink in value.

'Tis hard to calculate what a blow it would be to trade
in general, should every county but manufacture all the
several sorts of goods they use, it would throw our inland
trade into strange convulsions, which at present is perhaps,
or has been, in the greatest regularity of any in the
world.

What strange work must it then make when every
town shall have a manufacture, and every parish be a
ware-house; trade will be burthen'd with corporations,
which are generally equally destructive as monopolies, and
by this method will easily be made so.

Parish stocks, under the direction of Justices of Peace,
may soon come to set up petty manufactures, and here
shall all useful things be made, and all the poorer sort of

people

people shall be aw'd or byass'd to trade there only. Thus the shop-keepers, who pay taxes, and are the support of our inland circulation, will immediately be ruin'd, and thus we shall beggar the nation to provide for the poor.

As this will make every parish a market town, and every hospital a store-house, so in *London*, and the adjacent parts, to which vast quantities of the woollen manufacture will be thus transplanted, too great and disproportion'd numbers of the people will in time assemble.

Tho' the settled poor can't remove, yet single people will stroul about and follow the manufacturer; and thus in time such vast numbers will be drawn about *London*, as may be inconvenient to the government, and especially depopulating to those countries where the numbers of people, by reason of these manufactures are very considerable.

An eminent instance of this we have in the present trade to *Muscovy*, which however design'd for an improvement to the *English* nation, and boasted of as such, appears to be converted into a monopoly, and proves injurious and destructive to the nation. The persons concern'd removing and carrying out our people to teach that unpolish'd nation the improvements they are capable of.

If the bringing the *Flemings* to *England* brought with them their manufacture and trade, carrying our people abroad, especially to a country where the people work for little or nothing, what may it not do towards instructing that populous nation in such manufactures as may in time tend to the destruction of our trade, or the reducing our manufacture to an abatement in value, which will be felt at home by an abatement of wages, and that in provisions, and that in rent of land; and so the general stock sinks of course.

But as this is preparing, by eminent hands, to be laid

before

before this House as a grievance meriting your care and concern, I omit insisting on it here.

And this removing of people is attended with many inconveniences which are not easily perceived, as

1. The immediate fall of the value of all lands in those countries where the manufactures were before; for as the numbers of people, by the consumption of provisions, must where ever they encrease make rents rise, and lands valuable; so those people removing, tho' the provisions would, if possible, follow them, yet the price of them must fall by all that charge they are at for carriage, and consequently lands must fall in proportion.

2. This transplanting of families, in time, would introduce great and new alterations in the countries they removed to, which as they would be to the profit of some places, would be to the detriment of others, and can by no means be just any more than it is convenient; for no wise government studies to put any branch of their country to any particular disadvantages, tho' it may be found in the general account in another place.

If it be said here will be manufactures in every parish, and that will keep the people at home,

I humbly represent what strange confusion and particular detriment to the general circulation of trade *mention'd before* it must be, to have every parish make its own manufactures.

1. It will make our towns and counties independent of one another, and put a damp to correspondence, which all will allow to be a great motive of trade in general.

2. It will fill us with various sorts and kinds of manufactures, by which our stated sorts of goods will in time dwindle away in reputation, and foreigners not know them one from another. Our several manufactures are known by their respective names; and our serges, bayes and other goods, are bought abroad by the character and reputation of the places where they are made; when there

shall

shall come new and unheard of kinds to market, some
better, some worse, as to be sure new undertakers will vary
in kinds, the dignity and reputation of the *English* goods
abroad will be lost, and so many confusions in trade must
follow, as are too many to repeat.

3. Either our parish-stock must sell by wholesale or
by retail, or both; if the first, 'tis doubted they will make
sorry work of it, and having other business of their own
make but poor merchants; if by retail, then they turn
pedlars, will be a publick nusance to trade, and at last
quite ruin it.

4. This will ruin all the carriers in *England*, the wool
will be all manufactured where it is sheer'd, every body will
make their own cloaths, and the trade which now lives by
running thro' a multitude of hands, will go then through
so few, that thousands of families will want employment,
and this is the only way to reduce us to the condition
spoken of, to have more hands than work.

'Tis the excellence of our *English* manufacture, that
it is so planted as to go thro' as many hands as 'tis
possible; he that contrives to have it go thro' fewer, ought
at the same time to provide work for the rest—as it is it
employs a great multitude of people, and can employ more;
but if a considerable number of these people be unhing'd
from their employment, it cannot but be detrimental to
the whole.

When I say we could employ more people in *England*,
I do not mean that we cannot do our work with those we
have, but I mean thus:

First, It should be more people brought over from
foreign parts. I do not mean that those we have should
be taken from all common employments and put to our
manufacture; we may unequally dispose of our hands,
and so have too many for some works, and too few for
others; and 'tis plain that in some parts of *England* it is
so, what else can be the reason, why in our southern parts

of

of *England, Kent* in particular, borrows 20,000 people of other counties to get in her harvest.

But if more forreigners came among us, if it were 2 millions, it could do us no harm, because they would consume our provisions, and we have land enough to pro-duce much more than we do, and they would consume our manufactures, and we have wool enough for any quantity.

I think therefore, with submission, to erect manufac-tures in every town to transpose the manufactures from the settled places into private parishes and corporations, to parcel out our trade to every door, it must be ruinous to the manufacturers themselves, will turn thousands of families out of their employments, and take the bread out of the mouths of diligent and industrious families to feed vagrants, thieves and beggars, who ought much rather to be compell'd, by legal methods, to seek that work which it is plain is to be had; and thus this Act will instead of settling and relieving the poor, encrease their number, and starve the best of them.

It remains now, according to my first proposal page 37, to consider from whence proceeds the poverty of our people, what accident, what decay of trade, what want of employment, what strange revolution of circumstances makes our people poor, and consequently burthensom, and our laws deficient, so as to make more and other laws requisite, and the nation concerned to apply a remedy to this growing disease. I answer,

I. Not for want of work; and besides what has been said on that head, I humbly desire these two things may be consider'd.

First, 'Tis apparent, that if one man, woman, or child, can by his, or her labour, earn more money than will sub-sist one body, there must consequently be no want of work, since any man would work for just as much as would supply himself rather than starve.—What a vast difference then must there be between the work and the

work-men,

work-men, when 'tis now known that in *Spittle-fields*, and other adjacent parts of the city, there is nothing more frequent than for a journey-man weaver, of many sorts, to gain from 15*s.* to 30*s. per* week wages, and I appeal to the silk throwsters, whether they do not give 8*s.* 9*s.* and 10*s. per* week, to blind men and cripples, to turn wheels, and do the meanest and most ordinary works.

Cur Moriatur Homo, &c.

Why are the families of these men starv'd, and their children in work-houses, and brought up by charity; I am ready to produce to this Honourable House the man who for several years has gain'd of me by his handy labour at the mean scoundrel employment of tile making from 16*s.* to 20*s. per* week wages, and all that time would hardly have a pair of shoes to his feet, or cloaths to cover his nakedness, and had his wife and children kept by the parish.

The meanest labours in this nation afford the workman sufficient to provide for himself and his family, and that could never be if there was a want of work.

2. I humbly desire this Honourable House to consider the present difficulty of raising soldiers in this kingdom; the vast charge the kingdom is at to the officers to procure men; the many little and *not over honest methods* made use of to bring them into the service, the laws made to compel them; why are gaols rumag'd for malefactors, and the Mint and prisons for debtors, the war is an employment of honour, and suffers some scandal in having men taken from the gallows, and immediately from villains, and housebreakers made gentlemen soldiers. If men wanted employment, and consequently bread, this could never be, any man would carry a musket rather than starve, and wear the Queen's cloth, or any bodies cloth, rather than go naked, and live in rags and want; 'tis plain the nation is full of people, and 'tis as plain our people have no particular aversion to the war, but they are not

poor

poor enough to go abroad; 'tis poverty makes men soldiers, and drives crowds into the armies, and the difficulties to get *English*-men to list is, because they live in
plenty and ease, and he that can earn 20*s. per* week at an
easie, steady employment, must be drunk or mad when he
lists for a soldier, to be knock'd o'th'head for 3*s.* 6*d. per*
week; but if there was no work to be had, if the poor
wanted employment, if they had not bread to eat, nor
knew not how to earn it, thousands of young lusty fellows
would fly to the pike and musket, and choose to dye like
men in the face of the enemy, rather than lye at home,
starve, perish in poverty and distress.

From all these particulars, and innumerable unhappy
instances which might be given, 'tis plain, the poverty of
our people which is so burthensome, and increases upon us
so much, does not arise from want of proper employments,
and for want of work, or employers, and consequently,

Work-houses, corporations, parish-stocks, and the like,
to set them to work, as they are pernicious to trade,
injurious and impoverishing to those already employ'd, so
they are needless, and will come short of the end propos'd.

The poverty and exigence of the poor in *England*, is
plainly deriv'd from one of these two particular causes.

Casualty or Crime.

By casualty, I mean sickness of families, loss of limbs
or sight, and any, either natural or accidental impotence
as to labour.

These as infirmities meerly providential are not at all
concern'd in this debate; ever were, will, and ought to be
the charge and care of the respective parishes where such
unhappy people chance to live, nor is there any want of
new laws to make provision for them, our ancestors having
been always careful to do it.

The crimes of our people, and from whence their
poverty derives, as the visible and direct fountains are,

29   1. Luxury.

1. **Luxury.**
2. **Sloath.**
3. **Pride.**

Good husbandry is no *English* vertue, it may have been brought over, and in some places where it has been planted it has thriven well enough, but 'tis a forreign species, it neither loves, nor is belov'd by an *English-man*; and 'tis observ'd nothing is so universally hated, nothing treated with such a general contempt as a rich covetous man, tho' he does no man any wrong, only saves his own, every man will have an ill word for him, if a misfortune happens to him, hang him a covetous old rogue, 'tis no matter, he's rich enough, nay when a certain great man's house was on fire, I have heard the people say one to another, let it burn and 'twill, he's a covetous old miserly dog, I wo'nt trouble my head to help him, he'd be hang'd before he'd give us a bit of bread if we wanted it.

'Tho this be a fault, yet I observe from it something of the natural temper and genius of the nation, generally speaking, they cannot save their money.

'Tis generally said the *English* get estates, and the *Dutch* save them; and this observation I have made between forreigners and *English-men* that where an *Englishman* earns 20*s. per* week, and *but just lives*, as we call it, a *Dutch-man* grows rich, and leaves his children in very good condition; where an *English* labouring man with his 9*s. per* week lives wretchedly and poor, a *Dutch-man* with that wages will live very tolerably well, keep the wolf from the door, and have every thing handsome about him. In short, he will be rich with the same gain as makes the *English-man* poor, he'll thrive when the other goes in rags, and he'll live when the other starves, or goes a begging.

The reason is plain, a man with good husbandry, and thought in his head, brings home his earnings honestly to his family, commits it to the management of his wife, or otherwise disposes it for proper subsistance, and this man
30

with

with mean gains, lives comfortably, and brings up a family, when a single man getting the same wages, drinks it away at the ale-house, thinks not of to morrow, layes up nothing for sickness, age, or disaster, and when any of these happen, he's starv'd, and a beggar.

This is so apparent in every place, that I think it needs no explication; that *English* labouring people eat and drink, but especially the latter three times as much in value as any sort of forreigners of the same dimensions in the world.

I am not writing this as a satyr on our people, 'tis a sad truth; and worthy the debate and application of the nations physitians assembled in Parliament, the profuse extravagant humour of our poor people in eating and drinking, keeps them low, causes their children to be left naked and starving, to the care of the parishes, whenever either sickness or disaster befalls the parent.

The next article is their *sloath*.

We are the most *lazy diligent* nation in the world, vast trade, rich manufactures, mighty wealth, universal correspondence and happy success have been constant companions of *England*, and given us the title of an industrious people, and so in general we are.

But there is a general taint of slothfulness upon our poor, there's nothing more frequent, than for an *Englishman* to work till he has got his pocket full of money, and then go and be idle, *or perhaps drunk*, till 'tis all gone, and perhaps himself in debt; and ask him in his cups what he intends, he'll tell you honestly, he'll drink as long as it lasts, and then go to work for more.

I humbly suggest this distemper's so general, so epidemick, and so deep rooted in the nature and genius of the *English*, that I much doubt its being easily redress'd, and question whether it be possible to reach it by an Act of Parliament.

This is the ruine of our poor, the *wife mourns*, the

children

children *starve*, the husband *has work before him*, but lies at the ale-house, or otherwise *idles away* his time, and won't work.

'Tis the men that *wont work*, not the men that *can get no work*, which makes the numbers of our poor; all the work-houses in *England*, all the overseers setting up stocks and manufactures won't reach this case; and I humbly presume to say, if these two articles are remov'd, there will be no need of the other.

I make no difficulty to promise on a short summons, to produce above a thousand families in *England*, within my particular knowledge, who go in rags, and their children wanting bread, whose fathers can earn their 15 to 25*s. per* week, but will not work, who may have work enough, but are too idle to seek after it, and hardly vouchsafe to earn any thing more than bare subsistance, and spending money for themselves.

I can give an incredible number of examples in my own knowledge among our labouring poor. I once paid 6 or 7 men together on a *Saturday* night, the least 10*s.* and some 30*s.* for work, and have seen them go with it directly to the ale-house, lie there till *Monday*, spend it every penny, and run in debt to boot, and not give a farthing of it to their families, tho' all of them had wives and children.

From hence comes poverty, parish charges, and beggary, if ever one of these wretches falls sick, all they would ask was a pass to the parish they liv'd at, and the wife and children to the door a begging.

If this Honourable House can find out a remedy for this part of the mischief; if such Acts of Parliament may be made as may effectually cure the sloath and luxury of our poor, that shall make drunkards take care of wife and children, spendthrifts lay up for a *wet day*; idle, lazy fellows diligent; and thoughtless sottish men, careful and provident.

If

If this can be done, I presume to say, there will be no need of transposing and confounding our manufactures, and the circulation of our trade; they will soon find work enough, and there will soon be less poverty among us, and if this cannot be done, setting them to work upon woollen manufactures, and thereby encroaching upon those that now work at them, will but ruine our trade, and consequently increase the number of the poor.

I do not presume to offer the schemes I have now drawn of methods for the bringing much of this to pass, because I shall not presume to lead a body so august, so wise, and so capable as this Honourable Assembly.

I humbly submit what is here offered, as reasons to prove the attempt now making insufficient; and doubt not but in your great wisdom, you will find out ways and means to set this matter in a clearer light, and on a right foot.

And if this obtains on the House to examine farther into this matter, the author humbly recommends it to their consideration to accept, *in behalf of all the poor of this nation,* a clause in the room of this objected against, which shall answer the end without this terrible ruin to our trade and people.

FINIS.

A

VIEW

OF THE

Greenland TRADE

AND

Whale-Fishery.

WITH THE

𝕹ational and 𝕻rivate

ADVANTAGES thereof.

LONDON:

Printed for J. ROBERTS, near the *Oxford-Arms* in
Warwick-Lane. MDCCXXII.

TO

Sir John Eyles, *Bar.*

Sub-Governor of the *South-Sea* Company, *&c.*

SIR,

IT was by your commands signified to me in the following letter of the 13th of *July* last, that I drew up
a brief account of the *Greenland* Trade, for the perusal of
the Court of Directors of the *South-Sea* Company; and
you will, I hope, forgive me that I have taken the liberty,
to print both your letter, and the said account as it was
laid before them; being persuaded thereto from many
reasons, particularly in justification of my self, and as an
appeal to all the world for the truth of what is here laid
down, I having been supposed to mislead your judgment
by false allegations. I must have had the greatest as-
surance in the world to think of misguiding you, for tho'
you confess'd you was unacquainted with the trade, the
apt objections in the frequent conversations you allow'd
me on this subject, and the curious enquiries you made,
shew'd your judgment too penetrating to be deceiv'd; and
left me no room to expect, that any thing that was insinuating, and not grounded upon reason, could be imposed
upon you. Nor was there the least occasion for such an
attempt; the thing will speak for itself; and I am persuaded, whoever examines into the nature and circum-

3 stances

stances of the *Greenland* Trade, or considers the following sheets, as carefully and accurately as you have done; will be convinc'd, that I have laid down nothing, but what is true and practicable.

I am persuaded, and am sensible of your continued zeal in this affair; and as it will be a perpetual glory to you, that in so critical a juncture, you undertook the care and conduct of the *South-Sea* Company's distracted affairs; and that you have, (by standing boldly in support of reason, against wild and extravagant schemes, with so much steadiness and calm resolution) been an instrument in no small degree, in composing their affairs, and recovering their credit: It will be an addition to your character, that, even in the midst of all the difficulties upon you, greater than ever yet fell in weight upon one man in your station, you could have temper enough, or find time sufficient to employ your thoughts upon the enlargement of their trade: But you never made this objection, which was indeed the only one I fear'd; that you was already too much involved in other business to think of it.

Another reason I had for printing these sheets, is, that the nation in general may see, that this trade may be carried on from hence, equally at least, if not better, than from other nations; who, by the supineness of this kingdom, have it wholly in their hands: That the inestimable advantages the kingdom will receive by it, whatever befalls the particular undertakers, may be an inducement to some patriots to encourage it by the assistance of the Legislature, in whatever may, upon practice be found necessary.

These reasons I thought sufficient, though I have many others, for publishing these arguments about the carrying on the *Greenland* Trade, which I need not take up your time in relating particularly.

If

If I may have your excuse, I hope you will make my apologies to the Court of Directors, whose care and zeal for the Company's affairs, deserve the applause of the proprietors: And I am confident, nothing but fear of miscarriage in an attempt which has been successless to others, has been the occasion of an alteration in their thoughts, and their resolving, as they have done, not to carry it on.

I may seem too fond of my own opinion if I should say, that a little less precipitation in their thoughts, and a little more consideration in the merit or demerit of what I laid before them, might have given them a better opinion of it: But you gave me reason sufficient; the summer was far spent, and it was absolutely necessary to come to an immediate resolution, or else the proper vessels could not be built in time.

I have added to what was laid before the Court of Directors some further remarks, estimates and calculations which I have now collected, having omitted to mention them in the first state, through the haste and expedition with which you required it to be drawn.

I submit this wholly to your observation; and am with the highest deference and respect,

Your Honour's

most obedient,

and most Obliged

Humble Servant,

HENRY ELKING.

London,
Aug. 20. 1722.

5

The Letter of Sir *John Eyles*, written to the Author, and mention'd above, is as follows, *viz.*

L o n d o n, July 13. 1722.

Sir,

IT is now *seventeen months since you first discours'd me upon the subject of the whale-fishing, inviting me into a copartnership with several gentlemen who had thoughts of undertaking it : And I must own, the reasons you gave me, why it would be profitable to the undertakers, had almost determin'd me to engage with them. But as foreigners were now in the entire possession of this trade, originally carry'd on solely by the* English *; and all attempts that have been made from hence of late years, to recover it, have been fruitless ; I could not resolve upon it, till I had made a more strict enquiry and examination : When I found by the account you gave me, how extensive this trade might be made ; the great numbers of ships that are annually employ'd in it by our neighbours ; the multitudes of seamen train'd up thereby, and fitted for the service of their country ; that it is a trade carry'd on to desolate seas, open to all the world, unattended with the charges of ambassadors and consuls, factors, &c. that needed no capitulations with foreign powers, nor protection of convoys equal to what other trades do in time of war ; that the whole export is nothing but the product of labour, and the expence of provisions and wages for seamen ; I say, when I found these things, I took a new turn of thought, and consider'd*

7

this

this trade in another view. It appear'd to me so consider-able, that even the South-Sea *Company might undertake it; so national, that all reasonable encouragement might be expected from the legislature, when their aid and assistance might be wanting.*

In this way of thinking, it became my duty, in the station I am in, in that Company's service, to be well con-vinc'd, that I had good and sufficient ground to recommend it to the Court of Directors: I started to you all the diffi-culties and objections that occurr'd to me at several meetings, to which you gave me answers that seem'd to me full and satisfactory: You shew'd me plainly, by the methods you propos'd, that an hundred ships might be manag'd with the same ease as ten, and their stores effectually secur'd from waste and embezzlement: You left me at no loss in account-ing for the miscarriages of some late expeditions to the Greenland Seas, *and chalk'd out a sure way to avoid the errors they suffer'd by: To my objection concerning the cheapness of the* Dutch *navigation, the agility and better adaption of that people and country to this and other fish-ing trades, you gave me many good reasons to think it a great mistake; and that, consider'd in the whole, the* Dutch *navigation is dearer than ours: That we can be in no want of people equally proper and experienc'd in this trade; and that our river is far more convenient than any place in* Holland, *both in regard to the fitting out, and receiving the ships in return from their voyage: And in short, that we may have in almost every thing the advantage of foreigners: These and many other matters, too many to be particularly enumerated here, I question'd you upon, and you answer'd to my perfect satisfaction.*

Persuaded thus of the advantage this trade might be to the South-Sea *Company, the national service they would do by carrying it on; I did, now sixteen months since, propose*

it

it to the Court of Directors, who at that time so far ap-
prov'd of it, that they, in the month of September *last,*
recommended it to a General Court, who agreed to it, and
gave the Court of Directors sufficient powers.

From this time, the copartnership first propos'd by you
was no longer thought on; and I persuaded you to drop
that design, and to depend upon the South-Sea *Company.*
You did so, and have ever since been in reasonable expecta-
tion, that preparations would have been made this summer,
for setting out upon the trade next spring; and you are
not more surprized than my self, to find so great a back-
wardness in this affair.

Whether I had not capacity enough to see through the
fallacy of your answers to my enquiries, or to object to
the accounts you gave me, I know not; but I ought to
have some diffidence in my self, since I find now, at the
time this affair should have been in agitation, and ships
building for the purpose, some others, without whose con-
currence it is impossible to proceed, differ of late very
much in sentiments with me upon this subject.

What I have to desire of you, and is the occasion of
this letter, is, that you will lay before the Court of Direc-
tors, in writing, the substance of what you from time to time
have said to me, upon my examining into the nature of this
trade: If you draw it up under clear and distinct heads,
they may by frequent reading it, retain those arguments,
which in conversation or debate may slip the memory, or be
unobserv'd; and be thereby either convinc'd, as I think I
am, of the practicableness of it, or be able to shew me those
errors or fallacies in your notions, which I have not been
able to find out of my self.

I desire you to be as careful and correct as possible, and

that

that you will avoid putting down any thing that is insinuating only, and cannot be supported from reason or practice. We must very soon determine, either to carry or not to carry on this trade; and therefore the more expedition you dispatch this with, it will be the more acceptable to,

Sir,

Your Humble Servant,

JOHN EYLES.

To Mr. Henry Elking.

A
VIEW
OF THE
Greenland TRADE, *&c.*

THE *Greenland* trade hath in it all the qualificaticns that are needful to recommend it to this nation: It is qualified to enrich and make it more powerful: It is to be spoken of with regret, that though it was first discover'd by the *English*, it has been long since abandon'd to our more diligent neighbours the *Dutch*, and others; and this nation has suffer'd it to lie neglected, to their infinite loss and dishonour.

Though it has been generally suppos'd, it will be found upon examination a very great mistake, that the *English* cannot manage this trade, which the *Hollanders, Hamburgers, Bremers, French* and *Spaniards*, all carry on to advantage, and by which means they are made rich, even out of our pockets, who sit still and buy those goods of them for our ready money, which the *English* are every way better qualify'd to furnish to themselves, and even for export to other nations; as will be shewn in the following sheets.

Nor is it any just objection to the practicableness of this trade, to say, that it has been often attempted without success; since the reasons of that want of success, which

are

are fully examin'd in these sheets will appear to arise, not from any deficiency in the trade, but from the evident mismanagement of the undertakers; proceeding either from ignorance, want of stock, want of conduct, or of honesty.

It is a vulgar error, that the *Dutch* can build ships, or sail ships, or catch whales, better and cheaper than the *English.* Can they, who neither have timber of their own growth to build, nor iron, tar and hemp of their own growth to rig, or provisions of their own growth to victual their ships, nor sufficient seamen, harponeers and steersmen for the whale-fishing among their own subjects, ever manage a trade cheaper than the *English,* who have most of these materials and the provisions in their own country or plantations, and cheaper than the *Dutch;* and can, till their own men are taught, hire the artists at the same places, and upon as cheap terms as the *Dutch?*

The author of this Tract undertaketh to account for all the miscarriages of those gentlemen, who have formerly attempted this trade; and to prove even to demonstration, how every one of those false steps may be avoided, right and unerring measures be taken, and the trade be render'd prosperous and successful, even beyond what it has been, or can be, to the *Dutch* or any other nation.

In order to this, and to make every observing reader capable of making a judgment, both of what has been done by other nations, and may be done by us; the author has, from unquestion'd authorities, and from his own long experience, given here a clear, though brief account of the *Greenland* trade in general, and of every thing belonging to it, that may contribute to the successful carrying it on in this kingdom: Which account he has digested into several chapters or sections, for the more clear understanding the particulars; and those chapters appear under the following heads.

1. An

1. An account how the whale-fishery is, and ought to
be perform'd, from the first outset to the return of the
ships.

2. By whom this fishery is chiefly carried on, *viz.* by
the *Hollanders, Hamburgers* and *Bremers;* and how much
it appears to their advantage.

3. A brief recapitulation of what happen'd in the
infancy of the *Greenland* trade; how the *English* were
first in it, how they lost it, and what have been the causes
that all their attempts to retrieve it have been unsuccessful.

4. A full proof that *England* may retrieve this trade,
and are able to carry it on more to advantage than any
other nation; and all the known objections to the contrary
answer'd and remov'd.

CHAP. I.

*An Account how the Whale-Fishery is, and ought to be
perform'd, from the first Outset to the Return of the
Ships.*

ALL the necessary fishing instruments, such as harp-
ing-irons or harpoons, lances, cutting-knives, nose-
hooks, lines, shalloops, casks, &c. must be provided, and
the ships compleatly fitted, victuall'd and mann'd before
the end of *March;* and every thing being on board, and
the ships fallen down to *Gravesend,* and clear'd there,
must sail by the beginning of *April* for *Greenland.*

The

The vessels most proper for the whale-fishing, are those we call fly-boats, or cats, or hag-boats; and should be very strong built, and doubled at the bow, to resist the shocks of the ice. The size of those ships commonly used, are from 200 to 500 ton, little over or under; and they are supply'd with men and shalloops as follows:

	Ton.	Shalloops.		Men and Boys.
A Ship of	200 must have 4		and	29
	250 5			36
	300 6			43
	450 7			50

The particular qualifications of the men for a ship of about 300 ton, and six shalloops, are as follows, *viz.*

1 Chief Harpooneer, who commands the whole fishery.
1 Captain or master of the ship.
5 Other harpooneers.
6 Steersmen of the shalloops.
6 Managers of the lines.
1. Surgeon.
1. Boatswain.
1. Carpenter.
2. Coopers.
16. Common sailors.
2 or 8 Boys.

42 or 43 men in all.

The voyage to *Greenland* is generally performed in four or five weeks. The fishery begins with the month of *May*, and continues all the months of *June* and *July*: But whether they have a good fishing or a bad, they must come away and be clear of the ice in the month of *August*, so that in the month of *September* at farthest they must be expected home; but a ship that meets with a fortunate and early fishery in the month of *May*, may return in *June* or *July*.

The whale-fishing is carry'd on in the great Frozen Sea between the coasts of *Greenland* and *Spitzbergen*, in the

                                                    latitude

latitude of 70 to 80 degrees *north*; and as they have here no night, but see the sun always, during the season of the fishery, above the horizon, they divide the time not by day and night, but into three watches, allowing one third of the crew to be at rest for eight hours, when they turn out for the next; and so alternately they are upon duty sixteen hours, and asleep eight hours in every twenty four: And their eating-times are likewise divided thus, breakfast about four in the morning, dinner at noon, supper at eight in the afternoon; only with this exception, that when they are in pursuit of a whale, then all hands are called to help, without respect to sleeping-time, or eating-time, or any other business.

The whales are found among the ice, in the openings and vacancies between it; and thither the ships sail in quest of them, running boldly in between great floating islands of ice, which lye continually on either hand of them, commonly called fields of ice, and are often of many leagues circumference. To such large fields of ice they fasten their ships with a great hook, commonly called a nose-hook, and a hawser or tow-line; picking a hole first in the solid ice, wherein the hook taketh hold. And it is necessary to have ingenious and experienc'd commanders, who by their observations are able to judge upon what degrees of latitude to enter the ice, where and to what place of the ice to fasten the ship, where to stay or to remove, and where it is likely that whales will appear, if not discover'd immediately; and where 'tis proper to change places, to avoid being surrounded with ice; and how to preserve the ship from being lost and crush'd to pieces between the great islands of ice: Which are accidents that sometimes happen by carelessness or ignorance.

The reasons why the whales are found in great numbers between those openings of the ice is, because there they find their food in prodigious quantities, being small water insects, some like small shrimps, or snails without

shells;

15

shells; some of the shape of a spider, of the bigness of a grey-pea, and of a dark-brown colour, being a fatty, trainy, oily substance. The water-insects are no where seen but in those parts of the seas; and those only in places of 80, 100, or 120 fathom depth, which are crowded with them even from the surface to the bottom. It is supposed they breed among the weeds, or other things which nature furnishes at the bottom of the sea; for in deeper water the sea's clear, no insects are found, and consequently few or no whales can be expected there, these little creatures cou'd not be sufficient to serve as food to so vast a body as a whale, did he not find and swallow an immense quantity of them together.

As soon as the ships come near 70 degrees, and approach the ice, they immediately fit out their shalloops, and furnish every boat with lines, lances, harpoons, and all things necessary for the work; every shalloop or boat having six men, (*viz.*) one harpooneer, one steersmen, one manager of the lines, and three seamen to row, and six or seven lines on board, the length of which is 125 to 130 fathoms each.

When they are entred between the ice, and they see a whale, they row immediately up to him, as close as they can, and the steersman of the shalloop, must direct the same to the middle of the body, because the head is invulnerable, and towards the tail is dangerous. The harpooneer seeing himself able to reach the whale, casts the harpoon, or harping-iron, into his back, as near as is possible behind the head, because there it takes the surest hold, and doth not plow out so soon, as if cast nearer towards the tail.

The most critical time of striking the whales with the harpoon, is when in diversion they spout the water, which they do with great violence and noise, playing upon the surface of the water, without apprehension of disturbance.

The whale finding himself wounded, immediately

shoots

shoots under water, running away, notwithstanding his prodigious bulk, with the lines, as swift as a bird can fly. The shalloops following as fast as they can, in the mean time veering out the lines, which are tied one to another, and coiled up in the shalloop; and the other shalloops, upon a sign given, row up immediately, and keep close to the first, in order to furnish more lines, when they are wanted. Thus they follow, till the whale, who cannot live long under water, without air, appears again, then rowing up to him, strike another harpoon into him. The whale shoots away again, as before, but is seldom able to run off above one or two lines length at the second wound, but being tired, and losing much blood, comes up again, as before, and then fainting, they attack him with the lances, striking and sticking as many of them, and as deep as they can into his body. The lances penetrating into his entrails, put him into a great fury, but all the resistance he is able to make, is to throw his tail about in a terrible manner, and the skill of the steersmen in the shalloops is seen upon this occasion; for if they do not keep out of the reach of his tail, one blow of it, will dash the shalloop in a thousand pieces, but they dextrously avoid it, and keeping close to his sides, and continuing to wound him with the lances, he begins to spout blood instead of water, which is a signal of his being mortally wounded; as soon as he is dead, they cut off his tail, and fastning a line to the stump, joyfully tow him along, shouting and hollowing to their ship, and fasten the whale to the side of the same.

If they see more whales, they pursue their game with all their might, and with five or six shalloops, they may attack two whales at a time; and if two or three ships have agreed to fish in company, or to assist one another about the killing of one or more whales, they divide amongst them what they catch, according to agreement.

When they come to work on the dead whale, they

begin

begin with long and great knives to cut off the fat, which we call the blubber. This fat is all round about his body, upon his back and belly, to the thickness of six inches, something more or less, but about his under lips, a whale has sometimes blubber or fat, two or three foot thick, and his two fins also are very fat. The body of the whale serves them for a stage, and with irons fasten'd near to the heels of their shoes, called ice-spurs, they preserve and keep themselves from sliding off in the water. Thus they work upon him, artfully turning the body, till they have cut off the fat on all sides, and the fins, which we erroneously call whale-bones, out of his mouth, or upper jaws, where they grow in a very wonderful manner, and hard to describe, and are about 500 in number.

When the fins and the blubber are thus all cut away, and hoisted into the ship, they turn the rest of the body a-drift, leaving it to the sharks, bears, birds, and other voracious creatures, who always attend in great numbers for it, as their prey.

The blubber is hoisted over into the ship in large square pieces, after which it is cut upon the deck into small pieces, such as can easily go through the bung-holes in the hold of the ship, to the casks to which it is conveyed, or let down through a pipe, made of sail-cloth.

The whales are of different sizes; they commonly yield forty to fifty puncheons of blubber each whale; though there are some that yield sixty to eighty, even one hundred puncheons; and a whale of fifty puncheons, being commonly counted a very good whale, hath 1700 to 1800 hundred weight of fins in his mouth.

If a dead whale be met floating upon the sea, the property is to those who find it, and take first hold of the same; and to encourage the ships crew to be always very watchful, he who discovers, or first sees the dead whale, has a premium of a ducat, or half a guinea, for his discovery. The train oil of such a dead whale, especially if

it

it died of it self, is of a reddish colour, and not so valuable as of a whale that is immediately killed, but the fins are of equal goodness with those of another whale.

Besides the whales, there are several other monstrous fishes found and catch'd in those seas. Namely,

The pot-fish, or the *Sperma-Ceti* fish, called by the *French cachelot :* He is as big as the whale, having a monstrous large head, whereout they can get and fill 12 to 20 barrels of brains; and this brains, after purged and refined, they call (but very falsly) *sperma ceti.* Besides this, they cut from his body several puncheons of blubber; but he is not near so fat as the whale. This is a fish of prey, hath a row of great teeth in his mouth as white as ivory. One of these was caught last year, 1721, and before he was killed, vomited up, or cast out of his mouth a shark of 12 foot long, which it is supposed he had just taken, and not quite swallowed when he was surprized and kill'd. The spout-holes of this fish are at his nose, and not behind in the neck, like the whale. But this fish is seldom met with.

The fin-fish is as big as the whale too, and is distinguished from the whale by a large fin on his back. He is not so fat, nor hath such fins in his mouth as a whale; so that they never are thought worth the trouble of catching, or to venture the harpoons and lines upon him; being more nimble than the whale, he might run away with the lines, or endanger the shalloops.

Sometimes they meet with a fish called the unicorn, a very beautiful spotted creature, with a horn growing out of his upper jaw, and pointing strait forward, from 3 to 12 foot long, according to the growth of the fish; which is valued and sold as dear as ivory. This fish will yield one or two barrels of blubber, the train oil of which is whiter than that of the whale.

The morse or sea-cow, some call it the sea-horse, is found here too, both in the water and upon the ice. It is

as

as big as a large bullock, and has two large teeth in the
upper jaw sometimes half a yard long, hanging downwards,
and bending inward like a hook. With these teeth he
will attack men, and lay hold of a boat, and may sink it
or tear it to pieces, unless the men are nimble, and kill
him before he can do mischief. His skin is thick, but
spungy and porous : His two fangs are sold for ivory; and
they cut from a pretty large one about a puncheon of
blubber.

The seals, or dog-fishes, are often upon the ice in great
numbers, and they kill them very easily : One blow with a
staff upon their noses makes them fall. They yield very
good train; and the fat of 12 to 20 seals will fill a puncheon. Their skin is used by the trunkmakers, or dress'd
as leather, for several uses.

Many white bears are found upon the ice, swimming
from one island of ice to another : They feed upon fish,
and the flesh of the dead whales, after our fishermen have
turn'd them adrift as above. They kill them with lances,
or shoot them with musket-balls. Some of them are as
large as a cow : Their skin is valuable, and their fat yields
train-oyl too, but in small quantity.

When the fishery among the ice is over, the ships go
sometimes to the bays of *Spitzbergen*, and the men go
ashore to refresh themselves. There they find very good
deer, especially roebucks : They are very fat, and their
flesh is very delicious, occasion'd by the herbage and excellent fine grass, mix'd with several choice wholesome
simples, on the rocks and mountains in that country.
These creatures are very tame at first, till by hunting
and shooting them they are made more shy. Their
flesh is a great refreshment to the seamen after their
fishery; and they eat the venison boil'd with those wholesome herbs, and they eat sallads thereof, especially of

scurvy-grass,

scurvy-grass, which grows there in great quantity. But this diversion, and the pleasure of their repast, tempts them often to mispend some of that valuable time there, which ought to be wholly employ'd in the business of the voyage. This has sometimes been done to the great loss and disappointment of the employers; and must therefore by all the strictness imaginable be prevented, by those who hope for any success in these fishing expeditions.

CHAP. II.

By whom this Fishery chiefly is carried on; viz. by the Hollanders, Hamburghers, *and* Bremers; *and how much it appears to be to their advantage.*

WHILE all the *Netherland* provinces, tho' subject to the King of *Spain,* were govern'd by their own laws, and enjoy'd their ancient liberties, the greatest part of the commerce of these parts of the world was in the hands of the *Flemings;* particularly, they had the manufactures, the navigation, and the fisheries of every kind: And even to this day, the *Hollanders,* who are now masters of the said fisheries, sell their herrings in foreign markets under the name of *Flemish* herrings.

But when the King of *Spain* began, under the ministry of the duke *D'Alva,* to tyrannize and persecute, invading both the civil and religious liberties of the people, the inhabitants fled; and dispersing themselves into several parts, carry'd with them the trade also. Thus the manufactures came to *England,* and the navigation and fishery went to *Holland;* which province, with six others, maintaining their liberty, and *Spain* continuing to

oppress

oppress the rest, and the Duke of *Parma* taking the city of *Antwerp* in the year 1585, (which was to the *Flemings* then, what *Amsterdam* is now to the *Dutch*) was the fatal stroke and period of their trade and navigation.

Thus it is to be observed, that navigation, and the commerce attending it, never thrive but in countries free from exactions and impositions of absolute power : Free people alone are capable of carrying on those things. Hence it is, that the *Dutch* having maintain'd their liberty, drew to themselves the fishery of cod and herring ; and, extending themselves in trade, have, among other things, gotten likewise this most important article of the *Greenland*, or whale-fishery. For, except the two *Hanse* towns, *Bremen* and *Hamburgh*, free people like themselves, the greatest part of this trade is in their hands. The port of *Bayonne* in *France*, St. *Jean de Luz* and St. *Sebastian* in *Spain*, with the town of *Bergen* in *Norway*, all put together, send but about 20 ships a year on this trade : Whereas this very year, 1722. there have been sent to *Greenland*, for the whale-fishing,

180 Ships from *Holland.*
52 Ships from *Hamburgh.*
24 Ships from *Bremen.*

But that the vigor with which the *Hollanders* pursue this trade, and something of the gain they make by it, may appear ; and that the author of these sheets may not seem to speak without sufficient authority ; here under is a true list of the number of all the ships which have gone from *Holland* for the whale-fishing, from the year 1675 inclusive, to the present year 1722 exclusive ; with the number of whales they have kill'd, and the quantity of oil they have produced ; and is as follows :

N.B. There were sent to *Greenland* by the *Hollanders*, in the year 1670, 148 ships, which brought home 792 whales ; and in 1671, 155 ships brought 630½ whales : But in 1672, 1673, 1674, when they were engaged in war with *England* and *France*, they sent no ships at all, not being able to spare the seamen from their fleet.

VIZ.

Year.		Number of Ships sent out		Number of Whales killed		Puncheons of Train-Oil
1675	...	148	...	881½	...	36260
1676	...	145	...	808⅓	...	32347
1677	...	149	...	686	...	30050
1678	...	110	...	1118¾	...	44750
1679	...	126	...	831	...	39857
1680	...	148	...	1373	...	52406
1681	...	172	...	889	...	30306
1682	...	186	...	1470	...	62960
1683	...	242	...	1343	..	43540
1684	...	246	...	1185	...	44730
1685	...	212	...	1383¼	...	55960
1686	...	189	...	639	....	29543
1687	...	194	...	617	...	23211
1688	...	214	...	345	...	14600
1689	....	163	...	243	...	10120
1690	....	117	...	818½	...	34960
1691 No ships did go from *Holland*, being in war with *France.*						
1692	...	32	...	62	...	2748
1693	...	89	...	175	...	8480
1694	...	62	...	156¼	...	7562
1695	...	96	...	201	...	9106
1696	...	100	...	380	...	14975
1697	...	111	...	1274½	...	42281
1698	...	140	...	1488⅛	...	55985
1699	...	151	...	775½	..	30835
1700	...	173	...	907	....	36548
1701	...	207	...	2071¾	...	67507
1702	...	225	...	697¾	...	24388
1703	...	208	...	646½	...	24527
1704	...	130	...	651½	...	23701
1705	...	157	...	1664¼	...	52346
1706	...	149	...	452½	...	15299
1707	...	131	...	128	...	5431
1708	...	121	...	525⅓	...	20731
1709	...	127	...	190¼	...	8237
1710	...	137	...	62	....	3379
1711	...	117	...	630¼	...	20589
1712	...	108	...	370½	...	14203
1713	...	94	...	256	....	12854
1714	...	108	...	1234	....	37490
1715	...	134	...	696¼	...	25830
	Carried over			29328⅔		1149362

1716

Year	Number of Ships sent out		Number of Whales killed	Puncheons of Train-Oil
	Brought over		29328¾	1149632
1716	153	...	519	20216
1717	180	...	391	14463
1718	194	...	281¾	13103
1719	182	...	308	10100
1720	158	...	412¼	19092
1721	149	...	667⅓	23108
			32908½ Whales.	1250714 Punch. of T.O.

To the foregoing account is to be added the whalebone or fins which have been brought home with all this blubber ; and which from 32,908 ½ whales, must be more than forty millions of pound weight : By all which it is apparent, that in 46 years, the *Hollanders* have fish'd up out of the icy seas of *Greenland*, a vast treasure, amounting to no less than one hundred and fifty millions of *guilders*, or about fourteen millions pound *sterling*.

This account may well be surprizing to those who have hitherto had no just or right information of the trade of the *Greenland* whale-fishing ; and will put an end to any question, whether the same be worth while to be undertaken, or no ?

I might have added here, the like list of the ships from *Hamburgh,* since the year 1670, but it will be enough to say, that they, with about fifty ships yearly, have taken above 10,000 whales.

Nor hath it been less beneficial to those of *Bremen*, who about the year 1690, had but four or five ships, but encouraged since by the profits, they have augmented the number every year. And these two towns have so great a vent for those goods, by the *Elbe* and *Weser*, into the most considerable parts of *Germany*, that to supply them, their own ships are not sufficient, but they buy every year great quantities of oil and fins of the *Hollanders*, to supply the *German* markets.

As

As to the *Dutch,* their spice trade it self, which is their darling trade, is not in a national view, so advantageous to them, as this of the *Greenland* fishery. For all their *East-India* goods are purchased with money, whereas the *Greenland* fishery is carried on by a continual circulation of commerce ; and taking out no money, brings back such goods as draw money from all their neighbours. Nor are the goods this trade brings in, such as we call perishable commodities, or which will spoil or waste in the keeping, but they may be kept and laid up many years, without loss.

CHAP. III.

A brief Recapitulation of what happen'd in the infancy of the Greenland *Trade ; how the* English *were first in it ; how they lost it ; and what have been the causes that all their attempts to retrieve it have been unsuccessful.*

IT was about the year 1597, Queen *Elizabeth* then reigning, when the *English* having happily planted on the *eastern* coast of *North-America,* and flush'd with the success of their adventures that way, began to spread themselves into the *North* Seas, to make new discoveries, in search after the *north-east* passages to *China,* and the *north-west* passages to the *South-seas.*

In their searches this way, though they could not find either of the passages they look'd for, yet far from losing all their labour, they made other discoveries, which fully rewarded them for their diligence ; such their discoveries

were

were of the *North-Cape*, the coast of *Lapland*, and the port of *Archangel* in *Russia*, to the *east*; *Hudson's Bay*, *Davis-Streights*, and the coast of *Greenland*, to the *west*; and the *Frozen-Sea*, with the great island of *Spitsbergen* to the *North*, and other islands of less note.

Here they were agreeably surprized, with a discovery unexpected, of abundance of prodigious whales, and other sea-monsters, and in such multitudes, as encouraged them to make the first attempt at their fishing for, or catching them for their oil, which was then a valuable and scarce commodity in the world.

They began this trade in the year 1598, though with few ships, and advanced mightily in it, about the year 1608, and carried it on with very great success, without any rival, till the year 1612; then the *Hollanders*, in hopes of like advantages, sent the first ships to *Spitsbergen* or *Greenland*. But the *English* claiming the property, as the first discoverers, would not allow the *Dutch* should fish thereabouts, and share in so profitable a trade, and therefore attack'd their ships, *anno* 1613. took two of them, and brought them to *England*, with all the oil of the whales they had kill'd, and all their shalloops, fishing-tackle, &c. so that the *Dutch* valued their loss at 130,000 *guilders*, the said ships being full loaden, and having made a good voyage.

However, the *Dutch* went on with their trade, as the *English* did, though often bickering, till the year 1617, when the *English* attack'd them again, but came to be worsted; the *Hollanders* took one of the *English* ships, and carried her to *Holland*. But the *States-General*, willing to give no offence to King *James*, caused the ship to be restored, with all that was in her. And in order to prevent the like for the future, sent over a deputation to *England*, to treat upon the subject of the freedom of the fishery with his Majesty; who acting by pacifick councils, did not encourage his merchants to disturb the *Dutch*, nor

decide

decide that question as to the right; so it remained un-
determin'd, and both parties went on fishing as before.

The *English* merchants not being able to preserve an
exclusive trade, contented themselves with keeping possession of those bays and harbours in the island of *Spitsbergen*, which they had, and were then counted the best,
such as that now called *Clock Bay*, the *Safe-Harbour*, the
English-Bay, the *English-Harbour*, and several others.
The *Hollanders* settling more to the *north*, as at *North-
Bay, South-Bay, Holland-Bay, Amsterdam-Island*, and the
like. The *Danes* came afterwurds and placed themselves
between the *English* and the *Dutch*, at a place still called
the *Danish-Bay*. The *Hamburghers* came next, and they
pitch'd upon a place further *west*, call'd *Hamburgh-Bay*.
After them the *French* and *Biscayers*, who finding all the
rest settled, they were obliged to take possession further
north than the *Hollanders*, at a place called the *Biscay-
Hook*. And all of them, as the island was further discovered, and abundance of other bays and places found
out, shifted their stations as they found most for their
convenience; the island, and the fishery also, being more
than sufficient for them all.

At that time the whales having never been disturbed,
were taken in great numbers near the shore, and the
blubber being cut off, was immediately carried on shore,
and boil'd into train-oil on the spot, the ships carrying
nothing home with them, but the pure oil, and the fins:
Accordingly, warehouses were erected, coppers or caldrons
set up on shore, and all the business done there. And the
fishery it self was so plentiful, that other ships were
obliged to go, to bring the oil which they had, more than
the fishing-ships could bring away.

But time and change of circumstances shifted the
situation of the trade: For the whales, by little and little,
forsook the shore, whether because of their being disturbed
there, by the multitude of ships and shalloops, or that they

found

found greater quantities of the water-insects, which are their food, between the ice; or for what other cause, we know not. But they have ever since been found in the openings and spaces among the ice, and not in the bays as before; that is to say, not in any number; and hither the ships are obliged to follow them; and by this alteration, their warehouses and cookeries on shore, became useless: So that now the blubber is stow'd in puncheons on board, and carried directly home to their respective ports. The ruins of the warehouses and furnaces on shore, in the several bays of *Spitsbergen*, are still to be seen.

The fishery being now wholly managed upon the high sea, among the ice, made it more difficult and dangerous: and several ships were lost in the beginning, before they discover'd the nature and situation of the ice; and those ships that would not venture to follow the whales so far into the ice, returned often without catching any whales at all; which discouraged the merchants, who at that time carried on the trade in companies, and with a publick stock; that they separated and dissolved not only in *England*, but in *Holland*, and several other places.

But as the companies gave over that trade, several private merchants took it up, especially in *Holland*, and carried it on upon their particular accounts; and that with such success and advantage, that a great number of ships were sent to *Greenland*, many more than ever the companies did in any year before, and so it continues to this day.

As for *England*, the publick calamity of a civil war overspreading them at that time, was another cause that interrupted and discouraged the merchants in this, as well as in all their trades; so that this fishery hath been lost to them ever since, some particular attempts to retrieve it excepted.

There was one attempt made in the year 1694, which

at

at first gave good hopes of success, being undertaken by
a company, composed of very eminent merchants, with a
good capital and stock, and established by an Act of
Parliament in their favour, particularly giving them exclusive privileges, exempting them from paying any duties,
and their men from being press'd into the King's service,
&c.

But wanting due informations of the proper methods
of managing that whole affair; and which was worse,
being ill serv'd by almost all the people they employed,
both at home and abroad, pushing them into extravagant
and unnecessary expences, and irregular measures in every
thing, they were obliged to give over the undertaking,
their stock being wasted and embezzel'd. And this company, and even the whole body of merchants in the nation,
were discouraged from going on with, or making any further attempt of the same kind.

A brief Account of the particular mistakes of the Greenland *Company, and the ill conduct of their servants,
mention'd above, which may be assign'd as the reasons
of their miscarriage.*

1. Their ships were intrusted with and commanded by
persons unacquainted with the business, who had not only
the command of the ship, but also of the fishery; whereas
the chief harpooneer ought to command during the fishing.
that he may carry the ship where he knows is most proper
for the work; which defect occasioned their misfortunes;
for though they had some skilful foreign harpooneers, yet
for want of right conduct, they got no whales, or but few,
even when others made a good voyage.

2. Their captains had their certain pay, whether they
had success or not; whereas they should have been paid in
proportion to their fishery only: But not being so in-

terested

terested in the success of their voyage, when they found
it not easy to come to the whales among the ice, they went
away to *Spitsbergen*, to the bays, and diverted themselves
with hunting the deer, and left the shalloops to look for
whales, where few or none were to be found ; and thus
they ruin'd the voyages, consum'd the provisions, and
brought the company's stock in debt upon every voyage;
and the tallow, hides, and horns of the deer, which they
kill'd ashore, being allowed to them as a perquisite, they
found their pleasure and particular profit more, by killing
the deer, than catching of whales.

3. When they came home, the blubber of the few
whales they had taken, was not boiled to advantage ; the
cookery was managed slovenly, and wastfully; and the oil
was not well purg'd : The fins also were not well cur'd, nor
cleansed ; and when they came to market, they were
obliged to sell them considerably under the value of merchantable fins.

4. Their lines, fishing instruments, harpoons, casks, &c.
were not duly taken care of, or well preserved for further
service, but embezzell'd and spoil'd for want of care ; so
that when they should have been ready for the next year,
the company was obliged to buy uew, at a great and unnecessary expence.

5. In furnishing and fitting out their ships, it was the
same ; they victualled extravagantly, paid an exorbitant
and unusual price for their shalloops, and likewise for
their fishing instruments, and were at so many unnecessary
expences for incidents, both at their setting out, and
coming in, as may appear by their accounts yet to be
seen.

6. The last ship they employed, was unhappily lost in

the

the ice, after a prosperous fishery, having eleven whales on board. By all which disasters, the company's stock was wasted, and the gentlemen discouraged from raising any more, so that affair expired. And though by a subsequent Act of Parliament, *anno Annæ primo*, the trade was again laid open, yet no body hath since meddled with it.

CHAP. IV.

A full Proof that England *may retrieve this Trade, and are able to carry it on more to advantage than any other* Nation : *And all the known objections to the contrary, answered and removed.*

IT is a vulgar error, but so rivetted in the minds of ignorant people, that it will be very hard to persuade them to the contrary, that the *Dutch* can fit out their ships, and go to *Greenland*, and in a word, carry on the whale-fishery cheaper and to more advantage than the *English*.

If this were true, it might be one reason why it would be hard for the *English* to recover the *Greenland* trade, or indeed to carry on any trade at sea : But the contrary is manifest ; and I shall make it appear, that the *Dutch* are so far from being able to carry it on cheaper than the *English* ; that the *English*, on the contrary, are able to do it cheaper than the *Dutch*, in almost all the articles ; from the fitting out the ships, to the boiling of the blubber after they are come home.

If this be made out, then instead of its being an

argument

argument against it, it is an argument for the encouragement of the *English* to recover this trade. For example:

It is first alledged, that the *English* do not build ships so cheap as the *Dutch;* and it may in one sense be true; but it is answered, that the *English* build stronger than the *Dutch*, and their ships last longer, and are kept with less repair; which, as it is more than equivalent, so in the balance of the merchants books, it will appear that the *English* are the cheapest ships in the end: This is farther evident, by the conduct of the King of *Sicily*, (now *Sardinia*) the *French* nation, and the *Flemish East-India* Company, and what is most to be admired, even to the *Czar* of *Muscovy*, and others; who having occasion to furnish themselves with ships of war, and ships for long and hard voyages, to the *East-Indies*, *Mississippi*, &c. chose to build and buy them in *England*, rather than build or buy in their own country, or *Holland*, notwithstanding the difference of price, till the *English* government thought fit to pass an Act to prevent them.

If the natural situation of any country hinders the inhabitants from having the materials for their work so cheap as their neighbours, they must comply with their circumstances, and by the cheapness of their labour and living, make up the deficiency, if they can; and this is the case of the *Dutch*.

It is evident, they have not any thing relating to the building or fitting out a ship that is of their own growth; neither iron, timber, planks, masts, hemp, pitch or tar; nor for victualling, have they either flesh, fish, or corn; for bread and beer, all must be fetch'd at the expence of the first cost, freight, and other charges from foreign countries. The *English* have timber, planks, lead, iron, brass, pitch, tar, masts and yards, with corn for bread and beer, flesh, butter, cheese, rice, &c. all the produce of their own land and colonies: The only thing I meet with, in which the *Dutch* may be said to outdo us, is, that they have

saw-mills,

saw-mills, which we do not allow, because it is taking away the employment of the poor.   Having then so many of the materials of our own growth, which they must buy with money, why cannot we build as cheap as the *Dutch?* I say, we may build cheaper than they in the end, because our work is better and stronger, and the materials which are our own, are better than those used by the *Dutch.*

Besides, if it were true that the *Dutch* build as cheap, and as good to the merchant which is not, yet they being forc'd to buy all their materials, cannot build so much to the advantage of the publick interest, and general stock ; since speaking of that publick stock of the nation, so much of the timber, planks, and all the victuals, as is used in building and setting out of a ship in *England,* and is the growth of our own country, or of our plantations, costs indeed nothing at all to the publick ; because so much of our own growth as is sent abroad, is clear gain to the publick stock of the nation.

Nor have the *Dutch* (which may be surprizing to some) sufficient number of sea-men among their own subjects, for the work of the whale fishing : Nay not one half of them ; but they are obliged every year to have many thousands of the most necessary and most skilful, even such as commanders, harpooneers, steersmen, and sailors, from *Jutland, Holstein, Scotland, Norway, Bremen, Oldenburgh, Delmenhorst,* or *Friesland,* and the most and best men they have, are from thence ; who after the fishery is over, go to their habitations, and carry the money they have earn'd, back with them to their families, returning again in the season, as before : And the same men are as easy to be found by the *English,* and as willing to work for them, as for the *Hollanders.*

Again, which will perhaps seem as strange to some people, as the other, the wages of seamen is lower in *England,* than in *Holland.* For example : In *England,* the seamen are hired for 24 to 26 shillings *per* month,

33   when

when as in *Holland*, the ordinary pay is 16 to 18, or 20 *guilders per* month, which is from 30 to 36, or 40 shillings *sterling*. As to the commanders, harpooneers, and steersmen, they have no pay, but according to what they catch, every one having so much *per* puncheon on the oil they bring home. By which their interest being concern'd, their diligence is secured.

Thus that objection, which has been thought so very considerable, is removed ; *viz.* that *England* cannot build and victual ships as cheap as the *Dutch*, nor that they would not be able to find skilful hands enough for the carrying on the *Greenland* trade. On the contrary, as they are well able to find them in those countries, as above, so in a very few years, the *British* seamen will be as skilful in the business, as their teachers ; and as we are in no want of seamen, we shall not long need to send for any numbers of them from abroad. Besides, abundance of *North British* sailors are already expert in this work, having often serv'd in the *Dutch* ships at *Greenland ;* and on the first news of the *British* nation having undertaken to revive the whale-fishing, will flock to *London* for employment : So that *England* can never want people for their fishing, full as skilfnl as others.

But there is one particular more, in which the *English* have infinitely the advantage of the *Hollanders,* and this is in the easiness of their loading aud unloading the ships ; which is a very considerable article in the charge of the voyage. For example :

All who are acquainted with the situation of *Holland,* know that their ships for *Greenland,* before they set out, must ride at anchor between *Sardam* and *Amsterdam ;* and there they must take in their casks, victuals, and fishing-tackle ; which they must bring on board from their several distant warehouses, through the canals and sluices, in great lighter-boats ; even the very fresh water, which they must buy. When ready to sail, they must have pilots over the

Pampus,

Pampus, and through the *Zuider-Sea* to *Texel,* where she rides till a favourable wind brings her to sea; and the owner, or he who fits the ship out, must follow to *Texel,* to see if all the men are on board, and every thing ready for the voyage. And when they return, it is the like; with this addition, that the charge is so much greater, as their casks are now filled with blubber; require to be carry'd to the cookery, and from thence to *Amsterdam,* or other places; which lighteridges, and workmanship, pilotages, riding at anchor for several weeks, and keeping the sailors all that time in victuals and pay; is a very great charge for the owners, besides the spoiling of the casks and lines, and the leakage, caused by being so often removed from one place to another.

Whereas the situation of this river is so, that ships may load and unload at the warehouses and cookery, without paying any carriage, or lighters, or double workmanship; preserving thereby all the lines, casks and other materials, in a good condition, and prevent much leakage. And after a ship is clear'd at *Gravesend,* a favourable wind brings her to sea the next tide after. And in these articles, calculating all the particulars, it is plain, that *England* shall save at least, every *Greenland* voyage, 50*l.* upon every ship, which the *Dutch* are obliged to pay. And hereby, I doubt not, is sufficiently proved, that we can set out ships, and carry on the whale-fishing trade easier, better, and much cheaper than the *Hollanders.*

But the greatest encouragement and advantage for the undertakers, is the benefit of the custom which we enjoy by the importation; the train-oil being free imported, and the whale-fins paying 52*l. sterling per* ton less than when imported from other countries: So that the adventurers have (when hereby is added the duty upon exportation of the fins in *Holland,* the commission, brokeridge, weigh-money, freight, insurance, and other charges by loading and unloading them) a sure profit and addition in

the

the price of every ton of fins, of about 70*l. sterling* more
than any nation beyond sea enjoys; and is granted by the
legislature, to no other purpose, than to encourage the
inhabitants to this so advantageous trade.

And what by the increase and inlarging of this trade,
for the future will be brought home more than this nation
needs of train-oil and whale-fins, both very current and
valuable commodities beyond sea. And being no duty at
all upon train-oil, and all the three-pence *per* pound
whale-fins being drawn back when exported, we can provide all those parts of *Europe*, which now buy from the
Hollanders, with these commodities cheaper than they are
able to do. *Hamburgh* and *Bremen*, with all their ships,
have not enough to supply *Germany*, but must buy many
thousand puncheons of train-oil every year from *Holland*,
Flanders, *France*, and parts of the *Baltick Sea*, buy quantities of oil and soap boil'd of the *Greenland* oil; particularly, *Scotland* buys and consumes much of this soap.
And when the *Greenland* oil is imported directly, the
soap-boiling trade must certainly increase hereby, and the
North-Britons need not go to foreign markets, nor to buy
whalebone of them: And this is in *Ireland*, *Flanders*,
France, *Portugal*, *Spain*, *Italy*, *Germany*, and all other
countries of *Europe* a wanted commodity. How could
Holland set out else so great a number of ships, if all
Europe did not pay them for this their industry, having
but a small consumption themselves of all that they bring
home?

Though it is not easy to guess at a sum, yet it may not
be improper to observe here, and there is no doubt of it.
That we have paid to the *Hollanders*, in no more than half
a century since we quitted that trade, some millions of
money for those commodities, which our own men might
have fished up out of the seas, and which would have been
so much in our pockets, and at this time clear gain to the
publick stock. A treasure taken up out of the sea, is a

treasure

treasure gain'd : It must be so; it cannot be otherwise! And hereby it appears, that we bring home from *Greenland* no goods, but such as we can sell to several markets of *Europe* for money, or have such merchandize in exchange for it, as we should otherwise buy for money abroad: And any objection that might be moved that way, is removed.

And to speak further upon the surety of the advantage, both to the adventurers as to the publick stock, and the increase of trade and navigation, and of the money the said trade may keep and bring into the nation; it is certain, that we not only carry out our own product, but indeed we carry out nothing of value but provisions for the men, which they might be supposed to consume at home, if they did not go at all, especially when our own people come to be wholly employed, and so without carrying out any other produce, as above : The goods brought home, are caught out of the sea, *and is no more or less, than the sweat and labour of our people*, and the blessing of Almighty God; and so all the oil and whalebone that is brought home, is clear gain, except only the charges of the voyage.

No merchandize is given in the exchange for it,
No bills of exchange paid for it,
No money carried out to purchase it.

The charges of the fitting out a ship and of the whole voyage, is expressed in two articles, called in the stile of business,

Victuals and Wages,
Ware and Tear.

And these two will come for a ship with six shalloops, except what must be paid to the parteneer-officers, and steersmen, for their portions in the train-oil, and the

charges

charges of the cookery, by the return; *viz.* for victuals and wages, about 420*l. sterling*, for ware and tear, I reckon 180*l. sterling*, being in all both outset and return, 600*l. sterling*. This is often repay'd by one whale, that yields 50 to 60 punchions of trail-oil, and 18 or 1900 lbs. weight of fins, or more. And a ship bringing home 5 or 6, 10 or 12 whales, or a full loading of blubber and fins, it is easy to calculate to what considerable profit such a voyage doth amount to.

Much more might be said in commendation of this fishery and trade, but I doubt not this will satisfy any discerning reader; and that no body can make any further objections, or be longer prepossessed with imaginary discouragement: I am confident, that if any society of men, with a good stock, and a careful prudent management, would undertake it, they would greatly find their account in it; and the nation in general would reap so immense advantages by it, that it will naturally fall under the consideration of the legislature, to give all reasonable encouragements that may be wanting to promote it.

APPENDIX.

IT cannot be supposed that I have said in the foregoing chapters, all that the subject of the *Greenland* fishery will afford; to mention all the particulars, would fill a large volume, this trade being extensive beyond what most men imagine; I shall only, to what has been said, add some few remarks, which on second thoughts I could not omit.

As to the first head; *How the whale-fishery is perform'd ?* I should have given the method of boiling the blubber, and how to purge the same, to make it neat and clear train-oil; and also of cleaning the fins or whalebones to make them merchantable goods, after the return of the ships: But I think it sufficient at present to say, that the cookery of train-oil is done by the harpooneers, who know how to boil it to the most advantage; it being to their interest to do it well, because they are paid for the whole voyage, proportionably to the quantity of clear train-oil which they produce: The management of this cookery, and the particulars thereof, are too many to be set down here; the curious can only be satisfied, by seeing the regular method in which it is performed. The cleaning of the fins, is a work rather of labour, than of art, and is what most of the seamen that have used these voyages, are well acquainted with.

Belonging to the second head, *viz.* The advantages
which

which the Greenland *trade hath been to the* Dutch, *and
others :* It would make a book by it self, to describe all
the advantages in due form, and how the navigation of
Holland is increased hereby, and what a number of ships
they employ in consequence of it; by bringing in all the
materials necessary for the ships used in this fishery, being
timber, planks, deals, masts, caskstaves; hemp, pitch, tar,
iron, corn, beef, butter, salt, stock-fish, &c. voluminous and
bulky goods; and they, not having them of their own
growth, the same are brought by sea to their ports: And
again, by exporting the train-oil, and the whale-fins,
to the several ports of *Europe,* which they supply them
with; I say, what innumerable ships are hereby continually kept at sea, and what numbers of families are
hence maintain'd, are obvious to any who employ their
thoughts upon this subject.

And this trade has been a fund of seamen on any
emergency to the State, to furnish their fleets; and it had
been impossible for them to fit out their navy on several
particular occasions, without the aid of these *Greenland*
seamen, who being under emergencies of state, kept at
home, and not sent to *Greenland,* their fleets, have been
speedily mann'd, even to the surprize of the world; and
so they have often defended themselves against greater
powers, who have not so many seamen at hand, whereby
this fishery proves to be their great support, and contributes considerably to the maintenance of their state,
liberty and safety: And they are so sensible of the consequence of this trade to them, that by order of the *States*
in their daily publick prayers in all Churches, words to
this effect are inserted; (*viz*) That God will be graciously
pleased to bless their land, and in particular, *the great and
small fisheries.*

As to the third head, and *the causes of former miscar-*

riages

riages in the management of this trade: I think it is better to bury these things in a decent silence, than farther to enumerate past mistakes, and the disasters caused thereby. It will be sufficient that I have shewn, how the same may be certainly avoided for the future.

To the fourth chapter I have to add, relating to the products of this fishery, *viz.* train-oyl and whale-fins; that it is a great mistake to say of the first, that we have oyl enough, and that there will be no vent for what is imported from *Greenland;* when we know how many other parts of *Europe* want the train-oyl, and the soap boiled of the same. And if our own markets should be over-stock'd, and we send the oyl to foreign markets, we shall be able to sell as cheap, nay, even cheaper than the *Dutch*, and get more money by what we shall sell than they, according to the several before-mention'd reasons. Nor ought this trade to be merely for our own consumption, for that would but lessen the value and esteem of it, by reason that what will be consumed at home, will be but so much saved, and no addition to the publick stock: But the gain by exportations is what will increase our wealth and riches.

As to the whale-fins, it appears by the *Custom-house* books, that there hath been imported in the port of *London*, from the year 1715, to 1721, one year with another, about 150 tons yearly, even when the price hath been very dear; *viz.* 400*l. per* ton, little more or less, which is, one year with another, 60,000*l.* a year, over and above what is imported in all the other ports of *Great Britain* and *Ireland;* which may moderately be supposed to be 100 ton more. Then the sum paid for whalebone amounts to 100,000*l. per annum*, besides what probably may be run clandestinely: All which hath hitherto been clear loss to this nation, and clear gain to our neighbours.

But

But what an alteration will it be, and what may not such a trade come to in time ; when *England* shall not only import all this her self, but can supply other parts of *Europe* with the same as well as with train-oyl, whereby such a treasure as now is carry'd away to our neighbours, will be gotten and kept here at home? What an infinite number of seamen, tradesmen, and labouring poor people, both at sea and on shore, will be employ'd and maintain'd, by this trade? Which will afford and set to business the youth of our charity-schools, and in few years make room for great numbers of them ; and if they prove docile and tractable lads, they may be brought up to be steersmen, harpooneers, captains and commanders : And by a succession of such, this trade may be secured, never to be lost again. The number of seamen must increase continually, (much to the safety of our kingdom) because every year this fishery will take up boys ; that is to say, sturdy able youths, from fifteen to twenty years of age, and raw men who have never been at sea ; they being necessary for mean and ordinary uses : All which after two or three years service, may become expert and able seamen ; then other boys and raw men will be employ'd in their room ; so that this trade will be a *perpetual nursery* of seamen.

All our foreign commerce must be supported (whether in time of peace or war) at a great expence to the publick, by maintaining consuls, residents, ambassadors, governors and garisons, as well for correspondence and intelligence, as preservation and defence. But this trade and fishery is of a quite different nature ; it is carry'd on in the uninhabited parts of the world, in open and otherwise unfrequented icy seas, at the sole cost of the undertakers, without the least charge, burthen or incumbrance to the publick ; and therefore may justly claim more favour and encouragement than any other trade whatsoever.

How

How apprehensive the legislature always has been of the value of the fishery, appears by the several Acts of Parliament made for the encouragement of the same: And it is declared in the preamble of an Act, in the 14th year *Caroli* II. *" That the publick honour, wealth and " safety of this realm, as well in the maintenance and sup- " port of navigation, as in many other respects, doth in an " high degree depend upon the improvement and encourage- " ment of the fishery."* And particularly, to re-establish this *Greenland* trade and fishery, I refer the reader to the Acts made in the 25th year *Caroli* II. in the 4th and 5th year *Gulielmi* & *Mariæ*; in the 7th and 8th year *Gulielmi* III. and in the first year of Queen *Anne*; and it is hardly credible, that so many beneficial Acts, and the good intention of the legislature, till now, should have proved to be of no effect.

It remains yet to be said, that a further neglect of this fishery may be counted a dead loss to the nation, and is so far a weakning or a check to the growth of the strength of this kingdom: Nay, worse; because our neighbours get that which we neglect and pay for; growing in power and riches, when we sit still, and prove, by continuing so, as bad politicians as traders.

FINIS.

43

A N

A P O L O G Y

FOR THE

B U S I N E S S

OF

P A W N - B R O K I N G.

By a *P A W N - B R O K E R.*

Can there any Good Thing come out of Nazareth ?

L O N D O N:
Printed in the Year M.DCC.XLIV.

THE
BUSINESS
OF
PAWN-BROKING
Stated *and* Defended.

SECT. I.

SELF-DEFENCE is the first principle of the law of nature, the right of every man, and extends itself to every thing that is dear and valuable to a man. And of all that is thus sacred and inviolate, *moral character* justly challenges the next place to *conscious virtue and innocence*. An attack upon *moral character* is always found to awaken the utmost attention, and to excite the keenest grief and resentment; insomuch that a meek and tame submission to attacks of this kind is naturally and universally construed to be a symptom of guilt, or of a most abject and cowardly spirit: This consideration, it is humbly hoped, is a sufficient apology for the present publication of the following sheets.

If we may for the present only suppose, that it is no impossibility in nature, for a *pawn-broker* to be an honest and virtuous man, the reader may judge what grief and concern must seize him, upon reading the following

printed

printed vote; *viz. That leave be given to bring in a Bill for more effectually preventing the receiving stolen goods, by regulating the pawn-brokers;* which may be thought to imply that *pawn-brokers* are the *chief* and principal *receivers* of stolen goods.

A *receiver of stolen goods,* knowing or suspecting them to be such, is a character so vile and detestable, that words cannot aggravate, nor can any punishment well exceed its demerit.

But the more *black* and *heinous,* and the more extensive any charge is, the more solid, clear, and convincing, ought to be the proofs upon which it is supported.

As I intend this for a general vindication of the business of *pawn-broking,* I shall consider this important objection in its proper place, amongst other the most material objections that have, or can be, raised against the *business* or *profession.*   Before I proceed to the argument, I would premise,

1. That I do not pretend to vindicate the practices of all who call themselves *pawn-brokers;* for there are many ranked under the general name, whom we know nothing of and utterly disclaim: Many, who, thinking our business prodigiously gainful, if they have but a little money, take in pledges; and, for want of caution and experience, commit many oversights and indiscretions; the reproach whereof terminates upon the whole business.   Nor will I undertake to vindicate the practices of all who were regularly initiated into business, by serving an apprenticeship to it: And herein we are but upon a level with all other professions; for, I believe, there is no man so partial to his own business, as not to see and condemn the malpractices of some of his own profession.   It is therefore, for this and many other reasons, greatly to be wished, that a cool, sedate, and impartial inquiry should be made; and a wholesome, rational, and salutary regulation of this business should take place, by which it might be render'd

4   more

more safe and honourable to those that follow it, and more useful and beneficial to the public. The *pawn-brokers* desire nothing so much; and, if they may but hope to be heard without passion and prejudice, may perhaps be the most able to give light into a design or scheme of such a nature.

2. That as some parts of the following argument do admit of proof by figures, we shall, in those places, appeal to our reader's skill in arithmetic; which, surely, no force of prejudice (unless it should rise up to phrensy, or fanaticism) will be able to destroy: But, as to those particulars, that do not admit of figurative or mathematical demonstration, our reader must be content with arguments drawn from facts, probability, and analogy; and these will satisfy every judicious and honest inquirer as to those things, which do not in their own nature admit of any other medium of proof.

SECT. II.

WE begin this Section with the following *postulate.*

That it is no crime or immorality, nor any offence against the laws of the land, to receive a pledge or pawn (as a security for money lent) from the lawful owner, or from one deputed by the lawful owner; or, to the best of our knowledge, from such person; to restore it undiminish'd, and, to the utmost of our power, undamaged, upon the demand of such proprietor, or the person who had been deputed by such proprietor to pledge the same, upon re-payment of the money, for the security whereof such pledge or pawn was deposited: And further, that it is not unreasonable or unfit to receive some premium or profit,

5 *for*

for having supplied a person with money at all reasonable hours, and in such proportion as his necessity might require.

As no reasoning creature can refuse this *postulate*, we take it for granted; and shall proceed next to inquire, what the lowest *premium* (in the nature and reason of things) may be, which a *pawn-broker* must and ought to receive for the time, labour, expence, skill, and fortune, which his business requires.

For this purpose, I shall humbly submit the following propositions to consideration :

I. *That to lend one hundred, or one hundred and fifty pounds upon four hundred or five hundred distinct and different pledges, will take up four hundred times the quantity of time and trouble, that will be required to lend the same sum upon one single pledge.   Supposing therefore it may take a broker but ten minutes to examine the nature of the commodity, and to inquire as to property, &c. I believe that it will be found, that a week's time will be pretty well employed in lending money upon four or five hundred different pledges, allowing him to attend business fifteen hours in the day ; for he will not, in the whole week, (Sundays excepted) have above twenty hours to spare for the common offices of life.   But, supposing he should have very near as many pledges to re-deliver, besides keeping books for regular entries ; folding goods in such a manner, as may best preserve them, placing them in such order in his warehouses, that they may be found at a minute's warning, and keeping those warehouses in order, will require more hands than his own to execute.   It may therefore be reasonably supposed,*

II. *That such a person cannot perform his business as it ought to be done, without the help of two servants at least ; and, if these are, one or both, journeymen, wages must be*

6

paid

paid as well as they boarded; and, if both apprentices, the latter is of course.

III. *Supposing a person thus employed from week to week throughout the year, it will follow, that he cannot be at leisure to attend any other business for the support of himself and family.*

IV. *If this should prove a pretty near calculation of the number of pledges, which are (in common) received for the sum mentioned; it is easy to conceive, that much ware-house-room is required, a house larger than ordinary abso-lutely necessary; and, I suppose, proportional rent and taxes will be thought as necessary: It also follows, that the pawn-brokers really do, what the* Charitable Corporation *only pretended to; (viz.) Supply the poor with small sums; for, if four or five hundred different pledges are received for the sum of one hundred or one hundred and fifty pounds, the sums cannot be very large.*

V. *If a man of this business is single, he cannot possibly do without a maid-servant to do the business of the house; and such servant must have board and wages.*

VI. *He may find it convenient or necessary to marry; and, I take it for granted, may lay claim to the common and undeniable right of every man. I suppose, he and his family can no more live without food, raiment, and physic, than other people.*

VII. *If he has children, they must be fed, cloathed, educated, and put out into the world, as well as those of other men: And a pawn-broker is as much obliged as any other man, by the law of nature, and of his country, to perform this indispensible duty.*

VIII. Lastly, *He is obliged to contribute his proportion towards the support of Government, and the public expence.*

7 These

These propositions are most, if not all of them, self-evident; to attempt a proof of them would be an affront to my reader's understanding: I shall therefore draw a few corollaries, which necessarily follow from them: As,

First, That a *pawn-broker* must, at least, be allowed to make such advantages by his business, as may enable him to perform what is mentioned in the foregoing propositions. We have seen already, that he cannot attend any other business for the support of himself and family; and if his whole time, thought, labour, skill, and fortune, is hereby ingrossed, he may reasonably expect sustenance from it; it being the ordinance and appointment of God, *that man should live by his labour.*

Secondly, I infer, that those persons must be guilty of most flagrant injustice and oppression, who (by taking advantage of some laws hereafter to be mention'd) borrow money of a *pawn-broker,* and, upon repayment thereof, will not allow him such a *profit* or *premium,* as we shall presently prove indispensibly necessary, to enable him to discharge the obligations mentioned in the foregoing propositions.

This must needs be a complicated crime; for, if it be a *sin* or *vice,* by our words, actions; or omissions, to act, or speak; to contradict or counteract the truth of any known proposition whatever; or, in other words, *to act a lye**, in which the very formal nature of *vice* consists; what an aggravated offence must it be, to counteract the truth of so many self-evident propositions!

Let persons, thus acting, place themselves in our stead; sensible of the constant unavoidable charge we are at for rent, servants, and perhaps, a growing family; willing, by our labour and industry, to make some small provision against old age, and to put our helpless children (who may have no other resource) into some tolerable

8   way

---

* *Vide* Rel. of Nature delineated, *Sect.* I. *Propositions* 3, 4, &c.

way of beginning the world : Would not such persons think themselves cruelly treated, to be obliged to accept such a reward for their labour, as would not go above one third, or half-way, towards defraying their necessary charge? Again, if it is right and fit for any one man to treat us in this manner, it is right and fit for every man to do so : And what must be the consequence, but that we must necessarily wrong our creditors, not pay our rent, and other just demands mankind may· have upon us, commence bankrupts, and throw our families upon the parish? Certainly our most inveterate enemies will not say this is right and fit !

Thirdly, What monsters of iniquity must those be, who (under the authority and colour of the *law*) lay snares to oppress and plunder one of this business, for only getting such a profit by his business, as may enable him to discharge the obligations mentioned in the foregoing propositions !

We go on to the main point, (*viz.*) To find out (if possible) what *premium* or *profit* may, in the nature and reason of things, be suitable and fit for a *pawn-broker* to receive, in consideration of his labour, time, skill, and fortune. And here it will be necessary to state and vindicate the terms upon which we follow business at present : For this purpose I shall transcribe a passage from a public* paper, published about fourteen years ago, in which the *pawn-brokers* fairly and justly vindicated themselves from the false and vile aspersions, cast upon them by the then *Charitable Corporation,* who were, at that time, endeavouring to establish themselves upon our ruins : but were shamefully defeated, and afterwards fulfilled and accomplished, to the hurt and ruin of many families, what the *pawn-brokers* had predicted: But it has happened

to

---

* *Vide* Daily Post-Boy, *April* 26, 1731.

to the *pawn-brokers*, as the wise *Solomon* long ago observed, *Eccles.* ix. 14, 15, 16. *There was a little city, and few men within it ; and there came a great king against it, and besieged it, and built great bulwarks against it : Now there was found in it a poor wise man, and he by his wisdom delivered the city ; yet no man remembered that same poor man. Then said I, wisdom is better than strength : nevertheless (or altho') the poor man's wisdom is despised, and his words are not heard.*

The passage is as follows ; (*viz.*) " I shall only pro-
" pose the two following questions :

" *First*, Whether my time and labour does not intitle
" me to as good a reward as other men receive ?

" *Secondly*, Whether my having been subjected to the
" will and profit of another, for the term of seven years,
" may not deserve some consideration, as well as the ser-
" vitude of other men?

" I humbly conceive, these two are the principal *moral*
" grounds upon which a tradesman thinks he has a right
" to make considerable advantages of his money in trade,
" above what he can make of it by putting it out to
" interest. Now if it has been generally allowed, that
" this is an equitable way of judging, in relation to trade
" in general; it remains, that a reason be given, why I may
" not lay claim to a benefit, which all the rest of man-
" kind esteem their just right? Perhaps some profound
" reasoner will reply; But I am a fair trader, and you are
" not : I hope his stiling himself *fair*, and me *unfair*, will
" pass for nothing, till our actions are compared, and an im-
" partial judgment formed from them, and not from words.

" For which end, suppose I lend a person twenty
" shillings upon a pledge this day ; this person redeems
" his goods to-morrow (or he may let them lie a month,
" if he pleases) ; I expect six-pence profit for my time,
" trouble and laying out my money ; for this I am charged
" with getting 800 *per cent.* profit *per annum :* Now a fair

10   " trader

" trader lays out twenty shillings, sells his goods again for
" ready money, (it may be the same day) gets one shil-
" ling, and says he gets but five *per cent*.; whereas reckon
" his profits *per annum*, and they will amount to 1600 *per*
" *cent.* : My judgement is required as much to examine
" what I lend my money upon, as his is to inquire the
" worth of the commodity he buys; my money is as truly
" disbursed as his; and it takes me up as much thought
" and time to lend twenty shillings, as it does him to lay
" out twenty shillings.

" If any tradesman in *London* buys goods with ready
" money to-day, and sells them for ready money to-
" morrow, I ask, whether it would trouble his conscience,
" if he got sixpence *per* pound profit, which he calls $2\frac{1}{2}$ *per*
" *cent.* If any such person is to be found, let him cast the
" first *stone;* in this case he has security in his hands, as
" well as I. But here the fair trader objects, *You never*
" *make bad debts; you have always more than double*
" *security in your hands; I am exposed to contract bad*
" *debts, and meet with losses, which you are not liable to.*
" In answer to this, I say, you do not know what losses I
" am liable to; nor is it proper to acquaint every one with
" them, unless I had a mind to increase them.

" But more particularly to answer this objection—I
" allow, you meet with many losses in trade, and it is un-
" certain what a person may lose in a year's trading: But
" persons may, from a course of years, come to a general
" calculation of their losses, one year with another; and,
" I believe, it is a general rule with tradesmen, to allow
" so much a year for bad debts: Now, let any tradesman
" subtract this from his profits, and I will venture to
" compare profits with him; supposing us to have an
" equal sum of money in trade, and to return our stock as
" often.

" Now I will ingenuously show you what my profits in
" general are: I have three thousand pounds capital

" stock

" stock·in trade; I return this twice in a year, which
" amounts to six thousand pounds a year returns; I
" can make appear by my books, where I set down daily
" my returns, and the profit that day's return yields me,
" that at an average I do not make above nine *per cent.*
" profit of all my returns, by deliveries and sales: To
" explain this a little more particularly; I deliver, it may
" be, in a day, some things that have lain but one month
" in my hands; here is but two and a half *per cent.* profit.
" or, in sums, not quite two *per cent.*; others, that have
" been three, four, five, six, or twelve months, &c. Con-
" sequently, I sometimes do not get twelve-pence in the
" pound, sometimes eighteen-pence, and perhaps (tho'
" rarely) two shillings; but, take one day with another, one
" month with another I will prove (by my books, or upon
" oath) the truth of what I have just now asserted, *viz.*
" That I do not at most make above nine *per cent.* profit,
" upon all the returns I make in a year: The amount
" whereof is five hundred and forty pounds *per annum,*
" upon three thousand pounds capital stock in trade: Out
" of this is to be deducted my losses, the interest my
" money would produce out of trade, and the expences I
" must necessarily be at in negociating business; and as
" to these, let it be consider'd, that two-thirds, at least, of
" the monies I return, is in sums under twenty shillings,
" and any one may easily perceive the numbers of parcels
" and persons I must have to do with. Must not this
" require several servants, constant attendance, and daily
" care and fatigue?

　" Now, deduct one hundred and fifty pounds for the
" interest of my money; and I am certain no considerate
" person can allow much less than one hundred and fifty
" pounds more for the necessary charges I am at in nego-
" tiating business; there remains but two hundred and
" forty pounds to answer all losses, to keep myself, and
" those of my family that are not concerned in business,

　　　　　　　　　　　　　　" and

" and to lay up for posterity. Monstrous accumulation !
" supposing I had but one thousand pounds in trade, my
" profit would hardly amount to one hundred and eighty
" pounds *per ann.;* and what that will do, as to the
" charges of business, and keeping a family in the city
" of *London,* every one knows : But it is manifest
" there are multitudes of tradesmen in London, whose
" stocks do not exceed, if amount to, one thousand
" pounds, who live genteelly, and lay up money: Can
" they do this with one hundred and eighty pounds *per*
" *ann.?* If they cannot, whose profits must be largest ?

 " It will suffice to answer a seeming paradox in what
" I have asserted, that one thousand pounds in trade
" (allowing us to gain after the rate of thirty *per cent.*
" *per ann.* for small, and twenty *per cent. per ann.* for
" large sums) will not produce above one hundred and
" eighty pounds *per ann.;* if it be but considered, that
" one third part of our stock in trade, namely what
" has lain above twelve or fifteen months, pays no interest
" at all; for every *pawn-broker* knows, that not one
" parcel in ten is redeem'd after it has been so long time
" on our hands : and I shall give a demonstration by-and-
" by, that even plate, the most certain commodity we
" deal in, will not pay us twelve *per cent. per ann.* for the
" time we keep it ; which is two years at least."

Here it is granted, that, upon the present scheme of
our business, it is usual for small pledges to take after the
rate of thirty *per cent. per ann.* ; and the reason why a
broker can't do it for less, and get a living profit by his
business, is this—we, having no limited time for selling
pawns, are obliged (for fear of law-suits) to keep large
and perishing stocks by us ; which dead part of our stocks
eat up and devour a considerable part of the profit arising
from the live part of our stock : And it is a common and
notorious practice for knavish and designing people, to let
their goods lie three, four, or five years, without ever

coming

coming to make a demand of them ; on purpose, that the *pawn-broker* should (upon a presumption that the pledger is either dead, or has no thoughts of redeeming them) venture to sell them ; and so to have an opportunity of suing him, and recover whatever extravagant value they please to set upon them : This is almost daily practis'd, and not a little encourag'd, in the courts of law ; and there have been some people so artfully wicked, as to forswear their property in their own goods, so becoming evidences for themselves, and escaping payment of costs, if they are cast.

But if litigious people are not universally so dexterously wicked as this, they are frequently such worthless wretches, that a *pawn-broker*, if (by great good luck) he gets his cause, can have no other satisfaction for his costs of suit, than (if they don't run their country) to throw them into gaol ; which it is hardly worth his while to do. The lawyers very well know, that if a motion was made in court for security to be given by the plaintiff for costs of suit, in case he should be cast, it would not be regarded.

It is this vile and profligate part of mankind, aided and abetted by pettifogging attorneys, solicitors, bailiffs, and their followers, that are the people whom (for the most part) the *pawn-broker* is so unfortunate as to be engag'd against in law-suits : These wretches, having no scruples as to what they say or swear, provided it may help them to gain their cause ; and being plaintiffs ; have the opportunity of representing their cause in what light soever they please ; abuse the ear of the court, inflame juries, and carry their cause in triumph ; whilst the poor *pawn-broker* not only loses his cause, but incurs *infamy*.

Now was this difficulty removed, and was a *pawn-broker* allow'd by law to dispose of, and appropriate to his own benefit, any pledge, after he had kept it a *reasonably* limited time ; as, upon this consideration, he would not be oblig'd to keep so large a dead stock upon his hands, nor be liable to expensive and vexatious law-

14

suits,

suits, I think he may afford to lend small sums one-third cheaper than is now usually done, provided he is allow'd to take after the same *rate*, or whatever he and the *pledger* can agree upon, (not exceeding the same rate) for larger sums; and be allow'd one month's profit certain, tho' the pledge should happen to be redeem'd that day, or the next; which is not two *per cent.* upon the return, and cannot be thought unreasonable, because the chief labour and trouble is at the first taking of the pledge.

This reduction of the charge of borrowing small sums would be a great relief to the honest and industrious poor; who (as things are now situated) are obliged to pay dearer, on account of the wicked and designing part of mankind.

That a *pawn-broker* cannot do his business upon lower terms than those proposed, shall be next demonstrated.

We will suppose one of this profession married; and, with his own and his wife's fortune together, able to put two thousand pounds clear into trade; which, surely, is no contemptible beginning in almost any branch of business. Now every one knows, that two thousand pounds, after the rate of twenty *per cent.* will produce no more than four hundred pounds *per annum*, was it to be put out at once, and the interest to run on, without interruption, from the beginning to the end of the year. But it so happens in this business, that I may lend a person ten, twenty, or thirty pounds; which, in a month or two, he repays without any warning; by which means it may lie useless by me for another month or two. This must frequently happen of course: As an equivalent for which, we must suppose a *broker* cannot keep less than two hundred pounds running cash by him; consequently has but the *net* improvement of one thousand eight hundred pounds, which will amount but to three hundred and sixty pounds; from whence likewise must be deducted whatever he makes less than twenty

per

per cent. per annum, profit upon the goods he may have to sell, as well as what losses he may be liable to, from the various causes hereafter to be mentioned. For the present, I will only suppose forty pounds to be deducted from three hundred and sixty pounds; it will then be reduced to three hundred and twenty pounds. What this will do towards the support of a family, and laying up for posterity, we shall see presently: For which purpose I will lay before my *reader* the following Table of Calculation, made by the ingenious* Mr. *Vanderlint,* of the necessary charges of a middling tradesman's family, in the city of *London.* I will transcribe a passage from this author, which immediately precedes the Table itself: Says he;

" Another point, from whence I argue, that our trade
" is in a much worse state than it formerly was, shall be
" the following estimate of the necessary charge of a
" family in the middling station of life, consisting of a
" man, his wife, four children, and a maid-servant; so as,
" I think, a person that has such a family, and employs
" one thousand pounds of his own money in trade, ought
" to live. For, if such families must not have neces-
" saries enough, and I believe it will appear I have allowed
" no superfluities, I think we ought to give up trade, and
" find some other way to live. For trade terminates
" ultimately in the consumption of things; to which end
" alone trade is carried on : Therefore if those that employ
" in trade one thousand pounds of their own money shall
" not be able to supply such a middling family with need-
" ful and common things, what then becomes of the con-
" sumption of things? Or, in other words, what becomes
" of trade? For, to be sure, not one person in a good
" many is the real owner of such a sum. If therefore

" such

---

* A Wainscot Merchant. *Vide* his Essay on Trade.

" such families must retrench and abridge themselves of " common needful things, those in trade below them, in " this respect, must much more do so, if they have " families."

SECT. III.

An ESTIMATE of the necessary charge of a family in the middling station of life, consisting of a man, his wife, four children, and one maid-servant.

		Daily Expence		Weekly Expence			Yearly Expence
	d.	*s.*	*d.*	*l.*	*s.*	*d.*	
BREAD for seven persons *per* head, *per* day	0	0	5¼	0	3	0¾	
Butter	¾		5¼		3	0¾	
Cheese	¼		1¾		1	0¾	
Fish and flesh-meat	2½	1	5½		10	2½	
Roots and herbs, salt, vinegar, mustard, pickles, spices, and grocery, except tea and sugar	0½		3½		2	2½	
Tea and sugar	1		7		4	1	
Soap for the family occasions, and washing all manner of things, both abroad and at home	1½		10½		6	1½	
Threads, needles, pins, tapes, worsteds, bindings, and all sorts of haberdashery	0½		3½		2	0¼	
Milk one day with another			¾			5¼	
Candles about two pounds ½ *per* week the year round	—		—		1	3	
Sand, fuller's-earth, whiting, smallcoal, brickdust	—		—			2	
Ten-shilling small-beer, a firkin and a quarter *per* week	—		—		3	1½	
Ale for the family and friends	—		—		2	6	
Coals, between four and five chaldron *per annum*, may be estimated at	—		—		2	6	
Repairs of household goods, as table-linen, bedding, sheets, and every utensil, for household occasion	—		—		1	6	
Six shillings and two-pence weekly for seven persons amount to near				2	3	1¼	112 10 0

	l.	*s.*	*d.*
Brought over	112	10	0
Cloaths of all kinds for the master of the family - -	16		
Cloaths for wife, who can't wear much, nor very fine laces, with - - - - - -	16		
Extraordinary expence attending every lying-in, 10*l.* supposed to be about once in two years - -	5		
Cloaths for four children, at 7*l. per ann.* for each child -	28		
Schooling for four children, including every charge thereunto relating supposed to be equal, at least, to 10*s. per* quarter for each child - - - -	8		
The maid's wages may be - - - -	4	10	
Pocket expenses for the master of the family, supposed to be about 4*s. per* week - - - -	10	8	
For the mistress of the family, and for the four children, to buy fruit, toys, &c. at 2*s. per* week - -	5	4	
Entertainments in return for such favours from friends and relations - - - - -	4		
Physic for the whole family one year with another, and the extraordinary expence arising by illness, may exceed -	6		
A country lodging sometimes, for the health and recreation of the family; or, instead thereof, the extraordinary charge of nursing a child abroad; which, in such a family, is often needful - - - -	8		
Shaving, 7*s.* 6*d. per* quarter; and cleaning shoes, 2*s.* 6*d. per* quarter - - - -	2		
Rent and taxes may be somewhat more or less than -	50		
Expences of trade with customers, travelling-charges, Christmas-box money, postage of letters, &c. for the sake of even money, at least, - - - -	19	8	
Bad debts, which may easily be more than 2*l. per cent.* on the supposed capital of 1000*l.* - - -	20		
	315		

There must be laid up one year with another, for twenty years, in order to leave each child, and a widow, if there should be one, 500*l.* apiece -   -   -   -   75

One 1000*l.* therefore, by this estimate, should gain, one year with another -   -   -   -   -   390

" Which for the sake of a round sum (says this author)
" I will call forty *per cent. per ann.* in order to support
" such a family, and provide five hundred pounds apiece
" for four children and a widow, if there should be one
" left; which, if not, will augment each child's share but

     " one

" one hundred and twenty-five pounds. And here I sup-
" pose a man to live twenty years, from his marriage to
" his demise; which I take to be about the term one man
" or woman with another doth live. I do not mean by
" this, that no man or woman lives longer from the time
" of marriage than twenty years; I know many live much
" longer; but I am equally certain, that as many never
" reach this term as others live beyond it: And it will
" also many times happen, that five, six, seven, eight, or
" more children must be brought up by some parents;
" tho', perhaps, it will more frequently happen, that less
" than four will be raised by others.

" But those that shall happen to have seven or eight
" children, will find the 75*l. per ann.* supposed in this
" estimate to be laid up, in order to provide five hundred
" pounds apiece for four children, hardly sufficient to bear
" the extraordinary charge which so many more children
" will occasion in this rank of living: And, surely, it
" must be very hard, that the man who happens to have a
" numerous family (and many such there always are)
" should thereby be rendered not only uncapable to pro-
" vide any thing for them to set out in the world with,
" but be reduced in a course of years, as he certainly
" must, if a thousand pounds in trade will not produce, at
" least, forty *per cent. per annum.*"

This gentleman is far from saying, that tradesmen
can, at this time of day, make forty *per cent.* upon their
capital; but he proves they ought to do it, in order only
for a suitable decent support of their families; and to
provide for posterity in such proportion, that each child
may begin the world with the same advantage its parents
did. This must be an incontestable rule of right; for,
unless some such standard as this is fixed, we shall (every
generation growing poorer and poorer) dwindle by degrees
to a nation of beggars.

It is now time to bring our extorting *pawn-broker*,

with

with his twenty and thirty *per cent.* upon the stage again; and hear what he may have to say for himself. He pleads, " That if he has two thousand pounds in trade of his own, " he must either not spend what this Table of Calculation " allows, or he must provide nothing for his children, or " must, in old age, be beholden to the parish."

He is sensible, that the two last-mention'd articles, *viz. bad debts amounting to twenty pounds per ann.*; and the article of *expences with his customers, travelling charges, &c. amounting to twenty* per ann. *more,* may be said to be superfluous, by reason of the nature of his business. To this it is replied, that in this Table of Calculation nothing is allowed for the charge of servants in business. The reason of this omission is conjectur'd to be this; *viz.* " the large sums which are given with ap- " prentices in almost every trade, which will sufficiently " defray the charge of boarding apprentices for seven years " together :" But this is not our case; for we have, for the most part, but a trifling consideration, if any, with our apprentices; and yet few trades in *London* give better wages to journeymen than we do.

So that if I board a journeyman, and pay him twenty-five or thirty pounds yearly wages; and likewise board an apprentice, with whom I have had little or nothing; this will be more than an equivalent for the particulars mention'd in these two articles, tho', as to several of them, we come in for our share.

The sum of all is this—Mr. *Vanderlint,* a judicious and disinterested witness, proves, that a tradesman who has one thousand pounds of his own in trade, cannot support his family in a decent manner only, and lay up so much for each of his children, as may enable them to begin the world with the same advantage their parents did, unless he can make thirty-nine *per cent.* upon his capital.

The *pawn-broker* alleges, that upon the suppos'd scheme, he cannot make above sixteen *per cent.* upon his

capital;

capital; therefore cannot do that with two thousand pounds of his own in trade, which the above-cited author says, another tradesman with one thousand pounds of his own in trade ought to do.

Let us just compare these two cases:
The one with one thousand pounds capital

     must gain -   -   -   -   390*l. per ann.*

The other with two thousand pounds

     capital, cannot gain above -   -   320*l. per ann.*

Or, supposing no deductions at all, 400*l. per ann.* But I fear there must be larger deductions from four hundred pounds *per ann.* than I have made, since we are able to prove by our books, that we cannot make above sixteen *per cent.* upon our capital; tho' for small pledges we take after the rate of thirty *per cent. per ann.* or two and a half, upon the return within the month; which is occasion'd by our dead stock already mention'd.

It may be ask'd, how then is it possible for *pawn-brokers* to live at all? It is next to impossible to do it, with no more than two thousand pounds capital in trade.

But how do they come at so much money, since it can't be suppos'd many of them begin business with superior or equal fortunes to what is suppos'd?

I answer, if they were persons of such profligate principles and practices, as they are misrepresented to be, this question could not be answer'd; but (if it involves no contradiction in itself) to suppose a man of this business whose moral character is unblemish'd, the difficulty may possibly be solv'd; but of this hereafter.

I would here desire my reader to pause awhile, and take a review of the calculations, and see whether he can find any flaw, any artifice, or statagem, to impose upon him at unawares: If not, will he not stand amazed, at the opprobrious language so freely bestowed upon us? Is not here presented to his view a demonstration, as plain and certain as any one in *Euclid's Elements*, that,

21   upon

upon the scheme proposed, our gains cannot be half so large as those of other middling tradesmen? Nay, that they do not exceed what even the *farmer* must make of his produce; it being a maxim, that if a *farmer* does not make three rents, he cannot live.

From this calculation appears likewise the weakness and absurdity of some notable projectors, who are for reducing the premium to 5 or 10 *per cent. per ann.* These gentlemen would certainly deserve the thanks of the public, could they inform us, by what rule in arithmetic they can find it possible, upon these terms, for any *pawn-broker* only to defray the charge of house-rent and servants, and get such interest for his money as he might make of it, without any trouble, or loss of time : For, as to the support of himself and family, and making a provision for posterity, it seems, it is extortion and oppression in him, however laudable it may be in any other man.

But what treatment soever we may have met with from our fellow-creatures and fellow-subjects, the only return I shall make is, to desire them seriously to consider, that rash uncharitable censures are no marks of an honest and virtuous mind; and if they do not proceed from malice, yet no plea, either of ignorance or inconsiderateness, can justify them in *scandalizing* or *oppressing* any man; and that *defamation,* whether proceeding from malice, interest, rashness, or prejudice, is none of the least of crimes.

I shall proceed, in my next section, to state and consider the most material objections that have, or can be, made to this business.

SECT.

SECT IV.

I BEGIN with the most formidable and popular objection; (*viz.*)

Object. I. *This business gives harbour and encouragement to thieves.*

Answ. One may reasonably ask, upon what proof, or appearance of proof, so heinous a charge is supported? Have there been any discoveries made by accomplices? Has any unhappy wretch, under sentence of condemnation, brought these dark practices to light, and saved his own life, by bringing three or four *pawn-brokers* to their deserved punishment? Surely *Wild*, of infamous memory, (who may be supposed to have known better than most people who were the *receivers of stolen goods*) might have saved himself, as well as served the public, by only sacrificing the one tenth part of the *pawn-brokers* to its just resentment. Surprising it is, that no one malefactor (who is not quite seared and hardened against the terrors of death and its awful consequences) should ever (for the ease of his conscience) have opened such a scene of wickedness! Is it not strange, that none of our servants (either from love of justice, or from pique and revenge, if we have happened to have had any difference with them, or in hopes of a reward) should have discovered such mysteries of iniquity? Again, have there been discoveries made by search-warrants, of secret holes and hiding-places in their houses or warehouses, wherein quantities of goods have been concealed, of which no entry has been made in their shop-books; any forges for melting down gold or silver, to prevent a discovery? How do *pawn-brokers* behave towards constables, or others, upon any inquiry after stolen goods? Do they at once go and look for them; and, if possessed of them, produce them; or do

they

they deny such goods, which are afterwards found upon them? Have they any close conveyance at unseasonable hours, any under-factors to ship them for abroad, and vend them there?

But, supposing two or three men, of this business, were base and wicked enough to be guilty of some, or all, of these practices, would it follow, that all the rest of the business are guilty of the like? By no means; for, at this rate, not a trade in *London* but might be charged with such practices; for there have been more of almost every trade and business convicted thereof, than there have been *pawn-brokers:* We may defy our enemies to prove upon record, that three *pawn-brokers* have been convicted of such villainy, ever since such a business has been heard of in the nation.

Can any man in his senses suppose several hundreds of people, continually engaged in such practices, and this for these one hundred and fifty or two hundred years last past, and not three of them convicted; notwithstanding the vigilance of magistrates, the sharpness and severity of judges, and the prejudice and prepossession of juries?

Again, what stronger temptations are *pawn-brokers* under than other men, to be guilty of this vice? It must argue gross inattention, and want of reflection, to imagine, that a man who takes a pledge, and proposes to keep it two years, and whose warehouses are liable to be searched on a bare suspicion, should be under a stronger temptation to receive a stolen thing, than a man who buys any commodity, and, it may be, sells it again immediately, and is therefore not so liable to be detected. I would not be understood to cast the least reflection upon any set of tradesmen, (how liberal soever other tradesmen may have been in this respect towards us) when I say, a silversmith can more easily melt down and dispose of a piece of plate than a *pawn-broker* can; because, if it should at last be discovered, it would not

24   appear

appear so black in him as in one of us; it being his business to convert old plate into new; and is supposed to have bought it, and to have a right to do what he pleased with it; neither of which is our case.

Moreover, the *pawn-broker* (by sad experience) knows, what severity he must expect; and that any other tradesman may, with more hope of impunity, *steal a horse, than he look over the hedge.* In short, unless it can be proved, that we receive pawns with one hand, and buy in a clandestine manner, and at an unreasonable price, with the other, this charge is as weak as it is groundless.

It may perhaps be said, *if there were no receivers, there would be no thieves.*

But how does it follow, that *pawn-brokers* are the receivers? This doughty argument is of the syllogistic kind, and should stand thus:

If there were no receivers, there would be no thieves.

But *there are thieves;* and what is the fair and logical conclusion? Why, *ergo, there are receivers;* and not, *ergo, pawn-brokers are the receivers,* unless they are proved to be so.

And why must so illogical and hasty a conclusion be drawn from the premises? Are *pawn-brokers* men of such desperate fortunes and characters, as to run such hazards as these? Can it be thought that men, who have fortune and credit so great, as to command capital stocks of two, three, four, five, six, or eight thousand pounds; should stake their fortunes, families, reputation, and liberty, and run the risque of suffering fourteen years transportation, and this for the hope of getting two-pence, three-pence, six-pence, twelve-pence, or even twenty shillings, or five pounds? I take this opportunity to inform the world, (which is pleased to talk so very much, and understands so very little, of the nature of our business) that two or three thousand pounds capital stock in trade is no uncommon, nor any great matter with us: But shall in my turn, ask the in-

quisitive

quisitive world the following question; (*viz.*) That as it cannot be supposed, that many *pawnbrokers* have so great fortunes of their own to begin the world with, and that many of them have large credit; how comes it to pass, that a parcel of such contemptible and profligate wretches can obtain such credit? When I see this question fairly answered, I will give up the argument.

Again, is there no other possible way of disposing of stolen goods? No man that keeps an open shop, to buy as well as sell, in the whole nation? No ships to convey them to foreign parts? Or, is it impossible for gangs of thieves to send agents abroad with the goods they have stolen, and so preventing their rising up in judgment against them? Of this I am certain, that thieves must not be half so cunning as they are generally thought to be, if they can find any other way of disposing of goods, and yet chuse to pawn them, since they run a great risque, whether they may not be stopped (as they frequently are) at the *pawn-broker's*; but, if not, it often happens, that they are convicted several months after the robbery committed, by the goods being found at a *pawnbroker's*, and by the evidence of himself, or his servants; whereas had the things been sold outright, they might have passed through a great many hands, and no one would have owned their having ever been possessed of them, and so the criminal have escaped his deserved punishment. I am sure it must afford high delight, and exquisite diversion, to thieves and rogues, if they have had so much address, as to conceal their main resort and harbour, and the legislature should happen to be upon the wrong scent.

It may be urged, *that tho' it be allow'd, that* pawnbrokers *do not wickedly and designedly harbour and encourage thieves and villains, yet they may be accidentally the receivers of stolen goods, and so afford (tho' without and against their intention) encouragement to such villainy; and as a proof thereof, it may be said, that there is hardly a session, but more or less* pawn-brokers *are there, to give evidence concerning stolen goods.*

I would answer, since we are so often there, how comes it to pass, that our mysteries of iniquity are not there revealed, and some of us made examples of? Are we spared for our name's sake, or can we expect superior or equal mercy with a common thief?

But perhaps it is a manifest proof of the care and circumspection we make use of, that we are not all of us there every session, if it be but consider'd, that a *pawn-broker* must have but a small run of business, if he does not take in fifty distinct pledges, one day with another, throughout the year; which amounts to twelve hundred parcels of goods in a month. Now, supposing there are but five hundred *pawn-brokers* in *London*, the number of pledges, multiplied by the number of *pawn-brokers*, will amount to six hundred thousand pledges receiv'd in a month's time: Is it any thing surprising, that three, four, five, or even ten or twenty of these, should prove to be stolen? It is no such wonder, that *pawn-brokers* should be more frequently there than others; if it be but consider'd, that no one business in *London*, but this, depends intirely upon laying out money upon goods brought to their shops: For though a silversmith, goldsmith, and many other trades, keep open shops to buy, as well as to sell; yet it is not to be imagin'd, that what they accidently buy in their shops, bears any proportion to the other branches of their trade. Consider also, that the *pawn-broker* deals in a far greater variety of goods than other traders; and is, therefore, the more in danger of being imposed upon. I believe it will be found, that, instead of being even *accidental* encouragers of thieves, we are both *accidentally* and *voluntarily* the greatest detectors of them in the whole nation, and the greatest sufferers by them in every respect. How many persons, upon only advertising their goods, have had them restored,

27   and

and been deliver'd from a private and dangerous thief, by means of the *pawn-brokers* making a voluntary discovery of them! For which we may have sometimes (formerly) receiv'd the thanks of the court; but have generally found mankind so ungenerous and ungrateful, as to make us lose the money lent; unless they have been compell'd to the contrary, by their own advertisement; and even then not always, nor frequently without some litigation. Again, the *pawn-broker* frequently stops suspicious persons and things; and even, when he is so unhappy as to be imposed on, and receive a thing that is stolen, he is the chief sufferer: The owner has indeed the trouble of a prosecution, but has his goods again for nothing; so that the *pawn-broker* is in truth the person robbed, and the thief is detected and punish'd. What mighty encouragement do *pawn-brokers* give to thieves, or thieves to *pawn-brokers!*

Again, if any person will carefully peruse the sessions papers, he will find, that the goods, which any of us are concern'd about, are most commonly of such a trifling value, that no man can possibly think it worth his while to run any hazard, could he have had them for nothing. Strange that these trifles should come to light, when more valuable things cannot be discover'd! *What then becomes of them?* I answer, I know not; nor am under any more obligation to account for them, than any tradesman, who, at any time, buys goods in his shop. But this I know, that for upwards of twenty years I have been in the business, I never had six things offer'd to me, which have been advertis'd either at *Goldsmiths-Hall,* or in the public papers.

But there is one reason to be given, why we are not so liable to be impos'd upon in things of value, as in trifles; and that is, because it is usual to send home with strangers, who bring things of value; but which cannot be done for every trifling pledge of two or three shillings.

It may perhaps be alleg'd, *that if* pawn-brokers *would*
use

use more care and caution than they do, and more fre-
quently stop suspicious persons and things, they might
detect more thieves.

I answer, as to care and caution, it more behoves a
pawn-broker to exercise it, than any other man in the
whole nation : And can it be thought we are so blind to our
own safety and interests, as not to guard all in our power
against the loss of our money lent ; the being oblig'd to
attend the sessions, and sometimes to be catechiz'd in
open court, besides the danger of a malicious indictment ;
and this sometimes for refusing to part with the goods
without a prosecution ? Every one knows how easy a
matter it is to find a bill before a grand jury ; and tho'
a man is ever so honourably acquitted, yet it leaves a lasting reproach upon him to have been ever arraign'd, and
put upon a proof of his innocence, as to such flagrant
crimes as those under consideration. And, *as to dectect-*
ing more thieves than we do, I should be very glad to
know, who will protect me from *indictments,* actions of
trover, and for *false imprisonment ;* in case I should
happen to be too sanguine, and stop a person or goods
upon a mistaken suspicion ? Perhaps our adversaries
never dreamt of these things amidst all their visionary
slumberings. I have heard it suggested, *that we make*
private sales of goods, and so conceal stolen goods. I
answer, that we do generally sell wearing apparel, linen,
&c. in large quantities ; it may be, fifty, sixty, eighty, or
one hundred pounds-worth at a time : But those that buy
them are public dealers, who sell and distribute them to
the dealers in *Monmouth-street,* and other public places ;
so that it is not for the sake of concealing goods, that we
sell them in this manner, but because it is the only way
of vending them for despatch ; tho' most of the business
retail publicly in their own shops ; and we all sell jewels,
watches, and plate, in this manner. Once more, it may
perhaps be urged, *that it is expressly said, (in the Act of*

Parliament made in the first year of King James I.) *that we are harbourers and encouragers of thieves, and dishonest persons.*

To this it may be answered, that our ancestors, at that time, were greatly inclin'd to see *invisible* sights, and to believe *impossible* facts; for, in the very same session of Parliament, there was an Act made against *conjuration, witchcraft, and dealing with evil and wicked spirits;* by which it was made felony *to consult, covenant with, entertain, employ, feed, or reward, any evil and wicked spirit,* &c.

Now it is indisputable, that many hundreds, if not thousands, of poor superannuated women have been *legally* convicted, and suffer'd death, by virtue of this Act, for crimes impossible in nature to be committed: Yet never have three *pawn-brokers* been convicted of the crimes alleg'd against them in the other Act, tho' nothing, in the nature of things, renders such practices impossible, nor a discovery of them impervious. It is worth remarking, how different their fates! The one has had the sacrifice of hundreds, if not thousands, of lives, in confirmation of the suspicion our ancestors had of witches, conjurers, and the like; and yet so sceptical are we moderns, in these respects, that our legislature has, within these few years, repealed the *Act* as far as it extends to sorcery or witchcraft; if it had been possible in nature. But as to the other *Act* concerning *pawn-brokers,* or, as the Act calls them, *fripperers,* tho' there have never been three *fripperers* convicted upon this Act from that day to this, in confirmation of the suspicion our ancestors had of these men; yet it is as firmly believed by us moderns, that *pawn-brokers,* alias *fripperers,* arc receivers of stolen goods, as tho' scores or hundreds of them had been convicted, or confess'd themselves guilty of such practices. It is well if' we don't derive from our ancestors, and still retain, the happy faculty of seeing *invisibles,* and believ-

ing

iug *incredibles !* For my part, as I have not the gift of *second sight*, like the good people of the *Orcades*, it appears to me, *at first sight*, that if hundreds of *pawn-brokers* have been constantly harbouring and encouraging thieves and rogues for these hundred and fifty years last past; and this without being detected and punish'd; that they are an overmatch for the *Devil*. Till now, I never so much as suspected them to be *conjurers*; but begin to be in bodily fear, lest I should have been, for the greatest part of my life, a *conjurer*, without knowing any thing of the matter.

I heartily beg my reader's pardon, and hope he will excuse my prolixity upon this head at *this time*; which, at any other, would have been very impertinent; but as the principal present complaint against us is upon this topic, it was necessary to offer all that I think may be said, having the hard and almost impossible task of proving a *negative !* How far I have succeeded, must be left to consideration; and now I proceed to another objection.

Objection 2. *This business is rather prejudicial than serviceable to the public.*

Answer. I humbly conceive this to be a gross mistake, and to arise from the objector's ignorance of the sudden and unexpected disappointments and embarassments, which not only people of the lower rank, but even those of a higher station, are liable to. Can any one, who knows any thing of the world, be insensible of the many difficulties master-workmen of all sorts are plunged into, by being disappointed of their monies when due; and having, at the same time, journeymen to pay, who cannot be put off without their wages, or perhaps the want of a present supply for their family occasions? Can any one be ignorant of the distress which working people are expos'd to, from unforeseen accidents, sickness, and the like? How often from such causes, their goods

31   are

are liable to be seized for rent, by a needy or merciless landlord; or their persons, by an impatient creditor? How often are even gentlemen disappointed of their rents when due? Sometimes engag'd in tedious and expensive law or chancery-suits (where nothing can be done without the ready penny); yet in such streights do not care to expose their necessities to their friends or acquaintance, lest it should be to no purpose; or perhaps, lest (in gratitude) they should be oblig'd to return the favour at another time; and so run the hazard it may be, of losing the money lent.

But to put this matter out of dispute, we will only suppose two cases:

The first shall be, a person of higher rank, who may have a sudden occasion for twenty pouuds (there being no business of this nature); he is oblig'd to sell a parcel of plate, or any jewels: Will not this be a far greater damage to him, than paying after the rate of twenty *per cent. per ann.* one, two, three, or six months for the loan of such a sum (I choose to instance in plate, because every one justly thinks this to be attended with as little loss as any thing)? I say, supposing a gentleman selling seventy-three ounces of plate, he will lose, at least, six-pence *per* ounce in the fashion, and the six-pence *per* ounce duty (which all new plate pays to the king); which together will amount to one shilling *per* ounce at least: This loss will therefore come to three pounds thirteen shillings. And as to more curiously wrought plate, his loss in this will be far more in proportion, considering what he must have paid for the fashion of any plate, where the workmanship is something extraordinary.

Or if he should be oblig'd to sell a gold watch (not at all damag'd by wearing), which cost him twenty-five pounds; the very maker or seller of that watch, could not allow him above seventeen or eighteen pounds for it, if so much: I need not calculate what this loss will amount to.

Now,

Now, if he can pledge eighty ounces of plate for eighteen pounds, and redeem the pledge in a month's time, it will be but six shillings loss to him; or, if he cannot redeem it in less than six months' time, it will be but one pound sixteen shillings loss to him, or should he be, at last, oblig'd to dispose of it, he is at liberty to do this whenever he pleases : For none of us would refuse a goldsmith's buying it, even in our own shops.

But, if we take an instance from lower life, where there can be little or no opportunity to provide against sudden and unexpected accidents, which people of this class are more frequently exposed to; and suppose an inferior tradesman distress'd for want of such a sum as twenty or forty shillings to pay his journeymen or rent; or to support himself or family in sickness; or to go to market with for materials to work upon : Was there no such business as we are pleading for, what a happiness would such a man account it, that he could any where borrow such a sum as forty shillings, and traffick with it for three months together, for so small a charge as two shillings, and not be oblig'd to sell his own or wife's apparel, or household-goods, for it may be not one half of what they cost him? And would any impartial by-stander call him, that got the two shillings, an extortioner or oppressor; or would he not more justly deem them to be fools, or knaves, that so unjustly vilify'd their neighbour?

These two cases are supposed to arise from mere necessity; but I humbly apprehehend it may be made appear to be the interest of the small trafficker, sometimes to pledge his goods, tho' not driven thereto by mere necessity : By considering how much such a person may save by going to market with ready money, buying advantageous bargains unexpectedly, and the like. Suppose a man should save but ten *per cent.* in the purchase of any commodity, by going to market with ready money; if he has a pro-

bable

bable prospect of coming into his money in a reasonable time, it will be worth his while to pledge any goods he can spare, and to pay even after the rate of 20 *per cent. per ann.* for the loan: for, supposing him to lay out ten pounds, it saves him twenty shillings in the purchase; if he comes into his money, and redeems his goods in three months time, it is ten shillings clear in his pocket; and if he should not come into his money under six months time, he has had the chance of making a return or two of his money for nothing: For when he has redeemed his goods, and paid for the loan of the money, he is but where he was, had he gone to market upon credit.

It may likewise deserve consideration, whether some Acts of Parliament, made of late years, may not have so affected small credit, as to increase the necessity of this business. For, if small credit should happen to be thereby rendered so precarious, that the creditor should have very little better security for his debts than the honesty of the debtor, he will be apt to think it too dangerous and leaky a bottom to venture his property upon. And if the small trader cannot obtain credit, he must either go to market with ready money, or his business be at a stand; and, if he has not ready money of his own, will be under a strong temptation to apply to the *pawnbroker.* This consequence, I will be bold to say, is what our Legislature never once designed.

The truth is, every man is at liberty, whether he will come to our shops, or no. No one would come there, did he not find his account in it, or, at least, imagine he did so; since no man chuses an evil as such: And if, upon experiment, he finds himself mistaken, would he ever do so again?

Methinks our enemies would do well, to give some substantial reason, *whence it comes to pass, that such monsters and oppressors of mankind should ever have any business to do:* Yet so it is, that this business has found em-

ployment

ployment for its followers ever since commerce and trade began to lift up its head, and flourish in the nation. Again, how happens it, *that people should, for years together, think it better to pledge their goods as their occasions may require, and to pay such terrible interest for the loan, than at once to sell their goods, and buy others, when they had got money so to do?* Should it be said, *their pressing necessities put them upon it;* I answer, that necessity, the more pressing it is, the more sharp sighted; it being proverbially called, *the mother of invention.* This tempts me to think, that people have tried other experiments, but find none more eligible; nay, perhaps, have experienced, that no people will buy and sell with them for such a profit as we make of them.

If a poor man (thro' necessity) should be obliged to sell his coat for five or ten shillings; it cannot be supposed he could put another in the room of it for so little loss as one shilling; because the buyer of the one, and the seller of the other, would both get a profit out of him; whereas he may *pawn* his coat for five or ten shillings, let it lie a month or two, and redeem it again for three half-pence, three-pence, or, at most, six-pence loss; tho' the *ungodly* and *extorting pawn-broker* has got after the rate of thirty *per cent. per annum* for the loan.

Objection 3. *If pawn-brokers are allowed to sell goods pledged in any reasonably-limited time, and not to be accountable for the overplus that may remain, they will make vast advantages by what they may have forfeited for want of redemption; and the pledger will be most grievously oppressed.*

Answer. The pledger is at liberty to redeem his goods during the time limited; or, if he cannot, may be able to procure a friend to redeem them, and so have an opportunity of disposing of them as he thinks proper: Or, if not, may bring other tradesmen to buy them; who, upon

payment

payment of the charge due upon the *loan*, may have opportunity of buying them in our shops, which none of us at this time refuse, where we have no apprehensions of a snare laid for us by wicked and designing people; either of forcing the goods from us, without allowing us a reasonable and living profit by our business, or furnishing themselves with evidence to support an action of *trover*, should we venture to sell them; whilst they (if perishable goods) retain any of the least value; and so recover against us, by dint of swearing, a far greater value (besides costs of suit) than ever their goods cost them. I have known persons who have made it their business to go to *Monmouth-street*, and buy up for a very trifle, old-fashioned and scoured brocade-silk gowns, old-fashioned broad laces, or any thing that has an high-sounding name in a court, and *pawn* them, let them lie three or four years, and then sue the *pawn-broker*, if he refuses to pay them ten times the value of the goods, or even of what they cost them. I presume, the reader will easily perceive how careful and cautious we are obliged to be in the present situation; which care and wariness is no more than innocent self-defence, tho' it may have the appearance of artifice or cunning.

But, to give a further answer to this objection by a quotation from the public *paper already mentioned, it is in answer to the objection, " *That we lend so little upon* " *goods, that what we sell we gain immensely by.*" The reasons of this general mistake are;

" *First*, the considerable disparity between the price of " goods at the first hand, and the price of the same goods " when they come to be sold to the immediate wearer: " Commonly two or three profits are got out of them before " that comes to be the case. For instance: A weaver,

" perhaps,

---

* Daily Post-Boy, *April* 26, 1731.

" perhaps, sells a piece of silk to a mercer, at four shil-
" lings *per* yard; allows one yard in thirty for measure:
" This is, however, an advantage not universally known :
" This mercer, perhaps, sells this silk, by retale, at four
" shillings and six-pence, four shillings and nine-pence,
" or five shillings, *per* yard; consequently the buyer esti-
" mates the intrinsic worth of what quantity he buys after
" the rate he gave the *mercer* for it; not allowing for the
" loss that immediately accrues to the goods he buys, by
" separating that quantity from the rest of the piece, and
" consequently its being valued by all buyers but as a
" remnant; much less allowing for the gain the *mercer*
" has gotten out of it, and the loss the *buyer* must sus-
" tain, was he immediately to offer those goods to sale to
" the same, or any other *mercer;* who would certainly
" never give after that rate for a remnant, for which
" he can buy it in the whole piece from the weaver.
" Now I think every considerate man must allow, that a
" thing is intrinsically worth so much, and no more, than
" what it will fetch at a common market. Add to this
" the charge the wearer is at, in making up the goods for
" his own use; all which he supposes added to the in-
" trinsic worth thereof (which indeed is so for private
" use); but, as to a common market, is more than so
" much taken from it; because then, if exposed to sale,
" they will be valued but as second hand goods: Which
" leads me to observe;

" *Secondly*, the great and almost incredible difference
" between buying a thing new, and selling that thing at
" second hand. For instance: If you make you up a suit
" of superfine cloth cloaths, that shall cost you seven
" guineas; I defy you, tho' you had never worn them,
" to sell them to any dealer in second-hand cloaths for
" four pounds ten shillings; altho' they are now new
" and fashionable for colour and cut: What can you then
" suppose to sell this suit for a year and half hence?

" And

" And what must a *pawn-broker* lend upon them (who
" proposes to keep these goods two years before he ex-
" poses them to sale, and runs the hazard of the moth,
" &c. so as to get a moderate profit)? Surely, any one
" would think three guineas, or three pounds ten shil·
" lings, sufficient: Yet if a *pawn-broker* lends so much
" upon them, and keeps them two years, and then sells
" them; he is presently exclaimed against for not lending
" half the value of the goods; and people are apt, *rashly*
" and *falsely*, to charge the *broker*, as though he got clear
" as much as the goods cost them, more than he lent
" on them, from a mistaken *rate* of the intrinsic value of
" the goods from what they cost, and not from what they
" would sell for. Every one knows the various damages
" all sorts of new goods are liable to, by being kept so
" long a time: Woollens are in danger of the moths, silks
" of mildew; and even linen goods will soon decrease ten
" *per cent.* in their value by lying by, and thereby losing
" colour, &c.; which if any man disputes the truth of, let
" him make the experiment. It may here be objected,
" *as to plate and jewels, they do not grow worse by keeping.*
" I answer, even as to these, people use the same standard
" of judging as to their value, as they do in the other
" cases: Whereas it is indisputable, that they must lose
" considerably by selling; unless any one supposes gold-
" smiths or jewellers to trade for no profit. But, particu-
" larly, as to plate, every one knows, we lend, at least,
" four shillings *per* ounce; and upon sterling, four shil-
" lings and six-pence *per* ounce, be it old or new. Now,
" supposing I lend four shillings and six-pence *per* ounce,
" and sell it, after having been two years out of my money,
" for five shillings and six-pence; that is not above
" twenty-two and a half *per cent.* for two years; conse-
" quently but eleven and a quarter *per cent. per annum.*
" As to jewels, the value is precarious. It may be said,
" *no doubt but you take care to lend little enough upon all*

　　　　　　　　" *hazardous*

" *hazardous goods.* To which I reply; if I happen to
" offer a person less upon any sort of goods, than others
" of my business will lend, I must necessarily lose my
" customers; there being too many of our business for
" one person to lend just as he pleases upon goods; and
" it is impossible, in things whose values are uncertain,
" for us to hold together; and it would be somewhat sur-
" prising, if, amongst all our rogueries, we should be so
" very honest to one another, as not to undermine one
" another; since this is daily practised by the fair traders
" themselves: And it is the same thing for one of us to
" lend so much upon goods, as to leave no room for a
" living profit when he comes to sell those goods, thereby to
" get the more business to himself; as for any shop-keeper
" to underfall the market, in order to gain customers."

But what if it should be capable of proof, that, at this
time of day, we think ourselves well off, if, in commodities
of a perishable nature, we get our own principal money
lent, or five or ten *per cent.* more than our principal, after
we have been out of our money two years? I fear, others,
as well as myself, have frequently lost as much of our
principal by the goods we have had to sell.

This arises from the nature of perishable goods, change
of fashions, the number of brokers, the tricks and frauds
which the *pawn-broker* is liable to, who cannot be supposed to be an over-match for every man in his respective
calling, therefore must be often outwitted; and the urgent
necessities of the poor, who will go to five or six different shops to borrow six-pence extraordinary upon their
goods; nay, rather than disoblige a *customer,* we must
frequently lend more than we know the goods would sell
for at a common market, in hopes it may yet be worth
their while to redeem them; so far are we from having no
measures to keep with those we deal with.

Whatever the world may think, it is a certain truth,
that our selling bears a very small proportion to the

monies

monies we lend in a year: If any *pawn-broker* lends five or six thousand pounds *per annum,* his business must be ill-managed, and his pledges badly taken, if he sells more than five or six hundred pounds of goods in a year.

This assertion can indeed only be proved by our books, which we are far from being afraid of producing upon a proper occasion.

Again, if people are obliged to sell their goods, how can any law provide against the buyer's taking advantage of the seller's necessity? To prevent which, must such difficulties and embargoes be laid upon all commerce, that no man can proceed in his buiness? This reminds me of some surprising clauses in the *Charitable Corporation* Bill, for regulating lending money upon pledges. One clause, for instances, obliged every broker, to go, or send, to every person's house, to give proper notice of an intended sale, though the pledge was of never so small consequence. Another clause (if I am not mistaken) obliged him to make public sales by cant or auction, in which each individual pledge was to be sold and set down by itself. One would think, (with great submission) that the wisdom of our superiors should have first enacted a law to probibit any persons removing their habitations, that we might have known where to have found the pledger, in order to our obeying this law: It should likewise have provided a method for our paying a retinue of servants or porters, to go on these important errands; not to mention the charge of hiring a room or hall large enough for these public sales, paying the auctioneer, and clerks of undoubted fidelities and abilities, to register what every pledge was sold for, they being of such consequence, that four or five hundred of them may sell for eighty or a hundred pounds: It may be reasouably supposed, here would be work enough for a pretty many. It likewise might not bave been much amiss, if we had been insured customers for what we had to sell, since some of our goods can only be vended to

country.

country-dealers : How all this was to be done with the allowance of *ten per cent. per ann.* for all charges, I confess myself quite at a loss ; nay, can hardly think it practicable in its own nature, if we had been allowed *cent. per cent.* for so doing.

Objection 4. *But, was this business to be publicly allowed, it might prove a great means of helping bankrupts to money, and so be detrimental to trade in general.*

Answ. While there are so many of every business, who are ready to buy bargains of persons in bad circumstances, and who can afford to give much nearer the value of goods, than we can be supposed to lend upon them, as having an opportunity of selling them at a better market, coming into their money again so much sooner than we propose to do, running little or no hazard of damage, change of fashions, and the like; I say, while this is the case, there is not much danger from *pawn-brokers.* Besides, we are not over-forward of dealing with shopkeepers, lest we should happen to be brought in as creditors in a statute ; or if not, yet, in case a person breaks, we may have a great deal of trouble and vexation, with little or no profit.

But, lest any apprehension should arise from hence, it is an easy matter to insert a clause in the hoped-for regulation, to limit what *sum,* at any one time, or at various times, to any one person, a *pawn-broker* shall be suffered to lend upon piece goods; and to this the *pawn-brokers* have no objection.

I have not heard much complaint upon this head, from (our *quondam* very good friends and allies, in the common war with the *Charitable Corporation*) the good citizens of *London.* However, I raised this objection to prevent their being under any uneasiness, as to this point ; but have heard more complaints upon another head, which is the next objection.

Objection 5. *This business is found to give encouragement to various mechanics, to pawn other peoples goods; such as taylors, mantua-makers, &c. and journeymen workmen their master's goods, which they have to manufacture.*

Answ. This objection has more weight in it, and, perhaps, is better founded than all the rest put together.

But even here the law has provided a relief; for the owner may sue, and recover his goods without paying the *pawn-broker* the money lent; and this upon the evidence of the party who pledged them: And, if the *pawn-broker* knowingly encourages such practices, he deserves to lose his money; but if, on the contrary, he has been imposed on and abused, he has a right to *indict* the pledger for a fraud; and if the master-employer will not screen the criminal, but heartily join with the *pawn-broker,* to punish him to the utmost rigor of the laws; a few examples made, will be a great means of preventing these complaints for the time to come. The *pawn-brokers* desire no alteration of the laws (in this respect) in their favour; but only care should be taken against combinations betwixt master and man to *rob* the *pawn-broker,* which is no strange or unusual thing.

I wish some of us, especially young beginners, may not have afforded some reasons for complaints of this nature: But, nevertheless, it is highly unreasonable for a man who may have been hurt this way, to make no discrimination, whether this may have happened through ignorance or design: and to condemn the whole business, for what may be only the fault, or, perhaps, the misfortune, of one man. Yet how common is it to hear a man loading every one of the business with the foulest calumny and reproach; wreaking his revenge, upon all possible occasions, upon any one that falls in his way! And, if you can get him but cool enough, to give you the grounds or reasons of his vehement dislike, perhaps he will tell

you

you, that once he gave his coat, or his watch, to be mended, and they were *pawned*, and he was forced to redeem them.

If mankind knew but half the arts and contrivances to impose upon *pawn-brokers*, the great difficulty of distinguishing between the master-employer and the under-workman in many cases; and that a taylor, journeyman watch-maker, mantua-maker, or laundress, may have an opportunity of imposing upon the *pawn-broker* other peoples goods as their own, before his utmost vigilance can prevent it; I say, if mankind considered this, and were as backward to slander and reproach, as they are to praise and commend, much of the clamour and noise would cease. However I think, that if the *pawn-broker* loses the money lent, which I am certain he will do very quietly, where there is no appearance of a designed fraud and combination; and (as I said before) the master or employer would never screen the original cause of the mischief; a few examples made will silence any material complaints for the future.

It would likewise be a great means of preventing this mischief, if master-employers and others would always pay poor manufacturers, mantua-makers, taylors, and washer-women, as soon as their work is done. I durst to say, if any *pawn-brokers* have ventured knowingly to deal with these sort of people, they have been prevailed upon to do so by a plea of this nature, either true or false.

But if any person is so violently exasperated on this account, that nothing will satisfy him but the total extirpation of the *pawn-brokers*, root and branch; let him consider, that he has his remedy against the *pawn-broker* at law; whereas, if there was no such business, the under-workman, *&c.* will be under a violent temptation, upon pressing necessity, to sell his goods outright; and if the buyer happens to keep an open shop in the city of *London*, or

any

any other overt-market, he will find himself obliged to pay for his goods before he can recover them, if it be true (as I am informed) that goods (not being stolen) sold at an overt-market, are irrecoverable.

This interesting consideration may, perhaps, a little cool and moderate the heat and flame of those, who are *charitably* disposed to *set another man's house on fire, for the sake of roasting their own eggs.*

Objection 6. *But this business is an encouragement to idle and disorderly persons, who hereby having a ready supply, will not care for working while they have any thing left to pawn.*

Answ. This objection was heretofore very gravely urged against us, by the then managers of the *Charitable Corporation,* which fell much heavier upon themselves; for they proposed to supply all necessitous poor with sums as low as one shilling, two-thirds cheaper than we commonly do; and, consequently, gave just three times the encouragement to idle persons to pledge their goods that we do: And, if another corporation was to rise up, which took no more than five *per cent.* it would give six times the encouragement we do to such practices.

But this objection will have little weight, if it be considered, that the flourishing of all business depends upon quick returns; when trade is brisk, and every one in action, frequent occasions for money will arise, and the borrower will soon be in a capacity to repay the money lent, and will pay for the loan of it without grumbling or abatements : Whereas, when little or no trade is stirring, just the reverse of all this will be the truth of the case ; which, by the way, corrects a very great and general error, *viz.* "That our business is best when others are " upon the decline."

Whatever encouragement therefore our business may afford to idle and disorderly persons, I am sure they will

afford

afford no encouragement to the business; for if they should have any thing of their own, (which is much to be questioned) that was of value sufficient, if they pledge it, it is once for all, and we may never see their faces again till after two or three years time, when they are pretty secure they are sold; who (if they do nothing worse) will do us the favour of coming to scold and brawl, in order to get a small matter out of us for having disposed of their goods; tho' it is very possible, if not highly probable, we may have lost money by so doing.

Again, I suppose we are no more accountable for the abuse that may be made of our business than other men. Must not a vintner be allowed to sell wine, because people may make themselves drunk with it? Or must not an honest and skilful surgeon be suffered, lest he should indirectly prove an encouragement to the committing of whoredom? If this way of reasoning holds good, I fear it may be thought necessary to put a stop to all trade and commerce, lest it should corrupt that native simplicity and integrity, so conspicuous, for the most part, in places where the least traffick is carried on. In short, if any profession is to be charged with the abuses that have been made of it, either by some of themselves or others, the most sage, honourable, and reverend, will not escape severe censure.

Objection 7. *But almost every man says, that* pawnbrokers *are a sad and pernicious set of men: And what almost every body says, must be true.*

Answer. There was once a time when *Christians* themselves were every-where spoken against: And why? But because *Christianity* never had been examin'd with attention and impartiality. I intend no profane comparison, when I say the business I have been endeavouring to vindicate is indebted to the very same causes, for its being generally and vulgarly disliked; and it will be no difficult

45   matter

matter to account for the obloquy and reproach cast upon it, if we only consider, that mankind, thro' a strange petulancy of temper, are forward enough to condemn what they don't understand : That it is the interest of wicked and designing persons to blacken and defame us, in order, with the more ease, to make a prey of us : That others, to prevent the least suspicion of their having any dealings with us, *rave* and *exclaim*, whilst those who know and consider things, do not choose to defend or vindicate us, for fear of incurring the like suspicion.

Others, not considering the unavoidable charge of negociating business, ignorant of our losses, and perishing dead stocks, which we are obliged to keep, and comparing our profits with the *legal* interest of money, give a great loose to their rash and inconsiderate resentments : Others are greatly angry and displeased with us, because sometimes our interests and theirs happen to clash and interfere ; and every one knows, that self-interest is of a very inflaming nature, and a great provocative to zeal : And if it falls out, that a man of this happy temper and complexion of mind, happens to be upon a jury, it is ten to one but the rest of the pannel are kindled up to a flame by the zeal of this one man ; and shall not unfrequently bring in a verdict against the *pawn-broker*, in opposition to the directions of the court, to the law of the land, and the oath they have taken ; and justify themselves in so doing, to all their acquaintances, by " assuring them, " that the *pawn-brokers* are a pack of rogues and villains ; " and it is no great matter what becomes of them."

Add hereto ; that *pawn-brokers* are but men, and subjected to the common infirmities of human nature, mistakes, oversights, and indiscretions, for which no allowances are ever made or thought of. But if any one *pawn-broker*, or even his servant, happens to make the least trip, it is immediately construed roguery and design ; and not only the party concerned, but every man who is so

unhappy

unhappy as to follow the business, is involved in the same condemnation !

Objection 8. *Private men ought to conform to the laws of their country : And for such to live and act in defiance of such laws, is great presumption and insolence, and consequently immoral.*

Answer. There is a wide difference between violating the *letter*, and violating the *spirit*, and ultimate *design*, of a *law*.

There are two *laws*, which the *pawn-broker*, at first sight, may *appear* to *defy* and *oppose.*

The first (if that may he called the *law* of the *country*, which is only the traditional and repeated opinion of *sages* learned in the law) is this; *viz. "That it is not* lawful *" for a* pawnee, *ever to sell and appropriate to his own " benefit the* pledge *or* deposit, *notwithstanding the most " fair and open provisional contract had pass'd between the " pawnor and the* pawnee, *to settle the time of redemption " on forfeiture of the pledge."*

Which *maxim* or *adage*, it is humbly conceiv'd is founded upon this consideration ; "lest the *pawnee* should " take advantage of the *necessity* or *ignorance* of the " *pawnor*, and so over-reach and oppress him."

Now, if *common law* is founded upon *common sense*, I shall leave it to the *common sense* of my reader to determine ;

1. Whether the amount of this maxim is not this ; " lest *A* should oppress and plunder *B*, it shall be in the " power of *B* to oppress and plunder *A ?*

2. Whether this *maxim* is not built upon taking a point for certain and granted, which is disputable *ad in- " finitum; viz.* "That the *pawnor* (for the most part) " hath less *wit*, and more *honesty*, than the *pawnee ?"*

To the first query it may be replied, " that the " *pawnee* has his action for the debt against the *pawnor.*"

True ;

True; but suppose the *pawnor* is not to be found, or is so poor as not to be able to redeem the *pledge,* and so perverse as to refuse consent to the *sale* of the pledge, unless compell'd by *law;* the costs and charges whereof, the *pledge* nor the *pledger* are able to defray; or, if the sum borrow'd, will not hold the *borrower* to bail, what becomes of the *pledgee?* Or what is he the better for having a collateral (especially a perishable) *security* in his hands? Which question must likewise be left to the *common sense* of my reader. Once more, and I have done putting of questions.

Things standing thus, *viz.* If *A,* the *pawnee,* ventures to sell or dispose of the *pawn* or *deposit, B,* the *pawnor,* has an opportunity of suing *A* in *trover;* and if *A,* the pawnee, wants his money, or is doubtful or disatisfied with the *pawn* or collateral security, he may bring his action for the debt. It is, therefore, a point which the reader's *common sense* must determine, whether this *maxim of common law* is not a natural and apt foundation for expensive and vexatious law-suits?

For my part, I shall not presume to oppose my *common sense* to the *common sense* of those gentlemen who are *duly* and *publicly* authoriz'd interpreters of the law, because they may be able to assign wise and substantial reasons for their opinions, which never have occurr'd to me: And whom (notwithstanding the mistakes or miscarriages of some individuals) I look upon to be the guardians and repositaries of the laws and constitution of this realm; and consequently, of all that is dear and sacred to an *Englishman.*

Taking therefore this *maxim* as we find it, I shall only endeavour to show, that a *pawn-broker* (if he is an honest man) may violate the *letter,* without doing any injury to the *spirit* and *design* of this *law.*

For instance; if a *pawn-broker* keeps a *pledge* so long, as it will bear to be kept without perishing; or, if not

perishable,

perishable, till such *pledge* will only pay him a reasonable
and moderate profit, and less than other tradesmen expect for laying out their money; and never desires or
attempts to defraud a person of his pledge, because it
happens to be left for a small consideration, in a short
time after its being so pawned; but, on the contrary, keeps
such *pawn* year after year, in consideration of its value,
and in expectation of its being redeemed; and should
the same person find in his warehouse a perishable
pledge, which has lain so long as to be in manifest
danger of becoming of no value, either to the *pawnor*
or the *pawnee;* and by sale whereof, if he don't lose of
his principal, thinks himself tolerably well off, if he can
make five or ten *per cent.* above the principal, should
venture to sell it after he had kept it two years or more;
1 say, however such *man* may transgress the *letter,* he
cannot, by fair construction, be said to *sin* against the
true *intent, meaning,* and *spirit* of this *law.*

And that such a conduct is no impossibility in nature,
nay, that it may have taken place in fact, will best appear
by our books; and may likewise be credible, from what has
been already said in answer to Objection III., and by
this further consideration; *viz.* "That complaints have
" not been exhibited in the courts against the *pawn-*
" *brokers* for taking valuable *pawns,* and converting them,
" in three, six, or twelve months time, to their own
" benefit; but the suits commenced against them are,
" generally, for their having sold a *pledge,* tho' never
" demanded in three, four, or five years after it was
" left."

I proceed to consider the *statute-law,* which the *pawn-
broker* is supposed to live and act in defiance to; which
is the statute against *usury* and *extortion.*

And here the very same *excuse* may be alleged and
supported: For, if any man thinks the *pawn-broker's*
money, and the *legal* value thereof, the only thing to be

considered,

considered, he must be wilfully *blind*, or naturally *short-sighted*. For, to judge fairly and reasonably, his time, labour, servitude as an apprentice, and the expence of servants, warehouse-room, &c. must be taken into the account : And, when reasonable allowances are made for these, he will be found no more an *usurer* or *extortioner*, than he that lends his money at five *per cent.* and has no more charge or trouble, than to receive the produce as it becomes due; or than he that makes the most moderate profit by buying and selling goods in his shop.

A *farmer* is allowed to make three rents of his land : And why? Because one third goes to the landlord for rent; another third goes for the charges of cultivation; and the remaining third for the support of himself and family : and as a reward for his skill and daily labour, to fertilize and improve every *foot* of land.

The case of the *pawn-broker* is exactly *parallel.* The interest his money would produce out of trade, or which he must pay for money, if he borrows it, is one third; the charge of negociating business is another third; and the remaining third is for the support of himself and family, as a reward for his skill in his business, (which either is, or ought to be, very comprehensive) and his daily labour and care in laying out, and receiving in, shilling by shilling, or pound by pound, his capital stock : By which means multitudes of people are relieved in their distress and emergencies : And the honest *pawn-broker* is, perhaps, as useful and necessary a person in his place and station, and may as much deserve the countenance and protection of the public, as any other private man.

But, if any man thinks the statute against usury and extortion of such vast consequence to the safety and happiness of the community, that he cannot forgive the least violation of a tittle, jot, or letter therein contained, he would do well to consult the great Mr. *Locke's* discourse, intituled, *"Considerations of the Lowering of*

Interest,

Interest, and Raising the Value of Money;" and afterwards to read *Sect.* 7th, *Prop.* 4th and 9th, of " *The Religion of Nature delineated.*"

It is humbly apprehended, that, if it can be made appear, that this *business* is of indispensable necessity to the public, and may (under proper regulation) be rendered of great service to the *community*; and that our *country* cannot be supposed to require *impossibilities* at our hands; we are *tacitly* excepted from the *literal rigour* of this law, because our case is, in its own nature, exceptionable; and, we doubt not, will appear so to be, if coolly and impartially considered. Now, if so, it requires nothing but a signification of the explicit and open consent of our country to such *exception*, to justify us in what we do : But, surely, no *consent* of our country can justify an *immorality*; nor can any *determinations* thereof alter the *ratio's* and *habitudes* of things. It may therefore be presumed, that our country wants only to be duly and thoroughly informed of the true state of our case; which when done, we may hope, from its justice and clemency, to be treated like *men* and *Englishmen*. And as, by a Bill depending, our country has given us a plain intimation of its being at *leisure* to intend and examine us and our affairs, it cannot be deemed intruding or officious, to offer ourselves, and our affairs, to its scrutiny : Which if our country condescends to make, we humbly hope to vindicate ourselves in such a manner, as to remove its present seeming dislike; to awaken its attention and indignation against our *calumniators* and *oppressors*; and to convince the world, that the honest part of us have done nothing unworthy of *men, Englishmen,* or *Christians*.

CONCLUSION.

Having thus exhibited to the view and judgment of the public the reasons and grounds, upon which my own pri-

vate

vate judgment has determined in favour of the *business* or *profession*, I shall, with great serenity and composure, submit my private opinions to its discussion; and the more so, as my country, above all the nations of *Europe*, is justly renowned for free and impartial inquiry; and has, in so great and glorious a manner, broken in pieces the shackles of ignorance, superstition, and bigotry.

It is agreed on all hands, that a business of this nature, in some shape or other, is of absolute necessity: And it has been demonstrated, that private men cannot perform it upon lower terms than those proposed: And, for the public to permit and suffer any part of the community to be defrauded and harassed, defamed, oppressed and plundered, for not being *infallible*, or for not doing *impossibilities*, is the greatest reflection upon its wisdom and goodness.

Should it be said, that we are too officious, and have obtruded ourselves upon the public; it may be replied, that all trades, mysteries, and crafts have first existed, before they could possibly be taken notice of, and established; and, in this respect, are as much to be charged with intrusion as we. But our country has, many years ago, taken some notice of us; and seemed, at that time, chiefly intent upon affixing a true and proper *name* upon us, and regulating some imaginary *abuses ;* but has never yet signified its pleasure, that all business of this kind should totally cease: And what it doth not prohibit, it *tacitly* permits ; provided the thing done is not, in its own nature, *immoral*.

And the same demonstration, which proves that private *men* cannot perform this *business* under the terms proposed, will prove, with increased force, that no *bodies corporate*, or *monopolies*, can do what they may charitably pretend to ; *viz.* Supply the poor with small *sums*, upon pledges so low as one shilling, after the rate of ten *per cent. per annum.*

For,

For, if the private *pawn-broker* (trading upon his own stock) cannot do it, whose personal care and skill are employ'd in his business; why should it be thought possible for any body corporate to succeed better; since such body corporate must pay eighty, ninety, or an hundred pounds *per annum* interest for the sum of two thousand pounds, and must intirely trust to the fidelity and skill of hirelings and servants? And if they would answer the specious ends proposed, must have warehouses in all parts of the town; but cannot do these things at a cheaper rate than the private *pawn-broker*. It will therefore always be found, that, under colour of supplying the poor with small *sums*, a most pernicious and dangerous monoply will be erected, which will prove destructive and ruinous to the nation.

But nothing of this kind is to be apprehended from the private *pawn-broker*; who is always under the inspection of the magistrates and courts of law and justice: and, should he attempt to defraud or oppress his fellow-subject, is much more easily to be detected and punish'd, than bodies corporate, or their representatives. Add to this, that the *pawn-brokers*, when numerous and divided, will always have clashings and interferings of personal judgments and interests; which will effectually prevent any combinations against the common good.

Further, the establishment of such body corporate would be a manifest invasion of the *rights* of the *pawn-broker*; who, at least, can plead *prime occupance*, and the *prescription* of near two centuries in his own behalf; not to mention his having borne the heat and burthen of the day; his servitude as an *apprentice* and *journeyman*; having, perhaps, a long and high-rented lease upon his hands, and a numerous and dependent family: Upon all which accounts he has the best right of offering his service to his country.

Some late *advertisements*, and private whispers, make

me suspect, that something of a corporation-kind is in *embryo*; and not being able *otherwise* to account for the present sudden alarm of *pawn-brokers being the receivers of stolen goods:* For, tho' most frequent and audacious street-robberies have been committed of late; yet (upon the best inquiry I have been able to make) I do not find the *pawn-brokers*, either *accidentally* or *voluntarily*, to have been materially concerned in receiving the goods stolen: Which, one would think, should have opened the eyes of mankind, and have put them upon inquiring after some other *resource* and *harbour* for thieves and stolen goods, than the private *pawn-broker*.

But, if any corporation-schemeatist has thought to have taken the *pawn-brokers* napping, and so destroy them with a sudden stroke before they could call in the assistance of their *natural* allies: I will venture to tell him, that the *pawn-brokers never sleep*; for the world takes sufficient care, by a thorough application of *pinchings* and *tweakings*, to keep them from nodding, and forgetting themselves. Our enemies may sleep till they snore again; ay, and in their sleep may dream

> *Of Anthropophagi, and men whose heads*
> *Do grow beneath their shoulders!*

But it highly becomes us to keep awake, especially at this time; and, in our turn, to requite the favours we have so long and frequently received; and humbly present to the world an *anti-narcotic*, which may be safely taken at any *time*, or in any *place*; but promises sovereign effects, at the *bar*, the *bench*, the *guild*, and in *******

In a word: We would humbly address ourselves to those, who have it in their power to protect or suppress us; desiring to come to the light, that our deeds may be reproved, if they deserve it, or our innocence made to appear; being chearfully disposed to do any thing in our power, to give light into our business or practices, to those

who

who have a right to make such inquiry. We desire nothing more than a cool, considerate, and impartial examination: It is hoped, that none of us fear the most strict one that can be made; however, I know one that does not.

If it should, upon such inquiry, be found, that we are the men our enemies suggest, it is high time such vipers were intirely crushed; but, if not, it is as *timely* and *reasonable* that the *innocent* should be vindicated and protected, who have long groaned under unmerited *calumny* and *oppression.*

POSTSCRIPT.

LEST the good citizens of *London* should take umbrage at our stiling them our *friends and allies,* and should superciliously reject *alliance* and *amity* with us, or should be too hastily induced to join in the opposition, it may not be amiss to propose to them the following hints:

1. That should the private *pawn-broker* be suppress'd, the infallible consequence will be a *charitable corporation* or *petty-bank,* which, like all other monopolies, will begin with the most laudable pretences, but will infallibly rise by degrees to the most enormous height, and swallow up the trade of the nation; or (as heretofore) become a mighty bubble to draw in certain persons *charitably* disposed to relieve the poor, and, at the same time, get more interest for their money than any other fund will give.

Now, the private *pawn-broker* may be esteem'd a kind of advanc'd-guard, or out-work, which must be first demolish'd, before the common enemy can make his approaches.

2. the

2. The private *pawn-brokers* do cause, perhaps, a million of money to circulate in the channels of trade; which, otherwise, would be locked up in the public funds; or, what may be much worse, fall into the hands of a *charitable corporation.*

Whether small credit bears, at this time of the day, the most agreeable aspect? whether the ready money trade is so very considerable, as to bear the lopping-off so considerable a branch? or, whether there is too much ready money circulating in trade at this time? must be left to your consideration.

3. Whether, if the private *pawn-broker*, who is a sort of mountaineer, and, at present, possess'd of an important pass (tho' situated on a bleak, barren, and ingrateful soil) should be driven from thence, he may not retreat to the more warm and fertile plain, where there is already complaint for want of elbow room? And as he has, by thin diet, and frequent incursions upon him, been inur'd to hardship and fatigue, (whereby he may have acquir'd a robust and athletic constitution) may not prove a troublesome neighbour, and disturb their long and happy repose?

4. If the private *pawn-brokers* should be so regulated, as to be oblig'd to quit their posts of a sudden, one or other of these must be the consequence; either the *common enemy*, if prepared, will immediately get into possession; or, for want of such *supplement*, the suddenly distress'd and ungovernable multitude may possibly take it into their heads to be their own carvers: And, as *they* are not given to make the most nice, just, and accurate distinction as to *person* or *property*; the consequences may be as fatal one way as the other.

These hints may be enlarged in their own meditations: A word to the *wise* is enough.

FINIS.

EXTRACTS

FROM THE

WORKS

OF

Dr. FRANKLIN,

ON

Population, Commerce,

&c.

CONTENTS.

CONTENTS

FRANKLIN

ON

Population, Commerce, &c.

OBSERVATIONS CONCERNING THE INCREASE OF
MANKIND, PEOPLING OF COUNTRIES, &C.

Written in Pennsylvania, 1751.

1. TABLES of the proportion of marriages to births, of deaths to births, of marriages to the number of inhabitants, &c. formed on observations made upon the bills of mortality, christenings, &c. of populous cities, will not suit countries; nor will tables formed and observations made on full settled old countries, as Europe, suit new countries, as America.

2. For people increase in proportion to the number of marriages, and that is greater in proportion to the ease and convenience of supporting a family. When families can be easily supported, more persons marry, and earlier in life.

3. In cities, where all trades, occupations, and offices are full, many delay marrying till they can see how to bear the charges of a family; which charges are greater in cities, as luxury is more common; many live single during life, and continue servants to families, journeymen to trades, &c. Hence cities do not, by natural generation, supply themselves with inhabitants; the deaths are more than the births.

5   4. In

4. In countries full settled, the case must be nearly the same, all lands being occupied and improved to the height; those who cannot get lands, must labor for others, that have it; when laborers are plenty, their wages will be low; by low wages a family is supported with difficulty; this difficulty deters many from marriage, who therefore long continue servants and single. Only, as the cities take supplies of people from the country, and thereby make a little more room in the country, marriage is a little more encouraged there, and the births exceed the deaths.

5. Great part of Europe is fully settled with husband-men, manufacturers, &c. and therefore cannot now much increase in people. America is chiefly occupied by Indians, who subsist mostly by hunting. But as the hunter, of all men, requires the greatest quantity of land from whence to draw his subsistence, (the husbandman subsisting on much less, the gardener on still less, and the manufacturer requiring least of all) the Europeans found America as fully settled, as it well could be by hunters; yet these, having large tracts, were easily prevailed on to part with portions of territory to the new comers, who did not much interfere with the natives in hunting, and furnished them with many things they wanted.

6. Land being thus plenty in America, and so cheap, as that a labouring man, that understands husbandry, can, in a short time, save money enough to purchase a piece of new land, sufficient for a plantation, whereon he may subsist a family; such are not afraid to marry: for if they even look far enough forward to consider how their children, when grown up, are to be provided for, they see, that more land is to be had at rates equally easy, all circumstances considered.

7. Hence marriages in America are more general, and more generally early, than in Europe. And if it is reckoned there, that there is but one marriage *per annum* among 100 persons, perhaps we may here reckon two; and

if

if in Europe, they have but four births to a marriage, (many of their marriages being late) we may here reckon eight, of which, if one half grow up, and our marriages are made, reckoning one with another, at twenty years of age, our people must at least be doubled every twenty years.

8. But notwithstanding this increase, so vast is the territory of North America, that it will require many ages to settle it fully; and till it is fully settled, labor will never be cheap here, where no man continues long a laborer for others, but gets a plantation of his own; no man continues long a journeyman to a trade, but goes among those new settlers, and sets up for himself, &c. Hence labor is no cheaper now, in Pennsylvania, than it was thirty years ago, though so many thousand laboring people have been imported from Germany and Ireland.

9. The danger, therefore, of these colonies interfering with their mother country in trades, that depend on labor, manufactures, &c. is too remote to require the attention of Great Britain.

10. But, in proportion to the increase of the colonies, a vast demand is growing for British manufactures; a glorious market, wholly in the power of Britain, in which foreigners cannot interfere, which will increase, in a short time, even beyond her power of supplying, though her whole trade should be to her colonies. *   *   *   *

12. It is an ill-grounded opinion, that, by the labor of slaves, America may possibly vie in cheapness of manufactures with Britain. The labor of slaves can never be so cheap here, as the labor of working men is in Britain. Any one may compute it. Interest of money is in the colonies from 6 to 10 per cent. Slaves, one with another, cost 30*l.* sterling per head. Reckon then the interest of the first purchase of a slave, the insurance or risk on his life, his clothing and diet, expenses in his sickness and loss of time, loss by his neglect of business, (neglect is natural

to the man, who is not to be benefited by his own care or diligence) expense of a driver to keep him at work, and his pilfering from time to time, almost every slave being, from the nature of slavery, a thief, and compare the whole amount with the wages of a manufacturer of iron or wool in England, you will see, that labor is much cheaper there, than it ever can be by negroes here. Why then will Americans purchase slaves! Because slaves may be kept as long as a man pleases, or has occasion for their labor, while hired men are continually leaving their master (often in the midst of his business) and setting up for themselves. § 8.

13. As the increase of people depends on the encouragement of marriages, the following things must diminish a nation, viz. 1. The being conquered; for the conquerors will engross as many offices, and exact as much tribute or profit on the labor of the conquered, as will maintain them in their new establishment; and his diminishing the subsistence of the natives discourages their marriages, and so gradually diminishes them, while the foreigners increase. 2. Loss of territory. Thus the Britons, being driven into Wales, and crowded together in a barren country, insufficient to support such great numbers, diminished, till the people bore a proportion to the produce; while the Saxons increased on their abandoned lands, till the island became full of English. And, were the English now driven into Wales by some foreign nation, there would, in a few years, be no more Englishmen in Britain, than there are now people in Wales. 3. Loss of trade. Manufactures, exported, draw subsistence from foreign countries for numbers, who are thereby enabled to marry and raise families. If the nation be deprived of any branch of trade, and no new employment is found for the people occupied in that branch, it will soon be deprived of so many people. 4. Loss of food. Suppose a nation has a fishery, which not only employs great numbers, but

makes

makes the food and subsistence of the people cheaper : if another nation becomes master of the seas, and prevents the fishery, the people will diminish in proportion as the loss of employ and dearness of provision makes it more difficult to subsist a family. 5. Bad government and insecure property. People not only leave such a country, and, settling abroad, incorporate with other nations, lose their native language, and become foreigners; but the industry of those that remain being discouraged, the quantity of subsistence in the country is lessened, and the support of a family becomes more difficult. So heavy taxes tend to diminish a people. 6. The introduction of slaves. The negroes brought into the English sugar islands, have greatly diminished the whites there : the poor are by this means deprived of employment, while a few families acquire vast estates, which they spend on foreign luxuries; and, educating their children in the habits of those luxuries, the same income is needed for the support of one, that might have maintained one hundred. The whites, who have slaves, not laboring, are enfeebled, and therefore not so generally prolific; the slaves being worked too hard, and ill fed, their constitutions are broken, and the deaths among them are more than the births : so that a continual supply is needed from Africa. The northern colonies, having few slaves, increase in whites. Slaves also pejorate the families that use them; the white children become proud, disgusted with labor, and, being educated in idleness, are rendered unfit to get a living by industry.

14. Hence the prince, that acquires new territory, if he finds it vacant, or removes the natives to give his own people room;—the legislator, that makes effectual laws for promoting trade, increasing employment, improving land by more or better tillage, providing more food by fisheries, securing property, &c.;—and the man that invents new trades, arts or manufactures, or new improvements in

9   husbandry

husbandry, may be properly called *fathers of their nation* as they are the cause of the generation of multitudes, by the encouragement they afford to marriage.

15. As to privileges granted to the married, (such as the *jus trium liberorum* among the Romans) they may hasten the filling of a country, that has been thinned by war or pestilence, or that has otherwise vacant territory, but cannot increase a people beyond the means provided for their subsistence.

16. Foreign luxuries, and needless manufactures, imported and used in a nation, do, by the same reasoning, increase the people of the nation that furnishes them, and diminish the people of the nation that uses them. Laws therefore that prevent such importations, and, on the contrary, promote the exportation of manufactures to be consumed in foreign countries, may be called (with respect to the people that make them) *generative laws*, as, by increasing subsistence, they encourage marriage. Such laws likewise strengthen a country doubly, by increasing its own people, and diminishing its neighbors.

17. Some European nations prudently refuse to consume the manufactures of East India :—they should likewise forbid them to their colonies; for the gain to the merchant is not to be compared with the loss, by this means, of people to the nation.

18. Home luxury in the great increases the nation's manufacturers employed by it, who are many, and only tends to diminish the families that indulge in it, who are few. The greater the common fashionable expense of any rank of people, the more cautious they are of marriage. Therefore luxury should never be suffered to become common.

19. The great increase of offspring in particular families is not always owing to greater fecundity of nature, but sometimes to examples of industry in the heads, and industrious education, by which the children are enabled

better

better to provide for themselves, and their marrying early is encouraged from the prospect of good subsistence.

20. If there be a sect, therefore, in our nation, that regard frugality and industry as religious duties, and educate their children therein, more than others commonly do, such sect must consequently increase more by natural generation than any other sect in Britain.

21. The importation of foreigners into a country that has as many inhabitants as the present employments and provisions for subsistence will bear, will be in the end no increase of people, unless the new-comers have more industry and frugality than the natives, and then they will provide more subsistence, and increase in the country; but they will gradually eat the natives out. Nor is it necessary to bring in foreigners to fill up any occasional vacancy in a country; for such vacancy (if the laws are good, § 14, 16) will soon be filled by natural generation. Who can now find the vacancy made in Sweden, France, or other warlike nations, by the plague of heroism 40 years ago; in France, by the expulsion of the protestants; in England, by the settlement of her colonies; or in Guinea, by a hundred years' exportation of slaves, that has blackened half America? The thinness of the inhabitants in Spain is owing to national pride, and idleness, and other causes, rather than to the expulsion of the Moors, or to the making of new settlements.

22. There is, in short, no bound to the prolific nature of plants or animals, but what is made by their crowding and interfering with each other's means of subsistence. Was the face of the earth vacant of other plants, it might be gradually sowed and overspread with one kind only, as, for instance, with fennel: and were it empty of other inhabitants, it might, in a few ages, be replenished from one nation only, as, for instance, with Englishmen. Thus there are supposed to be now upwards of one million of English souls in North America (though it is thought scarce 80,000 have been brought over sea), and yet per-

haps

haps there is not one the fewer in Britain, but rather
many more, on account of the employment the colonies
afford to manufacturers at home. This million doubling,
suppose but once in 25 years, will, in another century, be
more than the people of England, and the greatest
number of Englishmen will be on this side the water.
What an accession of power to the British Empire by sea
as well as land? What increase of trade and navigation?
What numbers of ships and seamen? We have been
here but little more than a hundred years, and yet the
force of our privateers in the late war, united, was greater,
both in men and guns, than that of the whole British navy
in Queen Elizabeth's time. How important an affair then
to Britain is the present treaty* for settling the bounds
between her colonies and the French? And how careful
should she be to secure room enough, since on the room
depends so much the increase of her people?

23. In fine, a nation well regulated is like a polypus :
take away a limb, its place is soon supplied : cut it in two,
and each deficient part shall speedily grow out of the part
remaining. Thus, if you have room and subsistence
enough, as you may, by dividing, make ten polypuses out
of one, you may, of one, make ten nations, equally populous and powerful; or, rather, increase the nation tenfold
in numbers and strength.   *   *   *   *

*Remarks on some of the foregoing Observations, showing par-
ticularly the Effect which Manners have on Population.*

From Richard Jackson,† Esq. of London, to Benjamin
Franklin, Esq. at Philadelphia.

Dear Sir,
It is now near three years since I received your excel-
                         12   lent

---

* In 1751.

† An English barrister of eminence, and an intimate friend of
Dr. Franklin.

lent *Observations on the Increase of Mankind, &c.* in which you have with so much sagacity and accuracy shown in what manner, and by what causes, that principal means of political grandeur is best promoted ; and have so well supported those just inferences you have occasionally drawn, concerning the general state of our American colonies, and the views and conduct of some of the inhabitants of Great Britain.

You have abundantly proved, that natural fecundity is hardly to be considered, because the *vis generandi*, as far as we know, is unlimited ; and because experience shows, that the numbers of nations are altogether governed by collateral causes, and among these none of so much force as quantity of subsistence, whether arising from climate, soil, improvement of tillage, trade, fisheries, secure property, conquest of new countries, or other favorable circumstances.

As I perfectly concurred with you in your sentiments on these heads, I have been very desirous of building somewhat on the foundation you have there laid ; and was induced, by your hints in the twenty-first section, to trouble you with some thoughts on the influence manners have always had, and are always likely to have, on the numbers of people, and their political prosperity in general.

The end of every individual is its own private good. The rules it observes, in the pursuit of this good, are a system of propositions, almost every one founded in authority ; that is, deriving their weight from the credit given to one or more persons, and not from demonstration.

And this, in the most important as well as the other affairs of life, is the case even of the wisest and philosophical part of the human species ; and that it should be so is the less strange, when we consider, that it is perhaps impossible to prove that *being*, or life itself, has any other value than what is set on it by authority.

A confirmation of this may be derived from the ob-

servation,

servation, that, in every country in the universe, happiness is sought upon a different plan : and, even in the same country, we see it placed by different ages, professions, and ranks of men, in the attainment of enjoyments utterly unlike.

These propositions, as well as others framed upon them, become habitual by degrees, and, as they govern the determination of the will, I call them *moral habits*.

There is another set of habits, that have the direction of the members of the body, that I call therefore *mechanical habits*. These compose what we commonly call the *arts*, which are more or less liberal or mechanical, as they more or less partake of assistance from the operations of the mind.

The *cumulus* of the moral habits of each individual, is the manners of that individual ; the *cumulus* of the manners of individuals makes up the manners of a nation.

The happiness of individuals is evidently the ultimate end of political society ; and political welfare, or the strength, splendor, and opulence of the state, have been always admitted, both by political writers, and the valuable part of mankind in general, to conduce to this end, and are therefore desirable.

The causes that advance or obstruct any one of these three objects, are external or internal. The latter may be divided into physical, civil, and personal ; under which last head I comprehend the moral and mechanical habits of mankind. The physical causes are principally climate, soil, and number of subjects ; the civil, are government and laws ; and political welfare is always in a ratio composed of the force of these particular causes ; a multitude of external causes, and all these internal ones, not only control and qualify, but are constantly acting on, and thereby insensibly, as well as sensibly, altering one another, both for the better and the worse, and this not excepting the climate itself.

The

The powerful efficacy of manners in increasing a people is manifest from the instance you mention, the Quakers; among them industry and frugality multiply and extend the use of the necessaries of life; to manners of a like kind are owing the populousness of Holland, Switzerland, China, Japan, and most parts of Indostan, &c., in every one of which, the force of extent of territory and fertility of soil is multiplied, or their want compensated, by industry and frugality.

Neither nature nor art have contributed much to the production of subsistence in Switzerland, yet we see frugality preserves and even increases families that live on their fortunes, and which, in England, we call the gentry; and the observation we cannot but make in the southern part of this kingdom, that those families, including all superior ones, are gradually becoming extinct, affords the clearest proof that luxury (that is, a greater expense of subsistence than in prudence a man ought to consume) is as destructive as proportionable want of it; but in Scotland, as in Switzerland, the gentry, though one with another they have not one-fourth of the income, increase in number.

And here I cannot help remarking, by the bye, how well founded your distinction is between the increase of mankind in old and new settled countries in general, and more particularly in the case of families of condition. In America, where the expenses are more confined to necessaries, and those necessaries are cheap, it is common to see above one hundred persons descended from one living old man. In England, it frequently happens, where a man has seven, eight, or more children, there has not been a descendant in the next generation, occasioned by the difficulties the number of children has brought on the family, in a luxurious dear country, and which have prevented their marrying.

That this is more owing to luxury than mere want,

appears

appears from what I have said of Scotland, and more plainly from parts of England remote from London, in most of which the necessaries of life are nearly as dear, in some dearer, than London, yet the people of all ranks marry and breed up children.

Again : among the lower ranks of life, none produce so few children as servants. This is, in some measure, to be attributed to their situation, which hinders marriage, but is also to be attributed to their luxury and corruption of manners, which are greater than among any other set of people in England, and are the consequence of a nearer view of the lives and persons of a superior rank, than any inferior rank, without a proper education, ought to have.

The quantity of subsistence in England has unquestionably become greater for many ages ; and yet, if the inhabitants are more numerous, they certainly are not so in proportion to our improvement of the means of support. I am apt to think there are few parts of this kingdom that have not been at some former time more populous than at present. I have several cogent reasons for thinking so of great part of the counties I am most intimately acquainted with ; but, as they were probably not all most populous at the same time, and as some of our towns are visibly and vastly grown in bulk, I dare not suppose, as judicious men have done, that England is less peopled than heretofore.

The growth of our towns is the effect of a change of manners, and improvement of arts, common to all Europe ; and though it is not imagined that it has lessened the country growth of necessaries, it has evidently, by introducing a greater consumption of them, (an infallible consequence of a nation's dwelling in towns) counteracted the effects of our prodigious advances in the arts.

But however frugality may supply the place, or prodigality counteract the effects, of the natural or acquired

subsistence

subsistence of a country, industry is, beyond doubt, a more efficacious cause of plenty than any natural advantage of extent or fertility. I have mentioned instances of frugality and industry united with extent and fertility. In Spain and Asia Minor, we see frugality joined to extent and fertility, without industry; in Ireland we once saw the same; Scotland had then none of them but frugality. The change in these two countries is obvious to every one, and it is owing to industry not yet very widely diffused in either. The effects of industry and frugality in England are surprising; both the rent and the value of the inheritance of land, depend on them greatly more than on nature; and this, though there is no considerable difference in the prices of our markets. Land of equal goodness lets for double the rent of other land lying in the same county, and there are many years' purchase difference between different counties, where rents are equally well paid and secure.

Thus manners operate upon the number of inhabitants; but of their silent effects upon a civil constitution, history, and even our own experience, yield us abundance of proofs, though they are not uncommonly attributed to external causes; their support of a government against external force is so great, that it is a common maxim among the advocates of liberty, that no free government was ever dissolved, or overcome, before the manners of its subjects were corrupted.

The superiority of Greece over Persia was singly owing to their difference of manners; and that, though all natural advantages were on the side of the latter, to which I might add the civil ones; for though the greatest of all civil advantages, liberty, was on the side of Greece, yet that added no political strength to her, but in proportion as it operated on her manners; and, when they were corrupted, the restoration of their liberty by the Romans overturned the remains of their power.

Whether

Whether the manners of ancient Rome were at any period calculated to promote the happiness of individuals, it is not my design to examine; but that their manners, and the effects of those manners on their government and public conduct, founded, enlarged, and supported, and afterwards overthrew their empire, is beyond all doubt. One of the effects of their conquest, furnishes us with a strong proof, how prevalent manners are even beyond quantity of subsistence; for, when the custom of bestowing on the citizens of Rome corn enough to support themselves and families was become established, and Egypt and Sicily produced the grain that fed the inhabitants of Italy, this became less populous every day, and the *jus trium liberorum* was but an expedient that could not balance the want of industry and frugality.

But corruption of manners did not only thin the inhabitants of the Roman empire, it rendered the remainder incapable of defence long before its fall, perhaps before the dissolution of the republic; so that without standing disciplined armies, composed of men whose moral habits principally, and mechanical habits secondarily, made them different from the body of the people, the Roman empire had been a prey to the barbarians many ages before it was.

By the mechanical habits of the soldiery, I mean their discipline and the art of war; and that this is but a secondary quality appears from the inequality that has in all ages been between raw though well disciplined armies and veterans; and more from the irresistible force a single moral habit, religion, has conferred on troops, frequently neither disciplined nor experienced.

The military manners of the *noblesse* in France, compose the chief force of that kingdom; and the enterprising manners and restless dispositions of the inhabitants of Canada, have enabled a handful of men to harass our populous, and, generally, less martial colonies; yet neither

are

are of the value they seem at first, because overbalanced by the defect they occasion of other habits that would produce more eligible political good: and military manners in a people are not necessary in an age and country where such manners may be occasionally formed and preserved among men enough to defend the state: and such a country is Great Britain; where, though the lower class of people are by no means of a military cast, yet they make better soldiers than even the *noblesse* of France.

The inhabitants of this country, a few ages back, were to the populous and rich provinces of France, what Canada is now to the British colonies. It is true, there was less disproportion between their natural strength; but I mean, that the riches of France were a real weakness, opposed to the military manners founded upon poverty and a rugged disposition, compared to the character of the English; but it must be remembered, that at this time the manners of a people were not distinct from that of their soldiery; for the use of standing armies has deprived a military people of the advantages they before had over others; and though it has been often said, that civil wars give power, because they render all men soldiers, I believe this has only been found true in internal wars following civil wars, and not in external ones; for now, in foreign wars, a small army, with ample means to support it, is of greater force than one more numerous, with less. This last fact has often happened between France and Germany.

The means of supporting armies, and consequently the power of exerting external strength, are best found in the industry and frugality of the body of a people living under a government and laws that encouraged commerce; for commerce is at this day almost the only stimulus that forces every one to contribute a share of labor for the public benefit.

But such is the human frame, and the world is so constituted, that it is a hard matter to possess one's self of a benefit, without laying one's self open to a loss on some other side; the improvements of manners of one sort often deprave those of another: thus we see industry and frugality under the influence of commerce, which I call a commercial spirit, tend to destroy, as well as support, the government it flourishes under.

Commerce perfects the arts, but more the mechanical than the liberal, and this for an obvious reason; it softens and enervates the manners. Steady virtue and unbending integrity are seldom to be found where a spirit of commerce pervades every thing; yet the perfection of commerce is, that every thing should have its price. We every day see its progress, both to our benefit and detriment here. Things, that *boni mores* forbid to be set to sale, are become its objects, and there are few things indeed *extra commercium*. The legislative power itself has been *in commercio*, and church livings are seldom given without consideration, even by sincere Christians, and, for consideration, not seldom to very unworthy persons. The rudeness of ancient military times, and the fury of more modern enthusiastic ones, are worn off; even the spirit of forensic contention is astonishingly diminished, all marks of manners softening; but luxury and corruption have taken their places, and seem the inseparable companions of commerce and the arts.

I cannot help observing, however, that this is much more the case in extensive countries, especially at their metropolis, than in other places. It is an old observation of politicians, and frequently made by historians, that small states always best preserve their manners. Whether this happens from the greater room there is for attention in the legislature, or from the less room there is for ambition and avarice, it is a strong argument, among others, against an incorporating union of the colonies in America, or even a federal one, that may tend to the future reducing them under one government.

Their

Their power, while disunited, is less, but their liberty, as well as manners, is more secure; and, considering the little danger of any conquest to be made upon them, I had rather they should suffer something through disunion, than see them under a general administration less equitable than that concerted at Albany.

I take it, the inhabitants of Pennsylvania are both frugal and industrious beyond those of any province in America. If luxury should spread, it cannot be extirpated by laws. We are told by Plutarch, that Plato used to say, *It was a hard thing to make laws for the Cyrenians, a people abounding in plenty and opulence.*

But from what I set out with, it is evident, if I be not mistaken, that education only can stem the torrent, and, without checking either true industry or frugality, prevent the sordid frugality and laziness of the old Irish, and many of the modern Scotch, (I mean the inhabitants of that country, those who leave it for another being generally industrious,) or the industry, mixed with luxury, of this capital, from getting ground, and, by rendering ancient manners familiar, produce a reconciliation between disinterestedness and commerce; a thing we often see, but almost always in men of a liberal education.

To conclude: when we would form a people, soil and climate may be found at least sufficiently good; inhabitants may be encouraged to settle, and even supported for a while; a good government and laws may be framed, and even arts may be established, or their produce imported: but many necessary moral habits are hardly ever found among those who voluntarily offer themselves in times of quiet at home, to people new colonies; besides that the moral as well as mechanical habits, adapted to a mother-country, are frequently not so to the new settled one, and to external events, many of which are always unforeseen. Hence it is we have seen such fruitless attempts to settle colonies, at an immense public and

　　private

private expense, by several of the powers of Europe; and it is particularly observable, that none of the English colonies became any way considerable, till the necessary manners were born and grew up in the country, excepting those to which singular circumstances at home forced manners fit for the forming a new state. I am, Sir, &c.

R. JACKSON.

On the Price of Corn, and Management of the Poor.

To Messieurs the Public.

I am one of that class of people that feeds you all, and at present is abused by you all;—in short, I am a *farmer*.

By your newspapers we are told, that God had sent a very short harvest to some other countries of Europe. I thought this might be in favor of Old England; and that now we should get a good price for our grain, which would bring millions among us, and make us flow in money: that, to be sure, is scarce enough.

But the wisdom of government forbad the exportation.

Well, says I, then we must be content with the market price at home.

No, say my lords the mob, you sha'n't have that. Bring your corn to market if you dare;—we'll sell it for you, for less money, or take it for nothing.

Being thus attacked by both ends *of the constitution,* the head and the tail *of government,* what am I to do?

Must I keep my corn in the barn to feed, and increase the breed of rats?—be it so;—they cannot be less thankful than those I have been used to feed.

Are

Are we farmers the only people to be grudged the profits of our honest labor?—And why? One of the late scribblers against us, gives a bill of fare of the provisions at my daughter's wedding, and proclaims to all the world, that we had the insolence to eat beef and pudding!—Has he not read the precept in the good book, *Thou shalt not muzzle the mouth of the ox that treadeth out the corn;* or does he think us less worthy of good living than our oxen?

O, but the manufacturers! the manufacturers! they are to be favored, and they must have bread at a cheap rate!

Hark ye, Mr. Oaf;—the farmers live splendidly, you say. And pray, would you have them hoard the money they get? Their fine clothes and furniture, do they make them themselves, or for one another, and so keep the money among them? Or, do they employ these your darling manufacturers, and so scatter it again all over the nation?

The wool would produce me a better price, if it were suffered to go to foreign markets; but that, Messieurs the Public, your laws will not permit. It must be kept all at home, that our *dear* manufacturers may have it the cheaper. And then, having yourselves thus lessened our encouragement for raising sheep, you curse us for the scarcity of mutton!

I have heard my grandfather say, that the farmers submitted to the prohibition on the exportation of wool, being made to expect and believe that when the manufacturer bought his wool cheaper, they should also have their cloth cheaper. But the deuce a bit. It has been growing dearer and dearer from that day to this. How so? Why, truly, the cloth is exported; and that keeps up the price.

Now, if it be a good principle, that the exportation of a commodity is to be restrained, that so our people at

23   home

home may have it the cheaper, stick to that principle, and go thorough stitch with it. Prohibit the exportation of your cloth, your leather, and shoes, your iron ware, and your manufactures of all sorts, to make them all cheaper at home. And cheap enough they will be, I will warrant you—till people leave off making them.

Some folks seem to think they ought never to be easy till England becomes another Lubberland, where it is fancied the streets are paved with penny rolls, the houses tiled with pancakes, and chickens, ready roasted, cry, Come eat me!

I say, when you are sure you have got a good principle, stick to it, and carry it thorough. I hear it is said, that though it was *necessary and right* for the ministry to advise a prohibition of the exportation of corn, yet it was *contrary to law ;* and also, that though it was *contrary to law* for the mob to obstruct waggons, yet it was *necessary and right*. Just the same thing to a tittle. Now they tell me, an act of indemnity ought to pass in favor of the ministry, to secure them from the consequences of having acted illegally. If so, pass another in favor of the mob. Others say, some of the mob ought to be hanged, by way of example. If so,—but I say no more than I have said before, *when you are sure that you have got a good principle, go thorough with it.*

You say, poor laborers cannot afford to buy bread at a high price, unless they had higher wages. Possibly. But how shall we farmers be able to afford our laborers higher wages, if you will not allow us to get, when we might have it, a higher price for our corn?

By all that I can learn, we should at least have had a guinea a quarter more, if the exportation had been allowed. And this money England would have got from foreigners.

But, it seems, we farmers must take so much less, that the poor may have it so much cheaper.

This

This operates then as a tax for the maintenance of the poor. A very good thing, you will say. But I ask, why a partial tax? Why laid on us farmers only? If it be a good thing, pray, Messieurs the Public, take your share of it, by indemnifying us a little out of your public treasury. In doing a good thing, there is both honor and pleasure;—you are welcome to your share of both.

For my own part, I am not so well satisfied of the goodness of this thing. I am for doing good to the poor, but I differ in opinion about the means. I think the best way of doing good to the poor, is not making them easy *in* poverty, but leading or driving them *out* of it. In my youth I travelled much, and I observed in different countries, that the more public provisions were made for the poor, the less they provided for themselves, and of course became poorer. And, on the contrary, the less was done for them, the more they did for themselves, and became richer. There is no country in the world where so many provisions are established for them; so many hospitals to receive them when they are sick or lame, founded and maintained by voluntary charities; so many alms-houses for the aged of both sexes; together with a solemn general law, made by the rich, to subject their estates to a heavy tax for the support of the poor. Under all these obligations, are our poor modest, humble, and thankful? and do they use their best endeavours to maintain themselves, and lighten our shoulders of this burthen? On the contrary, I affirm that there is no country in the world in which the poor are more idle, dissolute, drunken, and insolent. The day you passed that act, you took away from before their eyes the greatest of all inducements to industry, frugality, and sobriety, by giving them a dependence on somewhat else than a careful accumulation during youth and health, for support in age or sickness. In short, you offered a premium for the encouragement of idleness, and you should not now wonder that it has had its effect in the in-

crease

crease of poverty. Repeal that law, and you will soon see
a change in their manners—*Saint Monday* and *Saint Tues-
day* will soon cease to be holidays. Six *days shalt thou
labor*, though one of the old commandments, long treated
as out of date, will again be looked upon as a respectable
precept; industry will increase, and with it plenty among
the lower people; their circumstances will mend, and
more will be done for their happiness by inuring them to
provide for themselves, than could be done by dividing all
your estates among them.

Excuse me, Messieurs the Public, if upon this *interesting* subject I put you to the trouble of reading a little of
my nonsense : I am sure I have lately read a great deal of
yours ; and therefore from you (at least from those of you
who are writers) I deserve a little indulgence.

I am yours, &c.   Arator.

On Smuggling, and its various Species.

Sir,

There are many people that would be thought, and
even think themselves, *honest* men, who fail nevertheless
in particular points of honesty; deviating from that
character sometimes by the prevalence of mode or custom,
and sometimes through mere inattention; so that their
honesty is partial only, and not *general* or universal. Thus,
one who would scorn to over-reach you in a bargain, shall
make no scruple of tricking you a little now and then at
cards; another that plays with the utmost fairness, shall
with great freedom cheat you in the sale of a horse. But
there is no kind of dishonesty, into which otherwise
good people more easily and frequently fall, than that of
defrauding government of its revenues by smuggling

when

when they have an opportunity, or encouraging smugglers by buying their goods.

I fell into these reflections the other day, on hearing two gentlemen of reputation discoursing about a small estate, which one of them was inclined to sell, and the other to buy; when the seller, in recommending the place, remarked, that its situation was very advantageous on this account, that being on the sea-coast in a smuggling country, one had frequent opportunities of buying many of the expensive articles used in a family, (such as tea, coffee, chocolate, brandy, wines cambrics, Brussels laces, French silks, and all kinds of India goods,) 20, 30, and in some articles 50 *per cent.* cheaper than they could be had in the more interior parts, of traders that paid duty. The other *honest* gentleman allowed all this to be an advantage, but insisted that the seller, in the advanced price he demanded on that account, rated the advantage much above its value. And neither of them seemed to think dealing with smugglers, a practice that an *honest* man (provided he got his goods cheap) had the least reason to be ashamed of.

At a time when the load of our public debt, and the heavy expense of maintaining our fleets and armies to be ready for our defence on occasion, makes it necessary not only to continue old taxes, but often to look out for new ones; perhaps it may not be unuseful to state this matter in a light that few seem to have considered it in.

The people of Great Britain, under the happy constitution of this country, have a privilege few other countries enjoy, that of choosing the third branch of the legislature; which branch has alone the power of regulating their taxes. Now whenever the government finds it necessary for the common benefit, advantage, and safety of the nation, for the security of our liberties, property, religion, and every thing that is dear to us, that certain sums shall be yearly raised by taxes, duties, &c. and paid into the public

27   treasury,

treasury, thence to be dispensed by government for those purposes, ought not every *honest man* freely and willingly to pay his just proportion of this necessary expense? Can he possibly preserve a right to that character, if by any fraud, stratagem, or contrivance, he avoids that payment in whole or in part?

What should we think of a companion, who having supped with his friends at a tavern, and partaken equally of the joys of the evening with the rest of us, would nevertheless contrive, by some artifice, to shift his share of the reckoning upon others, in order to go off scot-free? If a man who practised this, would, when detected, be deemed and called a scoundrel, what ought he to be called, who can enjoy all the inestimable benefits of public society, and yet by smuggling, or dealing with smugglers, contrive to evade paying his just share of the expense, as settled by his own representatives in parliament; and wrongfully throw it upon his honester and perhaps much poorer neighbours? He will perhaps be ready to tell me, that he does not wrong his neighbours; he scorns the imputation; he only cheats the king a little, who is very able to bear it. This however is a mistake. The public treasure is the treasure of the nation, to be applied to national purposes. And when a duty is laid for a particular public and necessary purpose, if through smuggling that duty falls short of raising the sum required, and other duties must therefore be laid to make up the deficiency; all the additional sum laid by the new duties and paid by other people, though it should amount to no more than a halfpenny or a farthing per head, is so much actually picked out of the pockets of those other people by the smugglers and their abettors and encouragers. Are they then any better or other than pickpockets? and what mean, low, rascally pickpockets must those be, that can pick pockets for halfpence and for farthings?

I would not however be supposed to allow in what I

have

have just said, that cheating the king is a less offence against honesty, than cheating the public. The king and the public in this case are different names for the same thing; but if we consider the king distinctly, it will not lessen the crime: it is no justification of a robbery, that the person robbed was rich and able to bear it. The king has as much right to justice as the meanest of his subjects; and as he is truly the common *father* of his people, those that rob him fall under the scripture woe, pronounced against the son *that robbeth his father, and saith it is no sin.*

Mean as this practice is, do we not daily see people of character and fortune engaged in it for trifling advantages to themselves? Is any lady ashamed to request of a gentleman of her acquaintance, that when he returns from abroad, he would smuggle her home a piece of silk or lace from France or Flanders? Is any gentleman ashamed to undertake and execute the commission? Not in the least. They will talk of it freely, even before others whose pockets they are thus contriving to pick by this piece of knavery.

Among other branches of the revenue, that of the post-office is, by a late law, appropriated to the discharge of our public debt, to defray the expenses of the state. None but members of parliament, and a few public officers, have now a right to avoid, by a frank, the payment of postage. When any letter not written by them or on their business, is franked by any of them, it is a hurt to the revenue; an injury which they must now take the pains to conceal by writing the whole superscription themselves. And yet such is our insensibility to justice in this particular, that nothing is more common than to see, even in a reputable company, a *very honest* gentleman or lady declare, his or her intention to cheat the nation of three-pence by a frank; and, without blushing, apply to one of the very legislators themselves, with a modest request, that

he

he would be pleased to become an accomplice in the crime, and assist in the perpetration.

There are those who by these practices take a great deal in a year out of the public purse, and put the money into their own private pockets. If, passing through a room where public treasure is deposited, a man takes the opportunity of clandestinely pocketing and carrying off a guinea, is he not truly and properly a thief? And if another evades paying into the treasury a guinea he ought to pay in, and applies it to his own use, when he knows it belongs to the public as much as that which has been paid in, what difference is there in the nature of the crime, or the baseness of committing it?

Some laws make the receiving of stolen goods equally penal with stealing, and upon this principle, that if there were no receivers there would be few thieves. Our proverb too, says truly, that *the receiver is as bad as the thief*. By the same reasoning, as there would be few smugglers, if there were none who knowingly encouraged them by buying their goods, we may say that the encouragers of smuggling are as bad as the smugglers; and that as smugglers are a kind of thieves, both equally deserve the punishments of thievery.

In this view of wronging the revenue, what must we think of those who can evade paying for their wheels and their plate, in defiance of law and justice, and yet declaim against corruption and peculation, as if their own hands and hearts were pure and unsullied? The Americans offend us grievously, when, contrary to our laws, they smuggle goods into their own country; and yet they had no hand in making those laws. I do not however pretend from thence to justify them: but I think the offence much greater in those who either directly or indirectly have been concerned in making the very laws they break. And when I hear them exclaiming against the Americans, and for every little infringement of the acts of trade, or ob-

struction

struction given by a petty mob to an officer of our customs
in that country, calling for vengeance against the whole
people as rebels and traitors, I cannot help thinking there
are still those in the world who can *see a mote in their
brother's eye, while they do not discern a beam in their own;*
and that the old saying is as true now as ever it was, *one
man may better steal a horse, than another look over the
hedge.*   **B. F.**

Observations on War.

By the original law of nations, war and extirpation
were the punishment of injury.   Humanising by degrees,
it admitted slavery instead of death; a farther step was,
the exchange of prisoners instead of slavery; another, to
respect more the property of private persons under conquest, and be content with acquired dominion.   Why
should not this law of nations go on improving?   Ages
have intervened between its several steps; but as knowledge of late increases rapidly, why should not those steps
be quickened?   Why should it not be agreed to, as the
future law of nations, that in any war hereafter the following description of men should be undisturbed, have the
protection of both sides, and be permitted to follow their
employments in security ? viz.

1. Cultivators of the earth, because they labor for the
subsistence of mankind.

2. Fishermen, for the same reason.

3. Merchants and traders in unarmed ships, who
accommodate different nations by communicating and
exchanging the necessaries and conveniences of life.

4. Artists and mechanics, inhabiting and working in
open towns.

It is hardly necessary to add, that the hospitals of
enemies should be unmolested—they ought to be assisted.

It

It is for the interest of humanity in general, that the occasions of war, and the inducements to it, should be diminished. If rapine be abolished, one of the encouragements to war is taken away; and peace therefore more likely to continue and be lasting.

The practice of robbing merchants on the high seas—a remnant of the ancient piracy—though it may be accidentally beneficial to particular persons, is far from being profitable to all engaged in it, or to the nation that authorises it. In the beginning of a war some rich ships are surprised and taken. This encourages the first adventurers to fit out more armed vessels; and many others to do the same. But the enemy at the same time become more careful; arm their merchant ships better, and render them not so easy to be taken: they go also more under the protection of convoys. Thus, while the privateers to take them are multiplied, the vessels subject to be taken, and the chances of profit, are diminished; so that many cruises are made wherein the expenses overgo the gains; and, as is the case in other lotteries, though particulars have got prizes, the mass of adventurers are losers, the whole expense of fitting out all the privateers during a war, being much greater than the whole amount of goods taken.

Then there is the national loss of all the labor of so many men during the time they have been employed in robbing; who besides spend what they get in riot, drunkenness, and debauchery; lose their habits of industry; are rarely fit for any sober business after a peace, and serve only to increase the number of highwaymen and house-breakers. Even the undertakers who have been fortunate, are, by sudden wealth, led into expensive living, the habit of which continues when the means of supporting it cease, and finally ruins them; a just punishment for their having wantonly and unfeelingly ruined many honest, innocent traders and their families, whose substance was employed in serving the common interest of mankind.

On the Laboring Poor.

To the Editor of * * * April, 1768.

Sir,

I have met with much invective in the papers for these two years past, against the hard-heartedness of the rich, and much complaint of the great oppressions suffered in this country by the laboring poor. Will you admit a word or two on the other side of the question ? I do not propose to be an advocate for oppression or oppressors. But when I see that the poor are, by such writings, exasperated against the rich, and excited to insurrections, by which much mischief is done, and some forfeit their lives, I could wish the true state of things were better understood, the poor not made by these busy writers more uneasy and unhappy than their situation subjects them to be, and the nation not brought into disrepute among foreigners, by public groundless accusations of ourselves, as if the rich in England had no compassion for the poor, and Englishmen wanted common humanity.

In justice, then, to this country, give me leave to remark, that the condition of the poor here is, by far, the best in Europe; for that, except in England and her American colonies, there is not in any country of the known world, not even in Scotland or Ireland, a provision by law to enforce a support of the poor. Every where else necessity reduces to beggary. This law was not made by the poor. The legislators were men of fortune. By that act they voluntarily subjected their own estates, and the estates of all others, to the payment of a tax, for the maintenance of the poor, incumbering those estates with a kind of rent charge for that purpose, whereby the poor are vested with an inheritance, as it were, in all the estates of the rich. I wish they were benefitted by this generous provision, in any degree equal

33   to

to the good intention with which it was made, and is continued. But I fear the giving mankind a dependance on any thing for support, in age or sickness, besides industry and frugality during youth and health, tends to flatter our natural indolence, to encourage idleness and prodigality, and thereby to promote and increase poverty, the very evil it was intended to cure; thus multiplying beggars instead of diminishing them.

Besides this tax, which the rich in England have subjected themselves to in behalf of the poor, amounting in some places to five or six shillings in the pound, of the annual income, they have, by donations and subscriptions, erected numerous schools in various parts of the kingdom, for educating, gratis, the children of the poor, in reading and writing; and in many of those schools the children are also fed and clothed. They have erected hospitals at an immense expense, for the reception and cure of the sick, the lame, the wounded, and the insane poor, for lying-in women, and deserted children. They are also continually contributing towards making up losses occasioned by fire, by storms, or by floods, and to relieve the poor in severe seasons of frost, in times of scarcity, &c. in which benevolent and charitable contributions no nation exceeds us.—Surely, there is some gratitude due for so many instances of goodness.

Add to this all the laws made to discourage foreign manufactures, by laying heavy duties on them, or totally prohibiting them, whereby the rich are obliged to pay much higher prices for what they wear and consume, than if the trade was open. These are so many laws for the support of our laboring poor, made by the rich, and continued at their expense: all the difference of price between our own and foreign commodities, being so much given by our rich to our poor; who would indeed be enabled by it to get by degrees above poverty, if they did not, as too generally they do, consider every increase of wages, only

as

as something that enables them to drink more and work less; so that their distress in sickness, age, or times of scarcity, continues to be the same as if such laws had never been made in their favor.

Much malignant censure have some writers bestowed upon the rich for their luxury and expensive living, while the poor are starving, &c.; not considering that what the rich expend, the laboring poor receive in payment for their labor. It may seem a paradox if I should assert, that our laboring poor do in every year receive *the whole revenue of the nation;* I mean not only the public revenue, but also the revenue or clear income of all private estates, or a sum equivalent to the whole.—In support of this position I reason thus: the rich do not work for one another. Their habitations, furniture, clothing, carriages, food, ornaments, and every thing, in short, that they or their families use and consume, is the work or produce of the laboring poor, who are and must be continually paid for their labor in producing the same. In these payments the revenues of private estates are expended, for most people live up to their incomes. In clothing or provision for troops, in arms, ammunition, ships, tents, carriages, &c. &c. (every particular the produce of labor), much of the public revenue is expended. The pay of officers, civil and military, and of the private soldiers and sailors, requires the rest; and they spend that also in paying for what is produced by the laboring poor. I allow that some estates may increase by the owners spending less than their income; but then I conceive that other estates do at the same time diminish, by the owners spending more than their income, so that when the enriched want to buy more land, they easily find lands in the hands of the impoverished, whose necessities oblige them to sell; and thus this difference is equalled. I allow also that part of the expense of the rich is in foreign produce or manufactures, for producing which the laboring poor of other nations

must

must be paid; but then I say, we must first pay our own laboring poor for an equal quantity of our manufactures or produce to exchange for those foreign productions, or we must pay for them in money, which money not being the natural produce of our country, must first be purchased from abroad, by sending out its value in the produce or manufactures of this country, for which manufactures our laboring poor are to be paid. And indeed if we did not export more than we import, we could have no money at all. I allow farther, that there are middle men, who make a profit, and even get estates, by purchasing the labor of the poor, and selling it at advanced prices to the rich; but then they cannot enjoy that profit, or the incomes of estates, but by spending them in employing and paying our laboring poor, in some shape or other, for the products of industry.—Even beggars, pensioners, hospitals, and all that are supported by charity, spend their incomes in the same manner. So that finally, as I said at first, *our laboring poor receive annually the whole of the clear revenues of the nation*, and from us they can have no more.

If it be said that their wages are too low, and that they ought to be better paid for their labor, I heartily wish that any means could be fallen upon to do it consistent with their interest and happiness; but as the cheapness of other things is owing to the plenty of those things, so the cheapness of labor is in most cases owing to the multitude of laborers, and to their under-working one another in order to obtain employment. How is this to be remedied? A law might be made to raise their wages; but if our manufactures are too dear, they will not vend abroad, and all that part of employment will fail, unless by fighting and conquering, we compel other nations to buy our goods whether they will or no, which some have been mad enough at times to propose. Among ourselves, unless we give our working people less employment, how can we for what they do pay them higher than we do? Out of what

fund

fund is the additional price of labor to be paid, when all our present incomes are, as it were, mortgaged to them? Should they get higher wages, would that make them less poor, if in consequence they worked fewer days of the week proportionably? I have said a law might be made to raise their wages; but I doubt much whether it could be executed to any purpose, unless another law, now indeed almost obsolete, could at the same time be revived and enforced; a law, I mean, that many have often heard and repeated, but few have ever duly considered. Six *days shalt thou labor.* This is as positive a part of the commandment, as that which says, *the* Seventh *day thou shalt rest;* but we remember well to observe the indulgent part, and never think of the other. *St. Monday* is generally as duly kept by our working people as *Sunday;* the only difference is, that instead of employing their time cheaply at church, they are wasting it expensively at the ale-house. I am, Sir, yours, &c.

MEDIUS.

---

*Plan for Benefiting distant unprovided Countries.**

By Messrs. Franklin and Dalrymple.

Aug. 29, 1771.

The country called in the maps *New Zealand,* has been discovered by the *Endeavour,* to be two islands, together as large as *Great Britain:* these islands named *Acpynomawée* and *Tovy-poennammoo,* are inhabited by a brave and generous race, who are destitute of *corn, fowls,* and *all quadrupeds,* except *dogs.*

37　　　　　　　　　　　　　　These

---

* These proposals were printed upon a sheet of paper, and distributed. The parts written by Dr. Franklin and Mr. Dalrymple are easily distinguished.

These circumstances being mentioned lately in a company of men of liberal sentiments, it was observed that it seemed *incumbent* on such a country as *this*, [England] to communicate to *all others* the conveniences of life which we enjoy.

Dr. Franklin, whose life has ever been directed to promote the true interest of society, said, "he would with all his heart *subscribe* to a voyage intended to communicate *in general* those benefits which we enjoy, to countries destitute of them in the remote parts of the globe." This proposition being warmly adopted by the rest of the company, Mr. Dalrymple, then present, was induced to offer to undertake the command on such an expedition.

On mature reflection this scheme appears the more honorable to the national character of any which can be conceived, as it is grounded on the noblest principle of benevolence. Good intentions are often frustrated by letting them remain indigested; on this consideration Mr. Dalrymple was induced to put the outlines on paper, which are now published, that by an early communication there may be a better opportunity of collecting all the hints which can conduce to execute effectually the benevolent purpose of the expedition, in case it should meet with general approbation.

On this scheme being shown to Dr. Franklin, he communicated his sentiments by way of introduction, to the following effect.

"Britain is said to have produced originally nothing but *sloes*. What vast advantages have been communicated to her by the fruits, seeds, roots, herbage, animals, and arts of other countries! We are by their means become a wealthy and a mighty nation, abounding in all good things. Does not some *duty* hence arise from us towards other countries still remaining in our former state?

"Britain is now the first maritime power in the world. Her ships are inumerable, capable by their form, size, and strength, of sailing all seas. Our seamen are equally bold, skilful and hardy; dexterous in exploring the remotest regions, and ready to engage in voyages to unknown countries, though attended with the greatest dangers. The inhabitants of those countries, our *fellow men,* have canoes only; not knowing iron, they cannot build ships : they have little astronomy, and no knowledge of the compass to guide them : they cannot therefore come to us, or obtain any of our advantages. From these circumstances, does not some duty seem to arise from us to them? Does not Providence by these distinguishing favors seem to call on us to do something ourselves for the common interest of humanity?

" Those who think it their duty to ask bread and other blessings daily from heaven, would they not think it equally a duty to communicate of those blessings when they have received them; and show their gratitude to their great Benefactor by the only means in their power, promoting the happiness of his other children?

" *Ceres* is said to have made a journey through many countries to teach the use of corn, and the art of raising it. For this single benefit the grateful nations deified her. How much more may Englishmen deserve such honor, by communicating the knowledge and use not of corn only, but of all the other enjoyments earth can produce, and which they are now in possession of. *Communiter bona profundere, Deum est.*

" Many voyages have been undertaken with views of profit or of plunder, or to gratify resentment; to procure some advantage to ourselves, or do some mischief to others : but a voyage is now proposed to visit a distant people on the other side the globe; not to cheat them, not to rob them, not to seize their lands, or enslave their persons; but merely to do them good, and make them, as far as in our power lies, to live as comfortably as ourselves.

" It seems a laudable wish that all the nations of the

earth

earth were connected by a knowledge of each other, and a mutual exchange of benefits: but a commercial nation particularly should wish for a general civilisation of mankind, since trade is always carried on to much greater extent with people who have the arts and conveniences of life, than it can be with naked savages. We may therefore hope in this undertaking to be of some service to our country, as well as to those poor people who, however distant from us, are in truth related to us, and whose interests do, in some degree, concern every one who can say *Homo sum,"* &c.

Scheme of a voyage by subscription, to convey the conveniences of life, as fowls, hogs, goats, cattle, corn, iron, &c. to those remote regions which are destitute of them, and to bring from thence such productions as can be cultivated in this kingdom to the advantage of society, in a ship under the command of Alexander Dalrymple.

Catt or bark, from the coal trade, of 350 tons, estimated at about - - - - - - - - - -	£2000
Extra expenses, stores, boats, &c. - - - - -	3000
	5000
To be manned with 60 men at 4*l.* per man per month	240
	12
	2880 per annum
	3
Wages and provisions 8640 for three years - -	8640
	13640
Cargo included, supposed - - - - - - -	£15000

The expenses of this expedition are calculated for *three* years; but the greatest part of the amount of wages will not be wanted till the ship returns, and a great part of the expense of provisions will be saved by what is obtained in

the

the course of the voyage by barter or otherwise, though it is proper to make provision for contingencies.

*   *   *   *   *   *   *

On the Institution in Holland to prevent Poverty.

" Craven Street, June 17th, 1772.

" To Mr. Maséres,

" Sir,

" I thank you for the pamphlet proposing to establish Life Annuities in parishes, &c.: I think it an excellent one. In compliance with your wish, page 25, 26, I send it back with a few marginal notes (perhaps of no great importance) made in reading it, requesting it may be returned to me.

" In page 118 of Dr. Price's Book on Annuities, second edition, you will find mention made of an institution in Holland. He had that information from me. Those houses are handsome neat buildings with very comfortable apartments; some form the sides of a square, with grass plats and gravel walks, flowers, &c., and some have little separate gardens behind each apartment. Those for men are called *Oude Mannen Hayzen,* for women *Oude Vrouwen Hayzen.* I think the different kinds sometimes make different sides of the same square. There is a chapel for prayers, a common kitchen, and a common hall, in which they dine together. Two persons such as best like one another, and choose so to associate, are generally lodged in one apartment, though in separate beds, that they may be at hand to assist each other in case of sudden illness in the night, and otherwise be mutually helpful. The directors have also a room to meet in, who form rules for the government of the house, hear complaints, and

rectify

rectify what is amiss. Gentlemen are directors of the *Oude Mannen Haus*, ladies of the *Oude Vrouwen Haus.* A committee of two are chosen every year, who visit often, see the rules observed, and take care of the management. At the end of the year, these are thanked off, and as an honorable memorial of their service, their names, with the year they served, are added to the gold-letter list on the walls of the room. All the furniture is neat and convenient, the beds and rooms kept clean and sweet by the servants of the house, and the people appear to live happily.

" These institutions seem calculated to *prevent* poverty, which is rather a better thing than *relieving* it : for it keeps always *in the public eye* a state of comfort and repose, with freedom from care in old age, held forth as an encouragement to so much industry and frugality in youth as may at least serve to raise the required sum (suppose 50*l.*) that is to intitle a man or woman at 50 to a retreat in these houses. And in acquiring this sum, habits may be acquired that produce such affluence before this age arrives, as to make the retreat unnecessary, and so never claimed. Hence if 50*l.* would (as by your table) intitle a man at 50 years of age to an annuity of 19*l.* 3*s.* 6*d*$\frac{1}{2}$, I suppose that in such a house, entertainment and accommodation to a much greater value might be afforded him, because the right to live there is not transferable, and therefore every unclaimed right is an advantage to the house, while annuities would probably be all claimed. Then it seems to me that the prospect of a distant annuity will not be so influencing on the minds of young people as the constant view of the comfort enjoyed in those houses, in comparison of which, even the payment and *receipt* of the annuities are *private transactions.*

" I write this in hopes you will, after consideration, favor me with your opinion whether (in addition to your plan, which will still have all its advantages for smaller

sums)

sums) one or more such houses in every county would not probably be of great use in still further promoting industry and frugality among the lower people, and of course lessening the enormous weight of the poor tax?

" I enclose a little piece I wrote in America to encourage and strengthen those important virtues, of which I beg your acceptance, and am, with great esteem,

" Sir, your most obedient humble servant,

" B. FRANKLIN."

Positions to be examined.

I. All food or subsistence for mankind arise from the earth or waters.

2. Necessaries of life that are not foods, and all other conveniences, have their values estimated by the proportion of food consumed while we are employed in procuring them.

3. A small people with a large territory may subsist on the productions of nature, with no other labor than that of gathering the vegetables and catching the animals.

4. A large people with a small territory finds these insufficient, and to subsist, must labor the earth, to make it produce greater quantities of vegetable food, suitable for the nourishment of men, and of the animals they intend to eat.

5. From this labor arises a *great increase* of vegetable and animal food, and of materials for clothing, as flax, wool, silk, &c. The superfluity of these is wealth. With this wealth we pay for the labor employed in building our houses, cities, &c. which are therefore only subsistence thus metamorphosed.

6. *Manufactures* are only *another shape* into which so much provisions and subsistence are turned, as were *equal*

in

in value to the manufactures produced. This appears from hence, that the manufacturer does not, in fact, obtain from the employer for his labor, *more* than a mere subsistence, including raiment, fuel, and shelter; all which derive their value from the provisions consumed in procuring them.

7. The produce of the earth, thus converted into manufactures, may be more easily carried to distant markets than before such conversion.

8. *Fair commerce* is, where equal values are exchanged for equal, the expense of transport included. Thus if it costs A in *England* as much labor and charge to raise a bushel of wheat, as it costs B in *France* to produce four gallons of wine, then are four gallons of wine the fair exchange for a bushel of wheat, A and B meeting at half distance with their commodities to make the exchange. The advantage of this fair commerce is, that each party increases the number of his enjoyments, having, instead of wheat alone, or wine alone, the use of both wheat and wine.

9. Where the labor and expense of producing both commodities are known to both parties, bargains will generally be fair and equal. Where they are known to one party only, bargains will often be unequal, knowledge taking its advantage of ignorance.

10. Thus he that carries 1000 bushels of wheat abroad to sell, may not probably obtain so great a profit thereon as if he had first turned the wheat into manufactures, by subsisting therewith the workmen while producing those manufactures: since there are many expediting and facilitating methods of working, not generally known; and strangers to the manufactures, though they know pretty well the expense of raising wheat, are unacquainted with those short methods of working, and thence being apt to suppose more labor employed in the manufactures than there really is, are more easily imposed on in their value,

and induced to allow more for them than they are honestly worth.

11. Thus the advantage of having manufactures in a country does not consist, as is commonly supposed, in their highly advancing the value of rough materials, of which they are formed; since, though six-pennyworth of flax may be worth 20*s.* when worked into lace, yet the very cause of its being worth 20*s.* is, that besides the flax, it has cost 19*s.* 6*d.* in subsistence to the manufacturer. But the advantage of manufactures is, that under their shape provisions may be more easily carried to a foreign market; and by their means our traders may more easily cheat strangers. Few, where it is not made, are judges of the value of lace. The importer may demand forty, and perhaps get thirty shillings for that which cost him but twenty.

12. Finally, there seem to be but three ways for a nation to acquire wealth. The first is by *war,* as the *Romans* did, in plundering their conquered neighbors. This is *robbery.*—The second by *commerce,* which is, generally, *cheating.*—The third by *agriculture,* the only *honest way;* wherein man receives a real increase of the seed thrown into the ground, in a kind of continual miracle wrought by the hand of God in his favor, as a reward for his innocent life, and his virtuous industry.

April 4, 1769. B. F.

Provision made in China against Famine.

Extract of a Letter to Dr. Percival.

I have somewhere read that in China an account is yearly taken of the number of people, and the quantities

of

of provision produced. This account is transmitted to the
Emperor, whose ministers can thence forsee a scarcity
likely to happen in any province, and from what province
it can best be supplied in good time. To facilitate the
collecting of this account, and prevent the necessity of
entering houses and spending time in asking and answering questions, each house is furnished with a little board
to be hung without the door, during a certain time each
year; on which board are marked certain words, against
which the inhabitant is to mark number or quantity,
somewhat in this manner :

Men,
Women,
Children,
Rice or Wheat,
Flesh, &c.

All under 16 are accounted children, and all above,
men and women. Any other particulars which the government desires information of, are occasionally marked
on the same boards. Thus the officers appointed to collect
the accounts in each district, have only to pass before the
doors, and enter into their book what they find marked
on the board, without giving the least trouble to the
family. There is a penalty on marking falsely, and as
neighbours must know nearly the truth of each other's
account, they dare not expose themselves by a false one,
to each other's accusation. Perhaps such a regulation is
scarcely practicable with us.*

46   *Note*

---

* The above passage is taken from Dr. Percival's Essays, vol. iii.
p. 25, being an extract from a letter written to him by Dr. Franklin,
on the subject of his observations on the state of population in
Manchester and other adjacent places. B. V.

Note respecting Trade and Manufactures.

Suppose a country, X, with three manufactures, as *cloth, silk, iron*, supplying three other countries, A, B, C, but is desirous of increasing the vent, and raising the price of cloth in favor of her own clothiers.

In order to this, she forbids the importation of foreign cloth from A.

A, in return, forbids silks from X.

Then the silk-workers complain of a decay of trade.

And X, to content them, forbids silks from B.

B, in return, forbids iron-ware from X.

Then the iron-workers complain of decay.

And X forbids the importation of iron from C.

C, in return, forbids cloth from X.

What is got by all these prohibitions?

Answer.—All four find their common stock of the enjoyments and conveniences of life diminished.

London, July 7, 1767.   B. F.

Notions concerning Trade and Merchants.

1. Were it possible for men, remote from each other, to know easily one another's wants and abundances, and practicable for them on all occasions conveniently to meet and make fair exchanges of their respective commodities, there would then be no use of the middle man or merchant; such a profession would not exist.

2. But since that is not possible, were all governments to appoint a number of public officers, whose duty and business it should be to inform themselves thoroughly of those wants and abundances, and to procure, by proper management, all the exchanges that would tend to increase the general happiness, such officers, if they could well discharge their trust, would deserve honors and salaries equivalent to their industry and fidelity.

3. But

3. But as in large communities, and for the more general occasions of mankind, such officers have never been appointed, perhaps from a conviction that it would be *impracticable* for such an appointment effectually to answer its purpose, it seems necessary to permit men, who, for the *possible profits* in prospect, will undertake it, to fetch and carry, at all distances, the produce of other men's industry, and thereby assist those useful exchanges.

4. As the persons primarily interested in these exchanges cannot conveniently meet to make known their wants and abundances, and to bargain for exchanges, those who transport the goods should be interested to study the probability of these wants, and where to find the means of supplying them; and, since there exist no salaries or public rewards for them in proportion to their skill, industry, and utility to the people in general, nor to make them any compensation for their losses arising from inexpertness or from accident, it seems reasonable that for their encouragement to follow the business, they should be left to make such profits by it as they can, which, where it is open to all, will probably seldom be extravagant. And perhaps by this means the business will be better done for the general advantage, and those who do it more properly rewarded according to their merits, than would be the case were special officers to be appointed for that service.

[The Essay that follows was originally published in 1774, and is the joint work of George Whately and Dr. Franklin. The original work was indeed written by the former, and communicated to the latter, who rarely ever perused a literary production without correcting, improving, or augmenting its force and value, from his own sources. The corrections and additions which were made by Dr. Franklin, produced an amicable controversy between them, who had the best claim to call himself the author of it, which was closed by a determination to publish it, without any name, but under this designation—" By a well wisher to the king and country."]

PRINCIPLES OF TRADE.

*Freedom and Protection are its best support; Industry the
only means to render Manufactures cheap.*

*Of Coins, Exchange, and Bounties, particularly the Bounty
on Coin.*

*Commerce is generally understood to be the basis on which the
power of this country hath been raised, and on which it must
ever stand.*

Tous les sujets doivent leurs soins, et leurs lumières, à l'état.

DEDICATION.

To all those who have the welfare and prosperity of
these kingdoms at heart, the following Essay, containing,
we hope, useful and incontrovertible principles on the subjects treated of, is very heartily and affectionately inscribed.

March, 1774.

CONTENTS.

PREFACE.

It is a vain imagination that we exist only for ourselves, or our particular country. The all-wise Creator
has ordained that *a mutual dependence* shall run through
all his works; and though our limited capacities will not
admit us fully to comprehend the nature and end of this
connected chain of things, yet we may, and indeed ought,

49

to

to inquire into and consider every thing which relates to our mutual dependence upon one another, and the springs and principles of our actions.

By this investigation we shall find that our wants, whether real or ideal, our passions, and our habits, are the springs of all our actions, and indeed the movers of the general intercourse and commerce between one man and another, one country and another.

Most writers upon trade have made it their business to support and explain some particular branches of traffic, or some favorite hypothesis. We shall, in the ensuing essay, use our best endeavors to remove from the friends of trade, and mankind in general, some prevailing prejudices, and to treat in a concise manner, upon a few self-evident principles, and general maxims, under a persuasion, that if such maxims and principles are just, all deductions and discussions whatever may be tried by their standard.

Some very respectable friends have indulged us with their ideas and opinions. It is with the greatest pleasure we, in this second edition, most gratefully acknowledge the favor; and must add, that should the public hold this performance in any estimation, no small share belongs to those friends.

-----

§ 1. Trade or commerce is the intercourse, as well between nation and nation, as between one man and another; by which we acquire whatsoever may be thought, or understood to be, of use or delight, whether real or ideal.

2. The spring or movement of such intercourse is, and ever must be, gain, or the hopes of gain; as neither the public, nor the individual, would intentionally pursue any unprofitable intercourse or commerce.

3. Gain being the principle of trade, the whole

mystery

mystery of trade must therefore consist in prosecuting methods whereby gain or advantage may be obtained.

In transactions of trade, it is not to be supposed that, like gaming, what one party gains the other must necessarily lose. The gain to each may be equal. If A has more corn than he can consume, but wants cattle, and B has more cattle, but wants corn, an exchange is gain to each; hereby the common stock of comforts in life is increased.

4. Freedom and protection are most indisputable principles whereon the success of trade must depend, as clearly as an open good road tends towards a safe and speedy intercourse; nor is there a greater enemy to trade than constraint.

5. Governments which have adopted those plain simple principles have been greatly benefited.

6. Were princes, in general, to abolish all sorts of prohibitory laws, trade in general would florish most in those countries where the happy situation, the mildness of the climate, the activity and industry of the inhabitants, would furnish means for a speedy and useful intercourse, reciprocally to supply any real or ideal want.

When princes make war by prohibiting commerce, each may hurt himself as much as his enemy. Traders, who by their business are promoting the common good of mankind, as well as farmers and fishermen, who labor for the subsistence of all, should never be interrupted or molested in their business, but enjoy the protection of all in the time of war as well as in time of peace.

This policy, those we are pleased to call barbarians, have, in a great measure, adopted; for the trading subjects of any power, with whom the emperor of Morocco may be at war, are not liable to capture, when within sight of his land, going or coming, and have otherwise free liberty to trade and reside in his dominions.

As a maritime power, we presume it is not thought
right

right that Great Britain should grant such freedom, except partially; as in the case of war with France, when tobacco is allowed to be sent thither under the sanction of passports.

7. We are no more to expect this, than that the whole world should be governed by the same laws. In our opinion, however, no laws which the art of man can devise, will or can hinder, or entirely stop the current of, a profitable trade; any more than the severest laws could prevent the satisfying of hunger, when any chance or opportunity offered to gratify it.

8. Nevertheless, so far as it is possible, according to the different modes and constitutions of each state, freedom and protection should be ever had in view by its respective government.

9. For whatever law is enacted, abridging a freedom or liberty, which the true interest of the state demands, or which does not grant protection where it may be wanted, must clearly be detrimental.

10. We are well aware, that in many cases, individuals may endeavor at an intercourse or trade, whereby the public, in one particular point, may seem injured; and yet it may be out of the power of the state to hinder it, without breaking in upon the freedom of trade; so that the Dutchman who, when Antwerp was besieged furnished arms, ammunition, and provision to the Spaniards, and gloried in it, though a chief magistrate of Amsterdam, was not so very wrong in his principles in general, as at first sight might appear: for this Dutchman ran the risk of losing his ammunition, &c. which, if taken, would have been indeed his loss, but a gain to the captors his countrymen; and if sold, and delivered to the enemy, brought profit to him, and in consequence to the state of which he was a member. This man, to evince how much he held freedom in trade to be essential, used a very strong figure; when owning his having furnished the

enemy

enemy of the state with ammunition, &c. he added; that he would, to prosecute his trade, sail through hell, at the risk of singeing his sails.

It is generally a vain imagination, that if we do not furnish an enemy with what he wants, he cannot be supplied elsewhere. Since we are to suffer the mischief he may do with it, why should we not receive the profit that arises on supplying it? Thus might the Dutchman have reasoned when he supplied the enemy with ammunition, &c.

11. We have, as a first principle, laid down what we apprehend every one must allow, that gain, or the hopes of gain, is the mover of all intercourse or trade. Herein, as above hinted, must be comprehended, all matters of use, in the first instance: and then, matters of ambition, delight, opinion: in one word, luxury.

12. Now things of real use can only be meat, drink, clothing, fuel, and habitation. The several particulars relative to these, every one's mind can suggest: to enumerate would almost be endless.

13. As to meat, in a country where corn, fruits, and cattle can be raised, and bred: the inhabitants must be wanting in industry, to cultivate the lands, or they cannot, in the common course of things, want help from their neighbors, for sustenance.

The same as to drink; if for it they will content themselves with the beverage made of their own corn and fruits.

And so of clothing; if they can be satisfied to be clad with the manufactures made from the produce of their own country.

As to fuel and habitation, there are very few countries which do not afford these articles.

14. The real want of all or any of these necessaries, must, and ever will be, an incentive to labor; either by every individual himself, in the community,

or by those, to whom an equivalent is given for their labor.

15. When ambition, delight, opinion, otherwise luxury, come to be considered, the field is extremely enlarged; and it will require a copious deliberation and ascertainment.

16. For luxury may be carried to such a height, as to be thought by some to be prejudicial to the state; though we, in a general sense, cannot well apprehend it can: inasmuch as what we call riches, must be the cause of luxury, taken in all its branches.

17. Now riches, as we conceive them, consist in whatever either a state or an individual have, more than is necessary, to procure the above essentials, which are only of real use, viz. meat and drink, and clothes, fire and shelter.

This more or abundance, from whatsoever cause it may proceed, after the bartering for, and procuring those essentials, would absolutely, and to all intents, be useless, and of no manner of avail, were it not that delight, and opinion, came in aid, to cause what we will call ideal wants; which wants, our passions, put into our make by the almighty hand that formed us, cause us to be almost as solicitous to provide for, and to supply, as if such wants were real.

18. We therefore must repeat, that from motives to acquire what may be thought of real or ideal use, spring the intercourse or trade between nations, as well as between individuals: and it seems to be self-evident that the produce of the land, and of industry in general, must supply all our wants: and consequently our trade.

19. Now, though it is hardly to be expected, as above hinted, that princes should allow of a general free trade or intercourse, because they seldom know their own true interest; yet it does not follow that fundamental maxims should not be attended to in governing an industrious

people.

people. Some of these principles we beg leave to expatiate on.

20. Land, to bring forth its increase, must be cultivated by man and beast. It is therefore the duty and interest of the state to rear both man and beast; and in their respective classes to nourish and cherish them.

21. Industry in all shapes, in all instances, and by all means, should be encouraged and protected: indolence by every possible method rooted out.

All that live must be subsisted. Subsistence costs something. He that is industrious produces by his industry, something that is an equivalent, and pays for his subsistence. He is therefore no charge or burden to society. The indolent are an expense, uncompensated.

There can be no doubt but all kinds of employment that can be followed without prejudice from interruptions; work that can be taken up, and laid down, often in a day, without damage; such as spinning, knitting, weaving, &c. are highly advantageous to a country: because, in them, may be collected all the produce of those fragments of time that occur in family business, between the constant and necessary parts of it, that usually occupy females; as the time between rising and preparing breakfast; between breakfast and preparing for dinner, &c. The amount of all these fragments is, in the course of a year, very considerable to a single family; to a state proportionably. Highly profitable therefore it is, in this case also, to follow that divine direction, gather up the fragments, that nothing be lost. Lost time is lost subsistence; it is therefore lost treasure.

Hereby, in several families, many yards of linen have been produced from the employment of these fragments only, in one year, though such families were just the same in number as when not so employed.

It was an excellent saying of a certain Chinese emperor, " I will, if possible, have no idleness in my do-

minions;

minions; for if there be one man idle, some other man must suffer cold and hunger." We take this emperor's meaning to be, that the labor due to the public, by each individual, not being performed by the indolent, must naturally fall to the share of others, who must thereby suffer.

22. Whatever can contribute towards procuring from the land, and by industry, a produce wherewith other nations may be supplied, ought highly to be encouraged.

23. Materials wanting in a country to employ its inhabitants, ought by all means to be procured. Gold and silver, those tokens of riches, used as such, and otherwise of little use, are not near so estimable. The bartering of them for such materials is manifestly advantageous.

24. These, as we apprehend, are incontrovertible principles, on which a wise government will found its resolutions.

25. That the use of the produce of other countries for ideal wants ought to be discouraged, particularly when the produce of the land, or of industry, are not given in exchange for them, has been strongly urged by many. On the grand principle of freedom in trade, we cannot well admit it: for it is plain the luxurious will use, and the trader, to prosecute his gain, will procure, such foreign produce: nor do prohibitory laws, or heavy duties, hinder. Nevertheless, to allow for a moment the doctrine, we will remark, that only the establishing it as a mode or fashion amongst the opulent and great, can possibly effectuate a disuse or discouragement

In fact, the produce of other countries can hardly be obtained, unless by fraud or rapine, without giving the produce of our land or our industry in exchange for them. If we have mines of gold and silver, gold and silver may then be called the produce of our land. If we have not, we can only fairly obtain those metals by giving for them the produce of our land or industry. When we have them, they are then only that produce or industry in another shape; which we may give, if the trade requires it, and our other produce will not suit, in exchange for the produce of some other country that furnishes what we have more occasion for, or more desire. When we have, to an inconvenient degree, parted with our gold and silver, our industry is stimulated afresh to procure more; that by its means we may contrive to procure the same advantage.

In this place it will be proper to observe upon an erroneous doctrine, which has been often strenuously insisted on, that the cheapness of provisions must render manufactures cheap; and that plenty of money conduces to the benefit of trade. We shall endeavor to prove that industry alone does both.

26. Providence has wisely ordained that there should be different occupations and pursuits amongst men, and that the rich and poor should be actuated by different wants, whether real or ideal. It is next to impossible that the rich should be without desires, or wishes for greater acquisitions; or the poor without being necessitated to acquire what must supply their real wants. If the rich curtail their desires, or wishes, their riches serve, in proportion to their not using them, no more than ore in an unworked mine. If the poor man, by *one* day's labor can supply his real wants for *two* days, and sits idle the half of his time, he may be considered in such idle time as a monk or a cripple with regard to the community. If a thirst for acquisition move the rich man, he industriously employs all his riches. If the scarcity of provisions compel the poor man to work his whole time, he assuredly, by his industry, must make more manufactures than only working half of it. Hence we conclude, that gain is the first mover; and industry, and the desire of supplying our wants, the intermediate movers of all

intercourse

intercourse or trade. We however must observe, that a government truly wise should always, as far as the general good allows, be as solicitous to procure plenty of provisions, whereby both man and beast may be kept in good health and strength, as to encourage industry. For industry cannot be sufficiently sustained without the strength arising from plenty of provisions.

The common people do not work for pleasure generally, but from necessity. Cheapness of provisions makes them more idle; less work is then done; it is then more in demand proportionally; and of course the price rises. Dearness of provisions obliges the manufacturer to work more days and more hours : thus more work is done than equals the usual demand; of course it becomes cheaper, and the manufactures in consequence.

27. As to plenty of money being a benefit to trade and manufactures, we apprehend every one conversant therein must know that the coin, by which we generally understand money, of every respective state, is by no means the mover of the intercourse or tradings of the world in general. Gold and silver in bullion, or in an uncoined mass, are rather more so; being, in point of value, a merchandise less liable to variation than any other. It is true that coin may be liable, in the fluctuation of trade, to be made a merchandise of; but as by constant use, the pieces of coin become lighter than their original weight, they thereby are less fit for merchandise. We therefore may say, that coins, in general, can no otherwise be useful, than as the common measure between man and man, as serving to barter against, or exchange for, all kinds of commodities. Certain it is that coins cannot be ranked amongst those things which are *only of real use.* Let us therefore suppose pieces of coin to be counters; and to simplify the matter still more, suppose every manufacturer to have of these counters any sum whatever, will it follow, that any sort of manufacture shall
be

be industriously attended to, or more work done than when no more counters than just enough to barter for the real wants of meat, drink, and clothes, &c. can be procured by labor? Surely no. It must be the desire of supplying our wants, which excites industry as above hinted, that alone sets that trade going, and only can procure plenty of manufactures.

28. It is, nevertheless, the duty of government to stamp coins or counters of different sorts and denominations, so that time, of all things the most precious, be not wasted in settling the respective exchangings amongst mankind. Nevertheless the plenty or scarcity of those coins cannot entirely depend on any government, but on the general circulation and fluctuation of trade, which may make them a merchandise, without the least detriment; as it must be allowed, that the precious metals gold and silver, of which such coins are principally composed, are no other than merchandise acquired from countries where there are mines, by those countries which have none, in exchange for the produce of their land, or of their manufactures.

29. That the welfare of any state depends on its keeping *all* its gold and silver, either in bullion or in coin, must be founded on a very narrow principle indeed. All republics we know of, wisely think otherwise. Spain, the grand source of silver, has of late years, very justly, allowed the free exportation of it, paying a duty, as in Great Britain lead and tin do : nor prior to this permission could their penal laws in Spain hinder its being exported; for it was a commodity which that kingdom was under a necessity of giving as an equivalent for what was furnished to them by other countries.

Could Spain and Portugal have succeeded in executing their foolish laws for " *hedging in the cuckoo*," as Locke calls it, and have kept at home all their gold and silver, those metals would, by this time, have been of little more

value

value than so much lead or iron. Their plenty would
have lessened their value. We see the folly of these
edicts; but are not our own prohibitory and restrictive
laws, that are professedly made with intention to bring a
balance in our favor from our trade with foreign nations
to be paid in money, and laws to prevent the necessity of
exporting that money, which, if they could be thoroughly
executed, would make money as plenty, and of as little
value; I say, are not such laws akin to those Spanish
edicts: follies of the same family?

30. In Great Britain, the silver coin bearing a disproportion to gold more than in neighboring states, of about
five in the hundred, must, by that disproportion, become
merchandise, as well for exportation, as for the manufactures at home, in which silver is employed, more than
if it remained in the mass uncoined. This might be
remedied without injuring the public, or touching the
present standard, which never should be done, only by
enacting that sixty-five shillings should be cut out of one
pound weight of standard silver, instead of sixty-two,
which are the number now ordained by law. We must
however remark, that, whenever by any extraordinary
demand for silver, a pound weight, bought even for sixty-
five shillings, can be sent abroad to advantage, or melted
down for manufactures, no prohibitory laws will hinder
its exportation or melting, and still becoming a merchandise.

31. Coiners have pointed out, though at the risk of
the gallows, a measure which we think would be advisable
in some degree for government to adopt. They coin and
circulate shillings of such weight as to gain ten to fourteen in the hundred, and upwards: as out of a pound of
standard silver they cut sixty-eight or seventy-one shillings. That these light shillings or counters are useful,
though the public be so greatly imposed on, is evident.
It must be presumed, that every thing is put in practice

by

by government to detect and stop this manifest roguery. If so, can it on the one hand be supposed the public purse should bear the burden of this fraud? yet, on the other hand, having no supply of legal shillings or counters, the utility of the illegal ones forces them, as it were, on the public. The power of the legislature to correct the erroneous proportion of five in the hundred, as above mentioned, is indubitable; but whether every private person possessed of these counters, or the public purse, should be obliged to bear the loss on a re-coinage, seems a difficult point to determine; as it may be alleged, that every private person has it in his power to accept, or refuse any coin, under the weight, as by law enacted, for each denomination. If the former, he does it to his own wrong, and must take the consequences. The individual, on the other hand, has to allege the almost total want of lawful counters; together with the impossibility or neglect of hindering those of an inferior weight from being suffered to be current. It may be submitted, that as the use of coin is for public utility, any loss which arises in the coin either by wearing, or even by filing and sweating, ought to be made good by calling in the coin after a certain number of years from the time of coinage, and receiving the money called in at the charge of the public. We are well aware what latitude such a resolution might give to the coiners of shillings, the filers, and the sweaters of gold; but taking proper measures beforehand, this evil might, we think, in a great degree be prevented.

32. In the beginning of his present majesty's reign, quarter guineas were wisely ordered to be coined; whereby the want of silver coin was in some degree supplied: which would still be more so, were thirds and two-thirds of guineas to be coined. We cannot conceive why this is not done; except that these denominations are not specified in his majesty's indenture with the master of

the mint; which in our humble opinion ought to be rectified.

33. We think it not improper here to observe, that it matters not, whether silver or gold be called the standard money ; but it seems most rational that the most scarce and precious metals should be the unit or standard.

That as to copper, it is fit for money, or a counter, as gold or silver, provided it be coined of a proper weight and fineness : and just so much will be useful as will serve to make up small parts in exchange between man and man, and no more ought to be coined.

As to paper circulating as money, it is highly profitable, as its quick passing from one to another is a gain of time, and thereby may be understood to add hands to the community : inasmuch as those, who would be employed in telling and weighing, will follow other business. The issuers or coiners of paper are understood to have an equivalent to answer what it is issued for, or valued at ; nor can any metal or coin do more than find its value.

§ It is impossible for government to circumscribe, or fix the extent of paper credit, which must, of course, fluctuate. Government may as well pretend to lay down rules for the operations, or the confidence, of every individual, in the course of his trade. Any seeming temporary evil arising, must naturally work its own cure.

34. As some principles relative to exchange have in our opinion been treated of in a very confused manner, and some maxims have been held out upon that subject, which tend only to mislead, we shall here briefly lay down what, according to our opinion, are self-evident principles.

35. Exchange, by bills, between one country or city and another, we conceive to be this. One person wants to get a sum from any country or city ; consequently has his bill or draft to sell : another wants to send a sum thither ; and therefore agrees to buy such bill or draft.

He

He has it at an agreed-for price, which is the course of the exchange. It is with this price for bills as with merchandise; when there is a scarcity of bills in the market, they are dear; when plenty, they are cheap.

36. We judge it needless to enter into the several courses and denominations of exchanges which custom hath established; they are taught at school. But we think we must offer a few words, to destroy an erroneous principle that has misled some, and confused others; which is, that by authority, a certain par, or fixed price of exchange, should be settled between each respective country; thereby rendering the currency of exchange as fixed as the standard of coin.

37. We have above hinted, that plenty and scarcity must govern the course of exchange; which principle, duly considered, would suffice on the subject; but we will add, that no human foresight can absolutely judge of the almost numberless fluctuations in trade; which vary, sometimes directly, sometimes indirectly, between countries: consequently no state or potentate can, by authority, any more pretend to settle the currency of the prices of the several sorts of merchandise sent to and from their respective dominions, than they can a par of exchange. In point of merchandise, indeed, where there is a monopoly of particular commodities, an exception must be allowed, as to such articles; but this is not at all applicable to trade in general; for the encouragement of which we cannot too often repeat that *freedom and security are most essentially necessary.*

38. Another specious doctrine, much labored by theorists, in consequence of that relating to the par is, that the exchange between any particular country being above or below par, always shows whether the reciprocal trade be advantageous or disadvantageous. It is, and must be allowed, that in trade nothing is given without adequate returns or compensations; but these are so

63   various

various and so fluctuating between countries, as often indirectly as directly, that there is no possibility of fixing a point from whence to argue; so that should there happen a greater variation than of two or three more in the hundred, at any certain period in the exchange, above or below what is called the par or equality of the money of one country to that of another, influenced by the fluctuations and circulations in trade, it does not follow, that a trade is advantageous or disadvantageous, excepting momentarily, if one may so say, which can be of no consequence to the public in general, as the trade from advantageous may become disadvantageous, and *vice versâ;* and, consequently, the deducing of reasons from what in its nature must be fluctuating, can only help to embarrass, if not mislead.

39. To return to trade in general. Our principles, we apprehend, may hold good for all nations, and ought to be attended to by the legislative power of every nation. We will not discuss every particular point: nor is it to our purpose to examine the pretended principles or utility whereon monopolies are generally established. That the wisdom of government should weigh and nicely consider any proposed regulation on those principles, we humbly judge to be self-evident; whereby may be seen whether it coincides with the general good. Solomon adviseth *not to counsel with a merchant for gain.* This, we presume, relates to the merchant's own particular profit; which, we repeat, must ever be the spring of his actions. Government ought, notwithstanding, to endeavor to procure particular informations from every one; not only from those actually employed, or those who have been concerned in particular branches of trade, but even from persons who may have considered of it theoretically and speculatively.

Perhaps, in general, it would be better if government meddled no farther with trade than to protect it, and let

it

it take its course. Most of the statutes, or acts, edicts, arrets, and placarts of parliaments, princes, and states, for regulating, directing, or restraining of trade, have, we think, been either political blunders, or jobs obtained by artful men for private advantage, under pretence of public good. When Colbert assembled some wise old merchants of France, and desired their advice and opinion, how he could best serve and promote commerce, their answer, after consultation, was, in three words only, *Laissez nous faire :* Let us alone. It is said, by a very solid writer of the same nation, that he is well advanced in the science of politics who knows the full force of that maxim—*Pas trop gouverner :* Not to govern too much. Which, perhaps, would be of more use when applied to trade, than in any other public concern. It were therefore to be wished, that commerce was as free between all the nations of the world, as it is between the several counties of England : so would all, by mutual communication, obtain more enjoyments. Those counties do not ruin one another by trade ; neither would the nations. No nation was ever ruined by trade ; even seemingly the most disadvantageous.

Wherever desirable superfluities are imported, industry is excited ; and therefore plenty is produced. Were only necessaries permitted to be purchased, men would work no more than was necessary for that purpose.

40. Though we waive a discussion on particular branches of trade, as the field is too large for our present purpose ; and that particular laws and regulations may require variation, as the different intercourses, and even interests of states, by different fluctuations, may alter ; yet, as what relates to bounties or premiums, which the legislature of Great Britain has thought fit to grant, hath been by some deemed, if not ill-judged, unnecessary ; we hope our time not ill bestowed, to consider of the fitness and rectitude of the principle on which we apprehend these bounties or premiums have been granted.

41. It

41. It must, we think, on all hands be allowed, that the principle whereon they are founded must be an encouragement tending to a general benefit, though granted on commodities, manufactures, or fisheries, carried on in particular places and countries, which are presumed or found to require aid from the public purse for farther improvement.

Of the bounties, some having had the proposed effect, are discontinued: others are continued, for the very reason they were first given.

In our opinion, no doubt can arise as to the utility of these grants from the public purse to individuals. The grand principle of trade, which is gain, is the foundation of bounties: for, as every individual makes a part of the whole public, consequently, whatever benefits the individual must benefit the public: hereby the wisdom of the legislature is most evident; nor should it in any wise be be arraigned, though ill success attended any particular commodity, manufacture, or fishery, for the encouragement of which bounties have been established.

We are well aware that it is not impossible the purpose of bounty may have been perverted, with a view to improper gain; but it is the duty of the legislature to use the proper measures for preventing such iniquity. This abuse, however, cannot be adduced as an argument against the benefit arising from allowing bounties.

42. These principles in regard to bounties or premiums, are applicable to most articles of commerce, except wheat and other grain, which we shall consider and enlarge on, as being of a complicated nature, and concerning which mankind have, at particular times, been divided in opinion.

43. It seems to us, that this bounty on grain was intended, not only to encourage the cultivating of land for the raising of it in abundance in this kingdom, for the use of its inhabitants, but also to furnish our neighbors,

whenever

whenever the kind hand of Providence should be pleased to grant a superfluity.

44. It never can be presumed that the encouragement by the bounty insures to the community an uninterrupted constant plenty; yet, when the grower of grain knows he may, by such bounty, have a chance of a foreign market for any excess he may have, more than the usual home consumption, he the more willingly labors and improves his land, upon the presumption of having a vent for his superfluity, by a demand in foreign countries; so that he will not probably be distressed by abundance; which, strange as it may seem to some, might be the case by his want of sale, and his great charges of gathering in his crop.

45. As there are no public granaries in this kingdom, the legislature could devise no better means than to fix stated prices under which the bounty or encouragement from the public purse should be allowed. Whenever the current prices exceeded those stipulated, then such bounty should cease.

46. Few consider, or are affected, but by what is present. They see grain, by reason of scanty crops, dear; therefore all the doors for gain, to the cultivators of it, must always be kept shut. The common outcry is, that the exporting our wheat furnishes bread to our neighbors cheaper than it can be afforded to our poor at home; which affects our manufacturers, as they can thereby work cheaper. To this last allegation we must refer to what we have said, section 26; though the former, that wheat is, by the bounty, afforded to our neighbours cheaper than to us at home, must in general be without foundation, from the several items of charge attending the exportation of grain, such as carriage, factorage, commission, porterage, &c. The freight paid to our own shipping, to which alone the bounty is restrained, must, when duly considered, very sufficiently counterbalance the bounty; so that more than what is given out of the public purse is put into the

67   pockets

pockets of individuals for the carriage, &c. : therefore we think we may well presume that, in general, grain exported comes dearer to the foreigner than to the consumer in Great Britain.

47. Nothing can be more evident, we apprehend, than that the superfluity of our grain being exported, is a clear profit to the kingdom, as much as any other produce of our labor, in manufactures, in tin, or any commodities whatsoever.

48. It behoves us, however, indubitably, to have an eye towards having a sufficiency of grain for food in this country, as we have laid down, section 26 : and were the legislature to enact, that the justices of the peace, at the Christmas quarter session, should have power to summon all growers of grain, or dealers therein, and upon oath to examine them as to the quantity then remaining; returns of which quantities should be made to the lords of the treasury, to be laid before parliament; the legislature would, upon such returns, be able to judge whether it would be necessary to enable his majesty, with the advice of his council, to put a stop to any farther exportation at such times as might be thought proper.

49. Or, it is submitted, whether the legislature would not act more consistent with the principle of granting bounties, by repealing the act allowing the present bounty on the several sorts of grain at the now fixed prices, and reduce these prices as follow :—

On wheat from forty-eight to thirty-six or thirty-two shillings.

On barley from twenty-four to eighteen or sixteen a quarter; and so in proportion for any other grain. In short, diminish the present standard prices, under which the bounty is granted, one quarter or one third.

50. In our humble opinion, this last method would be by much the most simple and eligible, as consistent with our grand principle of freedom in trade, which would be

cramped

cramped if dependent annually on parliamentary deliberation.

51. The advocates for not lowering the present stipulated prices that command the bounties from the public purse may allege, that our ancestors deemed them necessary, on the principle of granting any bounty at all, which we have above hinted, section 48. We do not controvert the wisdom of the principle for granting a bounty; for it must have been, and ever will be, an encouragement to cultivation; and consequently it would be highly improper wholly to discontinue it; nevertheless, if it has answered one great end proposed, which was cultivation and improvement, and that it is incontrovertible the cultivator has, by the improvements made by the encouragement of the bounty, a living profit at the reduced prices of thirty-two or thirty-six shillings, sixteen or eighteen, &c. as above, which probably, when our ancestors enacted the law for granting the bounty, they understood the cultivators could not have; it seems clear, that there ought to be the proposed change and reduction of the bounty prices, as above mentioned.

52. The French, intent on trade, have a few years since rectified a very gross mistake they labored under, in regard to their commerce in grain. One county or province in France should abound, and the neighboring one, though almost starving, should not be permitted to get grain from the plentiful province, without particular license from court, which cost no small trouble and expense. In sea-port towns wheat should be imported; and soon after, without leave of the magistrates, the owner should only have liberty to export one quarter or one third of it. They are now wiser; and through all the kingdom the corn trade is quite free; and what is more, all sorts of grain may be exported upon French bottoms only, for their encouragement; copying, we presume our law, whenever the market prices for three following days

shall

shall not exceed above forty-five shillings sterling for a quarter of wheat: our reason for mentioning this is only to show that other nations are changing their destructive measures, and that it behoves us to be careful that we pay the greatest attention to our essential interests.

In inland high countries, remote from the sea, and whose rivers are small, running from the country, not to it, as is the case of Switzerland, great distress may arise from a course of bad harvests, if public granaries are not provided, and kept well stored. Anciently, too, before navigation was so general, ships so plenty, and commercial connexions so well established, even maritime countries might be occasionally distressed by bad crops. But such is now the facility of communication between those countries, that an unrestrained commerce can scarce ever fail of procuring a sufficiency for any of them. If, indeed, any government is so imprudent as to lay its hands on imported corn, forbid its exportation, or compel its sale at limited prices, there the people may suffer some famine from merchants avoiding their ports. But wherever commerce is known to be always free, and the merchant absolute master of his commodity, as in Holland, there will always be a reasonable supply.

When an exportation of corn takes place, occasioned by a higher price in some foreign country, it is common to raise a clamor, on the supposition that we shall thereby produce a domestic famine. Then follows a prohibition, founded on the imaginary distress of the poor. The poor, to be sure, if in distress, should be relieved; but if the farmer could have a high price for his corn, from the foreign demand, must he, by a prohibition of exportation, be compelled to take a low price, not of the poor only, but of every one that eats bread, even the richest? The duty of relieving the poor is incumbent on the rich; but, by this operation, the whole burden of it is laid on the farmer, who is to relieve the rich at the same time. Of

the

the poor, too, those who are maintained by the parishes have no right to claim this sacrifice of the farmer; as, while they have their allowance, it makes no difference to them whether bread be cheap or dear. Those working poor who now mind business five or four days in the week, if bread should be so dear as to oblige them to work the whole six, required by the commandment, do not seem to be aggrieved so as to have a right to public redress. There will then remain, comparatively, only a few families in every district; who, from sickness or a great number of children, will be so distressed by a high price of corn, as to need relief; and these should be taken care of, by particular benefactions, without restraining the farmer's profit.

Those who fear that exportation may so far drain the country of corn, as to starve ourselves, fear what never did nor ever can happen. They may as well when they view the tide ebbing towards the sea, fear that all the water will leave the river. The price of corn, like water, will find its own level. The more we export, the dearer it becomes at home. The more is received abroad, the cheaper it becomes there; and as soon as these prices are equal, the exportation stops of course. As the seasons vary in different countries, the calamity of a bad harvest is never universal. If then all ports were always open, and all commerce free, every maritime country would generally eat bread at the medium price, or average of all the different harvests; which would probably be more equal than we can make it by our artificial regulations, and therefore a more steady encouragement to agriculture. The nations would all have bread at this middle price; and that nation which at any time inhumanly refuses to relieve the distresses of another nation, deserves no compassion when in distress itself.

We shall here end these reflections, with our most ardent wishes for the prosperity of our country, and our hopes that the doctrine we have endeavored to inculcate as to the necessity of protection and freedom, in order to insure success in trade, will be ever attended to by the legislature in forming their resolutions relating to the commerce of these kingdoms.

PREFACE TO THE APPENDIX.

The clamor made of the great inconveniences suffered by the community in regard to the coin of this kingdom, prompted me in the beginning of his majesty's reign to give the public some reflections on coin in general; on gold and silver as merchandize; and I added my thoughts on paper passing as money.

As I trust the principles then laid down are founded in truth, and will serve now as well as then, though made fourteen years ago, to change any calculation would be of little use.

Some sections in the foregoing essay of principles of trade, which might in this appendix appear like a repetition, have been omitted.

I always resolved not to enter into any particular deduction from laws relating to coin; or into any minutiæ, as to accurate nicety in weights. My intention was, and still is, no more than to endeavor to show, as briefly as possible, that what relates to coin, is not of such a complex, abstruse nature as it is generally made; and that no more than common justice with common sense are required in all regulations concerning it.

Perhaps more weighty concerns may have prevented government doing more in regard to coin, than ordering quarter guineas to be made; which till this reign had not been done.

But as I now judge by the late act relating to gold coin, that the legislature is roused, possibly they may consider still more of that, as well as of silver coin.

Should these reflections prove of any public utility, my end will be answered.

REFLECTIONS ON COIN IN GENERAL.

1. Coins are pieces of metal, on which an impression is struck; which impression is understood by the legislature to ascertain the weight and the intrinsic value, or worth of each piece.

2 The real value of coins depends not on a piece being called a guinea, a crown, or a shilling; but the true worth of any particular piece of gold or silver, is what such piece contains of fine or pure gold or silver.

3. Silver and copper being mixed with gold, and copper with silver, are generally understood to render those metals more durable when circulating in coins; yet air and moisture evidently affect copper, whether by itself or mixed with other metal; whereas pure gold or silver are much less affected or corroded thereby.

4. The quantity of silver and copper so mixed by way of alloy, is fixed by the legislature. When melted with pure metal, or added or extracted to make a lawful proportion, both gold and silver are brought to what is called standard. This alloy of silver and copper is never reckoned of any value. The standard once fixed, should ever be invariable; since any alteration would be followed by great confusion and detriment to the state.

5. It is for public convenience, and for facilitating the bartering between mankind for their respective wants, that coins were invented and made; for were there no coins, gold and silver might be made, or left pure; and what we now call a guinea's worth of any thing, might be cut off from gold, and a crown's worth from silver, and might serve, though not so commodiously as coin.

6. Hence it is evident that in whatever shape, form, or quality, these metals are, they are brought to be the most common measure between man and man, as serving to barter against or exchange for all kinds of commodities; and consequently are no more than an universal accepted merchandise;

chandise; for gold and silver in bullion, that is to say, in an uncoined mass, and gold or silver in coin, being of equal weight, purity, and fineness, must be of equal value, the one to the other; for the stamp on either of these metals, duly proportioned, neither adds to, nor takes from their intrinsic value.

7. The prices of gold and silver as merchandise, must in all countries, like other commodities, fluctuate and vary according to the demand; and no detriment can arise therefrom, more than from the rise and fall of any other merchandise. But if, when coined, a due proportion of these metals the one to the other, be not established, the disproportion will be felt and proved; and that metal wherein the excess in the proportion is allowed, will preferably be made use of, either in exportation or in manufacture; as is the case now, in this kingdom, in regard to silver coin, and which in some measure is the occasion of its scarcity.

For so long as 15 ounces and about one-fifth of pure silver in Great Britain are ordained and deemed to be equal to one ounce of pure gold, whilst in neighboring states, as France and Holland, the proportion is fixed only 14 and a half ounces of pure silver, to one ounce of pure gold, it is very evident that our silver, when coined, will always be the most acceptable merchandise, by near five in the hundred, and consequently more liable to be taken away or melted down, than before it received the impression at the mint.

8. Sixty-two shillings only are ordained by law to be coined from 12 ounces of standard silver; now, following the proportion above mentioned, of $15\frac{1}{5}$ to $14\frac{1}{2}$, no regard being necessary as to alloy, 65 shillings should be the quantity cut out of those 12 ounces.

9. No everlasting invariable fixation for coining can be made from a medium of the market price of gold and silver, though that medium might with ease be ascertained

so

so as to hinder either coined gold or silver from becoming a merchandise; for whenever the price shall rise above that medium, so as to give a profit, whatever is coined will be made a merchandise. This in the nature of things, must come from the general exchangings, circulation, and fluctuation in trade, and cannot be hindered; but assuredly the false proportions may be amended by the legislature, and settled as the proportion between gold and silver is in other nations; so as not to make, as now is the case, our coined silver a merchandise, so much to be preferred to the same silver uncoined.

10. What has been said seems to be self-evident; but the following calculations made on the present current price of silver and gold, may serve to prove beyond all doubt, that the proportion now fixed between gold and silver should be altered and fixed as in other countries.

By law, 62 shillings are to be coined out of one pound, or 12 ounces of standard silver. This is 62 pence an ounce. Melt these 62 shillings, and in a bar, this pound weight at market will fetch 68 pence an ounce, or 68 shillings the pound. The difference therefore between coined and uncoined silver in Great Britain is now nine and two-thirds per cent.

Out of a pound or 12 ounces of standard gold, 44 guineas and a half are ordained to be coined. This is $3l.$ $17s.$ $10\frac{1}{2}d.$ an ounce. Now the current market price of standard gold is $3l.$ $19s.$ an ounce, which makes not quite $1\frac{1}{2}$ per cent. difference between the coined and uncoined gold.

The state, out of duties imposed, pays for the charge of coining, as indeed it ought; for it is for public convenience, as already said, that coins are made. It is the current market price of gold and silver that must govern the carrying it to the mint. It is absurd to think any one should send gold to be coined that should cost more than $3l.$ $17s.$ $10\frac{1}{2}d.$ an ounce, or silver more than 62 pence the ounce; and as absurd would it be to pretend, that those prices *only* shall be the constant invariable prices. It is contended that there is not a proper proportion fixed in the value of one metal to another, and this requires alteration.

11. It may be urged, that should the legislature fix the proportion of silver to gold as in other countries; by ordering 65 shillings instead of 62 to be cut out of a pound of standard silver, yet still there would be 4¾ per cent. difference between coined and uncoined silver; whereas there is but about 1½ per cent. difference in gold.

On this we shall observe that the course of trade, not to mention extraordinary accidents, will make one metal more in request at one time than another; and the legislature in no one particular country, can bias or prescribe rules or laws to influence such demand; which ever must depend on the great chain of things, in which all the operations of this world are linked. Freedom and security only are wanted in trade; nor does coin require more, if a just proportion in the metals be settled.

12. To return to gold: it is matter of surprise, that the division of the piece called a guinea, has not been made smaller than just one half as it now is; that is, into quarters, thirds, and two-thirds. Hereby the want of silver coin might be greatly provided for; and those pieces, together with the light silver coin, which can *only now* remain with us, would sufficiently serve the uses in circulation.

In Portugal, where almost all their coin is gold, there are divisions of the moedas, or 27 shilling pieces, into tenths, sixths, quarters, thirds, halves, and two-thirds. Of the moeda and one-third, or 36 shilling piece, into eighths, quarters, and halves.

13. That to the lightness of the silver coin now remaining in Great Britain we owe all the silver coin we now have, any person with weights and scales may prove;

as

as upwards of 70 shillings coined in the reign of king William, or dexterously counterfeited by false coiners, will scarce weigh 12 ounces, or a pound troy.

14. All the art of man can never hinder a constant exportation and importation of gold and silver, to make up for the different calls and balances that may happen in trade; for were silver to be coined as above, 65 shillings out of a pound troy weight of standard silver; if those 65 shillings would sell at a price that makes it worth while to melt or export them, they must and will be considered and used as a merchandise; and the same will hold as to gold.

Though the proportion of about $14\frac{1}{2}$ of pure silver to one of pure gold, in neighboring states be *now* fixed, in regard to their coin, and it is submitted such proportion should be attended to in this kingdom, yet that proportion may be subject to alteration; for this plain reason, that should the silver mines produce a quantity of that metal so as to make it greatly abound more in proportion than it now does, and the gold mines produce no more than now they do, more silver must be requisite to purchase gold.

15. That the welfare of any state depends on its keeping *all* its gold and silver, either in bullion or in coin, is a very narrow principle; all the republics we know of, wisely think otherwise. It is an utter impossibility; nor should it ever be aimed at; for gold and silver are as clearly a merchandise as lead and tin; and consequently should have a perfect freedom and liberty, coined and uncoined, to go and to come, pass and repass, from one country to another, in the general circulation and fluctuation of commerce, which will ever carry a general balance with it: for we should as soon give our lead, our tin, or any other product of our land or industry, to those who want them, without an equivalent in some shape or other, as we should gold or silver; which it would be absurd to imagine can ever be done by our nation, or by any nation upon earth.

16. From

16. From Spain and Portugal come the greatest part of gold and silver: and the Spanish court very wisely permits the exportation of it on paying a duty, as in Great Britain lead and tin do, when exported; whereas heretofore, and as it still continues in Portugal, penal laws were enacted against the sending it out of the country. Surely princes by enacting such laws, could not think they had it in their power to decree and establish, that their subjects, or themselves, should not give an equivalent for what was furnished to them!

17. It is not our intention to descend into, or to discuss minutely, particular notions or systems, such as, *" That silver, and not gold, should be the standard money or coin."*

" That copper is an unfit material for money."

And *" That paper circulating as, and called artificial money, is detrimental."*

Yet as these doctrines seem to proceed from considering bullion, and money, or coin, in a different light from what we apprehend and have laid down, we will observe,

18. That it matters not whether silver or gold be called standard money; but it seems most rational, that the most scarce and precious metal should be the unit or standard.

19. That as to copper, it is as fit for money or a counter, as gold and silver, provided it be coined of a proper weight and fineness: and just so much will be useful, as will serve to make up small parts in exchanges between man and man.

20. That as to paper money, it is far from being detrimental; on the contrary, it is highly profitable, as its quick passing between mankind, instead of telling over, or weighing metal in coin, or bullion, is a gain of what is most precious in life, which is time. And there is nothing clearer than that those who must be concerned in counting and weighing, being at liberty to employ themselves on other purposes, are an addition of hands in the community.

The

The idea of the too great extension of credit, by the circulation of paper for money, is evidently as erroneous as the doctrine of the non-exportation of gold and silver in bullion or coin: for were it not certain, that paper could command the equivalent of its agreed-for value, or that gold and silver in bullion or coin exported, would be returned in the course of trade in some other merchandise, neither paper would be used or the metals exported. It is by means of the produce of the land, and the happy situation of this island, joined to the industry of its inhabitants, that those much-adored metals, gold and silver, have been procured: and so long as the sea does not overflow the land, and industry continues, so long will those metals not be wanting. And paper in the general chain of credit and commerce, is as useful as they are, since the issuers or coiners of that paper are understood to have some equivalent to answer for what the paper is valued at: and no metal or coin can do more than find its value.

Moreover, as incontestable advantages of paper, we must add, that the charge of coining or making it, is by no means proportionate to that of coining of metals; nor is it subject to waste by long use, or impaired by adulteration, sweating, or filing, as coins may.

A Thought concerning the Sugar Islands.

Should it be agreed, and become a part of the law of nations, that the cultivators of the earth are not to be molested or interrupted in their peaceable and useful employment, the inhabitants of the sugar islands would come under the protection of such a regulation, which would be a great advantage to the nations who at present hold those islands, since the cost of sugar to the consumer in those nations consists not only in the price he pays for it by the pound, but in the accumulated charge of all the taxes he pays in every war to fit out fleets and maintain

troops

troops for the defence of the islands that raise the sugar, and the ships that bring it home. But the expense of treasure is not all. A celebrated philosophical writer remarks, that when he considered the wars made in Africa for prisoners to raise sugar in America, the numbers slain in those wars, the numbers that, being crowded in ships, perish in the transportation, and the numbers that die under the severities of slavery, he could scarce look on a morsel of sugar without conceiving it spotted with human blood. If he had considered also the blood of one another, which the white natives shed in fighting for those islands, he would have imagined his sugar not as spotted only, but as thoroughly dyed red. On these accounts I am persuaded that the subjects of the Emperor of Germany, and the Empress of Russia, who have no sugar islands, consume sugar cheaper at Vienna and Moscow, with all the charge of transporting it, after its arrival in Europe, than the citizens of London and Paris. And I sincerely believe, that if France and England were to decide by throwing dice, which should have the whole of their sugar islands, the loser in the throw would be the gainer. The future expense of defending them would be saved : the sugars would be bought cheaper by all Europe if the inhabitants might make it without interruption ; and whoever imported the sugar, the same revenue might be raised by duties at the custom-house of the nation that consumed it. And on the whole, I conceive it would be better for the nations now possessing sugar colonies, to give up their claim to them, let them govern themselves, and put them under the protection of all the powers of Europe as neutral countries open to the commerce of all, the profit of the present monopolies being by no means equivalent to the expense of maintaining them.

REFLECTIONS

ON THE

FORMATION AND DISTRIBUTION

OF

WEALTH.

———

BY M. TURGOT,

COMPTROLLER GENERAL OF THE FINANCES OF
FRANCE,

IN 1774, 1775, AND 1776.

———

TRANSLATED FROM THE FRENCH.

LONDON:

PRINTED BY E. SPRAGG, FOR J. GOOD, BOOKSELLER,
NO. 159, NEW BOND STREET;

JOHN ANDERSON, NO. 62, HOLBORN HILL; and W. RICHARDSON,
ROYAL EXCHANGE.

1793.

REFLECTIONS

ON THE

FORMATION AND DISTRIBUTION

OF

WEALTH.

Ostendent terris hunc tantùm, fata. Æn. 6.

§ 1. *The impossibility of the existence of Commerce upon
the supposition of an equal division of lands, where every
man should possess only what is necessary for his own
support.*

IF the land was divided among all the inhabitants of a
country, so that each of them possessed precisely
the quantity necessary for his support, and nothing
more; it is evident that all of them being equal, no one
would work for another. Neither would any of them
possess wherewith to pay another for his labour, for each
person having only such a quantity of land as was necessary to produce a subsistence, would consume all he
should gather, and would not have any thing to give in
exchange for the labour of others.

§. 2. *The above hypothesis neither has existed nor could
continue. The diversity of soils and multiplicity of
wants, compel an exchange of the productions of the
earth, against other productions.*

This hypothesis never can have existed, because the
earth has been cultivated before it has been divided; the

3   cultivation

cultivation itself having been the only motive for a division, and for that law which secures to every one his property. For the first persons who have employed themselves in cultivation, have probably worked as much land as their strength would permit, and, consequently, more than was necessary for their own nourishment.

If this state could have existed, it could not possibly be durable; each one gathering from his field only a subsistence, and not having wherewith to pay others for their labour, would not be enabled to supply his other wants of lodging, cloathing, &c. &c., except by the labour of his hands, which would be nearly impossible, as every soil does not produce every material.

The man whose land was only fit to produce grain, and would neither bring forth cotton or flax, would want linen to cloath him. Another would have ground proper for cotton, which would not yield grain. One would want wood for his fire, and another be destitute of corn to support him. Experience would soon teach every one what species of productions his land was best adapted to, and he would confine himself to the cultivation of it; in order to procure himself those things he stood in need of, by an exchange with his neighbours, who, having on their part acquired the same experience, would have cultivated those productions which were best suited to their fields, and would have abandoned the cultivation of any other.

§. 3. *The productions of the earth require long and difficult preparations, before they are rendered fit to supply the wants of men.*

The productions which the earth supplies to satisfy the different wants of man, will not, for the most part, administer to those wants, in the state nature affords them; it is necessary they should undergo different operations,

4　　　　　　　　　　　　　　　　　and

and be prepared by art. Wheat must be converted into flour, then into bread; hides must be dressed or tanned; wool and cotton must be spun; silk must be taken from the cod; hemp and flax must be soaked, peeled, spun, and wove into different textures; then cut and sewed together again to make garments, &c. If the same man who cultivates on his own land these different articles, and who raises them to supply his wants, was obliged to perform all the intermediate operations himself, it is certain he would succeed very badly. The greater part of these preparations require care, attention, and a long experience; all which are only to be acquired by progressive labour, and that on a great quantity of materials. Let us refer, for example, to the preparation of hides: what labourer can pursue all the particular things necessary to those operations, which continue several months, sometimes several years? If he is able to do it, can he do it with a single hide? What a loss of time, of room, and of materials, which might be employed, either at the same time or successively, to tan a large quantity of skins! But should he even succeed in tanning a single skin, and wants one pair of shoes, what will he do with the remainder? Will he kill an ox to make this pair of shoes? Will he cut down a tree to make a pair of wooden shoes? We may say the same thing of every other want of every other man, who, if he was reduced to his field, and the labour of his own hands, would waste much time, take much trouble, be very badly equipped in every respect, and would also cultivate his lands very ill.

§ 4. *The necessity of these preparations, bring on the exchange of productions for labour.*

The same motive which has established the exchange of commodity for commodity, between the cultivators of lands of different natures, has also necessarily brought on the exchange of commodities for labour, between the cultivators and another portion of society, who shall have preferred the occupation of preparing and completing the productions of the earth, to the cultivation of it. Every one profits by this arrangement, for every one attaching himself to a peculiar species of labour, succeeds much better therein. The husbandman draws from his field the greatest quantity it is able to produce, and procures to himself, with greater facility, all the other objects of his wants, by an exchange of his superflux, than he could have done by his own labour. The shoemaker, by making shoes for the husbandman, secures to himself a portion of the harvest of the latter. Every workman labours for the wants of the workmen of every other trade, who, on their side, toil also for him.

§ 5. *Pre-eminence of the husbandman who produces, over the artificer who prepares. The husbandman is the first mover in the circulation of labour: it is he who causes the earth to produce the wages of every artificer.*

It must, however, be observed that the husbandman, furnishing every one with the most important and the most considerable objects of their consumption (I mean their food, and the materials of almost all manufactures) has the advantage of a greater degree of independence. His labour, among the different species of labour, appropriated to the different members of society, supports the same pre-eminence and priority, as the procuring of food did among the different works he was obliged, in his solitary state, to employ himself in, in order to minister to his wants of every kind. This is not a pre-eminence of honour or of dignity, but of *physical necessity*. The husbandman can, generally speaking, subsist without the labour of other workmen; but no other workmen can

6   labour

labour, if the husbandman does not provide him wherewith to exist. It is this circulation, which, by a reciprocal exchange of wants, renders mankind necessary to
each other, and which forms the bond of society: it is
therefore the labour of the husbandman which gives the
first movement. What his industry causes the earth to
produce beyond his personal wants, is the only fund for
the wages, which all the other members of society receive
in recompence for their toil. The latter, by availing
themselves of the produce of this exchange, to purchase
in their turn the commodities of the husbandman, only
return to him precisely what they have received. There
is here a very essential difference between these two
species of labour, on which it is necessary to reflect, and
to be well assured of the ground on which they stand,
before we trust to the innumerable consequences which
flow from them.

§ 6. *The wages of the workman is limited by the competition among those who work for a subsistence. He only
gains à livelihood.*

The mere workman, who depends only on his hands
and his industry, has nothing but such part of his labour
as he is able to dispose of to others. He sells it at a
cheaper or a dearer price; but this high or low price does
not depend on himself alone; it results from the agreement he has made with the person who employs him. The
latter pays him as little as he can help, and as he has the
choice from among a great number of workmen, he prefers the person who works cheapest. The workmen are
therefore obliged to lower their price in opposition to each
other. In every species of labour it must, and, in effect,
it does happen, that the wages of the workman is
confined merely to what is necessary to procure him a
subsistence.

7   § 7. *The*

§ 7. *The husbandman is the only one whose industry produces more than the wages of his labour. He, therefore, is the only source of all Wealth.*

The situation of the husbandman is materially different. The soil, independent of any other man, or of any agreement, pays him immediately the price of his toil. Nature does not bargain with him, or compel him to content himself with what is absolutely necessary. What she grants is neither limited to his wants, nor to a conditional valuation of the price of his day's work. It is a physical consequence of the fertility of the soil, and of justice, rather than of the difficulty of the means, which he has employed to render the soil fruitful. As soon as the labour of the husbandman produces more than sufficient for his necessities, he can, with the excess which nature affords him of pure freewill beyond the wages of his toil, purchase the labour of other members of society. The latter, in selling to him, only procures a livelihood; but the husbandman, besides his subsistence, collects an independent wealth at his disposal, which he has not purchased, but which he can sell. He is, therefore, the only source of all those riches which, by their circulation, animates the labours of society: because he is the only one whose labour produces more than the wages of his toil.

§ 8. *First division of society into two classes, the one* productive, *or the cultivators, the other* stipendiary, *or the artificers.*

Here then is the whole society divided, by a necessity founded on the nature of things, into two classes, both industrious, one of which, by its labour, produces, or rather draws from the earth, riches continually renewing,

which

which supply the whole society with subsistence, and with
materials for all its wants; while the other is employed
in giving to the said materials such preparations and forms
as render them proper for the use of man, sells his labour
to the first, and receives in return a subsistence. The
first may be called the *productive*, the latter the *stipendiary*
class.

§ 9. *In the first ages of society, the proprietors could not
be distinguished from the cultivators.*

Hitherto we have not distinguished the husbandman
from the proprietor of the land; and in the first origin
they were not in fact so distinguished. It is by the labour
of those who have first cultivated the fields, and who have
inclosed them to secure their harvest, that all land has
ceased to be common, and that a property in the soil has
been established. Until societies have been formed, and
until the public strength, or the laws, becoming superior
to the force of individuals, have been able to guarantee to
every one the tranquil possession of his property, against
all invasion from without; the property in a field could
only be secured as it had been acquired, by continuing to
cultivate it; the proprietor could not be assured of having
his field cultivated by the help of another; and that
person taking all the trouble, could not easily have comprehended that the whole harvest did not belong to him.
On the other hand, in this early age, when every industrious man would find as much land as he wanted, he
would not be tempted to labour for another. It necessarily follows, that every proprietor must cultivate his
own field or abandon it entirely.

§ 10. *Progress of society; all lands have an owner.*

But the land begins to people, and to be cleared more
and more. The best lands are in process of time fully

occupied

occupied. There remains only for those who come last, nothing but barren land, rejected by the first occupants. But at last, every spot has found a master, and those who cannot gaiu a property therein, have no other resource but to exchange the labour of their hands in some of the employments of the stipendiary class, for the excess of commodities possessed by the cultivating proprietor.

§ 11. *The proprietors begin to be able to ease themselves of the labour of cultivation, by the help of hired cultivators.*

Mean time, since the earth produces to the proprietor who cultivates it, not a subsistence only, not only wherewith to procure himself by way of exchange, what he otherwise wants, but also a considerable superfluity; he is enabled with this superfluity, to pay other men to cultivate his land. For among those who live by wages, as many are content to labour in this employment as in any other. The proprietor, therefore, might then be eased of the labour of culture, and he soon was so.

§ 12. *Inequality in the division of property: causes which render that inevitable.*

The original proprietors would (as I have already mentioned) occupy as much land as their strength would permit them with their families to cultivate. A man of greater strength, more laborious, more attentive about the future, would occupy more than a man of a contrary character. He, whose family is the most numerous having greater wants and more hands, extends his possessions further; this is a first cause of inequality.— Every piece of ground is not equally fertile; two men with the same extent of land, may reap a very different

10   harvest;

harvest; this is a second source of inequality.—Property in descending from fathers to their children, divides into greater or less portions, according as the descendants are more or less numerous, and as one generation succeeds another, sometimes the inheritances again subdivide, and sometimes re-unite again by the extinction of some of the branches; this is a third source of inequality. The difference of knowledge, of activity, and, above all, the œconomy of some, contrasted with the indolence, inaction, and dissipation of others, is a fourth principle of inequality, and the most powerful of all: the negligent and inattentive proprietor, who cultivates badly, who in a fruitful year consumes in frivolous things the whole of his superfluity, finds himself reduced on the least accident to request assistance from his more provident neighbour, and to live by borrowing. If by any new accident, or by a continuation of his negligence, he finds himself not in a condition to repay, he is obliged to have recourse to new loans, and at last has no other resource but to abandon a part, or even the whole of his property to his creditor, who receives it as an equivalent; or to assign it to another, in exchange for other valuables with which he discharges his obligation to his creditor.

§ 13. *Consequences of this inequality: The cultivator distinguished from the proprietor.*

Thus is the property in the soil made subject to purchase and sale. The portion of the dissipating or unfortunate, increases the share of the more happy or industrious proprietor; and in this infinite variety of possessions, it is not possible but a great number of proprietors must possess more than they can cultivate. Besides, it is very natural for a rich man to wish for a tranquil enjoyment of his property, and instead of employing his whole time

in toilsome labour, he rather prefers giving a part of his
superfluity to people to work for him.

§ 14. *Division of the produce between the cultivator and* *the proprietor.*   Net produce, *or revenue.*

By this new arrangement, the produce of the land
divides into two parts. The one comprehends the subsistence and the profits of the husbandman, which are the
rewards for his labour, and the conditions on which he
agrees to cultivate the field of the proprietor; the other
which remains, is that independent and *disposable* part,
which the earth produces as a free gift to the proprietor
over and above what he has disbursed; and it is out of
this share of the proprietor's, or what is called the *revenue,*
that he is enabled to live without labour, and which he
can carry wherever he will.

§ 15. *A new division of society into three classes. Cul-* *tivators, Artificers, and Proprietors, or the productive,* *stipendiary, and disposable classes.*

We now behold society divided into three branches;
the class of husbandmen, whom we may denominate cultivators; the class of artificers and others, who work for
hire upon the productions of the earth; and the class of
proprietors, the only one which, not being confined by a
want of support to a particular species of labour, may be
employed in the general service of society, as for war,
and the administration of justice, either by a personal
service, or by the payment of a part of their revenue,
with which the state may hire others to fill these employments. The appellation which suits the best with this
division, for this reason, is that of the *disposable* class.

§ 16. *Resemblance*

§ 16. *Resemblance between the two laborious classes.*

The two classes of cultivators and artificers, resemble each other in many respects, and particularly that those who compose them do not possess any revenue, and both equally subsist on the wages which are paid them out of the productions of the earth. Both have also this circumstance in common, that they only gain the price of their labour and their disbursements, and that this price is nearly the same in the two classes. The proprietor agreeing with those who cultivate his ground to pay them as small a part as possible of its produce, in the same manner as he bargains with the shoemaker to buy his shoes as cheap as he can. In a word, neither the cultivator, nor the artificer receives more than a bare recompense for his labour.

§ 17. *Essential difference between the two laborious classes.*

But there is this difference between the two species of labour; that the work of the cultivator produces not only his own wages, but also that revenue which serves to pay all the different classes of artificers, and other stipendiaries their salaries: whereas the artificers receive simply their salary, that is to say, their part of the productions of the earth, in exchange for their labour, and which does not produce any increase. The proprietor enjoys nothing but by the labour of the cultivator. He receives from him his subsistence, and wherewith to pay for the labour of the other stipendiaries. He has need of the cultivator by the necessity arising from the physical order of things, by which necessity the earth is not fruitful without labour; but the cultivator has no need of the proprietor but by virtue of human

13   conventions,

conventions, and of those civil laws which have guaranteed to the first cultivators and their heirs, the property in the lands they had occupied, even after they ceased to cultivate them. But these laws can only secure to the idle man, that part of the production of his land which it produces beyond the retribution due to the cultivators. The cultivator, confined as he is to a stipend for his labour, still preserves that natural and physical priority which renders him the first mover of the whole machine of society, and which causes both the subsistence and wealth of the proprietor, and the salaries paid for every other species of labour, to depend on his industry. The artificer, on the contrary, receives his wages either of the proprietor or of the cultivator, and only gives them in exchange for his stipend, an equivalent in labour, and nothing more.

Thus, although neither the cultivator and artificer gain more than a recompence for their toil; yet the labour of the cultivator produces besides that recompense, a revenue to the proprietor, while the artificer does not produce any revenue either for himself or others.

§ 18. *This difference authorises another distinction into the* productive *and* barren *classes.*

We may then distinguish the two classes not *disposable* into the *productive* class, which is that of the cultivators, or the barren class, which comprehends all the other *stipendiary* members of society.

§ 19. *How the proprietors may draw a* revenue *from their lands.*

The proprietors who do not cultivate their lands themselves, may adopt different methods of cultivating
14   them,

them, or make different agreements with those who cultivate them.

§ 20. *First method, or cultivation by labourers on wages.*

They may, in the first place, pay men by the day or
the year, to work their fields, and reserve to themselves
the whole of the produce; this includes a supposition that
the proprietor pays all advances, both for seed, and the
wages of the labourers, until after the harvest. But this
method requires great labour and assiduity on the part of
the proprietor, who alone can direct his men in their
labour, see that they employ their time well, and watch
over their fidelity, that they shall not carry away any part
of the produce.   It is true that he may pay a man of more
knowledge, and whose fidelity he knows, who, in quality
of manager and conductor, may direct the workmen, and
keep an account of the produce; but he will be always
subject to fraud.   Besides, this method is extremely
expensive, unless a large population, or want of employ in
other species of labour, forces the workmen to content
themselves with very low salaries.

§ 21.   *Second method, cultivation by slaves.*

In times not very distant from the origin of society, it
was almost impossible to find men willing to work on the
lands of another, because all the land not being as yet
occupied, those who were willing to labour, preferred the
clearing of new lands, and the cultivating them on their
own account; this is pretty much the case in all new
colonies.

In this situation violent men then conceived the expedient of obliging other men by force to labour for them.
They employed slaves.   These latter have had no justice

to

to look for, from the hands of people, who have not been able to reduce them to slavery without violating all the laws of humanity. Meantime, the physical law of nature secures to them their part of the productions which they have raised; for the master must necessarily nourish them, in order to profit by their labour. But this species of recompence is confined to mere necessaries for their subsistence.

This abominable custom of slavery has formerly been universal, and has spread over the greatest part of the globe. The principal object of the wars carried on by the ancients was, to carry off slaves, whom the conquerors either compelled to work for them, or sold to others. This species of thieving, and this trade, still continues, attended with all its cruel circumstances, on the coast of Guinea, where the Europeans encourage it by going thither to purchase negroes for the cultivation of their American colonies.

The excessive labour to which avaricious masters force their slaves, causes many of them to perish; and it becomes necessary, to keep up the number requisite for cultivation, that this trade should supply annually a very large number. And as war is the principal source which supplies this commerce, it is evident that it can subsist no longer than the people continue divided into very small nations, who are incessantly plundering each other, and every district is at continued war with its neighbours. Let England, France, and Spain carry on the most cruel hostilities, the frontiers alone of each state will be the only parts invaded, and that in a few places only. All the rest of the country will be quiet, and the small number of prisoners they could make on either side, would be but a weak resource for the cultivation of each of the three nations.

16   § 22 *Cultivation*

§ 22. *Cultivation by slaves cannot exist in great societies.*

Thus when men are formed into great societies, the recruits of slaves are not sufficiently numerous to support the consumption which the cultivation requires. And although they supply the labour of men by that of beasts, a time will come, when the lands can no longer be worked by slaves. The practice is then continued only for the interior work of the house, and in the end it is totally abolished ; because in proportion as nations become polished, they form conventions for the exchange of prisoners of war. These conventions are the more readily made, as every individual is very much interested to be free from the danger of falling into a state of slavery.

§ 23. *Slavery annexed to the land, succeeds to slavery properly so called.*

The descendants of the first slaves, attached at first to the cultivation of the ground, change their condition. The interior peace among nations, not leaving wherewithal to supply the consumption of slaves, the masters are obliged to take greater care of them. Those who were born in the house, accustomed from their infancy to their situation, revolt the less at it, and their masters have less need to employ rigour to restrain them. By degrees the land they cultivate becomes their country, they become a part of the nation, and in the end, they experience confidence and humanity on the part of their masters.

§ 24. *Vassalage succeeds to slavery, annexed to the land, and the slave becomes a proprietor. Third method ; alienation of the land for a certain service.*

The administration of an estate, cultivated by slaves, requires a careful attention, and an irksome residence.

17 The

The master secures to himself a more free, more easy, and more secure enjoyment of his property, by interesting his slaves in the cultivation of it, and by abandoning to each of them a certain portion of land, on condition of their paying him a portion of the produce. Some have made this agreement for a time, and have only left their serfs, or slaves, a precarious and revocable possession. Others have assigned them lands in perpetuity, retaining an annual rent payable either in provisions or in money, and requiring from the possessors certain services. Those who received these lands, under the condition prescribed, became proprietors and free, under the name of tenant, or vassal; and the ancient proprietors, under the title of lords, reserved only the right of exacting payment of the rent, and other stipulated duties. Thus it has happened in the greater part of Europe.

§ 25.   *Fourth Method.   Partial colonization.*

These lands, rendered free at the expence of rent, may yet change masters, may divide or reunite by means of succession and sale; and such a vassal may in his turn have more than he can cultivate himself. In general the rent to which those lands are subject, is not so large, but that, by cultivating them well, the cultivator is enabled to pay all advances, and expences, procure himself a subsistence, and besides, an excess of productions which form a revenue. Henceforth the proprietary vassal becomes desirous of enjoying this revenue without labour, and of having his lands also cultivated by others. On the other hand, the greater part of the lords grant out those parts of their possessions only, which are the least within their reach, and retain those they can cultivate with the least expence. The cultivation by slaves not being practicable, the first method that offers, and the most simple to engage free men to cultivate lands

which

which do not belong to them, was to resign to them such a portion of the produce, as would engage them to cultivate better than those husbandmen who are employed at a fixed salary. The most common method has been to divide it into equal parts, one of which belonged to the cultivator and the other to the proprietor. This has given place to the name (in France) of *metayer* (*medietarius*) or cultivator for half produce. In arrangements of this kind, which take place throughout the greatest part of France, the proprietor pays all contingencies; that is to say, he provides at his expence, the cattle for labour, ploughs, and other utensils of husbandry, seed, and the support of the cultivator and his family, from the time the latter enters into the *metairie* until the first harvest.

§ 26. *Fifth method. Renting, or letting out the land.*

Rich and intelligent cultivators, who saw to what perfection an active and well directed cultivation, for which neither labour nor expence was spared, would raise the fruitfulness of land, judged with reason that they would gain more, if the proprietors should consent to abandon, for a certain number of years, the whole of the harvest, on condition of receiving annually a certain revenue, and to be free of all expences of cultivation. By that they would be assured that the increase of productions, which their disbursements and their labour procured, would belong entirely to themselves. The proprietor, on his side, would gain thereby, 1st, a more tranquil enjoyment of his revenue, being freed from the care of advances, and of keeping an account of the produce; 2nd, a more equal enjoyment, since he would receive every year the same and a more certain price for his farm : because he would run no risk of losing his advances; and the cattle and other effects with which the farmers had stocked it, would become a security for his payment. On the other

hand

hand, the lease being only for a small number of years, if his tenant paid him too little, he could augment it at the expiration thereof.

§ 27. *The last method is the most advantageous, but it supposes the country already rich.*

This method of securing lands is the most advantageous both to proprietors and cultivators. It is universally established where there are any rich cultivators, in a condition to make the advances necessary for the cultivation. And as the rich cultivators are in a situation to bestow more labour and manure upon the ground, there results from thence a prodigious augmentation in the productions, and in the revenue of the land.

In Picardy, Normandy, the environs of Paris, and in most of the provinces in the north of France, the lands are cultivated by farmers; in those of the south, by the *metayers*. Thus the northern are incomparably richer and better cultivated than the southern provinces.

§ 28. *Recapitulation of the several methods of making lands productive.*

I have just mentioned five different methods by which proprietors are enabled to ease themselves of the labour of the cultivation, and to make their land productive, by the hands of others.

1. By workmen paid at a fixed salary.
2. By slaves.
3. By ceding their lands for rent.
4. By granting to the cultivator a determined portion, which is commonly half the produce, the proprietor paying the advances necessary for the cultivation.
5. By letting their land to farmers, who undertake to make all the necessary advances, and who engage to pay

to

to the proprietors, during the number of years agreed on, a revenue equal to its value.

Of these five methods, the first is too expensive, and very seldom practised; the second is only used in countries as yet ignorant and barbarous; the third is rather a means of procuring a value for, than abandoning of the property for money, so that the ancient proprietor is no longer any thing more than a mere creditor.

The two last methods of cultivation are the most common, that is, the cultivation by *metayers* in the poor, and by farmers in the richer countries.

§ 29. *Of capitals in general, and of the revenue of money.*

There is another way of being rich, without labour, and without possessing lands, of which I have not yet spoken, and of which it is necessary to explain the origin and connection, with other parts of the system of the distribution of riches in society, of which I have just drawn the outlines. This consists in living by what is called the revenue of money, or of the interest which is paid for the loan thereof.

§ 30. *Of the use of gold and silver in commerce.*

Gold and silver are two species of merchandize, like others, and less valuable than many of them, because they are of no use for the real wants of life. To explain how these two metals are become the representative pledges of every species of riches; how they influence the commercial markets, and how they enter into the composition of fortunes, it is necessary to go back again and return to our first principles.

§ 31. *Rise*

§ 31. *Rise of Commerce. Principle of the valuation of commercial things.*

Reciprocal wants first introduced exchanges of what we possessed, for what we stood in need of; one species of provision was bartered for another, or for labour. In exchanging, it is necessary that each party is convinced of the quality and quantity of every thing exchanged. In this agreement it is natural that every one should desire to receive as much as he can, and to give as little; and both being equally masters of what they have to barter, it is in a man's own breast to balance the attachment he has to the thing he gives, with the desire he feels to possess that which he is willing to receive, and consequently to fix the quantity of each of the exchanged things. If the two persons do not agree, they must relax a little on one side or the other, either by offering more or being content with less. I will suppose that one is want of corn and the other of wine; and that they agree to exchange a bushel of corn for six pints of wine. It is evident that by both of them, one bushel of corn and six pints of wine are looked upon as exactly equivalent, and that in this particular exchange, the price of a bushel of corn is six pints of wine, and the price of six pints of wine is one bushel of corn. But in another exchange between other men, this price will be different, accordingly as one or the other of them shall have a more or less pressing want of one commodity or the other; and a bushel of corn may be exchanged against eight pints of wine, while another bushel shall be bartered for four pints only. Now it is evident, that not one of these three prices can be looked on as the true price of a bushel of corn, rather than the others; to each of the dealers, the wine he has received was equivalent to the corn he had given. In a word, so long as we consider each exchange independent of any

other

other, the value of each thing exchanged has no other measure than the wants or desires of one party weighed with those of the other, and is fixed only by their agreement.

§ 32. *How the current value of the exchange of merchandize is established.*

Meantime it happens that many individuals have wine to dispose of to those who possess corn. If one is not willing to give more than four pints for a bushel, the proprietor of the corn will not exchange with him, when he shall know that another will give six or eight pints for the same bushel. If the former is determined to have the corn, he will be obliged to raise his price equal to what is offered by others. The sellers of wine profit on their side by the competition among the sellers of corn. No one resolves to part with his property, before he has compared the different offers which are made to him, of the commodity he stands in need of, and then he accepts of the best offer. The value of the wine and corn is not fixed by the two proprietors with respect to their own wants and reciprocal abilities, but by a general balance of the wants of all the sellers of corn, with those of all the sellers of wine. For those who will willingly give *eight pints* of wine for *a bushel* of corn, will give but four when they shall know that a proprietor of corn is willing to give *two bushels* for eight pints. The medium price between the different offers and the different demands, will become the current price to which all the buyers and sellers will conform in their exchanges ; and it will be true if we say, that six pints of wine will be to every one the equivalent for a bushel of corn, that is, the medium price, until a diminution of supply on one side, or of demand on the other, causes a variation.

§ 33.   *Commerce gives to all merchandize a current value
with respect to any other merchandize; from whence it
follows that all merchandize is the equivalent for a
certain quantity of any other merchandize, and may be
looked on as a pledge to represent it.*

Corn is not only exchanged for wine, but also for any
object which the proprietors of the corn may stand in
need of; as wood, leather, woollen, cotton, &c. it is the
same with wine and every other particular species. If a
bushel of corn is equivalent to *six pints* of wine, and a
sheep is equivalent to *three bushels* of corn, the same sheep
will be equivalent to eighteen pints of wine. He who
having the corn, wants the wine, may, without inconvenience, exchange his corn for a sheep, in order afterwards
to exchange the sheep for the wine he stands in need of.

§ 34.   *Every merchandize may serve as a scale or common
measure, by which to compare the value of any other.*

It follows from hence, that in a country where the
commerce is very brisk, where there are many productions
and much consumption, where there are great supplies
and a great demand for all sorts of commodities, every
sort will have a current price, having relation to every
other species; that is to say, that a certain quantity of
one will be of equal value to a certain quantity of any
others. Thus the same quantity of corn which is worth
eighteen pints of wine, is also the value of a sheep, a piece
of leather, or a certain quantity of iron; and all these
things have, in the transactions of trade an equal value.
To express or make known the value of any particular
thing, it is evident, that it is sufficient to announce the
quantity of any other known production, which will be
looked on as an equivalent for it. Thus, to make known
what a piece of leather of a certain size is worth, we may

say

say indifferently, that it is worth three bushels of corn, or eighteen pints of wine. We may by the same method express the value of a certain quantity of wine, by the number of sheep, or bushels of corn it will bring in trade.

We see by this, that every species of commodity that can be an object of commerce, may be measured, as I may say, by each other, that every one may serve as a common measure, or scale of comparison to describe the value of every other species, and in like manner every merchandize becomes in the hands of him who possesses it, a means to procure all others—a sort of universal pledge.

§ 35. *Every species of merchandize does not present a scale equally commodious. It is proper to prefer the use of such as are not susceptible of any great alteration in quality, and have a value principally relative to the number and quantity.*

But although all merchandize has essentially this property of representing any other, is able to serve as a common measure, to express its value, and to become a universal pledge to procure any of them by way of exchange, yet all cannot be employed with the same degree of facility for these two uses. The more susceptible any merchandize is to change its value by an alteration in its quality, the more difficult it is to make it a scale of reference for the value of others. For example, if eighteen pints of wine of Anjou are equivalent in value to a sheep, eighteen pints of Cape wine may be equivalent to eighteen sheep. Thus he who to express the value of a sheep, would say it is worth eighteen pints of wine, would employ an equivocal language, and would not communicate any precise idea, at least until he added some explanation, which would be very inconvenient. We are, therefore, obliged to choose for a scale of comparison, such commodities as being more commonly in use, and consequently of a value more gene-

rally

rally known, are more like each other, and of which consequently the value has more relation to the quantity than the quality.

§ 36. *For want of an exact correspondence between the value and the number or quantity, it is supplied by a mean valuation, which becomes a species of real money.*

In a country where there are only one race of sheep, we may easily take the value of a fleece or of a sheep by the common method of valuation, and we may say that a barrel of wine, or a piece of stuff, is worth a certain number of fleeces or of sheep. There is in reality some inequality in sheep, but when we want to sell them, we take care to estimate that inequality, and to reckon (for example) two lambs for one sheep. When it is necessary to treat of the relative value of other merchandize, we fix the common value of a sheep of middling age and quality, as the symbol of unity. In this view the enunciation of the value of sheep, becomes an agreed language, and this word *one sheep*, in the language of commerce, signifies only a certain value, which, in the mind of him who understands it, carries the idea not only of a sheep, but as a certain quantity of every other commodity, which is esteemed equivalent thereto, and this expression is more applicable to a fictitious and abstract value, than to the value of a real sheep; that if by chance a mortality happens among the sheep, and that to purchase one of them, you must give double the quantity of corn or wine that was formerly given, we shall rather say, that one sheep is worth two sheep, than change the expression we have been accustomed to for all other valuations.

§ 37. *Example of those mean valuations which become an ideal expression for value.*

There exists, in the commerce of every nation, many

examples

examples of fictitious valuations of merchandize, which are, as we may say, only a conventional language to express their value. Thus the cooks of Paris, and the fishmongers who furnish great houses, generally sell by *the piece*. A fat pullet is esteemed *one piece*, a chicken half a piece, more or less, according to the season : and so of the rest. In the negro trade in the American colonies, they sell a cargo of negroes at the rate of so much per negro, an *Indian piece*. The women and children are valued, so that, for example, three children, or one woman and two children are reckoned as one head of negro. They increase or diminish the value on account of the strength or other quality of the slaves, so that certain slaves are reckoned as two heads of negroes.

The Mandingo negroes, who carry on a trade for gold dust with the Arabian merchants, bring all their commodities to a fictitious scale, which both parties call *macutes*, so that they tell the merchants they will give so many *macutes* in gold. They value thus in *macutes* the merchandize they receive ; and bargain with the merchants upon that valuation. Thus in Holland they reckon by *bank florins*, which is only a fictitious money, and which in commerce is sometimes of a greater, sometimes of a less value than the coin which is denominated a *florin*.

§ 38. *All merchandize is a representative pledge of every object of commerce, but more or less commodious for use, as it possesses a greater or less facility to be transported, and to be preserved without alteration.*

The variation in the quality of merchandize, and in the different prices in proportion to that quality, which renders them more or less proper than others to serve as a common measure, is also more or less an impediment to their being a representative pledge of every other mer-

27 chandize

chandize of equal value. Nevertheless there is also, as to this last property, a very essential difference between the different species of merchandize. It is (for example) evident, that a man who possesses a piece of linen, is more certain of procuring for it, when he pleases, a certain quantity of corn, than if he had a barrel of wine of equal value: the wine being subject to a variety of accidents, which may in a moment deprive him of the whole property.

§ 39. *All merchandize has the two essential properties of money, to measure and to represent all value: and in this sense all merchandize is money.*

These two properties of serving as a common measure of all value, aud of being a representative pledge of all other commodities of equal value, comprehend all that constitute the essence and use of what is called money: and it follows from the details which I have just now given, that all merchandize is, in some respect, *money;* and participates more or less, according to its particular nature, of these two essential properties. All is more or less proper to serve as a common measure, in proportion as it is more or less in general use, of a more similar quality, and more easy to be divided into aliquot parts. All is more or less applicable for the purpose of a general pledge of exchange, in proportion as it is less susceptible of decay or alteration in quantity or quality.

§ 40. *Reciprocally all money is essentially merchandize.*

We can take only that which has a value for a common measure of value, that which is received in commerce in exchange for other properties; and there is no universal representative pledge of value, but something of equal value. A money of convention is therefore a thing impossible.

28

§ 41. *Different*

§ 41. *Different matters are able to serve and have served for current money.*

Many nations have adopted in their language and in their trade, as a common measure of value, different matters more or less precious. There are at this day, some barbarous nations, who make use of a species of little shells, called *cowries.* I remember to have seen when at college, some apricot stones exchanged and passed as a species of money among the scholars, who made use of them at certain games. I have already spoken of a valuation by heads of cattle; some of these are to be found in the vestiges of thé laws of the ancient German nations, who over-ran the Roman empire. The first Romans, or at least the Latins, their ancestors, made use of them also. It is pretended that the first money they struck in brass, represented the value of a sheep, and bore the image of that animal, and that the name of *pecunia* has obtained from *pecus.* This conjecture carries with it a great probability.

§ 42. *Metals, and particularly gold and silver, are the most proper for that purpose, and why.*

We are now arrived at the introduction of the precious metals into trade. All metals, as they have been discovered, have been admitted into exchange, on account of their real utility. Their splendor has caused them to be sought for, to serve as ornaments; their ductility and their solidity have rendered them proper for utensils, more durable and lighter than those of clay. But these substances cannot be brought into commerce without becoming almost immediately a universal money. A piece of any metal, of whatever sort, has exactly the same qualities as another piece of the same metal provided they are

both

both equally pure. Now the ease with which we can separate, by different chemical operations, a metal from other metals with which it is incorporated, enables us to bring it to a degree of purity, or, as they call it, to what standard we please ; then the value of metal differs only as to its weight. In expressing, therefore, the value of any merchandize by the weight of metal which may be had in exchange, we shall then have the clearest, the most commodious, and most precise expression of value; and hence it is impossible but it must be preferred in practice to all other things. Nor are metals less proper than other merchandize for becoming the universal token of all value that can be measured : as they are susceptible of all imaginable divisions, there is not any object of commerce, great or small, whose value cannot be exactly paid by a certain quantity of metal. To this advantage of accommodating itself to every species of division, they join that of being unalterable, and those which are scarce, as gold and silver, have a great value, although of a weight and size little considerable.

These two metals are then, of all merchandize, the most easy to ascertain their quality, to divide their quantity, and to convey to all places at the easiest expence. Every one, therefore, who has a superfluity, and who is not at the time in want of another useful commodity, will hasten to exchange it for silver, with which he is more certain, than with any thing else, to procure himself the commodity he shall wish for at the time he is in want.

§ 43. *Gold and silver are constituted, by the nature of things, money, and universal money, independent of all convention, and of all laws.*

Here then is gold and silver constituted money, and universal money, and that without any arbitrary agreement

among

among men, without the intervention of any law, but only by the nature of things. They are not, as many people imagine, signs of value; they have an intrinsic value in themselves, if they are capable of being the measure and the token of other values. This property they have in common with all other commodities which have a value in commerce. They only differ in being at the same time more divisible, more unchangeable, and of more easy conveyance than other merchandize, by which they are more commodiously employed to measure and represent the value of others.

§ 44. *Other metals are only employed for these uses, in a secondary manner.*

All metals are capable of being employed as money. But those which are too common have too little value in a large bulk to be employed in the current uses of commerce. Copper, silver, and gold, are the only ones which have been brought into constant use. And even copper, except among people to whom neither mines nor commerce have supplied a sufficient quantity of gold or silver, has never been used but in exchanges of small value.

§ 45. *The use of gold and silver, as money, has augmented their value as materials.*

It is not possible, but the eagerness with which every one has sought to exchange their superfluous commodities for gold and silver, rather than for any other commodity, must have augmented the value of these two materials in commerce. These are only thereby rendered more commodious for their employment as tokens, or common measure.

§ 46. *Variations in the value of gold and silver, compared with the other objects of commerce, and with each other.*

This value is susceptible of change, and in truth is
31 continually

continually changing; so that the same quantity of metal which answered to a certain quantity of such or such a commodity, becomes no longer equal thereto, and it requires a greater or less quantity of silver to represent the same commodity. When it requires more, it is said the commodity is dearer; when it requires less, tbat it is become cheaper; but they may as well say, that the silver is in the first case become cheaper, and in the latter dearer. Silver and gold not only vary in price, compared with all other commodities, but they vary also with each other, in proportion as they are more or less abundant. It is notorious, that we now give in Europe from fourteen to fifteen ounces of silver for one ounce of gold; and that in former times we gave only ten or eleven ounces.

Again, that at present in China, they do not give more than twelve ounces of silver for one ounce of gold, so that there is a very great advantage in carrying silver to China, to exchange for gold, to bring back to Europe. It is visible, that, in process of time, this commerce will make gold more common in Europe, and less common in China, and that the value of these two materials must finally come in both places to the same proportion.

A thousand different causes concur, to fix and to change incessantly the comparative value of commodities, either with respect to each other, or with respect to silver. The same causes conspire to fix and vary the comparative value, whether in respect to the value of each commodity in particular, or with respect to the totality of the other values which are actually in commerce. It is not possible to investigate these different causes, or to unfold their effects, without entering into very extensive and very difficult details, which I shall decline in this discussion.

§ 47. *The use of payments in money, has given room for the distinction of seller and buyer.*

In proportion as mankind became familiarized to the custom of valuing all things in silver, of exchanging all their superfluous commodities for silver, and of not parting with that money but for things which are useful or agreeable to them at the moment, they become accustomed to consider the exchanges of commerce in a different point of view. They have made a distinction of two persons, the buyer and the seller: the seller is him who gives commodities for money; and the buyer is him who gives money for commodities.

§ 48. *The use of money has much facilitated the separation of different labours among the different orders of society.*

The more money becomes a universal medium, the more every one is enabled, by devoting himself solely to that species of cultivation and industry, of which he has made choice, to divest himself entirely of every thought for his other wants, and only to think of providing the most money he can, by the sale of his fruits or his labour, being sure with that money to possess all the rest. It is thus, that the use of money has prodigiously hastened the progress of society.

§ 49. *Of the excess of annual produce accumulated to form capitals.*

As soon as men are found, whose property in land assures them an annual revenue more than sufficient to satisfy all their wants, among them there are some, who, either uneasy respecting the future, or, perhaps, only provident,

dent, lay by a portion of what they gather every year, either with a view to guard against possible accidents, or to augment their enjoyments. When the commodities they have gathered are difficult to preserve, they ought to procure themselves in exchange, such objects of a more durable nature, and such as will not decrease in their value by time, or those that may be employed in such a manner, as to procure such profits as will make good the decrease with advantage.

§ 50. *Personal property, accumulation of money.*

This species of possession, resulting from the accumulation of annual produce, not consumed, is known by the name of *personal property*. Household goods, houses, merchandize in store, utensils of trade, and cattle are under this denomination. It is evident men must have toiled hard to procure themselves as much as they could of this kind of wealth, before they became acquainted with the use of money; but it is not less evident that, as soon as it was known, that it was the least liable to alteration of all the objects of commerce, and the most easy to preserve without trouble, it would be principally sought after by whoever wished to accumulate. It was not the proprietors of land only who thus accumulated their superfluity. Although the profits of industry are not, like the revenue of lands, a gift of nature; and the industrious man draws from his labour only the price which is given him by the persons who pay him his wages; although the latter is as frugal as he can of his salary, and that a competition obliges an industrious man to content himself with a less price than he otherwise would do, it is yet certain that these competitions have neither been so numerous or strong in any species of labour, but that a man more expert, more active, and who practises more œconomy than others in his personal expences, has been

able

able, at all times, to gain a little more than sufficient to support him and his family, and reserve his surplus to form a little hoard.

§ 51. *Circulating wealth is an indispensible requisite for all lucrative works.*

It is even necessary, that in every trade the workmen, or those who employ them, possess a certain quantity of circulating wealth, collected before-hand. We here again are obliged to go back to a retrospect of many things which have been as yet only hinted at, after we have spoken of the division of different professions, and of the different methods by which the proprietors of capitals may render them of value; because, otherwise, we should not be able to explain them properly, without interrupting the connection of our ideas.

§ 52. *Necessity of advances for cultivation.*

Every species of labour, of cultivation, of industry, or of commerce, require advances. When people cultivate the ground, it is necessary to sow before they can reap; they must also support themselves until after the harvest. The more cultivation is brought to perfection and enlivened, the more considerable these advances are. Cattle, utensils for farming, buildings to hold the cattle, to store the productions, a number of persons, in proportion to the extent of the undertaking, must be paid and subsisted until the harvest. It is only by means of considerable advances, that we obtain rich harvests, and that lands produce a large revenue. In whatever business they engage, the workman must be provided with tools, must have a sufficient quantity of such materials as the object of his labour requires: and he must subsist until the sale of his goods.

§ 53. *First*

§ 53.   *First advances furnished by the land although uncultivated.*

The earth was ever the first and the only source of all riches: it is that which by cultivation produces all revenue; it is that which has afforded the first fund for advances, anterior to all cultivation.   The first cultivator has taken the grain he has sown from such productions as the land had spontaneously produced; while waiting for the harvest, he has supported himself by hunting, by fishing, or upon wild fruits.   His tools have been the branches of trees, procured in the forests, and cut with stones sharpened upon other stones; the animals wandering in the woods he has taken in the chace, caught them in his traps, or has subdued them unawares.   At first he has made use of them for food, afterwards to help him in his labours. These first funds or capital have increased by degrees. Cattle were in early times the most sought after of all circulating property; and were also the easiest to accumulate; they perish, but they also breed, and this sort of riches is in some respects unperishable.   This capital augments by generation alone, and affords an annual produce, either in milk, wool, leather, and other materials, which, with wood taken in the forest, have effected the first foundations for works of industry.

§ 54.   *Cattle a circulating wealth, even before the cultivation of the earth.*

In times when there was yet a large quantity of uncultivated land, and which did not belong to any individual, cattle might be maintained without having a property in land.   It is even probable, that mankind have almost every where began to collect flocks and herds, and to live on what they produced, before they employed

themselves

themselves in the more laborious occupation of cultivating the ground. It seems that those nations who first cultivated the earth, are those who found in their country such sorts of animals as were the most susceptible of being tamed, and that they have by this been drawn from the wandering and restless life of hunters and fishers, to the more tranquil enjoyment of pastoral pursuits. Pastoral life requires a longer residence in the same place, affords more leisure, more opportunities to study the difference of lands, to observe the ways of nature in the productions of such plants as serve for the support of cattle. Perhaps it is for this reason, that the Asiatic nations have first cultivated the earth, and that the inhabitants of America have remained so long in a savage state.

§ 55. *Another species of circulating wealth, and advances necessary for cultivation, slaves.*

The slaves were another kind of personal property, which at first were procured by violence, and afterwards by way of commerce and exchange. Those that had many, employed them not only in the culture of land, but in various other channels of labour. The facility of accumulating, almost without measure, those two sources of riches, and of making use of them abstractedly from the land, caused the land itself to be estimated, and the value compared to moveable riches.

§ 56. *Personal property has an exchangeable value, even for land itself.*

A man that would have been possessed of a quantity of lands without cattle or slaves, would undoubtedly have made an advantageous bargain, in yielding a part of his

37   land,

land, to a person that would have offered him in exchange,
cattle and slaves to cultivate the rest. It is chiefly by
this principle that property in land entered likewise into
commerce, and had a comparative value with that of all
the other goods. If four bushels of corn, the net produce of an acre of land, was worth six sheep, the acre
itself that feeds them could have been given for a certain
value, greater indeed, but always easy to settle by the
same way, as the price of other wares. Namely, at first
by debates among the two contractors, next, by the current price established by the agreement of those who exchange land for cattle, or the contrary. It is by the scale
of this current specie that lands are appraised, when a
debtor is prosecuted by his creditor, and is constrained to
yield up his property.

§ 57. *Valuation of lands by the proportion of their
revenue, with the sum of personal property, or the value
for which they are exchanged : this proportion is called
the price of lands.*

It is evident, that if land, which produces a revenue
equivalent to six sheep, can be sold for a certain value,
which may always be expressed by a number of sheep
equivalent to that value ; this number will bear a fixed
proportion with that of six, and will contain it a certain
number of times. Thus the price of an estate is nothing
else but its revenue multiplied a certain number of times;
twenty times if the price is a hundred and twenty sheep;
thirty times if one hundred and eighty sheep. And so the
current price of land is reckoned by the proportion of the
value of the revenue; and the number of times, that the
price of the sale contains that of the revenue, is called so
many years purchase of the land. They are sold at the
price of twenty, thirty, or forty years purchase, when on

purchasing

purchasing them we pay twenty, thirty, or forty times their revenue. It is also not less evident, that this price must vary according to the number of purchasers, or sellers of land, in the same manner as other goods vary in a ratio to the different proportion between the offer and the demand.

§ 58. *All capital in money, and all amounts of value, are equivalent to land producing a revenue equal to some portion of that capital or value. First employment of capitals. Purchase of lands.*

Let us now go back to the time after the introduction of money. The facility of accumulating it has soon rendered it the most desirable part of personal property, and has afforded the means of augmenting, by economy, the quantity of it without limits. Whoever, either by the revenue of his land, or by the salary of his labour or industry, receives every year a higher income than he needs to spend, may lay up the residue and accumulate it : these accumulated values are what we name a capital. The pusillanimous miser, that keeps his money with the mere view of soothing his imagination against apprehension of distress in the uncertainty of futurity, keeps his money in a hoard. If the dangers he had foreseen should eventually take place, and he in his poverty be reduced to live every year·upon the treasure, or a prodigal successor lavish it by degrees, this treasure would soon be exhausted, and the capital totally lost to the possessor. The latter can draw a far greater advantage from it ; for an estate in land of a certain revenue, being but an equivalent of a sum of value equal to the revenue, taken a certain number of times, it follows, that any sum whatsoever of value is equivalent to an estate in land, producing a revenue equal to a fixed proportion of that sum. It is perfectly the same whether the amount of this capital consists in a mass of

39   metal,

metal, or any other matter, since money represents all
kinds of value, as well as all kinds of value represent
money. By these means the possessor of a capital may at
first employ it in the purchase of lands; but he is not
without other resources.

§ 59. *Another employment for money in advances for enterprises of manufacture or industry.*

I have already observed, that all kinds of labour, either
of cultivation or industry, required advances. And I
have shewn how the earth, by the fruits and herbages it
spontaneously produces for the nourishment of men and
animals, and by the trees, of which man has first formed
his utensils, had furnished the first advances for cultivation; and even of the first manual works a man can perform for his own service. For instance, it is the earth
that provides the stone, clay, and wood, of which the first
houses were built; and, before the division of professions,
when the same man that cultivated the earth provided
also for his other wants by his own labour, there was no
need of other advances. But when a great part of society
began to have no resource but in their hands, it was necessary that those who lived thus upon salaries, should
have somewhat before hand, that they might either procure themselves the materials on which they laboured, or
subsist during the time they were waiting for their salary.

§ 60. *Explanation of the use of the advances of capitals in enterprises of industry; on their returns and the profits they ought to produce.*

In early times, he that employed labouring people
under him, furnished the materials himself, and paid from
day to day the salaries of the workmen. It was the cul-

tivator

tivator or the owner himself that gave to the spinner the hemp he had gathered, and he maintained her during the time of her working. Thence he passed the yarn to a weaver, to whom he gave every day the salary agreed upon. But those slight daily advances can only take place in the coarsest works. A vast number of arts, and even of those arts indispensable for the use of the most indigent members of society, require that the same materials should pass through many different hands, and undergo, during a considerable space of time, difficult and various operations. I have already mentioned the preparation of leather, of which shoes are made. Whoever has seen the workhouse of a tanner, cannot help feeling the absolute impossibility of one, or even several indigent persons providing themselves with leather, lime, tan, utensils, &c. and causing the requisite buildings to be erected to put the tan house to work, and of their living during a certain space of time, till their leather can be sold. In this art, and many others, must not those that work on it have learned the craft before they presume to touch the materials, lest they should waste them in their first trials? Here then is another absolute necessity of advances. Who shall now collect the materials for the manufactory, the ingredients, the requisite utensils for their preparation? Who is to construct canals, markets, and buildings of every denomination? How shall that multitude of workmen subsist till the time of their leather being sold, and of whom none individually would be able to prepare a single skin; and where the emolument of the sale of a single skin could not afford subsistence to any one of them? Who shall defray the expences for the instruction of the pupils and apprentices? Who shall maintain them until they are sufficiently instructed, guiding them gradually from an easy labour proportionate to their age, to works that demand more vigour and ability? It must then be one of those proprietors of capitals, or moveable accumulated

property

property that must employ them, supplying them with advances in part for the construction and purchase of materials, and partly for the daily salaries of the workmen that are preparing them. It is he that must expect the sale of the leather, which is to return him not only his advances, but also an emolument sufficient to indemnify him for what his money would have procured him, had he turned it to the acquisition of lands, and moreover of the salary due to his troubles and care, to his risque, and even to his skill; for surely, upon equal profits, he would have preferred living without solicitude, on the revenue of land, which he could have purchased with the same capital. In proportion as this capital returns to him by the sale of his works, he employs it in new purchases for supporting his family and maintaining his manufactory; by this continual circulation, he lives on his profits, and lays by in store what he can spare to increase his stock, and to advance his enterprize by augmenting the mass of his capital, in order proportionably to augment his profits.

§ 61. *Subdivision of the industrious stipendiary class, in undertaking capitalists and simple workmen.*

Thus the whole class employed in supplying the different wants of society, with an immense variety of works of industry, is, if I may speak thus, subdivided into two classes. The one, of the undertakers, manufacturers and masters, all proprietors of large capitals, which they avail themselves of, by furnishing work to the other class, composed of artificers, destitute of any property but their hands, who advance only their daily labour, and receive no profits but their salaries.

§ 62. *Another*

§ 62. *Another employment of capitals, in advances towards undertakings of agriculture. Observations on the
use, and indispensable profits of capitals in undertakings
of agriculture.*

In speaking first of the placing of capitals in manufacturing enterprizes, I had in view to adduce a more
striking example, of the necessity and effect of large
advances, and of the course of their circulation. But I
have reversed the natural order, which seemed to require
that I should rather begin to speak of enterprizes of agriculture, which also can neither be performed, nor extended, nor afford any profit, but by means of considerable advances. It is the proprietors of great capitals,
who, in order to make them productive in undertakings
of agriculture, take leases of lands, and pay to the owners
large rents, taking on themselves the whole burthen of
advances. Their case must necessarily be the same as
that of the undertakers of manufactures. Like them, they
are obliged to make the first advances towards the undertaking, to provide themselves with cattle, horses, utensils
of husbandry, to purchase the first seeds; like them they
must maintain and nourish their carters, reapers, threshers,
servants, and labourers, of every denomination, who subsist only by their hands, who advance only their labour,
and reap only their salaries. Like them, they ought to
have not only their capital, I mean, all their prior and
annual advances returned, but, 1st, a profit equal to the
revenue they could have acquired with their capital, exclusive of any fatigue; 2ndly. The salary, and the price
of their own trouble, of their risk, and their industry;
3rdly. An emolument to enable them to replace the effects
employed in their enterprise, and the loss by waste, cattle
dying, and utensils wearing out, &c., all which ought to
be first charged on the products of the earth. The over-

plus

plus will serve the cultivator to pay to the proprietor, for the permission he has given him to make use of his field in the accomplishing of his enterprize ; that is, the price of the leasehold, the rent of the proprietor and the clear product : for all that the land produces, until reimbursement of the advances, and profits of every kind to him that has made these advances, cannot be looked upon as a revenue, but only as a reimbursement of the expences of the cultivation, since if the cultivator could not obtain them, he would be loath to risk his wealth and trouble in cultivating the field of another.

§ 63.   *The competition between the capitalists, undertakers of cultivation, fixes the current price of leases of lands.*

The competition between rich undertakers of cultivation fixes the current price of leases, in proportion to the fertility of the soil, and of the rate at which its productions are sold, always according to the calculation which farmers make both of their expenditures, and of the profits they ought to draw from their advances. They cannot give to the owners more than the overplus. But when the competition among them happens to be more animated, they sometimes render him the whole overplus, the proprietor leasing his land to him that offers the greatest rent.

§ 64.   *The default of capitalists, undertakers, limits the cultivation of lands to a small extent.*

When, on the contrary, there are no rich men that possess capitals large enough to embark in enterprizes of agriculture; when, through the low rate of the productions of the earth, or any other cause, the crops are not sufficient to ensure to the undertakers, besides the reimbursement of their capital, emoluments adequate at least

to those they would derive from their money, by employing it in some other channel; there are no farmers that
offer to lease lands, the proprietors are constrained to hire
mercenaries or *metayers*, which are equally unable to
make any advances, or duly to cultivate it. The proprietor himself makes moderate advances, which only
produce him an indifferent revenue : If the land happens
to belong to an owner, poor, negligent, and in debt, to a
widow, or a minor, it remains unmanured; such is the
principle of the difference I have observed between provinces, where the lands are cultivated by opulent farmers,
as in Normandy and the Isle de France, and those where
they are cultivated only by indigent mercenaries, as in
Limousin, Angoumois, Bourbonnois, and several others.

§ 65. *Subdivision of the class of cultivators into under-*
   takers, or farmers, and hired persons, servants, and
   day-labourers.

Hence it follows, that the class of cultivators may be
divided, like that of manufacturers, into two branches,
the one of undertakers or capitalists, who make the advances, the other of simple stipendiary workmen. It
results also, that capitals alone can form and support
great enterprizes of agriculture, that give to the lands an
unvariable value, if I may use the expression, and that
secure to the proprietors a revenue always equal, and the
largest possible.

§ 66. *Fourth employment of capitals, in advances for*
   enterprizes of commerce. Necessity of the interposition
   of merchants, properly so called, between the producers
   of the commodities and the consumers.

The undertakers either in cultivation or manufacture,
draw their advances and profits only from the sale of the
fruits

fruits of the earth, or the commodities fabricated. It is always the wants and the ability of the consumer that sets the price on the sale; but the consumer does not want the produce prepared or fitted up at the moment of the crop, or the perfection of the work. However, the under-takers want their stocks immediately and regularly reim-bursed, to embark in fresh enterprizes : the manuring and the seed ought to succeed the crops without interruption. The workmen of a manufacture are unceasingly to be employed in beginning other works, in proportion as the first are distributed, and to replace the materials in propor-tion as they are consumed. It would not be advisable to stop short in an enterprize once put in execution, nor is it to be presumed that it can be begun again at any time. It is then the strictest interest of the undertaker, to have his capital quickly reimbursed by the sale of his crop or commodities. On the other hand, it is the consumer's interest to find, when and where he wishes it, the things he stands in need of; it would be extremely inconvenient for him to be necessitated to make, at the time of the crop, his provision for the whole course of a year. Among the objects of usual consumption, there are many that require long and expensive labours, labours that cannot be undertaken with profit, except on a large quantity of materials, and on such as the consumption of a small number of inhabitants of a limited district, may not be sufficient for even the sale of the work of a single manu-factory. Undertakings of this kind must then necessarily be in a reduced number, at a considerable distance from each other, and consequently very distant from the habi-tations of the greater number of consumers. There is no man, not oppressed under the extremest misery, that is not in a situation to consume several things, which are neither gathered nor fabricated, except in places con-siderably distant from him, and not less distant from each other. A person that could not procure himself the ob-

46   jects

jects of his consumption but in buying it directly from the hand of him that gathers or works it, would be either unprovided with many commodities, or pass his life in wandering after them.

This double interest which the person producing and the consumer have, the former to find a purchaser, the other to find where to purchase, and yet not to waste useful time in expecting a purchaser, or in finding a seller, has given the idea to a third person to stand between the one and the other. And it is the object of the mercantile profession, who purchase goods from the hands of the person who produces them, to store them in warehouses, whither the consumer comes to make his purchase. By these means the undertaker, assured of the sale and the re-acquisition of his funds, looks undisturbed and indefatigably out for new productions, and the consumer finds within his reach and at once, the objects of which he is in want.

§ 67. *Different orders of merchants. They all have this in common, that they purchase to sell again; and that their traffic is supported by advances which are to revert with a profit, to be engaged in new enterprizes.*

From the green-woman who exposes her ware in a market, to the merchants of Nantz or Cadiz, who traffic even to India and America, the profession of a trader, or what is properly called commerce, divides into an infinity of branches, and it may be said of degrees. One trader confines himself to provide one or several species of commodities which he sells in his shop to those who chuse; another goes with certain commodities to a place where they are in demand, to bring from thence in exchange, such things as are produced there, and are wanted in the place from whence he departed : one makes his exchanges in his own neighbourhood, and by himself, another by

means

means of correspondents, and by the interposition of carriers, whom he pays, employs, and sends from one province to another, from one kingdom to another, from Europe to Asia, and from Asia back to Europe. One sells his merchandize by retail to those who use them, another only sells in large parcels at a time, to other traders who retail them out to the consumers: but all have this in common that they buy to sell again, and that their first purchases are advances which are returned to them only in course of time. They ought to be returned to them, like those of the cultivators and manufacturers; not only within a certain time, to be employed again in new purchases, but also, 1. with an equal revenue to what they could acquire with their capital without any labour; 2. with the value of their labour, of their risk, and of their industry. Without being assured of this return, and of these indispensable profits, no trader would enter into business, nor could any one possibly continue therein: tis in this view he governs himself in his purchases, on a calculation he makes of the quantity and the price of the things, which he can hope to dispose of in a certain time: the retailer learns from experience, by the success of limited trials made with precaution, what is nearly the wants of those consumers who deal with him. The merchant learns from his correspondents, of the plenty or scarcity, and of the price of merchandize in those different countries to which his commerce extends; he directs his speculations accordingly, he sends his goods from the country where they bear a low price to those where they are sold dearer, including the expence of transportation in the calculation of the advances he ought to be reimbursed. Since trade is necessary, and it is impossible to undertake any commerce without advances proportionable to its extent; we here see another method of employing personal property, a new use that the possessor of a parcel of commodities reserved and accumulated, of a sum of money,

in

in a word, *of a capital*, may make of it to procure himself subsistence, and to augment, his riches.

§ 68. *The true idea of the circulation of money.*

We see by what has been just now said, how the cultivation of lands, manufactures of all kinds, and all the branches of trade, depend on a mass of capital, or the accumulation of personal property, which, having been at first advanced by the undertakers, in each of these different branches, ought to return to them again every year with a regular profit; that is, the capital to be again invested, and advanced in the continuation of the same enterprizes, and the profits employed for the greater or less subsistence of the undertakers. It is this continued advance and return which constitutes what ought to be called the circulation of money : this useful and fruitful circulation, which animates all the labour of society, which supports all the motion, and is the life of the body politic, and which is with great reason compared to the circulation of the blood in the human body. For, if by any disorder in the course of the expenses of the different orders of society, the undertakers cease to draw back their advances with such profit as they have a right to expect; it is evident they will be obliged to reduce their undertakings; that the total of the labour, of the consumption of the fruits of the earth, of the productions and of the revenue would be equally diminished; that poverty will succeed to riches, and that the common workman, ceasing to find employ, will fall into the deepest misery.

§ 69. *All*

§ 69. *All extensive undertakings, particularly those of manufactures and of commerce, must indispensibly have been very confined, before the introduction of gold and silver in trade.*

It is almost unnecessary to remark, that undertakings of all kinds, but especially those of manufactures, and above all those of commerce, must, unavoidably be very confined, before the introduction of gold and silver in trade; since it was almost impossible to accumulate considerable capitals, and yet more difficult, to multiply and divide payments so much as is necessary, to facilitate and increase the exchanges to that extent, which a spirited commerce and circulation require. The cultivation of the land only may support itself to a certain degree, because the cattle are the principal cause of the advances required therein, and it is very probable, there is then no other adventurer in cultivation but the proprietor. As to arts of all kinds, they must necessarily have been in the greatest languor before the introduction of money; they were confined to the coarsest works, for which the proprietors supported the advances, by nourishing the workmen, and furnishing them with materials, or they caused them to be made in their own houses by their servants.

§ 70. *Capitals being as necessary to all undertakings as labour and industry, the industrious man shares voluntarily the profit of his enterprize with the owner of the capital, who furnishes him the funds he is in need of.*

Since capitals are the indispensable foundation of all lucrative enterprizes; since with money we can furnish means for culture, establish manufactures, and raise a commerce, the profits of which being accumulated and

frugally

frugally laid up, will become a new capital : since, in a word, money is the principal means to beget money ; those who with industry and the love of labour are destitute of capital, and have not sufficient for the undertaking they wish to embark in, have no difficulty in resolving to give up to the proprietors of such capital or money, who are willing to trust them, a portion of the profits which they are in expectation of gaining, over and above their advances.

§ 71. *Fifth employment of capitals, lending on interest ;*
nature of a loan.

The possessors of money balance the risk their capital may run, if the enterprise does not succeed, with the advantage of enjoying a constant profit without toil ; and regulate themselves thereby, to require more or less profit or interest for their money, or to consent to lend it for such an interest as the borrower offers. Here another opportunity opens to the possessor of money, viz. lending on interest, or the commerce of money. Let no one mistake me here, lending on interest is only a trade, in which the lender is a man who sells the use of his money, and the borrower one who buys ; precisely the same as the proprietor of an estate, or the person who farms it, buys and sells respectively the use of the hired land. The Latin term for a loan of money or interest, expresses it exactly, *usura pecuniæ,* a word which adopted into the French language is become odious, by a consequence of false ideas being adopted on the interest of money.

§ 72. *False ideas on lending upon interest.*

The rate of interest is by no means founded, as may be imagined, on the profit the borrower hopes to make, with the capital of which he purchases the use. This rate

like

like the price of all other merchandize, is fixed by the
circumstances of buyer and seller; by the proportion of
the sum offered with the demand. People borrow with
every kind of view, and with every sort of motive. One
borrows to undertake an enterprize that is to make his
fortune, another to buy an estate, another to pay his
losses at play, another to supply the loss of his revenue,
of which some accident has deprived him, another to
exist on, in expectation of what he is able to gain by his
labour; but all these motives which determine the borrower, are very indifferent to the lender. He attends to
two things only, the interest he is to receive, and the
safety of his capital. He never attends to the use the
borrower puts it to, as a merchant does not care to what
use the buyer applies the commodities he sells him.

§ 73.   *Errors of the schoolmen refuted.*

It is for want of having examined the lending of
money on interest in its true point of view, that moralists,
more rigid than enlightened, would endeavour to make us
look on it as a crime. Scholastic theologists have concluded, that as money itself was not prolific, it was unjust
to require a premium for the loan of it. Full of these
prejudices they have fancied their doctrine was sanctioned
by this passage in the Gospel, *mutuum date nihil inde
sperantes:* Those theologians who have adopted more
reasonable principles on the subject of interest of money,
have been branded with the harshest reproaches from
those who adopt the other side of the question.

Nevertheless, there are but few reflections necessary
to expose the trifling reasons that are adduced to condemn
the taking of interest. A loan of money is a reciprocal
contract, free between both parties, and entered into only
by reason of its being mutually advantageous. It is evi-

dent, if the lender finds an advantage in receiving an interest for his money, the borrower is not less interested in finding that money he stands in need of, since otherwise he would not borrow and submit himself to the payment of interest. Now on this principle, can any one look on such an advantageous contract as a crime, in which both parties are content, and which certainly does no injury to any other person? Let them say the lender takes advantage of the wants of the borrower, to force the payment of interest, this is talking as absurd as if we were to say, that a baker who demands money for the bread he sells, takes advantage of his customer's wants. If in this latter case, the money is an equivalent for the bread the buyer receives, the money which the borrower receives to day, is equally an equivalent for the capital and interest he agrees to pay at the expiration of a certain time; for in fact, it is an advantage to the borrower, to have, during that interval, the use of the money he stands in need of, and it is a disadvantage to the lender to be deprived of it. This disadvantage may be estimated, and it is estimated, the interest is the rate. This rate ought to be larger, if the lender runs a risk of losing his capital by the borrower becoming insolvent. The bargain therefore is perfectly equal on both sides and consequently, fair and honest. Money considered as a physical substance, as a mass of metal, does not produce any thing; but money made use of in advances in cultivation, in manufacture, in commerce, produces a certain profit; with money we can acquire land, and thereby procure a revenue : the person therefore who lends his money, does not only give up the unfruitful possession of such money, but deprives himsel. of the profit which it was in his power to procure by it, and the interest which indemnifies him from this loss cannot be looked upon as unjust. The schoolmen, compelled to acknowledge the justice of these considerations, have allowed that interest for money may be taken, provided

the

the capital is alienated, that is, provided the lender gave up his right to be reimbursed his money in a certain time, and permitted the borrower to retain it as long as he was inclined to pay the interest thereof only. The reason of this toleration was, that then it is no longer a loan of money for which an interest is paid, but a purchase, which is bought with a sum of money, as we purchase lands. This was a mode to which they had recourse, to comply with the absolute necessity which exists of borrowing money, in the course of the transactions of society, without fairly avowing the fallacy of those principles, upon which they had condemned the practice: but this clause for the alienation of the capital, is not an advantage to the borrower, who remains equally indebted to the lender, until he shall have repaid the capital, and whose property always remains as a security for the safety of such capital; —it is even a disadvantage, as he finds it more difficult to borrow money when he is in want of it; for persons who would willingly consent to lend for a year or two, a sum of money which they had destined for the purchase of an estate, would not lend it for an uncertain time. Besides, if they are permitted to sell their money for a perpetual rent, why may they not lend it for a certain number of years, for a rent which is only to continue for that term? If an interest of 1000 livres *per annum* is equivalent to the sum of 20000 livres from him to keep such a sum in perpetuity, 1000 livres will be an equivalent for the possession of that sum for one year.

§ 74. *True foundation of interest of money.*

A man then may lend his money as lawfully as he may sell it; and the possessor of money may either do one or the other, not only because money is equivalent to a revenue, and a means to procure a revenue: not only because the lender loses, during the continuance of the

loan,

loan, the revenue he might have procured by it; not only because he risks his capital; not only because the borrower can employ it in advantageous acquisitions, or in undertakings from whence he will draw a large profit: the proprietor of money may lawfully receive the interest of it, by a more general and decisive principle. Even if none of these circumstances should take place, he will not have the less right to require an interest for his loan, for this reason only, that his money is his own. Since it is his own, he has a right to keep it, nothing can imply a duty in him to lend it; if then he does lend, he may annex such a condition to the loan as he chuses, in this he does no injury to the borrower, since the latter agrees to the conditions, and has no sort of right over the sum lent. The profit which money can procure the borrower, is doubtless one of the most prevailing motives to determine him to borrow on interest; it is one of the means which facilitates his payment of the interest, but this is by no means that which gives a right to the lender to require it; it is sufficient for him that his money is his own, and this is a right inseparable from property. He who buys bread, does it for his support, but the right the baker has to exact a price is totally independent of the use of bread; the same right he would possess in the sale of a parcel of stones, a right founded on this principle only, that the bread is his own, and no one has any right to oblige him to give it up for nothing.

§ 75. *Answer to an objection.*

This reflection brings us to the consideration of the application made by an author, of the text, *mutuum date nihil inde sperantes,* and shews how false that application is, and how distant from the meaning of the Gospel. The passage is clear, as interpreted by modern and reasonable divines as a precept of charity. All mankind are

bound

bound to assist each other; a rich man who should see his fellow creature in distress, and who, instead of gratuitously assisting, should sell him what he needed, would be equally deficient in the duties of christianity and of humanity.   In such circumstances, charity does not only require us to lend without interest, she orders us to lend, and even to give if necessary.   To convert the precept of charity into a precept of strict justice, is equally repugnant to reason, and the sense of the text.   Those whom I here attack do not pretend that it is a duty of justice to lend their money; they must be obliged then to confess, that the first words of the passage, *mutuum date*, contain only a precept of charity.   Now I demand why they extend the latter part of this passage to a principle of justice.   What, is the duty of lending not a strict precept, and shall its accessory only, the condition of the loan, be made one;   it would have been said to man, " It is free for you to lend or not to lend, but if you do lend, take care you do not require any interest for your money, and even when a merchant shall require a loan of you for an undertaking, in which he hopes to make a large profit, it will be a crime in you to accept the interest he offers you; you must absolutely either lend to him gratuitously, or not lend to him all?   You have indeed one method to make the receipt of interest lawful, it is to lend your capital for an indefinite term, and to give up all right to be repaid it, which is to be optional to your debtor, when he pleases, or when he can.   If you find any inconvenience on the score of security, or if you foresee you shall want your money in a certain number of years, you have no other course to take but not to lend: It is better for you to deprive this merchant of this most fortunate opportunity, than to commit a sin by assisting him."   This is what they must have seen in these five words, *mutuum date nihil inde sperantes*, when they have read them under these false prejudices.

Every

Every man who shall read this text unprejudiced, will soon find its real meaning; that is, "as men, as Christians, you are all brothers, all friends; act towards each other as brethren and friends; help each other in your necessities; let your purses be reciprocally open to each other, and do not sell that assistance which you are mutually indebted to each other, in requiring an interest for a loan which charity requires of you as a duty." This is the true sense of the passage in question The obligation to lend without interest, and to lend, have evident relation to each other; they are of the same order, and both inculcate a duty of charity, and not a precept of rigorous justice, applicable to all cases of lending.

§ 76. *The rate of interest ought to be fixed, as the price of every other merchandize, by the course of trade alone.*

I have already said, that the price of money borrowed, is regulated like the price of all other merchandize, by the proportion of the money at market with the demand for it: thus, when there are many borrowers who are in want of money, the interest of money rises; when there are many possessors who are ready to lend, it falls. It is therefore an error to believe that the interest of money in trade ought to be fixed by the laws of princes. It has a current price fixed like that of all other merchandize. This price varies a little, according to the greater or less security which the lender has; but on equal security, he ought to raise and fall his price in proportion to the abundance of the demand, and the law no more ought to fix the interest of money than it ought to regulate the price of any other merchandizes which have a currency in trade.

§ 77. *Money has in commerce two different valuations.*
One expresses the quantity of money or silver we give
to procure different sorts of commodities; the other
expresses the relation a sum of money has, to the in-
terest it will procure in the course of trade.

It seems by this explanation of the manner in which
money is either sold or lent for an annual interest, that
there are two ways of valuing money in commerce. In
buying and selling a certain weight of silver represents a
certain quantity of labour, or of merchandize of every
species; for example, one ounce of silver is equal to a
certain quantity of corn, or to the labour of a man for a
certain number of days. In lending, and in the commerce of money, a capital is the equivalent of an equal
rent, to a determinate portion of that capital; and reciprocally an annual rent represents a capital equal to the
amount of that rent repeated a certain number of times,
according as interest is at a higher or lower rate.

§ 78. *These two valuations are independent of each other,*
and are governed by quite different principles.

These two different methods of fixing a value, have
much less connection, and depend much less on each
other than we should be tempted to believe at first sight.
Money may be very common in ordinary commerce, may
hold a very low value, answer to a very small quantity of
commodities, and the interest of money may at the same
time be very high.

I will suppose there are one million ounces of silver in
actual circulation in commerce, and that an ounce of
silver is given in the market for a bushel of corn. I will
suppose that there is brought into the country in some

manner or other, another million of ounces of silver, and this augmentation is distributed to every one in the same proportion as the first million, so that he who had before two ounces, has now four. The silver considered as a quantity of metal, will certainly diminish in price, or which is the same thing, commodities will be purchased dearer, and it becomes necessary, in order to procure the same measure of corn which he had before with one ounce of silver, to give more silver, perhaps two ounces instead of one. But it does not by any means follow from thence, that the interest of money falls, if all this money is carried to market, and employed in the current expences of those who possess it, as it is supposed the first million of ounces of silver was; for the interest of money falls only when there is a greater quantity of money to be lent, in proportion to the wants of the borrowers, than there was before. Now the silver which is carried to market is not to be lent; it is money which is hoarded up, which forms the accumulated capital for lending; and the augmentation of the money in the market, or the diminution of its price in comparison with commodities in the ordinary course of trade, are very far from causing infallibly, or by a necessary consequence, a decrease of the interest of money; on the contrary, it may happen that the cause which augments the quantity of money in the market, and which consequently increases the price of other commodities by lowering the value of silver, is precisely the same cause which augments the hire of money, or the rate of interest.

In effect, I will suppose for a moment, that all the rich people in a country, instead of saving from their revenue, or from their annual profits, shall expend the whole; that, not satisfied with expending their whole revenue, they dissipate a part of their capital; that a man who has 100,000 livres in money, instead of employing them in a profitable manner, or lending them, consumes

them

them by degrees in foolish expences; it is apparent that on one side there will be more silver employed in common circulation, to satisfy the wants and humours of each individual, and that consequently its value will be lowered; on the other hand there will certainly be less money to be lent; and as many people will in this situation of things ruin themselves, there will clearly be more borrowers. The interest of money will consequently augment, while the money itself will become more plenty in circulation, and the value of it will fall, precisely by the same cause.

We shall no longer be surprised at this apparent inconsistency, if we consider that the money brought into the market for the purchase of corn, is that which is daily circulated to procure the necessaries of life; but that which is offered to be lent on interest, is what is actually drawn out of that circulation to be laid by and accumulated into a capital.

§ 79. *In comparing the value of money with that of commodities, we consider silver as a metal, which is an object of commerce. In estimating the interest of money, we attend to the use of it during a determinate time.*

In the market a measure of corn is purchased with a certain weight of silver, or a quantity of silver is bought with a certain commodity, it is this quantity which is valued and compared with the value of other commodities. In a loan upon interest, the object of the valuation is the use of a certain quantity of property during a certain time. It is in this case no longer a mass of silver, compared with a quantity of corn, but it is a portion of effects compared with a certain portion of the same, which is become the customary price of that mass for a certain time. Let twenty thousand ounces of silver be an equivalent in the market for twenty thousand measures of corn, or only for ten thousand, the use of those twenty thousand

ounces

ounces of silver for a year is not worth less on a loan than the twentieth part of the principal sum, or one thousand ounces of silver, if interest is at five per cent.

§ 80. *The price of interest depends immediately on the proportion of the demand of the borrowers, with the offer of the lenders, and this proportion depends principally on the quantity of personal property, accumulated by an excess of revenue and of the annual produce to form capitals, whether these capitals exist in money or in any other kind of effects having a value in commerce.*

The price of silver in circulation has no influence but with respect to the quantity of this metal employed in common circulation; but the rate of interest is governed by the quantity of property accumulated and laid by to form a capital. It is indifferent whether this property is in metal or other effects, provided these effects, are easily convertible into money. It is far from being the case, that the mass of metal existing in a state, is as large as the amount of the property lent on interest in the course of a year; but all the capitals in furniture, merchandize, tools, and cattle, supply the place of silver and represent it. A paper signed by a man, who is known to be worth 100,000 livres, and who promises to pay 100 marks in a certain time is worth that sum; the whole property of the man who has signed this note is answerable for the payment of it, in whatever the nature of these effects consists, provided they are in value 100,000 livres. It is not therefore the quantity of silver existing as merchandize which causes the rate of interest to rise or fall, or which brings more money in the market to be lent; it is only the capitals existing in commerce, that is to say, the actual value of personal property of every kind accumulated, successively saved out of the revenues and profits to be employed by the possessors to procure them new revenues and new profits. It is these accumu-

lated

lated savings which are offered to the borrowers, and the more there are of them, the lower the interest of money will be, at least if the number of borrowers is not augmented in proportion.

§ 81. *The spirit of œconomy continually augments the amount of capitals, luxury continually tends to destroy them.*

The spirit of œconomy in any nation tends incessantly to augment the amount of the capitals, to increase the number of lenders, and to diminish that of the borrowers. The habit of luxury has precisely a contrary effect, and by what has been already remarked on the use of capitals in all undertakings, whether of cultivation, manufacture, or commerce, we may judge if luxury enriches a nation, or impoverishes it.

§ 82. *The lowering of interest proves, that in Europe œconomy has in general prevailed over luxury.*

Since the interest of money has been constantly diminishing in Europe for several centuries, we must conclude, that the spirit of œconomy has been more general than the spirit of luxury. It is only people of fortune who run into luxury, and among the rich, the sensible part of them confine their expences within their incomes, and pay great attention not to touch their capital. Those who wish to become rich are far more numerous in a nation than those which are already so. Now, in the present state of things, as all the land is occupied, there is but one way to become rich, it is either to possess, or to procure in some way or other, a revenue or an annual profit above what is absolutely necessary for subsistence, and to lay up every year in reserve to form a capital, by means of which they may obtain an increase of revenue

or

or annual profit, which will again produce another saving, and become capital. There are consequently a great number of men interested and employed in amassing capitals.

§ 83. *Recapitulation of the five different methods of employing capitals.*

I have reckoned five different methods of employing capitals, or of placing them so as to procure a profit.

1st. To buy an estate, which brings in a certain revenue.

2d. To employ money in undertakings of cultivation; in leasing lands whose produce should render back, besides the expences of farming, the interest on the advances, and a recompense for the labour of him who employs his property and attention in the cultivation.

3d. To place a capital in some undertaking of industry or manufactures.

4th. To employ it in commerce.

5th. To lend it to those who want it, for an annual interest.

§ 84. *The influence which the different methods of employing money have on each other.*

It is evident that the annual returns, which capitals, placed in different employs, will produce, are proportionate to each other, and all have relation to the actual rate of the interest of money.

§ 85. *Money invested in land, necessarily produces the least.*

The person who invests his money in land let to a solvent tenant, procures himself a revenue which gives
him

him very little trouble in receiving, and which he may
dispose of in the most agreeable manner, by indulging all
his inclinations.   There is a greater advantage in the purchase of this species of property, than of any other, since
the possession of it is more guarded against accidents.
We must therefore purchase a revenue in land at a higher
price, and must content ourselves with a less revenue for
an equal capital.

§ 86.   *Money on interest ought to bring a little more income, than land purchased with an equal capital.*

He who lends his money on interest, enjoys it still
more peaceably and freely than the possessor of land, but
the insolvency of his debtor may endanger the loss of his
capital.   He will not therefore content himself with an
interest equal to the revenue of the land which he could
buy with an equal capital.   The interest of money lent,
must consequently be larger than the revenue of an estate
purchased with the same capital; for if the proprietor
could find an estate to purchase of an equal income, he
would prefer that.

§ 87.   *Money employed in cultivation, manufactures, or commerce, ought to produce more than the interest of money on loan.*

By a like reason, money employed in agriculture, in
manufactures, or in commerce, ought to produce a more
considerable profit than the revenue of the same capital
employed in the purchase of lands, or the interest of
money on loan: for these undertakings, besides the capital advanced, requiring much care and labour, and if they
were not more lucrative, it would be much better to
secure an equal revenue, which might be enjoyed without

labour.

labour. It is necessary then, that, besides the interest of the capital, the undertaker should draw every year a profit to recompence him for his care, his labour, his talents, the risque he runs, and to replace the wear and tear of that portion of his capital which he is obliged to invest in effects capable of receiving injury, and exposed to all kinds of accidents.

§ 88. *Meantime the freedom of these various employments are limited by each other, and maintain, notwithstanding their inequality, a species of equilibrium.*

The different uses of the capitals produce very unequal profits; but this inequality does not prevent them from having a reciprocal influence on each other, nor from establishing a species of equilibrium among themselves, like that between two liquors of unequal gravity, and which communicate with each other by means of a reversed syphon, the two branches of which they fill; there can be no height to which the one can rise or fall, but the liquor in the other branch will be affected in the same manner.

I will suppose, that on a sudden, a great number of proprietors of lands are desirous of selling them. It is evident that the price of lands will fall, and that with a less sum we may acquire a larger revenue; this cannot come to pass without the interest of money rising, for the possessors of money would chuse rather to buy lands, than to lend at a lower interest than the revenue of the lands they could purchase. If, then, the borrowers want to have money, they will be constrained to pay a greater rate. If the interest of the money increases, they will prefer lending it, to setting out in a hazardous manner on enterprizes of agriculture, industry, and commerce: and they will be aware of any enterprizes but those that produce, besides the retribution for their trouble, an emolu-

65 ment

ment by far greater than the rate of the lender's produce. In a word, if the profits, springing from an use of money, augment or diminish, the capitals are converted by withdrawing them from other employings, or are withdrawn by converting them to other ends, which necessarily alters, in each of those employments, the proportion of profits on the capital to the annual product. Generally, money converted into property in land, does not bring in so much as money on interest ; and money on interest brings less than money used in laborious enterprizes : but the produce of money laid out in any way whatever, cannot augment or decrease without implying a proportionate augmentation, or decrease in other employments of money.

§ 89. *The current interest of money is the standard by which the abundance or scarcity of capitals may be judged ; it is the scale on which the extent of a nation's capacity for enterprizes in agriculture, manufactures, and commerce, may be reckoned.*

Thus the current interest of money may be considered as a standard of the abundance or scarcity of capitals in a nation, and of the extent of enterprizes of every denomination, in which she may embark : it is manifest, that the lower the interest of money is, the more valuable is the land. A man that has an income of fifty thousand livres, if the land is sold but at the rate of twenty years purchase is an owner of only one million ; he has two millions, if the land is sold at the rate of forty. If the interest is at five per cent. any land to be brought into cultivation would continue fallow, if, besides the recovery of the advances, and the retribution due to the care of the cultivator, its produce would not afford five per cent. No manufactory, no commerce can exist, that does not bring in five per cent. exclusively of the salary and equivalents

for

for the risque and trouble of the undertaker. If there is a neighbouring nation in which the interest stands only at two per cent. not only it will engross all the branches of commerce, from which the nation where an interest at five per cent. is established, is excluded, but its manufacturers and merchants, enabled to satisfy themselves with a lower interest, will also sell their goods at a more moderate price, and will attract the almost exclusive commerce of all articles, which they are not prevented to sell by particular circumstances of excessive dearth, and expences of carriages, from the nation in which the interest bears five per cent.

§ 90. *Influence of the rate of interest of money on all lucrative enterprizes.*

The price of the interest may be looked upon as a kind of level, under which all labour, culture, industry, or commerce, acts. It is like a sea expanded over a vast country; the tops of the mountains rise above the surface of the water, and form fertile and cultivated islands. If this sea happens to give way, in proportion as it descends, sloping ground, then plains and vallies appear, which cover themselves with productions of every kind. It wants no more than a foot elevation, or falling, to inundate or to restore culture to unmeasurable tracts of land. It is the abundance of capitals that animates enterprize; and a low interest of money is at the same time the effect and a proof of the abundance of capitals.

§ 91. *The total Riches of a nation consists, 1. in the clear revenue of all the real estates, multiplied by the rate of the price of land. 2. in the sum of all the moveable riches existing in a nation.*

Real estates are equivalent to any capital equal to their annual revenue, multiplied by the current rate at which

lands

lands are sold. Thus if we add the revenue of all lands, viz.
the clear revenue they render to the proprietor, and to all
those that share in the property, as the lord that levies a
rent, the curate that levies the tythe, the sovereign that
levies the tax; if say I, we should add all these sums,
and multiply them by the rate at which lands are sold,
we would have the sum of all the wealth of a nation in
real estates.   To have the whole of a nation's wealth,
the moveable riches ought to be joined, which consist in
the sum of capitals converted into enterprizes of culture,
industry, and commerce, which is never lost; as all
advances, in any kind of undertaking, must unceasingly
return to the undertaker, to be unceasingly converted
into enterprizes, which without that could not be continued.   It would be a gross mistake to confound the immense mass of moveable riches with the mass of money
that exists in a state; the latter is a small object in comparison with the other.   To convince one's self of this,
we need only remember the immense quantity of beasts,
utensils, and seed, which constitute the advances of agriculture; the materials, tools, moveables, and merchan-
dises of every kind, that fill up the work-houses, shops,
and warehouses of all manufacturers, of all merchants,
and of all traders, and it will be plain, that in the totality
of riches either real or moveable of a nation, the specie
makes but an inconsiderable part: but all riches and
money being continually exchangeable, they all represent
money, and money represents them all.

§ 92. *The sum of lent capitals cannot be understood*
without a two-fold reckoning.

We must not include in the calculation of the riches
of a nation the sum of lent capitals; for the capitals
could only be lent either to proprietors of lands, or to

undertakers

undertakers to enhance their value in their enterprizes, since there are but these two kinds of people that can answer for a capital, and discharge the interest: a sum of money lent to people that have neither estate nor industry, would be a dead capital, and not an active one. If the owner of land of 400,000 livres borrows 100,000, his land is charged with a rent that diminishes his revenue by that sum. If he should sell it; out of the 400,000 livres he would receive, 100,000 are the property of the creditor. By these means the capital of the lender would always form, in the calculation of existing riches, a double estimate. The land is always worth 400,000*l.* when the proprietor borrows 100,000*l.* that does not make 500,000*l.* it only follows, that in the 400,000*l.* one hundred thousand belongs to the lender, and that there remains no more than 300,000*l.* to the borrower.

The same double estimate would have place in the calculation, if we should comprehend in the total calculation of capitals, the money lent to an undertaker to be employed in advance for his undertaking; it only results, that that sum, and the part of the profits which represents the interest, belongs to the lender. Let a merchant employ 10,000 livres of his property in his trade, and engross the whole profit, or let him have those 10,000 livres borrowed of another, to whom he pays the interest, and is satisfied with the overplus of profit, and the salary of his industry, it still makes only 10,000 livres.

But if we cannot include, without making a double estimate in the calculation of national riches, the capital of the money lent on interest, we ought to call in the other kinds of moveables, which though originally forming an object of expence, and not carrying any profit, become, however, by their durability, a true capital, that constantly increases; and which, as it may occasionally be exchanged for money, is as if it was a stock in store, which may enter into commerce and make good, when

69   necessary

necessary, the loss of other capitals. Such are the moveables of every kind; jewels, plates, paintings, statues, ready money shut up in chests by misers: all those matters have a value, and the sum of all those values may make a considerable object among wealthy nations. Yet be it considerable or not, it must always be added to the price of real estates, and to that of circulating advances in enterprizes of every denomination, in order to form the total sum of the riches of a nation. As for the rest, it is superfluous to say, though it is easy to be defined, as we have just done, in what consists the totality of the riches of a nation; it is probably impossible to discover to how much they amount, unless some rule be found out to fix the proportion of the total commerce of a nation, with the revenue of its land: a feasible thing, but which has not been executed as yet in such a manner as to dispel all doubts.

§ 93. *In which of the three classes of society the lenders of money are to be ranked.*

Let us see now, how what we have just discussed about the different ways of employing capitals, agrees with what we have before established about the division of all the members of society into three classes, the one the productive class of husbandmen, the industrious or trading class, and the disposing class, or the class of proprietors.

§ 94. *The lender of money belongs, as to his person, to the disposing class.*

We have seen that every rich man is necessarily possessor either of a capital in moveable riches, or funds equivalent to a capital. Any estate in land is of equal value with a capital; consequently every proprietor is a capitalist, but not every capitalist a proprietor of a real estate;

estate; and the possessor of a moveable capital may chuse to confer it on acquiring funds, or to improve it in enterprizes of the cultivating class, or of the industrious class. The capitalist, turned an undertaker in culture or industry, is no more of the disposing class, than the simple workmen in those two lines; they are both taken up in the continuation of their enterprizes. The capitalist who keeps to the lending money, lends it either to a proprietor or to an undertaker. If he lends it to a proprietor, he seems to belong to the class of proprietors, and he becomes co-partitioner in the property; the income of the land is destined to the payment of the interest of his trust; the value of the funds is equal to the security of his capital.

If the money-lender has lent to an undertaker, it is certain that his person belongs to the disposing class; but his capital continues destined to the advances of the enterpriser, and cannot be withdrawn without hurting the enterprise, or without being replaced by a capital of equal value.

§ 95. *The use which the money-lender makes of his interest.*

Indeed, the interest he draws from that capital seems to make him of the disposing class, since the undertaker and the enterprize may shift without it.   It seems also we may form an inference, that in the profits of the two laborious classes, either in the culture of the earth or industry, there is a disposable portion, namely, that which answers to the interest of the advances, calculated on the current rate of interest of money lent; it appears also that this conclusion seems to agree with what we have said, that the mere class of proprietors had a revenue properly so called, a disposing revenue, and that all the members of the other classes had only salaries or profits.

This

This merits some future inquiry. If we consider the thousand crowns that a man receives annually, who has lent 60,000 livres, to a merchant, in respect to the use he may make of it, there is no doubt of this being perfectly disposable, since the enterprize may subsist without it.

§ 96. *The interest of the money is not disposable in one sense, viz. so as the state may be authorized to appropriate, without any inconvenience, a part to supply its wants.*

But it does not ensue that they are of the disposing class in such a sense, that the state can appropriate to itself with propriety a portion for the public wants. Those 1000 crowns are not a retribution, which culture or commerce bestows gratuitously on him that makes the advance; it is the price and the condition of this advance, independently of which the enterprize could not subsist. If this retribution is diminished, the capitalist will withdraw his money, and the undertaking will cease. This retribution ought then to be inviolable, and enjoy an entire immunity, because it is the price of an advance made for the enterprize, without which the enterprize could not exist. To encroach upon it, would cause an augmentation in the price of advances in all enterprizes, and consequently diminish the enterprizes themselves, that is to say, cultivation, industry, and commerce.

This answer should lead us to infer, that if we have said, that the capitalist who had lent money to a proprietor, *seemed* to belong to the class of proprietors, this *appearance* had somewhat equivocal in it which wanted to be elucidated. In fact, it is strictly true, that the interest of his money is not more disposable, that is, it is not more susceptible of retrenchment, than that of money lent to the undertakers in agriculture and commerce.

But

But the interest is equally the price of the free agreement, and they cannot retrench any part of it without altering or changing the price of the loan.

For it imports little to whom the loan has been made: if the price decreases or augments for the proprietor of lands, it will also decrease and augment for the cultivator, the manufacturer, and the merchant. In a word, the proprietor who lends money ought to be considered, as a dealer in a commodity absolutely necessary for the production of riches, and which cannot be at too low a price. It is also as unreasonable to charge this commerce with duties, as it would be to lay a duty on a dunghill which serves to manure the land. Let us conclude from hence, that the person who lends money belongs properly to the disposable class as to his person, because he has nothing to do; but not as to the nature of his property, whether the interest of his money is paid by the proprietor of land out of a portion of his income, or whether it is paid by an undertaker, out of a part of his profits designed to pay the interest of his advances.

§ 97. *Objection.*

It may doubtless be objected, that the capitalist may indifferently either lend his money, or employ it in the purchase of land; that in either case he only receives an equivalent for his money, and whichever way he has employed it, he ought not the less to contribute to the public charges.

§ 98. *Answer to this objection.*

I answer first, that in fact, when the capitalist has purchased an estate, the revenue will be equal as to him, to what he would have received for his money by lending it; but there is this essential difference with respect to

73 the

the state, that the price which he gives for his land, does not contribute in any respect to the income it produces. It would not have produced a less income, if he had not purchased it. This income, as we have already explained, consists in what the land produces, beyond the salary of the cultivators, of their profits, and the interest of their advances. It is not the same with the interest of money; it is the express condition of the loan, the price of the advance, without which the revenue or profits, which serve to pay it, could never exist.

I answer in the second place, that if the lands were charged separately with the contribution to the public expences, as soon as that contribution shall be once regulated, the capitalist who shall purchase these lands will not reckon as interest for his money, that part of the revenue which is affected by this contribution. The same as a man who now buys an estate, does not buy the tythe which the curate or clergy receives, but the revenue which remains after that tythe is deducted.

§ 99. *There exists no revenue strictly disposable in a state, but the clear produce of lands.*

It is manifest by what I have said, that the interest of money lent is taken on the revenue of lands, or on the profits of enterprizes of culture, industry, and commerce. But we have already shewn that these profits themselves were only a part of the production of lands; that the produce of land is divided in two portions; that the one was designed for the salary of the cultivator, for his profits, for the recovery and interest of his advances; and that the other was the part of the proprietor, or the revenue which the proprietor expended at his option, and from whence he contributes to the general expences of the state.

We have demonstrated, that what the other classes of

society received, was merely the salaries and profits paid, either by the proprietor upon his revenue, or by the agents of the productive class, on the part destined to their wants, and which they are obliged to purchase of the industrious class. Whether these profits be now distributed in wages to the workmen, in profits to undertakers, or in interests of advances, they do not change the nature, or augment the sum of the revenue produced by the productive class over and above the price of their labour, in which the industrious class does not participate, but as far as the price of their labour extends.

Hence it follows, that there is no revenue but the clear produce of land, and that all other profit is paid, either by that revenue, or makes part of the expenditure that serves to produce the revenue.

§ 100. *The land has also furnished the total of moveable riches, or existing capitals, and which are formed only by a portion of its productions reserved every year.*

Not only there does not exist, nor can exist, any other revenue than the clear produce of land, but it is the earth also that has furnished all capitals, that form the mass of all the advances of culture and commerce. It has produced, without culture, the first gross and indispensible advances of the first labourers; all the rest are the accumulated fruits of the œconomy of successive ages, since they have begun to cultivate the earth. This œconomy has effect not only on the revenues of proprietors, but also on the profits of all the members of laborious classes. It is even generally true, that, though the proprietors have more overplus, they spare less; for, having more treasure, they have more desires, and more passions; they think themselves better ensured of their fortune; and are more desirous of enjoying it contentedly, than to augment it; luxury is their pursuit. The stipendiary class, and

chiefly

chiefly the undertakers of the other classes, receiving profits proportionate to their advances, talents, and activity, have, though they are not possessed of a revenue properly so called, a superfluity beyond their subsistence; but, absorbed as they generally are, only in their enter-prizes, and anxious to increase their fortune; restrained by their labour from amusements and expensive passions; they save their whole superfluity, to re-convert it in other enterprizes, and augment it. The greater part of the undertakers in agriculture borrow but little, and they almost all rest on the capital of their own funds. The undertakers of other businesses, who wish to render their fortune stable, strive likewise to attain to the same state. Those that make their enterprizes on borrowed funds, are greatly in danger of failing. However, although capitals are formed in part by the saving of profits in the laborious classes, yet, as those profits spring always from the earth, they are almost all repaid, either by the revenue, or in the expences that serve to produce the revenue; it is evident, that the capitals are derived from the earth as well as the revenue, or rather that they are but an accumulation of a part of the riches produced by the earth, which the proprietors of the revenue, or those that share it, are able to lay by every year in store, without consuming it on their wants.

§ 101. *Although money is the direct object in saving, and it is, if we may call it so, the first foundation of capitals, yet money and specie form but an insensible part in the total sum of capitals.*

We have seen what an inconsiderable part money forms in the total sum of existing capitals, but it makes a very large one in the formation of them. In fact, almost all savings are only in money; it is in money that the revenue is paid to the proprietors, that the advances and

profits

profits are received by the undertakers of every kind ; it is their money which they save, and the annual increase of capitals happens in money; but all the undertakers make no other use of it, than immediately to convert it into the different kinds of effects on which their enter-prizes turn; thus, money returns into circulation, and the greater part of capitals exist only, as we have already explained it, in effects of different natures.

FINIS.

EXTRACT

FROM

AN INQUIRY

INTO THE

Nature of the CORN LAWS;

with a View to the

NEW CORN-BILL

Proposed for Scotland.

EDINBURGH:

1777.

EXTRACT

FROM

AN INQUIRY

INTO THE

Nature of the CORN LAWS;

with a View to the

NEW CORN-BILL

Proposed for Scotland.

EDINBURGH:

1777.

EXTRACT

FROM

AN INQUIRY

INTO THE

Nature of the Corn Laws, &c.

I FORESEE here a popular objection. It will be said, that the price to the farmer is so high only on account of the high rents and avaricious extortions of proprietors. " Lower (say they) your rents, and the farmer " will be able to afford his grain cheaper to the consumer." But if the avarice alone of the proprietors was the cause of the dearth of corn, whence comes it, I may ask, that the price of grain is always higher on the west than on the east coast of Scotland? Are the proprietors in the Lothians more tender-hearted and less avaricious than those of Clyddesdale? The truth is, nothing can be more groundless than these clamours against men of landed property. There is no doubt, but that they, as well as every other class of men, will be willing to augment their revenue as much as they can, and therefore will always accept of as high a rent for their land as is offered to them. Would merchants or manufactures do otherwise? Would either the one or the other of these

3   refuse,

refuse, for the goods he offers to sale in a fair open way, as high a price as the purchaser is inclined to give? If they would not, it is surely with a bad grace that they blame gentlemen for accepting such a rent for their land as farmers, who are supposed always to understand the value of it, shall chuse to offer them.

It is not, however, the rent of the land that determines the price of its produce, but it is the price of that produce which determines the rent of the land; although the price of that produce is often highest in those countries where the rent of land is lowest. This seems to be a paradox that deserves to be explained.

In every country there is a demand for as much grain as is sufficient to maintain all its inhabitants; and as that grain cannot be brought from other countries but at a considerable expence, on some occasions at a most exorbitant charge, it usually happens, that the inhabitants find it most for their interest to be fed by the produce of their own soil. But the price at which that produce can be afforded by the farmer varies considerably in different circumstances.

In every country there is a variety of soils, differing considerably from one another in point of fertility. These we shall at present suppose arranged into different classes, which we shall denote by the letters A, B, C, D, E, F, &c. the class A comprehending the soils of the greatest fertility, and the other letters expressing different classes of soils, gradually decreasing in fertility as you recede from the first. Now, as the expence of cultivating the least fertile soil is as great, or greater than that of the most fertile field; it necessarily follows, that if an equal quantity of corn, the produce of each field, can be sold at the same price, the profit on cultivating the most fertile soil must be much greater than that of cultivating the others; and as this continues to decrease as the sterility encreases, it must at length happen, that the expence of cultivating

4

some of the inferior classes will equal the value of the whole produce.

This being premised, let us suppose, that the class F includes all those fields whose produce in oat-meal, if sold at fourteen shillings *per* boll, would be just sufficient to pay the expence of cultivating them, without affording any rent at all: That the class E comprehended those fields, whose produce, if sold at thirteen shillings *per* boll, would free the charges, without affording any rent; and that in like manner the classes D, C, B, and A, consisted of fields, whose produce, if sold respectively at twelve, eleven, ten, and nine shillings *per* boll, would exactly pay the charge of culture, without any rent.

Let us now suppose that all the inhabitants of the country, where such fields are placed, could be sustained by the produce of the first four classes, viz. A, B, C, and D. It is plain, that if the average selling price of oat-meal in that country was twelve shillings *per* boll, those who possessed the fields D, could just afford to cultivate them, without paying any rent at all; so that if there were no other produce of the fields that could be reared at a smaller expence than corn, the farmer could afford no rent whatever to the proprietor for them. And if so, no rents could be afforded for the fields E and F; nor could the utmost avarice of the proprietor in this case extort a rent for them. In these circumstances, however, it is obvious, that the farmer who possessed the fields in the class C could pay the expence of cultivating them, and also afford to the proprietor a rent equal to one shilling for every boll of their produce; and in like manner the possessors of the fields B and A could afford a rent equal to two and three shillings *per* boll of their produce respectively. Nor would the proprietors of these fields find any difficulty in obtaining these rents; because farmers, finding they could live equally well upon such soils, though paying these rents, as they could do upon the fields D

5 without

without any rent at all, would be equally willing to take the one as the other.

But let us again suppose, that the whole produce of the fields A, B, C and D, was *not* sufficient to maintain the whole of the inhabitants. If the average selling price should continue at twelve shillings *per* boll, as none of the fields E or F could admit of being cultivated, the inhabitants would be under the necessity of bringing grain from some other country, to supply their wants. But if it should be found, that grain could not be brought from that other country, at an average, under thirteen shillings *per* boll, the price in the home-market would rise to that rate; so that the fields E could then be brought into culture, and those of the class D could afford a rent to the proprietor equal to what was formerly yielded by C, and so on of others; the rents of every class rising in the same proportion. ·If these fields were sufficient to maintain the whole of the inhabitants, the price would remain permanently at thirteen shillings; but if there was still a deficiency, and if that could not be made up for less than fourteen shillings *per* boll, the price would rise in the market to that rate; in which case the field F might also be brought into culture, and the rents of all the others would rise in proportion.

To apply this reasoning to the present case, it appears, that the people in the Lothians can be maintained by the produce of the fields A, B, C, D, and E, but the inhabitants of Clyddesdale require also the produce of the fields F; so that the one is under the necessity of giving, at an average, one shilling *per* boll more for meal than the other.

Let us now suppose, that the gentlemen of Clyddesdale, from an extraordinary exertion of patriotism, and an inordinate desire to encourage manufactures, should resolve to lower their rents, so as to demand nothing from those who posssessed the fields E, as well as those of the class

6　　　　　　　　　　　　　　　　F, and

F, and should allow the rents of all the others to sink in proportion; would the prices of grain fall in consequence of this? By no means. The inhabitants are still in need of the whole produce of the fields F as before, and are under the necessity of paying the farmer of these fields such a price as to enable him to cultivate them. He must therefore still receive fourteen shillings *per* boll as formerly. And as the grain from the fields E, D, C, B, and A, are at least equally good, the occupiers of such of these fields would receive the same price for their produce. The only consequence, then, that would result from this quixotic scheme, would be the enriching one class of farmers at the expence of their proprietors, without producing the smallest benefit to the consumers of grain— perhaps the reverse, as the industry of these farmers might be slackened by this measure.

If, on the other hand, by any political arrangement, the price of oat-meal should be there reduced from fourteen to thirteen shillings *per* boll, it would necessarily follow, that all the fields of the class F would be abandoned by the plough, and the rents of the others would fall of course: but with that fall of rent, the quantity of grain produced would be diminished, and the inhabitants would be reduced to the necessity of depending on others for their daily bread. Thus it appears, that rents are not at all arbitrary, but depend on the market-price of grain; which, in its turn, depends upon the effective demand that is for it, and the fertility of the soil in the district where it is raised: so that lowering of rents alone could never have the effect of rendering grain cheaper.

A

TREATISE

ON THE

MARITIME LAWS

OF

RHODES.

———❦———

BY ALEXANDER C. SCHOMBERG, M.A.
FELLOW OF MAGDALEN COLLEGE, OXFORD.

═══════════

OXFORD:

SOLD BY D. PRINCE AND J. COOKE.

J. F. AND C. RIVINGTON, P. ELMSLY, AND
T. PAYNE AND SON, LONDON.
M.DCC.LXXXVI.

ADVERTISEMENT.

ANY research which tends to gratify a learned curiosity is at least innocent and amusing. If it serves at the same time to explain the manners and customs of a remote age, or to illustrate any trait of national character, it may justly be deemed both interesting and profitable. Few branches of literature can attain this important end so successfully as that which has for its subject the laws and polity of states; and there is none perhaps which has reflected stronger light upon public and domestic history, or proved a finer comment upon ancient philosophy and polite letters, than the liberal study of juridical antiquities. How far the truth of this observation may appear in the following pages I will not presume to say. They were originally designed to form a part of the illustrations annexed to the Chronological View, but finding the materials more copious than were at first imagined, I determined to lay them before the public in a separate treatise. By their judgment it must be determined how far an enquiry into the maritime laws of Rhodes may contribute to the amusement of the classical reader, or to the utility of the student of civil law.

A
TREATISE
ON THE
MARITIME LAWS
OF
RHODES.

THE Baron de Montesquieu has observed, that the laws of a well-regulated maritime state must necessarily be more varied and comprehensive than those of any other.* The reason is obvious. It is in such a state that the commercial spirit is usually found to be most active. This activity produces an extensive communication, which drawing together into one city the inhabitants of different countries, gives rise to a multitude of customs, interests and engagements, unknown to an inland people. " Dissimilitudo civitatum, says Tully, varietatem juris habeat necesse est.†　So that in order to adjust the controversies incident to this intercourse of nations, a peculiar jurisdiction is requisite, and certain principles of general jurisprudence must be adopted to conduct litigations and decide cases which do not fall within the reach of municipal polity.　To such an establishment Xenophon alludes, when, pointing out the means of encreasing the public revenue, he exorts his countrymen to erect a kind of maritime tribunal, and to bestow rewards upon such

5　　　　　　　　　　　　　　　　　of

---

* Esprit des Loix. Liv. 20. cap. 16.　　　† Pro Balbo. §. 13.

of the judges as should distinguish themselves by a diligent discharge of their function.*

That a people who so happily applied the principles of
sound philosophy and natural justice to the various exigencies of civil life, and who constructed a juridical system
more durable and extensive than their empire,† should
never have struck out any thing original in this essential
branch of legislation may appear somewhat singular. The
Romans did not even take the pains to digest or arrange
the materials which they borrowed; and while they carried
every other part of jurisprudence to the highest pitch of
accuracy and refinement, were content to stand indebted
to one of their provinces both for the form and matter of
their maritime code.

It is the purport of the following treatise to attempt
an elucidation of this point, by shewing that the conduct
of the Romans was perfectly consistent with their national
character and form of government; and that the peculiar
excellence of the Rhodian laws amply justified their
adoption.

It seems to be generally agreed that the Romans were
never very conspicuous as a *maritime power*, either in a
military or a commercial light. Many years had elapsed
from the foundation of their city before they became possessed of any thing that resembled a marine establishment, and though toward the latter age of the republic
we read of some very surprizing naval exertions, the sea

6   certainly

---

* Πόροι. p. 728. edit. Leunclav. The *Naval Duumvirs* had no
judicial authority at Rome; but in the lower empire there seems to
have been an officer like our *Consul*. Cod. Theodos. L. 7. De
Naviculariis.

† " Tanta sapientia fuisse Roma *in Jure constituendo* putanda
est, quanta fuit in his tantis opibus *Imperii* comparandis." *De Orat*
I. §. 44.

certainly was not their favourite element.* Polybius informs us that before the first Punic war, they had never been engaged in an action at sea, and being ignorant of the art of ship-building, had till that time been accustomed to navigate in hired vessels. The same writer indeed has given us some ancient treaties between Rome and Carthage, the first of which carries us back to the year of the city 245, and contains, among other curious particulars, certain restrictions on Roman fleets visiting the coasts of Africa, and on their trade both there and in the island of Sardinia; but it must be observed, that though this appears at first sight to contradict what has been asserted of their ignorance in naval matters, it will be found perfectly consistent, if we recollect the vicinity of these countries to the coast of Italy.† The constant wars in which Rome was involved with her neighbours, during the first five centuries, may be a reason why she paid so little attention to naval affairs. We find the smaller states of Italy very early on the sea, and engaged in considerable commerce for those times; particularly the Tarentines, Tyrrhenians, Spinetes and Liburnians, the latter of whom gave name to the most commodious kind of vessels used by the Romans. The city of Spina also, according to

7   Dionysius,

---

* It is worthy remark that there is no trace of any maritime law in the XII Tables, though at the time of the embassy into Greece, those of Rhodes may be supposed to have had very extensive influence.

Montesquieu's reason for this is perhaps too refined, see *Esprit des Loix*, Liv. 21. c. 9.

† Polybii. *Hist.* Lib. 3. cap. 22. et seq. He tells us these *Treaties* were copied by him with great difficulty from some obscure originals on brazen tablets in the Capitol. Barbeyrac, in his *Supplement* to the *Corps Diplomatique*, has given some acute remarks on them. Tom. i. Art. xcvii. ccli. ccxcvii. cccxxxii. and they have been ably illustrated by Professor Heyne in some *Gottingen Dissertations*, Anno. 1780.

Dionysius, became very powerful ; and some idea may be
formed of its opulence from the many rich presents
brought by this state to the temple at Delphi.

The encreasing power and haughtiness of Carthage at
last exciting the jealousy of Rome, taught her the necessity of supporting a marine force, and the famous victory
of Duillius, the first fruits of her application to naval
business, encouraged her to persevere in it.* By an
unexampled instance of exertion she in a few months
constructed a navy which enabled her to maintain a
superiority at sea, as is evident from her success soon
afterwards against the Macedonians, and from the event
of the third Punic war, which ended in the total destruction of her rival.†

After this she sent out a very respectable fleet against
the piratical confederacy, which had received considerable
strength by a junction with the ruined inhabitants of
Carthage and Corinth. They invested every part of the
Mediterranean, and hovering about the mouth of the
Tiber, effectually cut off the communication between
Rome, and Sicily, the principal granary of the city. It
was upon this occasion that Pompey was invested with the
sole command of the whole Roman navy, (a species of
authority never before entrusted to an individual) and with
a fleet of more than five hundred sail held absolute sway

8   over

---

* The singular privilege which Duillius enjoyed in consequence
of this victory, of being preceded at night by torches and music,
gave great offence to many of the graver Romans. Cicero mentions
his having often met him, when a boy, with this pompous attendance, and exclaims *tantum licentiæ dabat gloria !* De Senectute : and
Florus observes upon it, that it seemed to him, like " a diurnal
repetition of a triumph, which other conquerors were modest
enough to confine to a single day."   Lib. 2. cap. 2. §. 10.

† It was soon after the destruction of Carthage that Rome established a *trade* between *Utica* on the African coast and the island of
Delos, from whence she annually imported *slaves* into the city.

over the sea and the coasts, from the pillars of Hercules to the Thracian Bosphorous. He totally broke the piratical league, and, in order to prevent its reunion on the seas, settled its members in a large track of country at a great distance from the coast.*

The dominion of the sea became much more confirmed and extended under the emperors, some few of whom were naturally inclined to favour it. In the Code of Theodosius is a law of Constantine and Julian which confers the rank of knight upon those who had borne a naval command with honour; and another of Valentinian, which encourages persons of distinction to serve their country in that station. Dionysius of Halicarnassus terms Rome the mistress of the sea, not of the Mediterranean only, but of whatever parts were navigable, and says that she maintained considerable fleets.† The extent of her power 150 years after this, is specified by Appian, who mentions the islands of the Mediterranean and Egean seas; the Cyclades, Sporades, Cyprus, Crete, Rhodes and Lesbos, as subject to her; and in the days of Arcadius and Honorius we find she had large fleets constantly stationed at Alexandria, Carthage, Seleucia, and in the Euxine, besides others of smaller note in the ports of Italy and the islands.‡

It is extraordinary that with all this authority in their hands, the Romans should have been ignorant of the true advantages to be derived from naval power. In all their equipments, the principal object was to extend their empire, or to keep in awe the refractory provinces. Their fleets were seldom employed to open new communications, to discover new people, or to protect and encourage com-

9   mercial

---

* Florus, Lib. 3. cap. 6.   † Lib. 1.
‡ Cod. Lib. 12. tit. 60.   Cod. Theodos Lib. 8. tit. 7. §. 14. Cod. Lib. 12. tit. 24. §. 2.

mercial intercourse with distant climates. Except when they attended the corn ships from Sicily and Alexandria, or convoyed home the spoils of some conquered country, we never hear of their being upon the seas but for military purposes.* This (says a writer who cannot be too often quoted) was perfectly suitable with the national genius of " a people of soldiers, whose *trade* was their *sword,* and whose sword supplied all the advantages of trade, who brought the treasures of the world into their own exchequer, without exporting any thing but their personal bravery ; who raised the public revenues, not by the culture of Italy, but by the tributes of provinces; who had Rome for their mansion and the world for their farm. In consequence of this martial spirit, adds he, they lived on terms of defiance with all mankind. This proved fatal to factories and correspondence. The world was in arms, and insurances and under-writing were but a dead letter."† In a state where the military spirit thus pervaded every rank and condition of life, it was not probable that many should have either leisure or inclination for the pursuit of gain. *Quisque Hostem ferire, Murum ascendere, conspici dum tale facinus faceret properabat ; eas divitias, eam bonam famam, magnamque nobilitatem putabant* was the sketch which Sallust drew of the infant features of the republic, and the likeness was

10 tolerably

---

* This appears from the evidence of medals and inscriptions, where the emblems and titles are uniformly of a military cast. See Morisoti *Orbis Maritimus.* Lib. 1. cap. 26.

The corn traders were very early incorporated, and enjoyed privileges at Rome. Dig. lib. 3. tit. 4. et Cod. Theodos. tit. *De Naviculariis.* There were also officers appointed to superintend the distribution of this commodity, called *Præfecti Annonæ,* nearly upon the same plan as the French *Commissaires Des Vivres.* Dig. lib. 48. tit. 12. *De Lege Juliá, De Annoná.*

† Taylor's *Elements of Civil Law.* Art. *Property.* pp. 501. 504.

tolerably preserved even at the time he wrote,* except the contentions of the *forum* then engrossed almost as much of their attention as those of the *field.*

But the interests of commerce were not only neglected by the Romans: it appears from some of their best writers and from various regulations in the law books, that mercantile pursuits met with peculiar discouragement, and that trade, of whatever denomination, was expressly forbidden to men of noble or illustrious families; because, says Livy, " Quæstus omnis indecorus Patribus visus est," tho' in a law of Honorius, which forbids all men of family and fortune, or such as had borne any public offices, to engage in trade, a different reason is assigned, " Ut inter plebcios et negotiatores facilius fit emendi, vendendique commercium ;" † from the idea that a bargain is likely to be more just when the buyer and seller are on a level. The same honest principle, no doubt, which led the Greek Emperor to condemn to the flames a vessel richly laden which had been freighted by his wife.‡

As a further restriction, the merchant and mechanic were prevented by law from holding any dignity or exercising any office in the state; were forbidden to wear a sword, except on journeys, under certain restrictions; and

11   by

---

* *Bell. Catilin.* Every Roman was by birth a soldier, nor did he think it honourable to quit his profession, or exchange it for another, as long as he had vigour to pursue it. Cod. 4. 65. 31. *Canitiem* Galeâ premimus," says the poet. Though strictly speaking the time of necessary service (the *ætas robusta* or *militaris* as it is called) terminated with the xlvith year. D. 48. 5. 15.

† Liv. xxi. §. 63.

‡ Zonaras, lib. 3. Montesquieu has given an example of the truth of this maxim in the conduct of the Portuguese and Castilians on their East India settlements. *Esprit des Loix.* Liv. 20. cap. 18. Q. Claudius, a tribune, introduced a law, forbidding a man of senatorial rank, to possess a ship of more than 300 amphoræ burthen ; that being thought sufficient for carrying the produce of his estate. N.B. A Roman amphora contained about nine gallons.

by a still severer and more material exception, were, in
the article of marriage, deprived of the hopes of advancing their families to public honours or employments.*
In short, what Cicero says of trade (which some have, I
think with little reason, construed into a compliment) may
be considered as the general opinion of his countrymen.
" Mercatura si tenuis, sordida putanda est; sin magna et
copiosa, multa undique apportans, multisque sine vanitate
impartiens, *non est admodum vituperanda.*"† It cannot
be supposed that employments, so little respected or
              12   understood

---

* See a Constitution of Constantine. Cod. Lib. 5. tit. 27. §. 1.
† *De Officiis.* Lib. 1. These sentiments, which operated so
strongly against trade, are not the only instances of great resemblance between the institutions of Rome and Lacedæmon, where,
says Xenophon, traffic was confined to slaves or people of the lowest
class. Q. Was it by accident or design that Mercury was at Rome
regarded as the god of *thieves* as well as of *merchants* ?

I cannot forbear introducing in this place some sentiments
upon this subject, which notwithstanding the high character of the
person from whom they proceed, will not I believe be readily sub-
scribed to in this country.

Mr. Boswell asks Dr. Johnson, " What is the reason that we are
angry at a *trader*'s having opulence ?" *Johnson.* " Why, sir, the
reason is, (though I don't undertake to prove that there is a reason)
we see no qualities in trade that should entitle a man to superiority.
We are not angry at a soldier's getting riches, because we see that
he possesses qualities which we have not. If a man returns from a
battle, having lost one hand, and the other full of gold, we feel that
he deserves the gold ; but we cannot think that a fellow, by sitting
all day at a desk is entitled to get above us." *Boswell.* " But, sir,
may we not suppose a merchant to be a man of an enlarged mind,
such as Addison in the *Spectator* describes Sir Andrew Freeport to
have been ?" *Johnson.* " Why, sir, we may suppose any fictitious
character. We may suppose a philosophical day labourer, who is
happy in reflecting that by his labour he contributes to the fertility
of the earth, and to the support of his fellow creatures ; but we find
no such philosophical day-labourer. A merchant may, perhaps, be a
man of an enlarged mind ; but there is nothing in trade connected
with an enlarged mind." Boswell's *Journal of a Tour to the Hebrides.*
p. 409. This opinion, which would have been applauded at Rome

understood as *commerce* and *navigation* were by the Romans, would find a very conspicuous place in their political arrangements. It is true, many edicts to this purpose occur in the law books, but we look there in vain for any thing like a *mercantile* or *maritime code.*** Even those laws which are found dispersed in the *Corpus Juris Civilis* are thought not to be intended as general regulations, but to refer merely to the corn trade, which, being of the utmost consequence to a people whose territory was not adequate to the furnishing of a sufficient quantity for their own consumption, naturally forced the attention of the Legislature to this branch of commerce.†

I thought it necessary to premise thus much on a very copious and curious subject, not altogether unconnected with our present purpose, and shall now proceed to consider more at large the source from which the Romans derived their marine laws.

13 This

---

and Sparta, never can be admitted at London, Hamburgh or Marseilles.

* Dig. Lib. 14. tit. 1, 2. Lib. 47. tit. 9. Lib. 48. tit. 12. Cod. Justin. Lib. 4. tit. 33 et 63. Lib. 11. tit. 1. Cod. Theodos. *De Naviculariis.*

† See Suetonius *Vit. Claud.* cap. 19. Before the conquest of Egypt, Sicily and Sardinia were the granaries of Rome. After that event, the principal corn trade was carried on at Alexandria, and Augustus established a regular fleet for that purpose, which was called *Sacra*, or *Felix Embole ;* the *Sacred*, or *Happy Freight.* The ceremonies observed on its arrival at the mouth of the Tiber, are related with such circumstances as to give us the highest ideas of its importance. Seneca. Epist. 78. Suetonius, *in Vit. August.* §. 88.

This had been the case from the earliest age of the republic, for in the second year after the expulsion of the kings, when Porsenna struck terror into Rome, by his approach to reinstate the Tarquins, Livy says, "multa igitur blandimenta plebi ab senatu data ; *Annonæ* in primis habita cura, et ad *frumentum comparandum* missi, alii in Volscos, alii Cumas." Lib. 2. cap. 9. Suetonius speaking of some very pressing occasions to justify the use of slaves in the army reckons, *a tumult in a time when supplies of corn are scanty. Vit. Aug.* §. 25.

This honour is due to the island of Rhodes, the extraordinary wisdom and justice of whose naval code, gained it admission into the most celebrated system of polity that ever was devised; whence, being partially adopted in the Eastern Empire, it has imperfectly descended to these times, and may be traced in most of the naval codes now in use.

Though Cicero's observation, " Qui *mare* tenet, eum necesse est rerum potiri," * appears not to have been much understood at Rome, in his days, it was nevertheless founded on reason and fact, and has been since justified by many striking examples. History, I believe, scarcely offers an instance of an industrious maritime people, however inconsiderable in point of territory, who have failed to arrive at great political consequence.†

I might confirm this remark by the examples of some ancient and modern states, which must occur to my reader's recollection, but shall confine myself to that single one which is immediately connected with our subject.

There is no writer extant who treats expressly of the Rhodians; what we would know of them therefore must be collected by fragments from various sources; fortunately their extensive connections, and their activity for so many years in the affairs of Greece and Rome, has given them such a respectable place in history, that the materials are not so scanty or unconnected as might be conceived.

The Isle of Rhodes, lies in the Mediterranean Sea,

14   about

---

* *Ad Atticum.* Lib. 10. Ep. 1.

† What Censorinus, in Appian, says to the Carthaginian deputies, cannot be taken as a serious argument. It was the interest of the Romans to persuade them that a *maritime situation* was disadvantageous, and the earnestness with which he addresses them proves what was his real opinion of the matter. Appian. Lib. 8. *De rebus Punicis*, §. 86. edit. Schweighæuser. 1785.

about seven leagues from the coast of Lycia and Caria, and is described as part of Asia Minor. Its original inhabitants, according to the best accounts, were Cretans of the race of Hercules; for, though they are frequently called descendants of the Dorians, and were themselves fond of being so considered, it is well known, that colony did not settle in the island till after the Trojan war.* At this early period they appear to have been a powerful and industrious people. Homer, in his celebrated catalogue of the confederated fleet dwells with peculiar satisfaction on the "nine vessels which were brought by Tlepolemus from this island," and from what he says at the conclusion of his little history of its original settlement, it may be supposed then to have been in a flourishing condition † Pindar has also spoken in very high terms of Rhodes, and figuratively describes its wealth and fertility by saying that "the sun collected together clouds which poured down showers of gold upon it," ‡ the same image that is used by Homer on the like occasion. Strabo

15   informs

---

* Strabo Geograph. Lib. 14. Pausanians. Lib. 9. Diodorus Siculus. Lib. 5. cap. 13. Aristides. Ροδιοις, Περι ομονοιας. p. 568. edit. Jebb. Oxon. 1722. At the conclusion of this oration, Aristides, urging them strongly to unanimity, says, "I am particularly pained that you, who are so tenacious of your original language, as not to admit a single expression, but what is *Doric*, in a matter of so much moment as the welfare of your state, which depends on your unanimity, should be so little solicitous of preserving the *Doric Harmony*." Loc. cit. p. 571.

† Iliad. B. 653.

‡ Olymp. Od. 7. Il. B. 670. The Halia, a celebrated festival at Rhodes, was not derived, as many have imagined, from αλς the sea, but from the Doric αλιος, for ηλιος, the sun, to whom the island was dedicated: and it must be observed as something singular, that the Rhodians, though for so many ages a maritime people, never offered any sacrifice or celebrated any rites to the sea.

Pindar calls Rhodes τριπολιν νασον, from the three cities, Jalyssus, Lindus and Camirus, which it originally contained ; for the informs us, that in times of remote antiquity, by reason of its superiority on the seas, the wisdom of its laws and the industry of its inhabitants, no country in the world exceeded Rhodes, and adds that it was this maritime excellence alone which afterwards supported its influence for so long a time among the ancient states, and strengthened its alliances with the Greeks and Romans.*

The fame which this island acquired, by its numerous seminaries of learning, is known to every classical reader. Thither Æschines retired, and opened that school of Rhetoric to which, after his death, the greatest characters in Rome resorted.† Cicero and Pompey both studied there, and Julius Cæsar, we are told, having put to sea for that purpose, was taken on his voyage by pirates.‡ But it was not alone the cultivation of eloquence, philosophy, and the Greek language which attracted such a number of visitants; the pure temperature of the climate, the fertility of the soil, and the luxurious refinements of the capital city, which once might be said to have rivalled Athens herself, conspired to render Rhodes a desirable retreat.§   To this happy condition of the island a variety.

16   of

---

city, that bears the name of the island, was first built during the Peloponnesian war, by the same architect, according to Strabo, who constructed the Piræus at Athens. *Geog.* Lib. 14. p. 964. edit. Amstelod. 1717.

* Loc. cit.

† See his Epistle to Philocrates, in which he describes his voyage ; and Plutarch, *In vit. Demosthen.*

‡ He was forced to remain in captivity, says Suetonius, forty days, " non sine summâ indignatione, cum uno Medico et cubiculariis duobus." Lib. 1. §. 4.

§ Strabo. Lib. 14. Athenæi Deipnosoph. §. 13. In Cicero's familiar epistles, Brutus says to Cassius " Quid ergo est, inquis, tui consilii ? Dandus est locus fortunæ ; cedendum ex Italiâ, migrandum Rhodum." Lib. 11. Ep. 1. And in another of Matius to Cicero, " Mihi quidem si optata contingent, quod reliquum est vitæ in otio Rhodi degam." Lib. 11. Ep. 28. The emperor Tiberius passed seven

of writers have given testimony; but in a more particular manner the sophist Aristides, in his two orations to the inhabitants. To him I refer my readers,* and hasten to what is more properly our concern, its *maritime* consequence and power.

Here we shall meet with numerous confirmations of Cicero's remark.† In what light the Rhodians were considered by the Athenians, who of all the Grecian states, stood the highest in naval power, may be collected from a variety of facts in the history of that people, but more particularly from a spirited oration of Demosthenes, wherein he labours to persuade his countrymen that it is both for their honour and their interest to deliver those islanders from the oppressive oligarchy under which they groaned; and although at that time they had very little reason to expect any favour from the Athenians, justly dissatisfied with their conduct in the social war, yet of such consequence did this orator consider their alliance, that perhaps there is not extant a more laboured piece of eloquence than that which he delivered upon this occasion.‡ It did not fail to have its proper effect, and the Rhodians became once more a free people.§ From this

17   time

---

years of his life there, upon which occasion Manilius has the following complimentary lines.

" Virgine sub castâ felix terrâque marique
Est Rhodos, hospitium recturi principis orbem :
Tumque Domus vere solis, cui tota sacrata est
Cum caperet lumen magni sub Cæsare mundi."

Lib. 4. 763. edit. Bent. 1739.

* Loc. cit.   † See p. 340.

‡ Περι της των Ρωδιων ελευθεριας. See also Isocrates, *For the Peace.*

§ Ant. Xtm 350. Some writers, it is true, give another account of this matter, asserting, that it was to the death of the famous Artemisia, who had conquered their island and governed it with great rigour, and not to the eloquence of Demosthenes, that Rhodes

time the situation of their affairs was very flourishing, and
their alliance was courted successively by almost all the
contending Princes; yet, upon the most prudent principles of policy, seldom adopted by powerful states, they
persevered in observing such a strict neutrality, that we
do not hear of their being actively engaged in any dispute
for more than 40 years.* Thus they naturally increased
in wealth and power, while their neighbours, constantly
engaged in obstinate and expensive wars, were gradually
wasting their strength and revenue. They became however at last (as might reasonably be expected) an object
of jealousy, and by refusing to join Antigonus, who had
earnestly solicited their assistance against Ptolemy, this
prince turned his whole force upon them in that famous
siege, which gave rise to more ingenious instruments of
destruction than any upon the records of antiquity.†
Notwithstanding the shock they received from such a
formidable attack, in their subsequent wars with the
Byzantines and Macedonians they still maintained their
usual superiority at sea; and, near a century after, in a
naval engagement off the island of Chios, gave Philip the
severest overthrow he ever experienced.‡   It was to them
18   that

---

was indebted at this time for its freedom.   See Aul. Gellius. Lib. 10.
c. 18.   Strabo. Lib. 14.

* It was this policy which induced them to make a voluntary
submission to Alexander the Great, whose arms they knew were irresistible, and under whose protection they had nothing to fear. Quint.
Curtius. Lib. 4.   Diodorus tells us—This conqueror had a peculiar
affection for Rhodes, and deposited his will in the Archives of that
city.

† Ant. Xt   304. 303.   Campbell, *Political Survey*. Vol. 1. p. 33.
very justly observes that, their *commercial interests* naturally connected them with Ptolemy. Diodorus Sic. Lib. 20.   Plutarch. in vit.
Demetrii.   Polyæni *Strateg*. Lib. 4. cap. 6.

‡ Polybius. Lib. 16. The whole account of this naval action is
worth consulting, for it abounds with instances of singular courage

that the eyes of Greece were turned for protection against the oppressive requisition of the Byzantines, who attempted to impose a tax upon all ships which entered their sea; and Polybius declares of them at this period, that they conducted their enterprizes with such a degree of activity and zeal, that he will not scruple to pronounce them the most powerful and opulent state of Greece.*

The very essential service they rendered the Romans, by harassing and checking the naval armaments of the Carthaginians, promoted and confirmed a long alliance between them; an alliance to which, it is probable, that Rome was indebted for all the maritime skill she afterwards possessed. Livy has recorded a speech made by the Rhodian ambassadors to the Roman Senate, which carries with it an air of haughtiness and independence very unusual in addresses to that powerful people.† The subject of their embassy was nothing less than to insist that the Romans should make peace with Perseus, against whom, while they thought the cause was just, they had materially assisted them; and at the same time a second embassy to the same purpose was dispatched to the army in Macedonia, threatening that they would turn their arms against the Romans if they refused to comply with their requisition. The consequences, however, proved extremely humiliating to the Rhodians; the principal partisans of Perseus were put to death, and the ambassadors were obliged to appear before the senate habited in mourning, and to plead forgiveness for their insolence in a strain very opposite to their address in the preceding year.‡

19   Not

---

and skill, and conveys to us a very advantageous idea of the naval power of the Rhodians.

    * Lib. 4. cap. 5.   † Lib. 44.

  ‡ Ut supra. Lib. 45. Gellius has preserved some fragments of a speech of Cato in behalf of the Rhodian Ambassadors; among

Not long after this, Cicero speaks of them as of a people, " Quorum usque ad nostram memoriam disciplina navalis et gloria remansit," * though they had then very visibly begun to decline both in power and wealth, and a few years after were so far reduced that, notwithstanding they retained, according to the historian, their naval skill, they suffered a defeat at sea from the very people whom they had taught to make use of a marine force.† Thenceforth they took a less splendid part ; for though their island continued to possess all its natural and acquired advantages, a fruitful soil, commodious ports and arsenals, stately edifices and schools of learning, yet the national character was much degenerated from what it was in those days when, with a laudable spirit of patriotic jealousy, they would say as Aristides afterwards encouraged them in vain to say ; " We are Rhodians. Will any nation, Greek or Barbarian, contend with us on points of honour or nobility, we will contend with them, we will exceed them." ‡ Marcus Antonius was a great admirer of the

20   Rhodians

---

which are the following remarkable words. " Rhodienses superbos esse aiunt, id objectantes quod mihi a liberis meis minime dici velim. Sint sane superbi. Quid id ad nos attinet ? idne irascimini si quis superbior est quam nos ?" Lib. 7. cap. 3.

 * Pro Lege Maniliâ.

 † Appian. Lib. 4. De Bellis civilibus, §. 72. edit. Schweighæuser. 1785.

 ‡ Ælius Aristides. Ροδιοις, περι Ομονοιας. p. 566. Tom. 1. edit. Jebb. Oxon. 1722.

 C. Cassius, 41 years before Christ, plundered the city of all its pictures and statues, leaving only that of Apollo, upon which he observed, in derision, that he had left the Rhodians nothing but the sun. How contrary this to the conduct of Demetrius upon a like occasion, who not only abstained from plunder, but, at the end of the siege, delivered to his enemies all the military machines which they had constructed ! Plut. *Vit. Dem.* See also, his well known behaviour to Protogenes. The conduct of Cassius is still more reprehensible, when we are told that he received his education in the island. Appian, ut supra. The historian's whole account of the general's

Rhodians it is said, and attempted to restore them to some degree of power, but they made such an ill use of his indulgencies that he was obliged to repeal them.*   Under the first emperors little occurs to illustrate their history.   That their condition could not have been very flourishing we may infer from an observation which Tacitus has made upon them, that the Romans granted them liberty and deprived them of it, according as they were found to deserve it by readily fulfilling their engagements as allies in war, or to forfeit it by their internal seditions.†   And notwithstanding Pliny, who wrote at the beginning of Vespasian's reign, calls Rhodes " Civitas *Libera* et pulcherrima," ‡ we find, that under this very emperor it became for the first time a Roman Province.§ In this state it remained, under the Greek empire, till the 7th century, when, together with other islands in those seas, it yielded to the arms of the Saracens. We have very short and imperfect accounts of this part of the Rhodian history, and few events occur worthy of being separately recorded.

21

It

---

conference with his old præceptor Archelaus, who was sent to deprecate his vengeance, is highly interesting. §. 67.

* Appian, ut supra. Lib. 5. §. 7. He bestowed upon them some islands in the Mediterranean, which they so severely oppressed with taxes, that they were withdrawn from their jurisdiction in the following year. *Loc. cit.* The prevailing vices of the Rhodians seem to have been luxurious living and a haughty spirit; the natural consequences of great wealth and a long series of prosperity. Athen. *Deip*. 10 & 14, 15.

† Tacit. *Annal*. Lib. 12. Yet, in the reign of Augustus, the name of a citizen of Rhodes was purchased at a considerable price, an example of which Athenæus has given us in Posidonius the Stoic.

‡ Lib. 5. cap. 31.

§ Suetonius, *in vit. Vespas*. cap. 8. Orosius. Lib. 7. For some curious specimens of Rhodian coins, see Huberti Goltzii *Græciæ universæ Numismata*. Tab. xxiii. xxiv.

It may not be improper to mention, that soon after Vespasian's death the island was desolated and the city totally destroyed by an earthquake. This melancholy event is spoken of by Pausanias,* and by Capitolinus in his life of Antoninus Pius, during whose reign it happened, but in a more particular manner by Aristides the Sophist, who had studied there, and retained a strong affection for the place.† His description of the calamity is extremely picturesque and affecting. He expatiates largely on the irreparable loss which all the civilized world must feel from the destruction not only of so many noble specimens of architecture, sculpture, painting, and military engines, but from being deprived of the advantage which they enjoyed of such commodious harbours and arsenals as those of Rhodes. For he adds "of all these, and various other splendid ornaments, which at once declared the surprising opulence and strength of the place, no vestige remains. Nothing now is visible but the bare rock on which the city stood!"‡

Though the humanity of Antoninus Pius induced him to attempt the restoration of Rhodes, and great sums of money were expended on the work, there is every reason to think this was but partially executed, and extended only to cleansing the harbour and rebuilding the magazines;§

22

for

---

* Lib. 2. cap. 7. Lib. 8. cap. 43.

† *In Rhodiac.* p. 553, edit. Jebb. et Περι ομονοιας, p. 571.

‡ Ut sup. passim. In the same Oration he recommends it to them to send emissaries to different countries for the purpose of collecting contributions for restoring the city, p. 360, and again Περι ομονοιας, p. 274. a custom not uncommon in other instances of the same kind in ancient times; and which, as Polybius observes, had been practised before by the Rhodians on a similar occasion with great success. Lib. 5.

§ Pausanias, *Arcad.* lib. 8, dwells upon this admirable trait in Antonine's character, which had shewn itself upon many other occasions.

for from this period it is mentioned as a convenient and much frequented port : but we hear nothing of the learning, the valour, or the opulence of its inhabitants. After groaning long under the Saracen yoke, it seemed to recover something of its ancient spirit in the hands of its next possessors, the famous Hospitalers or Knights of St. John of Jerusalem, who maintained their ground from the opening of the 14th century till the year 1521 ; when, after incredible efforts of bravery and skill, they were finally driven out by the victorious arms of Solyman the Magnificent. Since that time the island has remained in the hands of the Turks.* It is not to our present pur-

23 pose

---

* Before the Hospitalers were dispossessed, they were known by the name of *Knights of Rhodes.* After their expulsion they wandered in search of a place of settlement for more than eight years, and being at last put in possession of *Malta* by Charles the Fifth, they adopted the name of that island, which they still maintain, together with a very watchful jealousy over the Turks, and inhabitants of the Barbary Coast. If we may rely on the public papers, the ancient spirit of these islanders has not yet forsaken them ; for we there read of a very gallant action with a superior number of Tunisian Gallies, in which the Maltese admiral obtained a complete victory. *Morning Chron.* Dec. 9. 1785.

It is somewhat singular that the history of this people, which exhibits such a splendid detail of events, should remain so little known. Their unparalleled exertions for almost two centuries against the infidels ; the admirable traits of civil wisdom in their government; the characters and the conduct of an illustrious succession of Grand Masters, whose extensive alliances rendered them respectable at all the courts of Europe, and formidable to that power, whose arms were then irresistible in the East, necessarily furnish very striking and instructive examples. Their last attempt to repel the infidels, though unsuccessful, abounds with more instances of true magnanimity than are to be met with in any other history of so short a period. See Jac. Bosio. *Istoria della Sac. religione et ill^{ma} militia di San. Giov. Gierosolim,* part. 2. lib. 1. and particularly lib. 2. part. 2. for an epistolary address of the Grand Master to all the Christian princes of Europe. Their history is also written by l'Abbè Vertot, in 4 vols. 8vo.

N.B. The *Hospitalers* came into England about the year 1100, and

pose to dwell on the history of those religious militants,
it is sufficient to observe, that although (agreeably to the
spirit of their institution) they never encouraged commercial intercourse among themselves, they have always been
very strenuous defenders of the traffic carried on in their
seas by other powers; and that their expulsion from
Rhodes must consequently have proved detrimental to the
Levant trade, of which they constantly professed themselves the protectors.*

That nations of much higher antiquity than the
Rhodians had cultivated the art of navigation both with
military and commercial views, and had carried it to a
considerable perfection, there is the clearest evidence.
Eusebius has given them the fourth place only in his
catalogue of maritime states, who obtained the sovereignty
of the sea, and fixes it at about 900 years before the
Christian Æra, almost two centuries prior to the foundation of Rome.†

But though the Rhodians cannot claim the honour of
being the earliest *navigators,* they have an undoubted
right to a much nobler praise, that of being the *first
legislators of the sea:* for there is nothing upon record
which can lead us to suppose any of those maritime
powers which preceded them had ever appeared in that
                           24   **character,**

---

were held in such esteem that their Superior was the first lay baron,
and had a seat among the lords in parliament. At the Reformation
they shared the fate of the other religious orders, and were totally
suppressed, 32 Hen. VIII. c. 24.

 * Morgan's Hist. of Algiers, vol. 1.

 † The first in order are the Cretans, 1406 years before Christ:
next are the Lydians, 1179: thirdly the Thracians 1000 ; and
fourthly the Rhodians, 916 years before Christ ; which, according
to the Marbles, is the age in which Homer flourished. Euseb. *Chro-
nicon.* Lib. 2. This part of his information, the chronologist tells
us, he derived from a work of Castor the Rhodian Περι των θαλασ-
σοκρατησαντων.

character. There is therefore great truth as well as spirit in the assertion of an ancient jurist—"That to erect as it were a throne for justice, on the ocean, and to teach her to regulate the transactions of man on that unstable element, with the same firmness and precision as on land, was a grand and an *original* idea of the Rhodians." * It is impossible to fix with any certainty the precise time when these celebrated sea laws were first compiled. Harmenopulus of Thessalonica, a juridical writer of the 12th century, gives them the pre-eminence over all others as well in *antiquity* as authority, but does not tell us at what period they first appeared.† The most general opinion seems to be that they were probably compiled about nine centuries before the Christian Æra, or soon after that time, when, as we have already seen, Rhodes first acquired the superiority on the seas, and maintained it for the space of 24 years.‡ There are some indeed who have called in question their great antiquity, attributing them to that age when the city of Rhodes was founded; which, according to Strabo, was in the days of the administration of Pericles at Athens, consequently five centuries later than is usually conceived. But the geographer in the very chapter which contains this information, seems to have been aware that a conjecture of this sort might arise, and therefore warns his readers not to date the naval skill of the Rhodians from this event; for, says he, they were very famous as a sea-faring people even before the institution of the Olympiads.§ After all,

25 as

---

* Docimus. *In Tractat. Tactatuum.* Tom. 9. p. 642.
† Procheiridion Juris. Lib. 2. tit. 11.
‡ Eusebius ut supra. The learned Selden says they were compiled in the days of Jehosaphat, which agrees with this period. *Mare clausum.* Lib. 1. cap. 10.
§ Strabo. *Geograph.* Lib. 14. The first Olympiad, according to the received mode of reckoning at present, was 776 years before

as there is no express authority for the date of these laws, this part of their history must rest solely upon conjecture; nor can we boast of much accurate information on a point of greater moment, the time of their reception at Rome, and the degree of influence they held there; though here indeed our authorities are somewhat more clear and satisfactory.

Before the æra of imperial Rome the subject is entirely involved in obscurity. From what Cicero says in admiration of the naval discipline of Rhodes,[*] no inference, I think, can be drawn of its regulating the Roman marine at that time; indeed, from the silence of this writer in many places, where he had an opportunity of introducing some notices of those laws, it may be presumed they were not collectively extant at Rome in his days, though it appears probable that many of them were separately admitted before that period.[†] If any reliance can be placed on those fragments of imperial edicts, usually prefixed to what is called a collection of Rhodian laws, we must fix their first formal reception at Rome in the reign of Tiberius Claudius, whose sanction appears at the head of the compilation.[‡] There is certainly no emperor under whom an event of this sort was more likely to happen. We have numerous instances of his attention to maritime affairs, and of his particular affection for Rhodes. In the Roman code are two Acts of Senate ratified by

26

him,

Christ, which makes Strabo's account coincide with that of Eusebius, and with the conjecture of Selden.

[*] Pro Lege Maniliâ.   [†] Dig. Lib. 14. tit. 2. De Jactu.

[‡] These fragments, as well as the laws themselves, are in Greek. They are adopted by Leunclavius in his *Jus Græco Romanum*, and by Peckius in his *Collection of the Rhodian Laws:* though many are inclined to suspect their authenticity. Gothofred thinks them an epitome of some larger Edicts at the head of an original compilation made by Michael Psellus, or some writer of that epitomizing age. *De Imperio Maris*, cap. 8.

him, for protecting the persons and property of the shipwrecked.* Suetonius has recorded various other acts for
the regulation of commerce and the improvement of sea
ports, especially that most material of all to the Roman
people, the port of Ostia.† To this may be added the
great privileges granted by him to such as should build
merchant ships, and that remarkable indulgence with
which he induced the corn-traders to put to sea in the
winter.‡ His regard for the Rhodians appeared upon a
variety of occasions, and of this he gave them a most
signal proof, by restoring them their liberties when he was
laying many of the neighbouring states under heavy
restrictions.§

From the words of this emperor's edict in favour of
the Rhodian laws, it appears, that a body of mariners and
merchants had petitioned him to give the laws of contribution, which hitherto had been partially applied, a general
extent.‖ In consequence of which, by the advice of Nero,
commissioners were sent to Rhodes to make the strictest
enquiries into their maritime code, and from the articles
specified in their commission it certainly must have been
very comprehensive. They were to consult all the laws
respecting mariners, ship's masters, merchants and passengers ; freight, partnership and bargains ; trusts and
pledges ; and besides this were to observe the form of

27   their

---

* Cod. Lib. 11. Tit. 4. 5. *De Incendio, Ruinâ, Naufragio.*

† The situation of this port shews, that not only the trade, but,
in a great measure, the subsistence of Rome, must have depended
upon it.

‡ " Negotiatoribus *certa Lucra* proposuit, *suscepto in se damno,* si
cui quid per tempestates accidisset." Sueton. *Vit. Claud.* cap. 18.
Some writers think they discover the origin of *Insurance* in this Act
of Claudius. Molloy. *De Jure Maritimo et Navali.* B, 2. cap. 7.
§. 1.

§ Sueton. ut sup. cap. 25.

‖ See this matter fully explained below, where the *law* of *ejection*
is treated of.

their vessels, the manner of constructing them, and to make enquiries into every circumstance that had any connection with naval matters.*

This commission Claudius confirmed by a public decree, and delivered it signed with his own hand to the consul Antoninus.   There are some who contend that the whole of this transaction is to be referred to the reign of Tiberius, the successor of Augustus Cæsar, founding their opinion upon the great affection which this emperor had for Rhodes, and the favour he shewed to its magistrates and men of learning.†   But plausible as this appears, the supposition is destroyed by the very words of the edict, which are so plain that it is surprising any doubt should have arisen on the subject.   In the first place it was made at the suggestion of Nero, the successor of Claudius, whose partiality for that island was manifested on a variety of occasions.   It is reported of him, when he dispatched Crato into Greece to collect the most curious works of art and bring them to Rome, that he excepted Rhodes, and ordered him to remove nothing out of that island. Tacitus says, that it was in a great measure owing to his persuasion too that Claudius restored its liberties.‡

28   In

---

* *Jus Navale Rhodiorum*, in Principio. Allowing the authenticity of this Edict, Rome is more indebted to Greece for legislation than is usually imagined by those who only take into consideration the embassy which produced the decemviral code.

† The emperor himself resided in the island seven years. See p. 342, Note.

‡ Annal. Lib. 12. It was probably on this occasion that the following epigram was written.

Ωs παρος, αελιου, νυν καισαρος ή Ροδος ειμι

Νασος, ισον δ' αυχω φεγγος απ' αμφοτερων,

Ηδη σβεννυνυμεναν με νεα κατεφωτισεν ακτις

Αλιε, και παρα σον φεγγος ελαμψε Νερον.

Πωs ειπω ; τινι μαλλον οφειλομαι ; os μεν εδειξεν

Εξ αλος, όs δ' ηδη ρυσατο δυομενην.

Lib. 1. Antholog. Antiphili Epig. cap. εις νησους.

In the next place we are told the edict was delivered to the Consul Antoninus, who can be no other than that Q. Aterius Antoninus, the colleague of D. Junius Silanus, during whose office, according to Tacitus, Rhodes obtained her freedom.*

After Tiberius Claudius, the next sanction which the Rhodian laws are supposed to have received, was from Vespasian, who in general terms is said to have confirmed them by an act of senate, in the consulship of Laurus and Agrippinus. There appears, however, to be something suspicious in the account, for it not only wants the concurrence of historians, none of whom take the least notice of the event, but the names of the consuls under whom it took place are not to be met with in the Fasti Consulares.†

From Trajan they seem to have received no fresh authority, for neither this emperor or Adrian are recorded to have done more than express their general approbation of them in the senate.‡ The last fragment in this collection is a rescript of Antoninus Pius, which as it is well authenticated, will be more particularly considered below, in treating of the law *De Jactu,* of which it forms one of the most curious paragraphs.

We may reasonably ask, why laws once established by

29   proper

Nero was at this time only sixteen years old.

Theo, Phœbus, once, now Cæsar I obey,
In splendour equal to the God of Day,
O'er my deserted isle new lustre streams,
And Nero's glories darken Phœbus' beams !
Say, most my partial thanks shall Phœbus claim,
Or shall I reverence most a Nero's name ?
That gave me first from ocean's gulf to rise,
This rais'd my sinking glory to the skies !

* Loc. cit. A.D. 55.
† Gothofred. *De Imperio Maris.* cap. 10.
‡ In the Code, Lib. 11. tit. 4, 5. *De incendio,* &c. is a law of

proper authority, should afterward require such frequent confirmation? and this can be explained only by supposing it to have been a necessary declaration of the emperor's good will towards the island, whenever it was restored to forfeited liberty: an act, the frequency of which we have had occasion already to remark.* Thus it appears that the binding authority of the Rhodian Laws at Rome depended solely on the imperial sanction, from which, it must be observed, that the influence they derived was merely conditional, and was not permitted to operate to the contradiction or derogation of the national laws. They were considered, as the laws of Oleron are by many of the maritime states of Europe, in the light of *ratio scripta*, as *voluntary*, not as *necessary* law; and, as a code of equity and general justice, were applied in all naval suits, with the exception, however, of some particular laws, whose features were too severe to gain them admission into a system of polity so mild and reasonable as that of Rome.† Upon this head a jurist of the Greek empire has observed, that there seems to have been two evils which attended the original Rhodian laws, namely, the dishonesty of those who were to interpret and apply them; and that, which attends all human institutions, an obscurity in their meaning from the necessary revolutions in the customs and manners of the world. The first evil gave rise to that cloud of glosses and conceits which have obscured, rather than elucidated, the original; and from the other have proceeded those

30   various

Adrian, which ordains, that the plunder of a wreck shall be repaid by the proprietor of the land on which the ship was cast.

* p. 32.

† One of the laws rejected by the Romans, as unreasonably severe, was that which condemned to immediate sale any ship of war driven into a foreign port, even though no dispute subsisted between the parties.

various laws which sprang up, as occasion required, and which having never been formed into a separate body, it is now become difficult, and, in most cases, impossible to distinguish from the ancient code.* It is much to be lamented that so valuable a system of marine regulations, should not have survived in better condition. " Justinian, (as Molloy expresses it) was an obsequious admirer of the Rhodian laws and incorporated them into his inestimable pandects."† Still we must regret, that they do not appear there in their original form and language. They are scattered so promiscuously over this immense compilation, and are besides so involved in the questions and interpretations of the jurists, that for want of being properly specified by name, when they occur, they cannot with any certainty be selected from that body of maritime law which gradually accumulated under the emperors. I am aware that many ingenious civilians have exhibited a collection of naval regulations under the denomination of the Rhodian laws, and have accompanied it with learned observations; and moreover that this collection has been adopted without scruple by some excellent writers on maritime affairs as authentic.‡ Simon Schardius published it in the middle of the sixteenth century, with a Latin translation in 41 distinct titles, from a MS., he tells us, in the great Pithou's library, and this is the same

31   copy

---

* Docimus. *In Calcem Græco-Romani.* Edit. Freher.
† Introduction to his Book " *De Jure Maritimo et Navali.*"
‡ Morisoti. *Orbis Maritimus,* Lib. 1. cap. 30. A book rich in materials for that great desideratum, a good commercial history; which being, as Montesquieu has observed, a history of the *communication of mankind*, must necessarily abound in events the most interesting and important, that can occupy the attention of a social being: he adds in the next chapter, that, the history of luxury would make a splendid part of this narrative. *Esp. des Loix.* Liv. 21. cap. 5 et 6. Postlethwayte's Translation of M. Savary's Dictionary of Commerce. Vol. 2. Art. Rhodes.

copy which has been used by Marquhard, Freher, and Leunclavius, in their editions of the *Jus Græco-Romanum*. Some few years after Schardius, a collection of the same kind was published imperfectly by Pet. Peckius, whose work has been since completed by Binnius from a MS. in the library of Nic. Heinsius.* But, after all, it is scarcely probable that these laws in their present form should be of Rhodian extraction; for, though they are said to have been selected from Justinian's laws, they will be found upon comparison to bear very little analogy to any maritime cases in the Pandects. Add to this, that the Greek in which they are written is far from being pure. It abounds with those barbarisms which the language contracted at Constantinople. Balduin, in short (a profound antiquary and an accurate civilian) does not hesitate to pronounce at once of them (somewhat too harshly indeed) that they are " crude farragoes of naval matters."† They

32   form

---

* There is a MS. of these laws in the Bodleian library, num. 264. 18. presented among others to the University, at the instance of Archbishop Laud, by Sir Thomas Roe, ambassador from King James I. to the Great Mogul, and afterwards to the Ottoman Court.

† *De Lege Rhodiâ Comment.* p. 193. edit. Basil. To save those, who wish to consult these cases, the trouble of searching for them through the Corpus Juris Civilis, I have here set down with their proper references some of the principal titles, that bear any relation to navigation and commerce. De Negotiis gestis. Dig. lib. 3. tit. 5.— Nautæ. Cauponis, Stabularii ut recepta restituant, 4. tit. 9.— De Exercitoriâ Actione, 14.—tit. 1. et Cod. lib. 4. tit. 25—Ad Legem Rhodiam, de Jactu, cod. tit. 2.—De Institoriâ Actione, eod. tit. 3. et C. 4. tit. 25.—De nautico fænore, 22. tit. 2. et C. 4. tit. 33.—De incendio, ruinâ et naufragio, 47. tit. 9.—De commerciis et mercatoribus, C. 4. tit. 63.—De annonis et tributis, C. 10. tit. 16.—De Classicis, C. 11. tit. 12.—De litorum et itinerum custodiâ, C. 12. tit. 45.—De naviculariis, seu naucleris, publicas species transportantibus, C. 11. tit. 1.—De prædiis et omnibus rebus naviculariorum, eod. tit. eod.—De navibus non excusandis, eod. tit. 3.—Ne quid oneri publico ponatur, eod. tit. 4.—De naufragio, eod. tit. 5.—De nauticis usuris, Authent. Collat. 8. tit. 6.

form a complete title in the Basilical Code and from this circumstance together with much internal evidence (notwithstanding that they are said to be extracted from the 14th book of the Pandects) it is highly probable that they are a compilation of the 9th or 10th century.* It is not necessary to enter into a particular exposition of them. For this I must refer my reader to some of the works I have mentioned, particularly to that of Vinnius, in whose commentaries he will find much historical and juridical information. The whole collection consists of 51 articles, all of them immediately relative to maritime affairs. The form however in which they are presented to us appears to be rather defective in point of order and perspicuity. In some places, for instance, laws of the same tendency are separated by those of a very opposite complexion, and in others, articles are connected together, whose subjects do not seem to bear any affinity.† To consider it as a marine code, it is far from being complete, but if we allow its pretensions to originality and view it as a remnant saved from the wreck of time and barbarism, it certainly affords an extremely valuable specimen of ancient jurisprudence, since fortunately there are very few circumstances of any considerable importance for which it does not in some measure provide. Such as for the hiring and freighting of ships—the transporting of passengers and goods—the delivering of things received in good condition—the borrowing and trusting of money

33   for

Besides these there are some others, of which little more than the bare titles are extant, that relate chiefly to the wages, privileges, and punishments of seamen.

* Lib. 5. 3. tit. 8.

† This is the case with Articles 9 and 10, which are separated from the rest, on ejection and shipwreck, by a variety of laws respecting contracts, freight, &c. neither is there any obvious correspondence between the 7th, 8th and 9th articles. Basilic. Lib. 53. tit. 8.

for sea voyages—the duties, wages &c. of mariners, and
above all, the rate and quality of contributions for losses
in common danger and for the salvage of goods : indeed if
we even agree to pronounce it a compilation of the lower
empire, its value will still be great, as we may fairly
conclude it to have been used as an epitome or manual
formed out of some original code. The objection made
to its present form, might easily be removed, as it is
capable of very methodical arrangement. The whole for
instance, might not improperly be divided into two parts,
mercantile law and nautical law; and each of these be
considered under the two separate heads of *civil* and
criminal jurisdiction. In the first part would be comprized
all those articles which have any reference to *commercial
intercourse,* such as freight, average, salvage, loans,* and
all bargains respecting contingencies to which a vessel is
liable before its departure during the voyage, and on its
return to port.† To the second part would belong such
laws as regulate the conduct of the master, the mariners,
and the passengers, towards each other; their management and care of the vessel, and the privileges, duties,
and wages, allotted to their several stations.‡ When
this arrangement was made, the second distribution into
criminal and judicial law would be obvious,§ and if into

34

this

---

* The ancients always observed a distinction between the interest
of money lent by land and by sea ; the latter (called by the moderns
Bottomry) was by them termed *Fœnus Nauticum,* which, on account
of the great hazard of the lender, was permitted to be exceedingly
high. See this fully treated of, Dig. Lib. 22. tit. 1. *De usuris,*
&c. and tit. 2. *De Nautico Fœnore;* and, for the modern practice,
Molloy, *De Jure Marit et Navali.* Book 2. chap. 11.

† See, in particular, Art. 9. 11. from 16. to 24. 27. 37. 42. 43. 44.
45. 46. and Articles 10. 27. 29. 30. 32. 41. which treat of shipwreck.

‡ particularly Art, from 1 to 8. and 12. 13. 15. 34. 36. 38. 48. 50.
51.

§ The laws which may strictly be called *penal,* are contained in
the eight first Articles, and in Articles 12. 13. 15. 38. 48. 50. 51.

this collection were incorporated under their proper heads, all the other sea laws which occur in the Roman code, such as the opinions and commentaries of the old jurists in the Pandects with the imperial constitutions contained in the code and novels, we should then obtain perhaps some clear idea of what at present lies in a very dark and deranged condition, the state of the *ancient maritime law*.*

It is worthy of remark that among the Rhodian laws, those of shipwreck and distress at sea occur most frequently. The arts of ship-building and of navigation, though zealously cultivated by many nations of antiquity, were, if compared with their present state, extremely rude and imperfect. The outward form and structure of their ships was ill contrived for security or expedition, even in the most prosperous weather, and rendered them in tempests totally unmanageable ; nor was it much improved by the shape or disposition of the sails and rigging.† If to these defects we add the moderate skill of mariners, for the most part confined to particular coasts, ignorant of any fixed principles of their art and unassisted by that infallible guide of modern navigators, the compass : can we be surprized at the caution with which they entered on a voyage ? or at the extreme care of the legislature in preparing them to surmount the various accidents to

35   which

---

* Dr. Zouch's small but comprehensive work, *Descriptio Juris et Judicii Maritimi*, is too elementary, though perhaps if it were published with a commentary and notes illustrative of modern sea laws and usages, it would sufficiently answer the purpose. Peckius and Schardius are too much occupied in verbal criticism to afford any satisfactory expositions of their subject. See their editions of *the Naval Laws of Rhodes*.

† Montesquieu has treated particularly of this matter. *Esprit des Loix*. Liv. 21. 6. and recites many curious facts of commercial geography.

which they were so liable?* What is here advanced
must not be understood to contradict any former asser-
tions of the nautical skill which many nations of antiquity
displayed; for it is founded merely on a comparison of
their efforts with the improved exertions of modern days.
Whoever consults the remarkable facts on this head collected with infinite labour and discernment, by Huet, in
his instructive *History of the Navigation and Commerce
of the Ancients*, must be struck with the number, bold-
ness and extent of naval expeditions carried on under such
disadvantageous circumstances. In short considering
the various obstacles which those early mariners had to
encounter, and the few motives to encourage them,
instead of arraigning their ignorance, we ought rather to
admire the progress they made in an art, which, of all
others, most requires the accumulated labour, ingenuity
and experience of ages to bring it to any degree of
perfection†.

Though it was my original design to have confined
these enquiries to some leading historical facts relative to
the ancient sea laws, I cannot avoid giving the following
specimen of their wisdom and equity. The celebrated
law of ejection, as it is called,‡ which forms the second title

in

---

* See the writers *De re Navali*, in the 11th vol, of Gronovius's
Thesaurus Antiquitatum Græcarum, particularly Lazarus Bayfius,
who has given plates of various kinds of ships and naval implements,
from antique marbles, medals, and bas reliefs. The curious reader
will also find much information with respect to the state of the
ancient marine establishment in the 22d and six following chapters
of the first Book of Morisotus, with a good collection of naval coins
and inscriptions.

† Piracy was not the least of the dangers which attended Navigation in those days. Justin says, that, among many nations,
" *Latrocinium Maris* Gloriæ habeatur." Lib. 43. cap. 3. and Montesquieu gives some good reasons for their contracted intercourse by
Sea. Liv. 21. 7.

‡ *De Lege Rhodiâ*, De Jactu.

in the fourteenth Book of the Digests, has always been considered as an extract of indubitable authenticity. It contains various provisions for security against danger and for reparation of losses sustained at sea, particularly in cases of shipwreck. Each of the articles of which it is composed, appears to have been derived from some original code of Rhodian law, and is illustrated by the comments and opinions of the most learned jurists. From their works they were again selected by the compilers of the Digests, and arranged by them in their present form. The adversaries of Justinian might here perhaps with some shew of justice give vent to the spirit of *anti-tribonianism*; for there is great reason to suppose that many other articles of similar tendency, which occur in the imperial law, were drawn from the same source, though it is in this article alone that any such acknowledgment, either express or implied, can be found. It would be well also if on this occasion as on many more, the carelessness and inaccuracy of the compilers were the only things complained of by their enemies, who have seldom omitted an opportunity of imputing to their disingenuity those losses, which more candid minds would attribute to the natural decay of time, and the ravages of barbarism.* But to return.

It is provided by the Rhodian law, that "if for the sake of lightening a ship in danger at sea an *ejection* shall take place, that which was given up for the general good, shall be replaced according to the proportion of what is saved, by *a general contribution*."† Nothing can be
more

---

* An ingenious civilian, now living, speaking of Justinian's being suspected to have destroyed the original works from which his compilers copied, humourously compared his conduct to that of a clumsy artist, who having been employed to paint the sign of a badger, set persons to destroy all the badgers in the neighbourhood, with a view of preventing a discovery of his unskilful imitation.

† Dib. Lib. 14. Tit. 2. *De Lege Rhodiâ, De* Jactu. § 1.

more equitably devised than this law, which has by its
intrinsic merit gained admission into all the marine codes
of succeeding times.*   To render this act of *ejection*
perfectly legal, it must be observed, that the three following cases ought to concur : First, the ship must be in
evident danger of perishing with her cargo, secondly, the
resolution taken by the captain on this occasion, must be
in consequence of a consultation held with his officers
and crew on the subject, and lastly, the ship and cargo
must appear to have been saved by these means.

Agreeably to these three axioms it is to be concluded,
that the partial loss, thus voluntarily incurred to prevent
a total one of the ship and cargo, ought to be equally
borne by the ship and her remaining lading.†   After this
general position, we have a variety of cases stated, and
some particular rules and exceptions specified.   For
instance, " they, whose property has suffered *ejection* upon
the foregoing terms, shall have action against the master
of the ship, and the master against those who saved their
property in consequence of the *ejection,* in order that the
loss may fall equal." ‡

This is in exact conformity with a well known maxim
at this day, namely, that as the *common law* looks upon

38

the

---

* " William the Conqueror and Hen. 1st, made and ratified this
law, concerning goods cast overboard by mariners in a storm, in
imitation of the ancient Rhodian law, *De Jactu*."   Molloy, *De Jure
maritimo et navali.* Book 2 chap. 6.   See also Miege's *Laws of Oleron.*
Art. 8, 9, 10 the *Wisbuy Laws,* Art. 20, 21, 38, 46. and the laws of
the *Hanse Towns,* Tit. 8, 9. with Reinold Kuricke's Commentary.
N.B.—All these may be found in Malyne's *Lex Mercatoria.*

† Beauw. *Lex Mercatoria.*   Article *Salvage.* p. 135, &c.   And
this conforms with the rule of modern practice, which holds that
average is only admissible in cases where the loss of one man's goods
contributes to the safety of another's, and not in all cases of a
partial loss at sea.   Shower's *Cases* in *Parliament.* 20.

‡ Tit. 2. § 2.

the goods and cargo as a pledge for the freight, so the
marine law looks upon them as a security for answering
any average or contribution, and with this view, the
master is bound not to deliver the goods till the contribution is settled, they being tacitly obliged for the one as
well as the other.*

" For any damage sustained by the ship and its tackle
by a storm, no contribution can be demanded; any more
than an artificer who shall break or injure his tools, can
require reparation from the person for whom he was
working."† " But if (as it is specified afterwards) this
damage did not arise by storm, but was voluntarily
incurred, and with the general consent; then, in conformity with the first clause, it must come into the contribution." ‡

" Every kind of goods, even jewels, money, &c. which
could not have been a burthen to the ship, are nevertheless not exempted from contribution. Indeed it should
seem reasonable that their proportion ought to be greater
according to their value. But apparel in use, provisions,
and all things necessary for the sustenance of the crew,
are exempt."

" In settling the terms of contribution, the goods lost,
are not to be valued at what they might fetch if carried
to market, but according to the original price they were
purchased at; and on the contrary the goods, which are
to contribute, must be estimated not at what they originally cost, but at what they will sell for. Quoniam (as
it is expressed) *detrimenti* non *lucri* sit præstatio." §

39   " When

---

* Molloy. Book 2. chap. 6. §. 7.

† Tit. 2. §. 2. Molloy. *Loc. cit.*   ‡ Tit. 2. §. 2.

§ The modern custom has been, that if goods are thrown over
before half the voyage is complete, then they are to be valued at the
price they cost; if after half the voyage, then at the price which
goods of the same quality shall sell for at the place of the ship's

" When in order to lighten a ship coming into port, part of the cargo is put into a skiff or boat, and this shall perish in the sea, the ship being saved, a contribution is required, to indemnify those, whose property was thus, as if by *ejection*, sacrificed for the general good. But if the ship perish and the boat be preserved, no contribution is to take place ; because it is never allowed but where ships arrive safe." *

If in a storm by an ejection of one man's property the ship be saved for a time and afterwards perish, and it so happen that the goods then on board are picked up by divers,† they must be contributory to the ejected goods,

40　　　　　　　　　　　which

---

discharge. In many cases, however, the Rhodian law still continues in force. Beauw. Loc. cit. Molloy. Loc. cit.

* By the law of the Admiralty, if a ship be lost before her unloading, no freight shall be paid, but every one must bear his part of the loss, and in such case even the mariners lose their wages. Molloy. B. 2. Chap. 4. and B. 2. Chap. 3. 6. 7. For, as it is observed, *freight* is the *mother of wages*, and wherever freight is due wages are due also, and *vice versa*, provided the mariners have honestly performed their parts. 1. 3 & 4.

† *Divers*, called by the ancients *Urinatores*, were incorporated at Rome in the same society with the fishermen, as appears from two inscriptions in Gruter ;

FL. ANNIO ANNÆO LEMONIA FORTUNATO PISCATOR URINATORI. P. CCCLIV. and again. TI. CLAUDIO ESQUIL. SEVERO DECURIALI LECTORI PATRONO CORPORIS PISCATORUM ET URINATORUM. P. CCCXCI. They are alluded to by Manilius in these lines,

" Corpora qui mergunt undis ipsumque sub antris
　Nerea et aquoreas conantur visere nymphas,
　Exportantque maris prædas, et rapta profundo
　Naufragia, atque imas avidi scrutantur arenas."

　　　　　　　　　　　　　　　Astronom. Lib. 5. v. 431. see also
a highly coloured description, beginning with

　　" Cæruleus ponto cum se Delphinus in astra
　　" Erigit" &c. and ending at v. 448.
and by Lucan,

　　　　　— " animam servare sub undis.
　Scrutarique stretum, si quid mersisset arenis." Lib. 3. v. 697.

which on the contrary if recovered are not liable to the
same conditions; because the goods which *sunk with the
ship,* were not, as in the case of those *ejected,* sacrificed
for the general safety. And here a question is put,
" whether goods which have received injury on board be
liable to contribution, because it seems unreasonable for a
person to suffer doubly?" It is answered, " that the
person is to contribute according to the reduced value of
his property from the injury it has sustained." Another
question then arises, " whether if the damage has accrued
to him in consequence of an *ejection,* which has exposed
his goods to the weather, or has broken them by violent
usage, he is to contribute." And it is decided, " that he
is to deduct from the rate of the contribution the amount
of his own damages and to contribute the remainder."
But then again it is said, " suppose the damage is greater
than the rate of contribution—in that case the damaged
property must be brought into the average; for it is very
immaterial whether it had been totally spoiled, or thrown

41 overboard,

The first institution of corporate, or, collegiate bodies at Rome,
appears to have been by Numa, who in order to unite the Romans
and Sabines more closely, took away the distinctions which had subsisted between them, and distributed the two people indiscriminately
into separate fraternities, according to their different trades. Plutarch. *in Numa.* p. 155. edit. Bryan. For full information on this
subject consult Dig, 3, tit. 4, and 47. tit. 22, and 46. tit. 1. 22, with
Taylor's *El. of Civ. Law. art. Senatus-consultum Marcianum.* p. 567
—573.

The rate of *salvage* was thus settled by the ancients, as appears
in the collection of Rhodian laws. A person saving any part of a
wreck at sea, shall have one *fifth* of what he saves. Art. 45. and a
third, a *half,* or a *tenth,* according to the depth of water. A *tenth* for
salvage on the coast, and a *fifth* for him, who saving himself, brings
something to shore. Art. 47. see also Beauw. *Lex Mercat.* art. *Salvage,*
p. 135 &c. for the modern practice. A proportion is also given
according to the bulk of the salvage, gold and silver paying less than
coarse and burthensome goods. Art. 40.

overboard, and if in the latter case a recompense be made to the owners, it is but just in the former, when the injury can be proved to have happened in consequence of an *ejection.*" *

" If a ship be cast away, the goods saved from wreck are not liable to contribution, for the same reason that property saved in a boat is exempt: and because as it is elsewhere said; property thus saved, belongs as entirely to the owner, as if it had been rescued from fire."

" If by the violence of a storm, or any other accident, the masts and rigging be damaged or destroyed, and the captain put into port to make a temporary refitment, for this expence no contribution can be required."

There appears to be something unreasonable in this, for the expence of refitting was certainly incurred for the safety of the cargo. There is much more equity in the rule at present observed, which enjoins, that although the charges of bringing a ship into port are not to be brought into an average, yet when this is done from indispensable necessity, to escape a storm, to refit and so forth, then even the wages and provisions are brought into an average, and all the expences occasioned by this necessity are discharged by general contribution.†

" Goods cast overboard to lighten the ship make no *derelict,* but are to be restored to their owners if found, just as in the case of a burthen which a weary man has laid by the road side, while he rests himself or goes in search of assistance."‡

42

" If

---

* Lib. 14. Tit. 2 §. 4.   † Beauw. p. 137.

‡ It is necessary to state the following distinctions which are observed in property lost at sea. *Wreck* is properly applied to goods, which, when a ship is sunk, or otherwise perished, are driven to land by the sea. " *Quæ naufragio ad terram appelluntur.*" For if the goods are found floating on the sea, they are called *flotsam.* When they are cast overboard to lighten a ship, which notwithstanding this, afterwards perishes, they are, *jetsam;* and *lagan* or *ligan,* when

" If you freight a ship, and your goods, without your consent, and no necessity compelling, be put on board another ship, in worse condition than the first, and are lost, you have action against the master with whom the agreement was made; but the action will not lie, if both the ships perish in the voyage." The present rule is, that if there be extreme necessity and an empty ship is passing by, the master may transfer the goods, and if that ship perish, his conduct is unimpeachable; but then it must appear that the ship seemed *probable* and *sufficient*." *

These are the principal clauses in that title of the Digests, *De Lege Rhodiâ de jactu*, which as they all relate to one point of maritime justice, I have thought proper to select. There are a few others intermixed with them upon different subjects, such as *contracts*, *piracy* and *freight*, which it is not here necessary to mention. But what has rendered this title particularly curious, is a small historical fragment, there inserted, from some collection of Rhodian laws by Volusius Mæcianus, a jurist of the 3d century. It is a rescript of Antoninus Pius in answer to a petition of Eudæmon, a merchant of Nicomedia, to that emperor, wherein he states, that being shipwrecked among the Cyclades, his property was seized upon by the officers

43　　　　　　　　　　　　　　　of

---

having been ejected and sunk to the bottom, the mariners with an intent to get them again, fasten to them a buoy to mark the place where they may be found. The *Court of Admiralty* therefore cannot hold plea of *wreck*, but it must be tried before the king's justices at common law, as being *infra corpus comitatus*, the proper jurisdiction of the Admiralty being *supra altum mare*. 1. Instit. 260. and a note of Selden on Fortescue *de laud. leg. Ang*. Cap. 32. & 2 Instit. 168. But of the other three, *flotsam, jetsam*, and *ligan*, the Admiralty hath jurisdiction. Bracton lib. 3. fol. 120.

Derelict, differs from each of these in being goods cast into the sea without any hope or likelihood of ever recovering them, and are so wilfully given up by the owner. Molloy. B. 2. Chap. 5. §. 4.
* Molloy. Book 2. chap. 4. §. 5.

of revenue.* He addresses the emperor by the title of
sovereign, Κυριος and he is answered in the true spirit of
a Roman, who considered the world as one country, of
which Rome was the principal city.† Εγω μεν του κοσμου
κυριος, ὁ δε νομος της θαλασσης. Τῳ νομῳ των Ροδιων
κρινεσθω τῳ ναυτικῳ. " I am sovereign of the world,
it is true, nevertheless controversies at sea must be
determined by the maritime laws of Rhodes, except (as
he adds) in cases where they contradict our own laws." ‡
This answer has given rise to various controversies
on the authority of the Rhodian laws at Rome; and
to innumerable disputes whether the emperors claimed
any dominion upon the seas. There certainly is
nothing here which implies a denial of this part of
the imperial power; for as Gothofred justly observes,
" non *imperium*, sed *judicium* tantum legi Rhodiæ,
hac lege committit," § and even this is with limitations, for it is no longer admissible than while it agrees
with the laws of Rome. The same writer gives the
following rational paraphrase of this answer, " you have

44 done

---

* The Cyclades were islands terrible to mariners and appear to
have been notorious for shipwrecks. Virgil says of them
—— " Sparsasque per æquor
Cyclades et crebris legimus freta concita terris"
Æn. 3. 237.
and Horace frequently mentions them in this light. See lib. 1. Od.
1, lib. 3. Od. 29, et 1. 14.

† " Gentibus est aliis tellus data limite certo ;
" *Romanæ* spatium est *Urbis* et *Orbis* idem."
Ov. *Fast.* lib. 2, v. 243.

‡ The application of the Rhodian law to this particular case was
in every light proper : for we are told, there was a separate governour
over the five provinces of Scythia, Mysia, Caria, the Cyclades, and
Cyprus, but that in maritime cases the governour of Rhodes had
supreme jurisdiction. See *Novel* 41, Tit. *De Quæstoribus, id est,
Præfectis Insularum*. et Nov. 50. et 163. Tiberius, during his retirement there, acted with this power. Sueton, *Vit. Tib.*

§ De Imperio Maris. cap. 7.

done right, Eudæmon, in applying to me for redress; conceiving, as it appears you did by calling me in your petition *Lord of the World,* that I might extend my authority at pleasure over the seas : But there are certain laws of Rhodes established at Rome for regulating naval matters, and therefore, they must decide in this case." *

45   Were

---

* The emperor's delicacy in this matter deserves our attention. It is well known that the ancient laws gave wreck to the sovereign. Dig. Lib. 49. tit. 14. *De Jure Fisci.*

"Quicquid conspicuum, pulchrumque est æquore toto,

" *Res Fisci* est ubicumque natat."

Juvenal Sat. 4. v. 54. and upon this subject

many laws and edicts occur, see *De Incendio, Ruinâ,* &c. Dig. Lib. 47, tit. 9. et Dig. 43. 12, 13, 14, 15. et *De acquir. possess. et rerum Dominio.* et Cod. lib. 11. Tit. 4 and 5.

Antoninus, very humanely altered this rule, declaring, that in cases of distress "Fiscus meus sese non interponat. Quod enim jus habeat fiscus in alienâ calamitate, ut de re tam luctuosâ compendium sectetur ?" Cod. Lib. 11, tit. 5. *De Naufragiis.*

This reminds us of an ordonnance of Louis the XIVth, which sets aside the old law, and permits the proprietors of shipwrecked goods to reclaim them within a year and a day, paying the expence of salvage. *Ordon. de la Marine* Art. 29, tit. 9, Liv. 4. and we are informed that even after this prescribed time the claimers might recover them. "Le Roi & M. L'Amiral ayant toujours eu la gran-deur d'âme d'admettre les réclamations, quoique faites *hors du tems prescrit.*" Valin, *Sur L'Ord. de la Marine,* loc. cit.

Wreck, originally in this country was given to the crown for two main reasons of common law. 1st, That the property of all goods must be in some person. 2d, That such goods as no person can claim property in, do belong to the king by his prerogative, and when navigation and commerce were less common and perfect, it was difficult to prove in whom the property of wrecks at sea was. Others have given as a reason, that wreck was bestowed on the king to indemnify him for his charges in scouring the sea of pirates. 2 Instit. 167. Wreck may belong to the *subject* either by grant from the king or by prescription. 2 Instit. 168. Anciently, wreck of the sea, &c. was " primi inventoris, quasi totius populi, sed postea ad regem translata fuerunt, quia non modo totius populi, sed Reipub-licæ etiam caput est." 2 Instit. 168. *Doctor and Student.* Dial. 2, chap. 51.

Were it necessary, a variety of testimonies might be brought, to shew that the emperors were actually considered and claimed to be held lords of the sea, and that even private persons, by their permission, enjoyed peculiar privileges upon that element. But I refer my reader to the 13th chapter of Gothofred's excellent treatise, *De Imperio Maris*, and to the 25th and 36th chapters in the 1st Book of Selden's *Mare clausum*, a work which has given the fullest answer to those modern disputants who, by ingenious refinements and hasty interpretations, have

46   attempted

The laws of Oleron are very severe on the plunderers of a wreck. See Art. 24, 25, 28, 30, 31. They are to suffer excommunication, and capital punishment, without the protection of any custom or statute whatever, and if they do violence to the persons of the shipwrecked, they are to be plunged into the sea till they are half dead, and then to be drawn out and stoned to death. " A lord of a manor, who shall connive at these proceedings shall have his goods sold for pious uses, and he himself shall be fastened to a stake in the midst of his mansion house, which is then to be set on fire at the four corners, and burnt to the ground, and a market to be established on the spot, for the sale of hogs, and swine, to all posterity."

But by Stat. West. 1. cap. 4. & 17. E. 2. c. 11. If a man, a dog, or a cat, escape alive, or the party to whom the goods belong, claim within a year and a day, they are his; and this royal claim was renounced by Rich. I, in the isle of Oleron. *Ol. Laws*, cap. 47. Hoveden's *Annals*, fol. 678. By a law of Sicily A.D. 1221 the plunder of shipwrecked goods was made capital. *Pragmatic. Regni Siciliæ*. Panorm. 1647.

Indeed a person under these circumstances was an object of protection by the laws of almost all the civilized states of antiquity.

ΝΑΥΑΓΟΣ ηκω ξενος, ΑΣΥΛΗΤΟΝ γενος

" Being a shipwrecked stranger, I am a person who ought not to be plundered." Euripid. *Helen*. ver. 456.

And the acute author of *Observations on the Statutes chiefly the more ancient*, thinks it " much to the honour of humanity, that in every part of the globe, where any sort of civil policy prevails, making prisoners those who are shipwrecked on their coasts, is peculiar to Japan ; nor was this barbarian practice introduced among them till after the expulsion of the Portuguese, who had made very unjustifiable attempts on their religion and government." p. 17.

attempted to deny, that any nation or prince, ever did or
can, with justice, claim an exclusive right over the seas.
I cannot, however, quit the consideration of this law
without taking notice of a very singular correction of
Antoninus's answer given us by Samuel Petit. Instead
of ο δε *ΝΟΜΟΣ* της θαλασσης, he reads, ο δε *ΑΝΕΜΟΣ*,
which he thus explains; "with regard to your shipwreck
I can give no redress, nor is it in my power to prevent
it in future. I am lord of the *land* it is true, but the
wind commands the sea; and he then proceeds, as to a
second clause in the answer, to refer him to the Rhodian
code for relief against his plunderers." *

47   Having

---

* Miscellan. 3, cap. 11.

With respect to the argument *De Maris Dominio*, there are very
early records that nations of high antiquity, claimed and held an
exclusive sovereignty over certain seas; for example, it is shewn in
the conditions of that treaty between Athens and Lacedæmon in the
fourth Book of Thucydides, and in those which are to be found in
the third Book of Polybius, between Rome and Carthage. The
inferences which can be drawn from the opinions of the Roman
lawyers on this article are very indecisive, for if one has asserted,
"Mare esse in primævo jure quo omnia erant *communia*." another
contends, "Videmus, de jure gentium, in Mare esse *regna distincta*,
sicut in terrâ."

Dion Chrysostom in his 34th oration says, that Trajan, in extending certain privileges to Tharsus, gave her right and dominion over
the river (Cydnus) and over the adjacent seas, and in Dig. Lib. 4. tit,
De rerum Divisione, we find the emperor Antoninus communicating
the same right to the fishermen of Formia. The exclusive privileges
enjoyed by private individuals on the sea, for the purposes of luxury,
were derived also from imperial authority, and serve for frequent
topics of ridicule, though never of complaint, to the Roman writers;
which would scarcely be the case, had they been considered as usur-
pations. See Pliny, *Hist. Nat.* Lib. 9. cap. 54. Sallust, *Bell. Catilin.*
§. 17. Martial. Lib. 10, Epig. 30.

For what regards our own country in this dispute, it may be
proved, by many ancient records, and by a series of undeniable
evidence brought down through various ages, that the kings of
England did very early claim to be, and were acknowledged sovereigns
of the sea, so much of it at least, as is the object of the controversy.

Having thus endeavoured historically to trace the origin, progress and influence of the Rhodian laws at Rome, in as clear a manner as the imperfection of the materials will permit, and to give a slight specimen of their character, it remains to enquire in a summary way, what was their fate after the dissolution of the Roman

48   empire

---

4 Instit. 142. Selden. *Mare Clausum.* c. 27. For I apprehend the warmest advocates for exclusive privilege thereon, never attempted to extend it either to the Atlantic, or the Southern Ocean. Thus king Edgar is said *Quatuor maria vindicare,* and Sir J. Burroughs cites a record in the Tower, having for its title " Of the Sovereign of the *English Seas,* and the Office of Admiral thereon." *Sovereignty of the British Seas asserted.* p. 7. and Edward III. calls himself and his predecessors, " Domini Maris *Anglicani* circumquaque et etiam Defensores" Selden, notes on Fortesc. c. 32. The extent of this dominion was particularly ascertained by a treaty at Westm. Feb. 9. 1673-4, to be from Cape Finisterre, to the middle point of the Land Van Staten in Norway.

The duty of the *flag,* which is a consecutive acknowlegment of this dominion, is as old as the reign of king John, since whose time it has been constantly asserted by his successors. This mark of respect indeed had always appeared to foreigners so unquestionably our right, that the first instance of its being inserted as an article in any treaty was in the year 1653. *Treaty of Peace between the Commonwealth of England, and the United Provinces.* Art. 15.

It is worthy of remark that, at the very time when the warmth of this controversy had excited a general jealousy concerning the *imperium Maris,* the Venetians asserted their right over the Adriatic in a memorable instance. They insisted upon, and obtained the privilege of transporting from Naples to Trieste, the king of Spain's sister, who was espoused to the king of Hungary, threatening, that if the Spaniards should presume to send any ships into their gulph for this purpose, they would attack them as enemies to the republic. A.D. 1630. Pancius. *De Dominio Maris Adriatici.* L. 2, c. 6, and thus by one illustrious example they effectually put to silence all the learned arguments of their adversaries.

N.B.—A fruitless attempt was made about half a century ago, to revive the controversy by Mons. Deslande in his *Essay on maritime power,* to which he appears to have been instigated by the Count de Maurepas, intendant of the French marine.

empire had produced a total change in the inhabitants, manners and language of Europe.

The successive inundations of northern barbarism in the 5th and 6th centuries, and the ravages of the Saracens on the coasts and islands of the Mediterranean sea in the 7th, necessarily gave a check to every species of liberal communication, and thus proved equally fatal to the interests of literature and of commerce. The latter in particular received a very severe blow, by the extinction of the Indian trade, which had long been the principal branch carried on in the Greek empire, by the way of Egypt. This was effectually cut off when the Saracens took possession of Alexandria. It is not however to be understood that commercial intercourse was totally obstructed. It still feebly subsisted, but the mode of carrying it on was changed. The merchant, unwilling to transport his property over an element infested by a lawless enemy, to whose arms most of the maritime powers had yielded, and finding the principal ports and harbours either deserted or in possession of a people more inclined to plunder than traffic, sought other channels of communication.

The exchange of commodities was, during this period, chiefly transacted by means of inland traders or travelling merchants, who for this purpose established staples and enterpots, and thus contributed to aggrandize many of those towns which since have made so conspicuous a figure in Germany and the Netherlands.* The foundation of many new commercial states was also laid in these ages, and, as the ancient channels became dry or obstructed, fresh sources of trade began to open on the western and southern coasts of Europe.†

The

---

* Anderson's History of Commerce. Vol. 1, p. 432.
† Anderson ut supra p. 235. Cedreni *Compend. Hist.* Par. 2. p. 477. Edit. Paris. Ockley's *Conquests of the Saracens.*

The conquests of Charlemagne in Italy, and his establishment of Christianity in the north, are considered, by some writers, as the causes of the revival of maritime commerce, since at the same time that he diffused a liberal and communicative spirit by the introduction of the true religion, he removed in a great measure the principal obstacles to its gratification, by scowering the sea of pirates and rendering that passage from the north to the south more safe and commodious.

But perhaps we are to look further back for the true cause. The furious ravages of Attila, the Hun, in the 5th century, compelled many of the distressed inhabitants of Italy to seek for safety in the marshes and islands at the northern extremity of the Adriatic,* whence, in less than four hundred years after their settlement, arose the magnificent mart of Venice.† As early as the beginning of the 8th century, we hear of her with a powerful fleet, defending the Exarchate of Ravenna against the Lombards,‡ and soon after this, defeating the views of Charlemagne, who, jealous of the preference which she gave to the Greek emperors, had sent a large armament into the Adriatic.§ It is to this state, in fact, that we are indebted for the revival of the commercial spirit in Europe. She seems first to have encouraged it in her neighbour and powerful rival, Genoa, by whose communication of the rich commodities of the East, a similar zeal was excited among the nations on the Baltic, who were themselves at last enabled to contend with them both, for the balance

50   of

---

* Jornandes. *De Rebus Geticis.*

† The reader may compare Cassiodorus Epist. 12, lib. 12, with lib. 12, Ep. 24. and consult Montesquieu *Esp. Des. Loix*, Liv. 20. c. 5.

‡ Essai de L'Histoire du Commerce de Venice, and Muratori, *Antichita Italiane.* Dissertazioni, 25ᵗᵃ & 26ᵗᵃ.

§ Loc. cit.

of commercial power.* The superiority however of the
Italian cities must be confessed ; for at the time when the
Hanseatic towns, having run their career of glory, were
gradually disuniting and yielding to the arms of neighbouring princes, Venice of herself was able to sustain, and
in some measure defeat, the most formidable league suddenly raised against her, that is to be met with in the
history of modern times.†

If, during the period called the middle ages, any form
of maritime justice was acknowledged, it probably was
such as those fragments of the Rhodian code, preserved
in the Roman law, afforded. A variety of causes contributed to preserve an active intercourse between the
Italian provinces and Constantinople, where many parts
of Justinian's compilation were still read in the Greek
language, and where a new body of jurisprudence had
recently been formed, into which the laws of Rhodes were
admitted.‡ We have no authority for supposing that any

51   new

---

* De Mailly. *Histoire de Gennes.*

It must be observed that I here speak of *maritime* commerce
only. Inland traffic was promoted and established by very different
means. Montesquieu traces it, rather whimsically, from the introduction of Aristotle's works, which first taught mankind to confound
the lending upon interest with *usury*, Περι Πολιτειας, lib. 1. cap. 9,
10. and encouraged a spirit of persecution against the Jews, who,
wearied with proscriptions, confiscations, and extortions, at length
found it necessary to render their property *invisible*. They invented
a secret and compendious mode of negotiation by bills of exchange
and paper currency, and thus gave, as it were, a soul to mercantile
communication. Esp. des. Loix, Liv. 21. cap. 16.

† Maimbourg, Histoire de la Ligue. The League of Cambray, to
which I allude, took place in the year 1510, a period when the naval
powers of Denmark and Sweden had greatly weakened the Hanseatic
confederacy, and when the French and English, by withdrawing
their principal cities from the alliance, threatened, for a time, its
total annihilation.

‡ The Codes of Leo and Constantine, Lib. 53. tit. 8. *See Chronological View of Roman Law*, p. 67.

new system had been drawn up more early than the close of the 11th century. At that time the people of Amalfi had risen into great repute for skill in navigation, and activity in trade. They were respected by all their neighbours on the Mediterranean coasts, and enjoyed peculiar privileges in the east.* To this people we owe the first code of modern sea laws, called, from the place of its compilation, Tabula Amalfitana. The authority of this code was acknowledged by all the maritime states, on those seas, and continued in force for more than four hundred years, as may be inferred from the following words of Marino Freccia, a writer at the close of the 16th century—" Hinc in regno, non lege Rhodia, maritima decernuntur, sed Tabula quam Amalfitanam vocant, omnes controversiæ, omnes lites, ac omnia Maris discrimina, eâ lege, eâ sanctione *usque ad hæc tempora* finiuntur." † Yet, at the time this author wrote, its influence was not so extensive as formerly. As trade increased, various other ports of the Mediterranean acquired their share of it, and, becoming powerful and opulent, were impatient of receiving laws from a neighbouring rival. Each therefore, as occasion offered, set up for its own legislator, and decided in particular cases, according to regulations of its own, still however referring to the Amalfitan table in

52

points

---

* See Du Fresne's notes on Anna Comnena's History, p. 234. edit. Paris.

By permission from the Caliphs they founded the famous hospital of St. John, at Jerusalem, whose knights, as we have seen, became inhabitants of Rhodes, and proved powerful protectors of that commerce, to which they were indebted for their existence. The honour of inventing the compass is also by some attributed to the people of Amalfi. Gemelli Carreri's *Voyages*, Book. 1. chap. 1. Giannone *1st. di Napoli*, Lib. 7, cap. 3.

† In Lib. *De Sub feudis*. *De Officio Admir*. Lib. 1..Num. 8. This writer, p. 327, tells us that Amalfi was a Metropolitan See, as early as the year 904.

points of public concern. The sources of maritime law, being thus multiplied, produced in process of time such confusion and contradiction in the administration of justice, that, at a general assembly, it was at last agreed to digest the separate laws of each community into one body. Accordingly, making use of the Amalfitan table as a basis, they formed a superstructure of all such regulations as appeared useful and consistent in the various laws of Marseilles,* Pisa, Genoa, Venice, Barcelona,† Aragon and the Morea, and published them about the close of the 14th century, under the name of *Consolato del Mare,* a code which, to this day, retains most of its original authority.‡ Whoever is at all acquainted with the general spirit of this code will not hesitate in pointing to the source whence it was derived. In many particular articles we may discover the exact features of its original; and this internal evidence added to the reasons already assigned for such a conclusion, afford, I think, very presumptive proof, that some parts at least of the Amalfitan table were copied from such fragments of the Rhodian laws as are preserved in the pandects of Justinian.§

While trade and navigation in the south were thus regulated by two codes, the *Table of Amalfi* and the

---

* Marseilles, at this day, one of the busiest ports in Europe, was founded almost six centuries before Christ by a Greek colony, and is celebrated as a place of great wealth and splendour by many ancient writers. Strabo Lib. 4. Tacitus in *Vit. Agricolæ.* Cicero *Orat. pro Val. Flocco.* Montesquieu *Esp. Des Loix Liv.* 20. c. 5.

† Some are of opinion that the laws of Barcelona claim the honour of being the basis of modern mercantile jurisprudence. See Robertson's *State of Europe.* p. 351.

The account I have given above, is founded upon the opinion of Giannone. *Ist di Napoli.* Lib. 11. cap. 6. and of Freccia, Loc. cit.

‡ Zouch's *Admiral Jurisdiction.* Welwood's *Abridgment of sea laws.* Giannone, ut supra. The best edition of the *Consolato del Mare* was published at Venice in 1567.

§ Ante page 377.

Consolato del Mare, the spirit of commerce had revived in another quarter of Europe, and the influence of these ancient sea laws was seen to diffuse itself on the western coasts and among the nations on the Baltic. The state of maritime justice among the inhabitants of those regions, before the 12th century, may easily be imagined. It was suited well enough perhaps to the contracted intercourse of the times, but must have been soon found inadequate to the purposes of that extensive communication which now began to be opened.

About the year 1194, king Richard I, on his return from the Holy Land, rested for some time in the isle of Oleron in the Bay Aquitain, or, as it is now called, of Biscay, and having been convinced, perhaps during his perilous voyage, of the great inconveniences to which merchants and mariners in that quarter of the world were perpetually exposed for want of a maritime code, he there gave orders for a work of this kind to be compiled. Such, according to the best authorities, was the origin of the laws of Oleron, so justly celebrated for their wisdom and equity, and for being the model of all the sea laws in the west of Europe.* Jealous of the lustre which our country derives from this circumstance, the French

54 writers

---

* Godolphin in an "appendix to his View of the Admiralty Jurisdiction," has given a collection of them in 47 articles. Selden thinks, that Richard published them, not as duke of Aquitaine, but by his right at that time, as king of England, to superintend and direct all transactions on those seas. *Mare Clausum.* cap. 24. which perfectly agrees with the opinion of another very learned English civilian, who says of these laws, that "the western world received them from the English, by way of deference to the *sovereignty of our kings in the British Ocean,* and to the judgment of our countrymen in sea affairs." Sir Leoline Jenkins's *Charge to the Cinque Ports.* p. lxxxvii.

Henry II, about 20 years before, had promulgated a law of wreck in that island, which was adopted by his son. Rymer's *Fœdera* Tom. 1. p. 12. 20. Hen. II. A.D. 1174.

writers have not been backward in asserting a superior claim to this code. It was drawn up, they say, in the French language, published in an island on the coast of France, and intended solely for the service of that nation; since throughout the whole, no mention is made of the Thames, or any river or port in England or Ireland, but all is referred to Bourdeaux, St. Malo, and other sea ports of France.* But no argument founded on the place where it was compiled and promulgated can, I think, be adduced in favour of their opinion, when it is considered that the isle of Oleron, with other territories in those parts of France, was then annexed to the crown of England; consequently, these laws were as much English laws as if Richard had published them in London. This may also serve to answer the other part of their argument, for ·besides that it was more natural to insert the names of places in the neighbourhood, than of such as were remote, it must be obvious that Bourdeaux and St. Malo were as much a part of the king's dominion, as any sea ports in England or Ireland. As to the language in which they are written, it is no other than what was frequently adopted by our kings in their legal acts and ordinances, and cannot therefore be used as a reasonable proof in this particular instance. "I call them the laws of Oleron, says a great civilian, not but that they are *peculiarly enough English*, being long since incorporated into the customs and statutes of our Admiralties; but the equity of them is so great, and the use and reason of them is so general, that they are known and received all the world over by that rather than by any other name."† With respect to the latter part of this observation it must be remarked, that greater latitude is here given to those laws, than writers in general have

55   been

---

* Miege's, *Sea Laws.* p. 3.   † Sir Leoline Jenkins. loc. cit.

been willing to allow them. For it has been asserted,
that their influence never extended further than over the
western seas of Europe, and even in these was more
particularly confined to the coasts of France and Great
Britain, and it is added, that their authority, in this part
of the world,.very much resembled that of the Rhodian
laws in the Mediterranean.   " The sea laws instituted at
Oleron, says Molloy, never obtained any other, or greater
force than those of Rhodes formerly did, that is, they
were esteemed for the reason and equity found in them,
and applied to the case emergent." *   Their warmest
admirers, in short, have limited their authority to that
ocean which extends from the Straits of Gibraltar to the
coast of Norway. These laws are said to have received
amendment and confirmation twice during the reign of
Edward III, particularly by the verdicts given in the
famous inquisition at Queensborough, in the year 1376,†
but since that time their influence has gradually become
feeble and contracted; and as laws, more conformable to
modern custom, have been introduced, even the subject of
many articles has long ago grown entirely obsolete.‡   In
France they seem to have been originally admitted nearly

upon

---

* Molloy, *De jure maritimo et navali*, Introduction. Grotius. *Flor.
Spars. in Jus Justinian.* p. 17.

† The Inquisition at Queensborough was held before two admirals, and the Lord Warden of the Cinque Ports, (an officer of high
antiquity, as appears from a summons in the time of Ed. 1 see
Brady's *Appendix.* No. 6.) and the verdicts there given by 18 expert
seamen, appointed for the purpose of examining the maritime code,
were confirmed by the king's letters patent. Sir Leol. Jenkins's
Speech in behalf of the jurisdiction of the Admiralty. vol. 1. p. lxxvii.
Molloy. loc. cit. Selden, in his notes on Fortescue *De laud. leg. Ang.*
cap. 32. considers Roughton's translation, called, *De Officio Admiralitatis*, rather, as a monument of antiquity than authority, and ascribes
it, with a copy of the Roll of Oleron (communicated to him by Sir
Walter Raleigh) to the time of Henry VI.

‡ Anderson's *History of Commerce.* vol. 1. p. 96.

upon the same footing as in this country, and afterwards to have experienced similar revolutions. By an ancient record, entitled *Droits et Pré-éminences de l'Amiral*, this officer is enjoined in the 10th title to found his decisions on the laws of Oleron. In some subsequent records a more extensive scope is given him, and the Oleron laws are often superseded by public edicts and local usages; most of them have been variously modified, and some parts abrogated by royal ordonnances;* yet they still maintain a place in their marine code, and hold, as with us, a limited authority in nautical controversies.†

Various are the materials of which the maritime law of England is at present composed. Besides the rules of Oleron, the 'indisputable basis of the structure, many useful principles have been adopted from the laws of Rhodes and from the Roman civil law. " Julis Civilis vel Cæsarii usus, ab antiquis seculis etiam nunc retinetur in Foro Maritimo seu Curiâ Admiralitatis." ‡ And surely it may be considered as a fortunate coincidence, that the works of Justinian should begin to diffuse their light over Europe at the very time when commerce, by bringing together the inhabitants of distant climates, had created new situations and new interests among men, which rendered some volume of natural justice absolutely necessary.§ To the species of law just mentioned may also be

57   added

---

* Particularly by Charles VI, Lewis XII, Francis I, and Henry III.

† Reglemens et Ordonnances sur la fait de l'Amirauté, published at Rouen in the years 1543. 1554. 1594. 1602. 1604. See also 12 articles of the Marble Table 1673, (so called, from the place where the admiralty sessions are held every week at Paris,) and the final regulations in the year 1681 Liv. 1. tit. 2. *Ordonnances de la marine.*

‡ Selden *Dissert ad Fletam.* cap. 8. and Sir J. Hayward's *Life of Edward* VI, p. 29.

§ During the 12th and 13th centuries, academies for the study of the *Roman Civil Law* were established in almost every country in Europe. That of Irnerius at Bologna erected A.D. 1150 seems to

added some municipal institutions and customs peculiar
to certain places on the sea coasts ; " the whole, as Blackstone observes, being corrected, altered and amended by
acts of parliament and common usage; so that out of this
composition a body of jurisprudence is extracted, which
owes its authority only to its reception here *by consent
of the crown and people.*" *

The first case in our law, extant, relative to marine
jurisdiction, occurs in the reign of Edward I, and is
preserved in an old record in the Tower, which speaks of
the king's sovereignty on the seas, and the jurisdiction of
his deputy, the admiral, as being, even then, *du temps
dont il n'y a de mémoire.*†

58

But

---

have been the parent of all the rest. The schools of Montpelier,
Toulouse, and Orleans, in which Azo and Accursius taught, spread
this science over *France;* and in the same age, Vacarius, whom
Selden calls a disciple of the Bolognese academy, *Dissert. ad Flet.*
cap. 7. read lectures on the civil law at Oxford. "Tunc (speaking of
this æra) leges et causidici in *Angliam* primo vocati sunt, quorum
primus, magister Vacarius hic in *Oxenfordiâ* legem docuit." Duck,
De usu &c. l. 2. c. 8. §. 27 from a MS. in the Cotton Library, and he
afterwards shews, that the study was much cultivated in England,
especially in this university. *Ut supra* from §. 28. to 38. The same
period, so propitious to *jurisprudence,* proved equally favourable to
commerce. The foundation of the great mercantile commonwealth of
the Hanse Towns was laid. An immense number of cities in different parts of Europe received their charters of independence.
The Oleron and Wisbuy Laws were promulgated, coinage and manufactories improved, and various other channels opened, through which
to facilitate and extend the communication of mankind. Anderson's
Hist. of Commerce. vol. 1. B. 3.

* Commentaries. B. 3. chap. 7. §. 3. see more particularly stat. 28.
Hen. VIII. 5. Eliz. c. 5. 13. Car. II. 9. 2. W. and M. 2. 22 and 31.
Geo. II. in the two last of which, the laws for regulating his majesty's
navies and forces by sea were collected and formed into one code.

N.B.—Duck thinks, that many parts of our maritime law are
copied from the *Consolato del Mare.* De usu &c. l. 2. c. 8. §. 25.

† Selden's notes on Fortescue, cap. 32. 1 Inst. 439. 4 Inst. *Jurisdiction of Courts.* c. 22.

But whatever may have been the nature of the antiquity of this officer's power, it is generally agreed that the *Court of Admiralty*, in which he presides, was not formed into a regular establishment till the time of Edward III, when that authority, which had before been very irregularly exercised, became more permanent and defined.* To discountenance the opinion of those, who,

59   not

---

* Selden Loc. cit.

Though there be no doubt that the office of admiral is of very high antiquity, there appears no express mention of it before the close of the 13th century 25 Ed. I. nor in our printed law does it occur till, 8. Ed. II. Rymer's *Fœd.* tom. 1. p. 176. Selden, *ut sup.* In the beginning of the following century, we meet with two or more admirals at the same time, who are described as holding jurisdiction over the north and south seas, distinguished by the mouth of the Thames. But in 10. Rich. II. the office of *sole admiral* of England was conferred for the first time by the king's letters patent on Rich. Fitzallen jun. Earl of Arundel and Surry. Spelman's *Glossary.* voc. Admiral. Fædera. tom. 2. p. 162. 4. Inst. 75. Hale. C.L. 36. Since then it has been considered of high dignity, and its authority variously modified and limited, particularly by stat. 28. Hen. VIII. and 5. Eliz. c. 5. It is at present exercised by persons stiled, Lords Commissioners for executing the Office of Lord High Admiral of Great Britain and Ireland. stat. 2. W. and M. c. 2. and stat. 22. Geo. II. c. 3. which adds, that no sentence shall be valid unless the major part of the commissioners present be of the privy council.

In *France*, the admiral is always a prince or a person of high birth and quality. He sits in the king's house, and there holds his court, which used to be the case with the admirals of England. This court is composed of a lieutenant general, who presides, a particular lieutenant, three counsellors, the king's advocate and soliictor, a chief register, and two serjeants, all appointed by the admiral, but holding their commissions of the king.

The admiralty of Holland is divided into the five colleges of Amsterdam, Rotterdam, Hoorn, Middleburgh, and Harlingen. That of Amsterdam is composed of 12 lords, or counsellors. Of these, one is deputed by the nobility of Holland; the cities of Amsterdam, Leyden, Haarlem, Gouda, and Eadam depute one each, and the other six are chosen by the six other provinces. The rest of the colleges are nearly upon the same principle. Each of them has its particular officers, namely, an advocate fiscal, a receiver general, a commissary,

not distinguishing between the *office* itself and the *place* where it was exercised, have carried this institution into a much more remote period, it may be sufficient to refer to Britton, who, in the introduction to his book on the *Ancient Pleas of the Crown* Temp. Ed. I. will be found not to have enumerated the *Admiralty* among the courts of Justice at that time. This omission Lambard accounts for, by saying that the office, afterwards delegated to the admiral, was then in the king himself, and was exercised by him, or by some lawyers who attended him; and he is inclined to place the origin of the *Admiral's Court* in the days of Edward III, both on account of his reign being remarkable for its naval and mercantile operations, and because by a statute 2 Richard II. which regulates the proceeding of that court, the king establishes it upon the same footing as in his grandfather's time, as if he meant by these words to reduce it to its *original* authority.* In what this authority consisted, it is not difficult to form a general idea, though some particular articles of jurisdiction have been very warmly disputed.† It seems to have had the exercise both of *criminal* and *civil* justice over all maritime persons, and in all causes properly maritime.‡ This it continued to hold till 28 Hen. VIII. when it appearing inconsistent with the genius of the

60 English

---

an overseer of the sailors, a commissioner of sales, a treasurer, who is paymaster, a grand provost, with secretaries and officers for the inspection of passports, and the receipt of duties.

N.B.—They may pass final sentence in all civil matters under 600 florins, but, above this sum, an appeal lies from their sentence to the assembly of the states general. Postlethwayte, *Dict. of Trade and Commerce*, vol. 1. p. 21.

* Archeion. p. 48.

† Sir Ed. Coke's *Jurisdiction of Courts*, 4. Inst. c. 22 and 23. Zouch's *Jurisdiction of the Admiralty asserted.* Godolphin's *View of the Admiralty Jurisdiction.*

‡ Sir Leoline Jenkins's *Speech in behalf of the Admiralty Jurisdiction.* vol. 1. p. lxxvii.

English constitution to admit of proceedings in criminal suits without a jury, a statute was passed which enacted, that for the future all cases of marine felonies should be tried before commissioners nominated by the Lord Chancellor, according to the laws of England.* Among these commissioners, two common law judges are constantly appointed, who, as Blackstone observes, in effect try all the prisoners, and " this, he adds, is now the only method of trying marine felonies in the court of admiralty; the judge of the admiralty still presiding therein, as the Lord Mayor is the president of the sessions of *Oyer* and *Terminer* in London." † It is not to my present purpose to enter particularly into the civil practice of this court, the extent of its authority, or the forms of its proceedings. Perhaps I may be thought to have carried my reader already too far from the main object of the enquiry, I shall only add therefore, how in all contests respecting this court, it should be remembered, that although the proper region of its jurisdiction is said to be *super altum mare*, it is not the *place* only, but *the nature of the case*, happening within such a place, that creates the jurisdiction; and therefore if a contract of marriage or a testament be made at sea, or if a lease or any obligation be *sealed* there, the *common law* shall have cognizance of it, and not the *admiralty*, because *the case, though on the high sea, is not properly maritime*. And so on the contrary, in a case of which the admiralty hath *original* jurisdiction, though circumstances afterwards arise properly the objects

61 of

---

* It had been attempted in 8. Hen. VI. but the royal assent not being obtained, it miscarried.

N.B.—The jurisdiction of the *Cinque Ports* was not included in this statute, for this was always considered as distinct from, and independent of the Lord High Admiral's Court. Sir L. Jenkins. ut supra.

† Commentaries. B. 4. c. 19.

of *common law*, yet shall the *maritime law* prevail : thus in the case of *Sandys*, and the *East-India Company*, it was the opinion, that if it were an *admiralty cause*, the matter being transacted *infra corpus comitat*, was not material, for that a person might be taken up by execution out of the admiralty, upon sentence there, in any county of England.*

If from the west, and from the coasts of the Mediterranean, we turn our attention to the northern parts of Europe, we shall there discover an industrious, and active people, adopting similar schemes of legislation on the shores of the Baltic. The same causes, no doubt, which gave rise to the laws we have already described, operated also in the production of that body of marine law, known by the title of the *Wisbuy Code*, from an opulent city of that name in the isle of Gothland, where it was promulged. It is hardly possible to settle the exact age of this compilation. Different writers, as guided by their particular prejudices, have ascribed it either to a very late, or a very early period. According to some, the inhabitants of Gothland carried on an active trade, and were, on other accounts, a respectable people, as far back as the 9th century, and from this circumstance they infer that these laws must be of very high antiquity, and were the model by which those of Oleron were framed. Others, with the best authority on their side, bring forward the bright age of this island, and the foundation of its capital city, to the middle of the 12th century, and retort, in favour of the Oleron laws, a strong charge of imitation

62

on

---

* Skinner's Rep. Term. Hill. 35. Car. II. 9. 13. Rep. 53. 1. Sid. 158. 1. Salk. 35. Zouch ut sup. Assert. 3. For the practice of the Admiralty court, consult an excellent little work Clarke's *Praxis Curiæ Admiralitatis*, the 8vo edit. of 1743. with notes ; and for valuable political information on the subject of maritime law Wynne's edition of Sir L. Jenkins's works, his life in vol. 1. and the letters at the end of vol. 2.

on the compilers of the northern code.* But which ever
has the best claim to originality, it is certain that these
two codes bear a very striking resemblance to each other,
not only in the general spirit, but even in the very letter
of some particular laws, a circumstance which may
perhaps be accounted for, without fixing the imputation
of plagiarism on either, by referring them both to one
common source, the laws of Rhodes. The probability of
such a conclusion, strengthened with much internal evidence, will appear by reflecting upon the great communication that was opened, in the 12th century, between the
Baltic and the Mediterranean coasts, when the inhabitants
of the South began to exchange the luxurious produce of
their climate, for the coarser, but equally useful commodities of the north.† It was not possible for an intercourse, where so many different claims, and such opposite
interests were concerned, long to subsist without having
recourse to some standard of justice, by which commercial
and nautical controversies might be adjusted. The salutary effects of those sea laws, already mentioned as pre
vailing in the south, must have strongly recommended
them to the notice of a rising nation of mariners, destitute
(as it is natural to suppose they were) of civil, or commercial maxims, and that spirit of universal equity, by
63 which

---

* Lambecii. *Origines Hamburgenses.* page 12. Cleirac *Us' et
Coustumes de la mer.* See also *Fasciculus de Jure nautico,* p. 682
and Olaus Magnus. Hist. Lib. 10. cap. 16. Welwood's assertion that
" the laws of Oleron were afterwards translated into Dutch by the
people of Wisbuy, to serve them in their traffic on the coast of Holland " is to be understood, not of the code here in question, but of
some particular laws which they found it necessary to adopt, to
regulate their intercourse with this newly-erected nation of traders.
Abridgment of Sea Laws. p. 13.

† Spain, Italy, and the Levant, furnished the northern traders
with spices, drugs, fruits, wine, cotton, &c. from whom they in return
obtained, among other necessary articles, iron, copper, flax, hemp,
and timber.

which they are characterized, rendered them alike applicable to naval suits in the Gulph of Venice, or of Finland. The commendation which Grotius has bestowed on the laws of Wisbuy implies a degree of excellence in them not often found in the polity of rude nations, and conforms exactly with what has constantly been applied to the Rhodian laws. " Quæ de maritimis negotiis *Insulæ Gothlandiæ Habitatoribus* placuerunt, tantum in se habent, tum æquitatis, tum prudentiæ, ut omnes oceani accolæ eo, non tanquam proprio, sed velut *gentium jure,* utantur." * Their authority is also described by a northern historian in the following words. " In omni navigantium controversiâe, præsertim a Consulatu Wisbycensi petitur et datur jus et fententia definitiva, quid unicuique permittendum vel auferendum erit." And the extent of their influence is afterwards thus clearly defined by the same writer. " Leges maritimæ et decisiones omnium controversiarum singulariter longe lateque usque ad *Columnas Herculis* et *ultimum mare Scythicum,* exeâ (i.e. Lege Wisbycensi) petuntur, et datæ observantur." † It is greatly to the honour of these ancient laws, that having for many ages enjoyed unrivalled authority in all the maritime tribunals of the north, they were thought worthy of being adopted by the legislators of the Hanseatic league, and acknowledged as the basis of their compilation.‡ Reinold Kuricke, a learned commentator on this

work,

---

* Prolegomena ad Procopium. p. 64.

† Olaus Magnus Hist. lib. 2. cap. 24. and lib. 10. cap. 16. It is not improbable, that since, by this account, the laws of Oleron and Wisbuy must have been indifferently used in many places, the dispute of originality might have proceeded from the inaccuracy of quoting them in those ignorant ages.

Wisbuy was in the 12th century a place of extraordinary splendour, and the many noble specimens of art, found there even at this day, may serve to justify the description given by Olaus.

‡ The society of the Hanse Towns began to be formed about the

work, informs us that before the close of the 16th
century, notwithstanding their extensive commerce, the
65 Hanse

beginning of the 13th century, for the protection of the Baltic trade,
and for more than 300 years was considered as a most formidable
maritime association. The nature, and extent of its original institution, are not easily ascertained. It seems to have consisted only
of a few considerable towns, situated on the Baltic Sea, at the head
of which were the cities of Lubec and Hamburgh. Mutual interest
was at first the only bond of their connection : a code of laws, and a
regular form of government was afterwards established, magistrates,
and other officers, with their respective tribunals appointed, a public
treasury erected, fleets and armies levied, and the union of the whole
confederacy cemented by the strongest political obligations. In the
14th century, which may be considered as the æra of its glory, the
Hanseatic League comprized 64 cities, which had as many more in
alliance with them. It was divided into four separate districts, 1st
The Vandalic, over which (and indeed over the whole) Lubec presided.
In this district were contained all the German cities along the Baltic
coast, from the Elbe, to the Oder. The 2nd district of the Rhine, at
the head of which was Cologne, comprised the countries of Cleves,
Overyssel, Gueldre, and the Circle of Westphalia. Brunswic formed
the 3d district and had under it most of the principal cities of Upper
and Lower Saxony. The last district was that of Prussia headed by
the city of Dantzic, and containing most of the towns from the
Vistula to the Gulph of Finland. Thus was this powerful confederacy, besides a very extensive inland territory possessed of a sea coast
of more than twelve hundred miles in Germany only, and had in
alliance many large cities in England, France and Italy. In consequence of these advantages, it for many years almost monopolized
the trade of the North, and, by preserving its alliances unshaken
bore a considerable part in the politics of Europe. Secure of effectual
protection, the Hanseatic States claimed exclusive privileges in trade
to the detriment of others ; they arrested the ships of different nations
upon the most frivolous pretences ; imprisoned the merchants, and
refused to release them without exorbitant ransoms : But as their
prosperity had naturally awakened the jealousy of their neighbours,
their arrogance contributed to inflame it, and in the end raised up
against them a combination which gradually effected their ruin
The dissolution of the confederacy however turned greatly to the
advantage of some of its parts. The cities of Hamburgh and Lubec,
in particular, gained in opulence what they had lost in power.
Finding themselves no longer at the head of an ambitious league,

Hanse Towns had never published any code of maritime law, but were entirely governed by those of *Wisbuy* and *Oleron*. At a general meeting at Lubec, in the year 1614, it was agreed to extract from them whatever should be thought most useful, to adopt such of the Rhodian laws as were extant, and, with the addition of certain local usages, to form the whole into a systematic arrangement under 15 titles, which should comprise a penalty for every offence, and an equitable rule of decision for every dispute incident to the Baltic trader.*

66   Having

---

which had enabled them to exercise a kind of commercial despotism over their neighbours, they adopted milder maxims of trade, and contenting themselves with a peaceful interchange of commodities, preserved their liberties and political consequence. Davenant has drawn a very splendid picture of the state of Hamburgh at the close of the last century, and ranks her as the third commercial city in Europe, London and Amsterdam being, as he says, the only ports that could claim pre-eminence. See his *Discourses on the Public Revenue and Trade of England*, Part II. An accurate account of the Hanseatics would make an interesting part of the *Commercial History*, formerly mentioned as a great desideratum. The writers who treat expressly of them are, Angelius a Werdenhagen, in a latin work, *De Rebus-publicis Hanseaticis*, 3 vol. 12°. and Knipschildius, *Tractatus Hist-politico-Juridicus, de Juribus Civitatum Imperialium.* Lib. i. cap. 4.

Many important facts also may be gathered from Lambecius *Origines Hamburgenses*, from the northern historians, from Guicciardini's *History of the Low Countries*, where their principal comptoir was established, and from Anderson's *History of Commerce*.

* What has been advanced of the strong resemblance between the Oleron, Wisbuy and Hanseatic Codes, will be confirmed by referring to the following articles in each, which contain indisputable proofs of imitation.

Oleron.	Wisbuy.	Hanse.
Art. 1, 2	Art. 13, 14, 15	Tit. 2
7	19	14 - Art, 2.
8, 9, 10	12, 20, 21, 38	8, 9, 10,
14	26. 50. 67. 70	
18	31	
19	32	4 - Art. 21

Having thus briefly pointed out the origin and nature of those several maritime codes, in which any traces of the Rhodian laws can be discovered, I shall only further observe, it is no small proof of their superior excellence, that being transplanted out of their native soil, in Greece, they have flourished in very opposite climates and situations, and that though conveyed, as we have seen, in a mutilated condition, from one extremity of Europe to the other, yet amidst all the revolutions in government and trade, their authority has been confirmed, and their equity acknowledged in every country which has at any time been the seat of naval, or commercial empire.

67

Besides these more striking instances, others might be selected which have a slighter, though a sufficient resemblance, to justify the supposition, that they were copied from each other; though upon the same principle, as we have shewn, they may all three be referred back to the *Consolato del Mare*, and from thence to the one general source of maritime justice, The Ancient Laws of Rhodes. Compare, in particular, Titles 8 and 9, *Jur. Hanseatic*, edit. Kuricke, with the *Rhodian Law*, De Jactu.

THE END.

A

DISSERTATION

ON THE

POOR LAWS.

BY A

WELL-WISHER TO MANKIND.

———————————

LONDON:

PRINTED FOR C. DILLY IN THE POULTRY.

M.DCC.LXXXVI.

A

DISSERTATION

ON THE

POOR LAWS.

SECT. I.

TO a man of common sensibility nothing can be more
distressing, than to hear the complaints of wretchedness, which he hath no power to redress, and to be
daily conversant with misery, which he can neither fly
from, nor relieve.   This at present is the situation of the
clergy, who, in virtue of their office, are obliged to visit
the habitations of the poor.   Here they see helpless infancy and decrepit age, the widow and the orphan, some
requiring food, and others physic; all in such numbers,
that no private fortune can supply their wants.   Such
scenes are more distressing, when, as it sometimes happens, the suffering objects have been distinguished for
industry, honesty, and sobriety.   The laws indeed have
made provision for their relief, and the contributions are
more than liberal which are collected for their support;
but then, the laws being inadequate to the purposes for
which they were designed, and the money collected being
universally misapplied, the provision, which was originally

3   made

made for industry in distress, does little more than give encouragement to idleness and vice. The laws themselves appear beautiful on paper, and will be the admiration of succeeding ages, when, in the revolution of empires, the whole fabric of our government shall be dissolved, and our nation, as a separate kingdom, shall exist no more. These laws, so beautiful in theory, promote the evils they mean to remedy, and aggravate the distress they were intended to relieve. Till the reign of Q. Elizabeth they were unknown in England; and to the present moment, they have never been adopted by any other kingdom upon earth. It has been most unfortunate for us, that two of the greatest blessings have been productive of the greatest evils. The revolution gave birth to that enormous load of debt, under which this nation groans; and to the reformation we are indebted for the laws which multiply the poor.

At the dissolution of the monasteries, the lazy and the indigent, who were deprived of their accustomed food, became clamorous, and, having long since forgot to work, were not only ready to join in every scheme for the disturbance of the state, but, as vagrants, by their numbers, by their impostures, and by their thefts, they rendered themselves a public and most intolerable nuisance. To stop their mouths, and to make them employ their hands in honest labour, was the intention of that day. But at the same time the laws took under their protection some objects of distress, who for near two hundred years, from a noble kind of pride, refused the proffered aid, or received it with reluctance; and who at the present moment would be more effectually relieved, if no other laws existed but the first great laws of human nature, filial affection, and the general benevolence of mankind. The world it must be confessed, is wicked enough: yet amidst all their wickedness men seldom want compassion, unless the circumstances in which they find themselves are peculiarly

4   distressing.

distressing. Should we " in the straitness of a siege
behold men eating the flesh of their sons and of their
daughters; should we see among them a man tender and
delicate, whose eye should be evil towards his brother and
towards the wife of his bosom, and towards the remnant
of his children, so that he should not give to any of them
of the flesh of his children whom he should eat;" * we
must not from such instances conclude that all men, or
even most men, are destitute of mercy and compassion,
or that man in general can be kind and beneficent only by
compulsion. No doubt in every district will be found
some, who are strangers to the finer feelings of the human
heart; but at the same time in every district will be found
some, who are endued with generosity of soul; and others,
who under the influence of piety will rejoice to relieve the
wants and distresses of their fellow creatures. In every
place some will be distinguished for benevolence, others
for brutality; but in general man is what his situation
makes him. Is he happy himself in the enjoyment of
ease and affluence? In such circumstances " he will be
eyes to the blind and feet to the lame; he will be a father
to the poor; the blessing of those that are ready to perish
will come upon this man: he will cause the widow's heart
to leap for joy."† Let the same man be straitened in his
circumstances, let him be burthened with taxes, let him
be harassed by the clamours and distracted by the inces-
sant demands of the most improvident and lazy of the
surrounding poor; and he will have little inclination to
seek for objects of distress, or to visit the sequestered
cottage of the silent sufferer. It is generally found, that
modest worth stands at a distance, or draws nigh with
faltering tongue and broken accents to tell an artless tale;
whilst the most worthless are the most unreasonable in
5   their

---

* Deut. xxviii. 53.
† Job. xxix.

their expectations, and the most importunate in their soli-
citation for relief. If the latter, from any imperfection of
our laws, get abundantly too much, the former must of
necessity obtain too little. If, agreeable to the general
practice of the labouring poor, a man, previous to his
marriage, or whilst his family is small, has made no provision for his future wants; if all, to whom he might
naturally look for aid, are in the same circumstances with
himself; and if the charity of those among his neighbours, who are distinguished for benevolence, nay, of all
who have the common feelings of humanity, is exhausted;
if they who are most willing are least able to relieve him;
we must expect to see distress and poverty even among
those who are worthy of compassion. This at present is
the case in England. There never was greater distress
among the poor: there never was more money collected
for their relief. But what is most perplexing is, that
poverty and wretchedness have increased in exact proportion to the efforts which have been made for the comfortable subsistence of the poor; and that wherever most is
expended for their support, there objects of distress are
most abundant; whilst in those countries or provincial
districts, where the least provision has been made for their
supply, we hear the fewest groans. Among the former
we see drunkenness and idleness cloathed in rags; among
the latter we hear the chearful songs of industry and
virtue.

If laws alone could make a nation happy, ours would
be the happiest nation upon earth: idleness and vice could
not exist; poverty would be unknown; we should be like
a prosperous hive of bees; all would have enough and
none too much. The reverse of this we find to be the
case: poverty and vice prevail, and the most vicious have
access to the common stock. If a man has squandered
the inheritance of his fathers; if by his improvidence, by
his prodigality, by his drunkenness and vices, he has dis-

6

sipated

sipated all his substance; if by his debaucheries he has ruined his constitution, and reduced himself to such a deplorable condition that he hath neither inclination nor ability to work; yet must he be maintained by the sweat and labour of the sober and of the industrious farmer, and eat the bread which should be given only to virtue in distress. If in all cases, this bread, so ill bestowed, were superabundant; if the industrious farmer were himself in ease and affluence: the grievance would yet be tolerable. But in this day it often happens that the industrious farmer is opprest with poverty. He rises early, and it is late before he can retire to his rest; he works hard and fares hard; yet with all his labour and his care he can scarce provide subsistence for his numerous family. He would feed them better, but the prodigal must *first* be fed. He would purchase warmer cloathing for them, but the children of the prostitute must *first* be cloathed. The little which remains after the profligate have been cloathed and fed, is all that he can give to those, who in nature have the first claims upon a father. If this evil could be stemmed, whilst the present laws subsist, he might yet have hope; but when he considers, that all the efforts, which have been made in his own parish or in others, have been vain, and that the evil is constantly increasing, he is driven to despair of help, and fears that he shall be himself reduced to work for daily hire. It will be evident that his fears are not altogether groundless, if we consider, that even in parishes, where no manufactures have been established, the poor rates have been doubling, some every fourteen years, and others nearly every seven years; whilst in some districts, where the manufactures are carried on to a considerable extent, the poor rates are more than ten shillings in the pound upon the improved rents. That the distress does not arise from the high price of corn, will be clear, if we consider, what may perhaps hereafter be more fully stated, that although for these two

hundred

hundred years the price of wheat has fluctuated between wide extremes, yet upon comparing the average prices within that period, the ancients did not find a cheaper market than the moderns. If we take the average of the sixty years which terminated at the commencement of the present century, we shall find the price of wheat to have been six shillings and four pence halfpenny per bushel, whereas in the subsequent sixty years it was only five shillings; and for the last twenty years, ending with the year 1782, not more than six shillings and sixpence : yet during that long period in which provisions were the cheapest, the poor rates were continually advancing. That the distress does not arise from the high price of soap, leather, candles, salt, and other small articles needful in a family, will appear not only from the superior advance in the price of labour (in the proportion of six to four within a century),[*] but from hence, that where the price of labour is the highest and provisions are the cheapest, there the poor rates have been the most exorbitant. In Scotland they have no legal provision for the poor, yet labour is cheaper and corn is dearer than they are in England.

SECT. II.

UNDER the best administration, the laws relating to the poor give occasion to much injustice; under the worst, they are too often the instruments of oppression and revenge. If the intentions of the magistrate are good, his compassion may be ill directed; but if at any time his judgment is blinded by his passions, in the keenness of his resentment for some real or imaginary affront, he is apt to forget the purpose for which the administra-

8   tion

---

[*] Sir William Petty, P. Arithmetic.

tion of the poor laws was committed to his care, and to abuse his power, by granting, when the property of his own tenants is not to be affected by it, the most ample relief to the most unworthy objects. This indeed would seldom happen, if none but gentlemen of a liberal education were put into the commission of the peace; or if, agreeable to the original constitution of our government, this office were elective. But should the wisest and the best of men be chosen, yet we could not expect that such would every where be found willing to devote their time and whole attention to the administration of those laws, whose natural tendency is to increase the number of the poor, and greatly to extend the bounds of human misery.

SECT. III.

ALL who are conversant with Tacitus have admired the extent of his knowledge, the shrewdness of his remarks, and the nervous strength of his expression. In a speech which he puts into the mouth of the Roman emperor Tiberius, we find this passage : " Languescet industria, intendetur socordia, si nullus ex se metus aut spes, & securi omnes aliena subsidia expectabunt, sibi ignavi, nobis graves."* Hope and fear are the springs of industry. It is the part of a good politician to strengthen these: but our laws weaken the one and destroy the other. For what encouragement have the poor to be industrious and frugal, when they know for certain, that should they increase their store it will be devoured by the drones ?† or what cause have they to fear, when they are assured, that if by their indolence and extravagance, by their drunkenness and vices, they should be reduced to want,

9   **they**

---

* L. ii. p. 73, 74, edit. Els.   † Hesiod, 302.

they shall be abundantly supplied, not only with food and raiment, but with their accustomed luxuries, at the expence of others. The poor know little of the motives which stimulate the higher ranks to action—pride, honour, and ambition. In general it is only hunger which can spur and goad them on to labour; yet our laws have said, they shall never hunger. The laws, it must be confessed, have likewise said that they shall be compelled to work. But then legal constraint is attended with too much trouble, violence, and noise; creates ill will, and never can be productive of good and acceptable service: whereas hunger is not only a peaceable, silent, unremitted pressure, but, as the most natural motive to industry and labour, it calls forth the most powerful exertions; and, when satisfied by the free bounty of another, lays a lasting and sure foundation for good will and gratitude. The slave must be compelled to work; but the freeman should be left to his own judgment and discretion; should be protected in the full enjoyment of his own, be it much or little; and punished when he invades his neighbour's property. By recurring to those base motives which influence the slave, and trusting only to compulsion, all the benefits of free service, both to the servant and to the master, must be lost.

It is universally found, that where bread can be obtained without care or labour, it leads through idleness and vice to poverty. Before they discovered the gold and silver mines of Peru and Mexico, the Spaniards were distinguished among the nations of Europe for their industry and arts, for their manufactures and their commerce. But what are they now? a lazy, poor, and miserable people. They have been ruined by their imaginary wealth. The declension of the Spaniards has been attributed to the expulsion of the Moriscoes; and the blow was certainly severe, but not altogether adequate to the effect. The number expelled was more than six hundred thousand,

10   besides

besides those who died by the sword, by famine, or by the sentences of the Inquisition. The principal charge brought against them was their obstinate adherence to the Mahometan religion: the political reason assigned for their expulsion was, that by their industry, temperance, and frugality, they were able to work cheaper than the Spaniards, whilst by their sobriety they contributed little to the public revenue: but the real cause of this impolitic measure was an order from the Pope, that these infidels should be converted at the expence of the Spanish clergy. The Archbishop of Valentia was to pay three thousand six hundred ducats yearly, and the other bishops in proportion to their incomes, for the support of an Arabic mission.* Thus the temperate, the frugal, and the industrious, being banished from the kingdom, whilst the indolent found a constant influx of gold and silver from abroad, the whole nation sunk by degrees into the present state of torpid inactivity. It is more than one hundred and seventy years since this event, and yet in all that time Spain has not recovered her population. The quantity of gold and silver imported annually into Cadiz and Lisbon has been reckoned six millions sterling.† Here we find a sufficient cause for the decay of their industry and arts.

Our poor began only to appear in numbers after the dissolution of the monasteries. Then it was they first attracted notice; but they had existed long before, always most abundant in the vicinity of the religious houses. At the present moment we are told, that in Naples six thousand Lazaroni are daily fed by the monastic orders, under the specious name of charity, not upon a sudden emergency, but statedly, and as the only means of their subsistence. As a peace offering this may be politic and wise,

11   well

---

* Geddes, Account of the Moriscoes.
† Smith, Wealth of Nations

well calculated to conciliate the good opinion of the un-
thinking mind, and to command the admiration of the
vulgar; but at the same time it is inconsistent with the
most established principles of political œconomy: for as
industry and frugality are the only foundation of national
prosperity; so temperance and labour are the only source
of happiness and wealth to individuals. A learned Jesuit,
who has lately written and is now publishing an elegant
defence of that society, assumes great merit from this
circumstance, that instead of extorting for themselves a
scanty pittance from the vitals of the people, such was the
benevolence of these holy fathers, and such the abundant
wealth of their establishments, that they relieved all in
the surrounding villages, who made application to their
charity. Their intentions, no doubt, were good, but their
bounty must have been misapplied. He, who statedly
employs the poor in useful labour, is their only friend;
he, who only feeds them, is their greatest enemy. Their
hopes and fears should centre in themselves: they should
have no hope but from their own sobriety, diligence,
fidelity, and from the well-earnt friendship of their employers; and then their only fear would be the fear of
forfeiting by their misconduct, that favour and protection
which would be their principal resource in times of sickness and distress.

SECT. IV.

A WISE legislator will endeavour to confirm the
natural bonds of society, and give vigour to the first
principles on which political union must depend. He will
preserve the distinctions which exist in nature independent
of his authority, and the various relations which, antece-
dent to his creation, connected man to man. He will
study the natural obligations which arise from these rela-

tions, that he may strengthen these connections by the sanction of his laws. Among the first of these relations stands the relation of a servant to his master; and the first duty required from a servant is prompt, chearful, and hearty obedience. On this condition alone can the connection be preserved, as without due subordination all government must end. But our laws tend to weaken these bonds, and to destroy this subordination, by compelling the occupier of land to find employment for the poor. With this provision, what have they to fear when discharged from service? If one will not employ them, another must. If the work be slighted or neglected, if it be deserted in the pressing hour, or spoiled in the execution, it is to little purpose for the master to complain; he can have no redress. Does he seek relief from the civil power? The unequal contest is begun, and the remedy will be worse than the disease. Both the servant and the master know when the work is ill performed, or when the servant has not earnt his wages, even when legal proof is wanting. If then the master has no other remedy, he is at the mercy of his servants; he must connive at their neglects, and bear their impertinence with patience. There is no alternative but this, or to maintain them without work. The appeal in this case to a magistrate is from a superior tribunal to the inferior, from the stronger to the weaker. Where the natural sanctions are sufficient to secure obedience without disturbing the peace and good order of society; there a wise legislator will be careful not to interfere, lest, by weakening these, without being able to substitute better in their place, he should stop the course of justice and protect the guilty. The wisest legislator will never be able to devise a more equitable, a more effectual, or in any respect a more suitable punishment, than hunger is for a disobedient servant. Hunger will tame the fiercest animals, it will teach decency and civility, obedience and subjection, to the most brutish, the most

13 obstinate,

obstinate, and the most perverse. A good servant need
not be afraid of wanting work. If one master should
dismiss him from his service, others will be happy to
receive him. But should a man be notorious for a thief,
and for spoiling or neglecting work; should he be either
so false, so vicious, or so ill-tempered, that no master
would be willing to employ him; it would certainly be just
that he should suffer hunger till he had learnt to reform
his conduct. There are perhaps few parishes which cannot produce some of this untoward disposition. Indeed
it is the general complaint of farmers, that their men do
not work so well as they used to do, when it was reproach-
ful to be relieved by the parish.

S E C T. V.

IT may seem strange in a country where agriculture,
arts, manufactures, and commerce, are most flourishing, all of which have a mutual and corresponding influence on each other, to say that the laws discourage
manufactures; yet this may be said of the poor laws in
England. By our present system we prevent their introduction, check their progress, and hasten their departure.
If the rental of a parish were not bound to provide for
the increasing poor, every gentleman of landed property
would be solicitous to have manufacturers established on
his estates, in order to consume the produce of his lands.
By multiplying the consumers he would enhance the value
of all the various products of the soil: he would enjoy
the monopoly of hay and pasture, and share with all his
neighbours to a given distance in the sale of corn. But
when he considers that manufactures fluctuate, that the
benefit which he is to derive from them will not bear
proportion to the burthen which he must entail upon his
property; he will rather wish to keep them at a conve-

nient distance. The principal benefit he can expect is, that the value of his pastures should be doubled : but even whilst the manufacture prospers, the demands of the poor, both upon his arable and pasture, will be more than doubled, and when it fails, the poor's rate will swallow up the whole. The surrounding parishes will reap the chief advantage : he will have the happiness to see them flourish ; but the load and burthen of the poor will remain upon his own estate. " Sic vos non vobis fertis aratra, boves."*

In every parish, as the law now stands, they who have legal settlements, have the monopoly of labour, because the labouring poor are confined to their respective parishes. This provision is perfectly consistent with the whole system of our poor laws, and was designed not only to prevent the evils which naturally arise from vagrancy, and which might be equally prevented by more wholesome laws ; but to protect each parish from intruders, who might become chargeable either for themselves or for their children. This provision is productive of considerable evils, which the legislature has never yet been able to remove : for not only have the industrious poor been restrained from seeking employment where they would otherwise have been received with joy, and confined to their own parishes, in which they were regarded with an evil eye ; but for want of competition the price of labour to the manufacturer has been much enhanced. With a certificate, indeed, the poor are per-mitted to reside iu any parish where work is to be had, but then a certificate is not easily obtained. Now it is evident that by raising the price of labour you must directly check the progress of the manufactures ; and by experience it is found, that the same effect arises indirectly to a more considerable extent ; for in proportion as you advance the wages of the poor, you diminish the quantity of their work. All manufacturers complain of this, and

15   universally

---

* Virgil's Complaint.

universally agree, that the poor are seldom diligent, except when labour is cheap, and corn is dear.   It must be confessed that too many of them have some little resemblance to the animal described by travellers under the name of Nimble Peter; a creature so inactive, that, when he has cleared one tree, he will be reduced to skin and bones before he climbs another, and so slow in all his motions, that even stripes will not make him mend his pace."* Drunkenness is the common vice of poverty; not perhaps of poverty as such, but of the uncultivated mind; for it is the characteristic of unpolished nations to be fond of intoxicating liquors.   Whatever be the cause, it is notorious, that with the common people the appetite for strong drink is their prevailing appetite.   When therefore, by the advance in wages, they obtain more than is sufficient for their bare subsistence, they spend the surplus at the ale-house, and neglect their business.   Is a man drunk one day?   He will have little inclination to work the next.   Thus for every drunken fit two days are lost.   By frequent repetition the habit is confirmed, and, by reducing the number of working days, their value is enhanced. In proportion to this loss, the price of labour will be raised.   As long as men have nothing to fear, either for themselves or for their families, this practice will prevail.   Where the price of labour is advanced, the industrious and the sober will by degrees acquire a taste for luxury.   They will not be contented with bare subsistence, with a sufficient quantity of coarse yet wholesome food, with warm but home-spun garments, and with healthy but unfurnished cottages; they will contract habits of refinement, which, when suffered to promote their industry, will be useful both to themselves and to the public; but which, in all cases, will have a tendency to keep up

16   the

* Dampier, Vol. ii. Part ii. p. 61.

the price of labour, and to advance the price of all those articles which they consume. Even they who do not work must eat, and, by increasing the demand for corn, will enhance its value, and consequently the price of labour. In this case action and re-action are equal, but not opposite. The high price of labour raises the value of provisions, and the high price of provisions enhances the value of labour. They are both increased by the present system of our poor laws, and have both a tendency to check the progress of manufactures, and to hasten their departure. The most specious argument produced against granting a free trade to the sister kingdom was, that, having labour cheap, and not being burthened with a poor's rate, she would be able to undersell us in the market, and thereby ruin our manufactures. Should England repeal the present laws, and make a better provision for the frugal, the sober, and the industrious, among the poor, Ireland could no longer boast of this advantage.

Manufactures always seek the cheapest countries. As they are leaving the southern counties and travelling to the north, so in time will they leave the north, and, to a considerable degree, quit the kingdom, unless some wise regulations are established for the better relief and government of the labouring poor.

The poor laws to a certain degree discourage improvements in agriculture; for it is certain, that more waste land would be taken into tillage, if gentlemen were not alarmed by the increasing burthen of the poor. Against the claims of the church, provision has been made by an exemption from tythes for seven years; but the demands of the poor admit of no exemption. Monied men have greatly the advantage over the owners and occupiers of land, as being free from those heavy taxes, which the latter pay to the king, to the church, and to the poor. When the poor's rate amounts to ten shillings, or even to

four

four shillings in the pound, who will be at the expence of clearing, fencing, breaking up, manuring, cropping, the waste and barren parts of an estate? Certainly no gentleman can do it with a view to profit. In Scotland the sums are immense which have been expended for this purpose; but in England a man of property would choose rather to take the public for his debtor, than to be himself a debtor to the poor; more especially as it is not possible for him to conjecture what will be the extent of this unlimited rent-charge upon his estate. Were it not for this incumbrance agriculture would certainly be pushed much farther than it has ever been, and many thousand acres of the poorer commons, heaths, and moors, would be inclosed and cultivated. The best writers have complained, that by a tax, similar in its operation to our poor's tax, agriculture in France has been depressed, the assessment being made in proportion to their stock in trade. The conduct of the French in this respect is not more absurd than ours. How widely different has been the operation of our land-tax! It has been a spur to industry, because from the beginning the proportion has been never changed. To be consistent in principle, the legislature should either limit the sum to be collected for the poor, or if agriculture is to be effectually checked, they should equalize the land-tax. Had this tax followed our improvements with a tight grasp, and with a watchful eye, like the church, and like the poor, England would not at this day discover the smiling aspect which all foreigners admire, when they every where behold our vallies cloathed with flocks, and our hills with corn. A wise politician will study to remove every obstacle which can retard the progress of improvement: but such is the system of our laws, that the greater the distress among the poor, the less will be the inducement to cultivate our more stubborn and unprofitable lands.

S E C T. VI.

A DISTINGUISHED writer of the present century has clearly stated some advantages which the community derives from the introduction of luxury, and would from thence conclude, that private vices are public benefits. His conclusion we cannot grant him; nor can we allow the premises, if by luxury be meant any thing inconsistent with morality. If in our idea of luxury we include only the comforts and conveniences of life, then a taste for luxury must be productive of industry and virtue, must increase the happiness of individuals, and promote the welfare of the state. If men were contented to go naked, to lie under hedges, and, according to the fiction of the poets, to feed on acorns, there would be none to labour till the acorns were consumed. In general the industry of man bears proportion to his real or imaginary wants. Could the landlord be contented with the produce of his native soil, he would cultivate only what would be sufficient for the consumption of his family; or could the labourer be contented with what was barely sufficient to satisfy his hunger, when he no longer felt the cravings of his appetite, he would cease to labour. But as their wants are multiplied, the master is willing to employ more workmen, and the workman himself is reconciled to constant labour. There was a time when the inhabitants of Europe had neither rum, brandy, spices, tea, sugar, nor tobacco: they now covet these, and these new desires have produced new efforts to gratify them. There was a time when they had neither linen, shoes, nor stockings; they now feel the want of these, and receive them as the rewards of industry. But supposing that, with these new desires, they could obtain not only linen, shoes, and stockings, but spices, spirits, tea, sugar, and tobacco, without care or labour, what encouragement would they have to industry? By

19   the

the present system of our poor laws, at least as they are
now administered, the benefits which arise from luxury,
in promoting industry among the labouring poor, are lost;
and the most improvident may rest assured, that he shall,
at all events, share these superfluities with the most active
and laborious; and that in times of scarcity his wants
shall be the *first* supplied, and his comfort the *first* consulted. To be consistent, the legislature should make the
same provision for farmers, manufacturers, and merchants;
that in case, by their profusion or neglect of business,
they should be insolvent, their debts might all be paid,
and themselves, together with their families, might be
supported in the style and manner to which they had been
accustomed; all out of the revenues of the state, or by
special rates to be collected; not by voluntary donations,
but by compulsive payments, and not merely from the
opulent, but from those who had themselves been strug-
gling with poverty and want: nay, to be consistent, they
should pass a law that no man should reap the fruit of
his indiscretion; or, to be perfectly consistent, they
should repeal all penal statutes.

Hesiod, in his Georgics, or didactic poem on agriculture, describes with beautiful simplicity the excellent
effects of emulation, representing two kinds of strife and
contention among men; the one productive of violence,
the other of peace, harmony, and plenty. The one is
intent only upon plunder, whilst the other seeing wealth
as attendant upon industry, is induced to labour, in order
to obtain those comforts which the diligent only can
command.

Εις ετερον γαρ τις τε ιδων εργοιο χατιζων
Πλουσιον, ος σπευδει μεν αρομμεναι ηδε φυτευειν,
Οικον τ’ευ θεσθαι· ζηλοι δε τε γειτονα γειτων
Εις αφενον σπευδοντ’· αγαθη δ’ερις ηδε βροτοισι.

E και Ημ. 21.

This principle has been perverted by our laws; and

now

now the person who excites the envy and emulation of the lazy and improvident, is not the man who by his activity is acquiring affluence, but the indolent poor in every parish, who by his impudence and by his importunity has obtained the most ample and the most unmerited relief. This our poet has described as the natural emulation among beggars. Καὶ πτωχὸς πτωχῷ φθονέει.

SECT. VII.

IT seems to be a law of nature, that the poor should be to a certain degree improvident, that there may always be some to fulfil the most servile, the most sordid, and the most ignoble offices in the community. The stock of human happiness is thereby much increased, whilst the more delicate are not only relieved from drudgery, and freed from those occasional employments which would make them miserable, but are left at liberty, without interruption, to pursue those callings which are suited to their various dispositions, and most useful to the state. As for the lowest of the poor, by custom they are reconciled to the meanest occupations, to the most laborious works, and to the most hazardous pursuits; whilst the hope of their reward makes them chearful in the midst of all their dangers and their toils. The fleets and armies of a state would soon be in want of soldiers and of sailors, if sobriety and diligence universally prevailed: for what is it but distress and poverty which can prevail upon the lower classes of the people to encounter all the horrors which await them on the tempestuous ocean, or in the field of battle? Men who are easy in their circumstances are not among the foremost to engage in a seafaring or military life. There must be a degree of pressure, and that which is attended with the least violence will be the best. When hunger is either felt or feared, the desire of obtaining bread will quietly dispose the mind to undergo the greatest hardships, and will sweeten the severest labours. The peasant with a sickle in his hand is happier than the prince upon his throne.

Now a fixed, a certain, and a constant provision for the poor weakens this spring; it increases their improvidence, but does not promote their chearful compliance with those demands, which the community is obliged to make on the most indigent of its members; it tends to destroy the harmony and beauty, the symmetry and order of that system, which God and nature have established in the world. The improvident among the poor have been advancing in their claims: they now begin to understand that they have a legal right to all. When this, which hitherto has been only felt, shall be clearly seen, and universally acknowledged, nothing will remain but to cast lots, who among the active and the virtuous shall perform the vilest offices for the indolent and vicious.

S E C T. VIII.

OUR poor laws are not only unjust, oppressive, and impolitic, nor are they merely by accident inadequate to the purpose for which they were designed; but they proceed upon principles which border on absurdity, as professing to accomplish that which, in the very nature and constitution of the world, is impracticable. They say, that in England no man, even though by his indolence, improvidence, prodigality, and vice, he may have brought himself to poverty, shall ever suffer want. In the progress of society, it will be found, that some must want; and then the only question will be this, Who is most worthy to suffer cold and hunger, the prodigal or the provident, the slothful or the diligent, the virtuous or the vicious? In the South Seas there is an island, which from the first

discoverer

discoverer is called Juan Fernandes. In this sequestered spot, John Fernando placed a colony of goats, consisting of one male, attended by his female. This happy couple finding pasture in abundance, could readily obey the first commandment, to increase and multiply, till in process of time they had replenished their little island.* In advancing to this period they were strangers to misery and want, and seemed to glory in their numbers : but from this unhappy moment they began to suffer hunger; yet continuing for a time to increase their numbers, had they been endued with reason, they must have apprehended the extremity of famine. In this situation the weakest first gave way, and plenty was again restored. Thus they fluctuated between happiness and misery, and either suffered want or rejoiced in abundance, according as their numbers were diminished or increased; never at a stay, yet nearly balancing at all times their quantity of food. This degree of æquipoise was from time to time destroyed, either by epidemical diseases or by the arrival of some vessel in distress. On such occasions their numbers were considerably reduced; but to compensate for this alarm, and to comfort them for the loss of their companions, the survivors never failed immediately to meet returning plenty. They were no longer in fear of famine : they ceased to regard each other with an evil eye; all had abundance, all were contented, all were happy. Thus, what might have been considered as misfortunes, proved a source of comfort; and, to them at least, partial evil was universal good.

When the Spaniards found that the English privateers resorted to this island for provisions, they resolved on the total extirpation of the goats, and for this purpose they put on shore a greyhound dog and bitch.† These in their

23   turn

---

* Dampier, Vol. i. Part ii. p. 83.   † Ulloa, B. ii. C. 4.

turn increased and multiplied, in proportion to the quantity of food they met with; but in consequence, as the Spaniards had foreseen, the breed of goats diminished. Had they been totally destroyed, the dogs likewise must have perished. But as many of the goats retired to the craggy rocks, where the dogs could never follow them, descending only for short intervals to feed with fear and circumspection in the vallies, few of these, besides the careless and the rash, became a prey; and none but the most watchful, strong, and active of the dogs could get a sufficiency of food. Thus a new kind of balance was established. The weakest of both species were among the first to pay the debt of nature; the most active and vigorous preserved their lives. It is the quantity of food which regulates the numbers of the human species. In the woods, and in the *savage state*, there can be few inhabitants; but of these there will be only a proportionable few to suffer want. As long as food is plenty they will continue to increase and multiply; and every man will have ability to support his family, or to relieve his friends, in proportion to his activity and strength. The weak must depend upon the precarious bounty of the strong; and, sooner or later, the lazy will be left to suffer the natural consequence of their indolence. Should they introduce a community of goods, and at the same time leave every man at liberty to marry, they would at first increase their numbers, but not the sum total of their happiness, till by degrees, all being equally reduced to want and misery, the weakly would be the first to perish.

To procure a more ample, certain, and regular supply of food, should they cut down their woods and take to *breeding cattle,* this plenty would be of long continuance; but in process of time its limits would be found. The most active would acquire property, would have numerous flocks and numerous families; whilst the indolent would either starve or become servants to the rich, and the

community

community would continue to enlarge till it had found its natural bounds, and balanced the quantity of food.

Should they proceed to *agriculture*, these bounds would be much extended, and require ages before the straitness would be felt again. In process of time a compleat division of labour would take place, and they would have not only husbandmen, but artists, manufacturers, and merchants, monied men and gentlemen of landed property, soldiers and men of letters, with all their servants, to exchange their various commodities and labours for the produce of the soil. A noble author, in the north of Britain, is of opinion, that " a nation can scarce be too populous for husbandry, as agriculture has the singular property of producing food in proportion to the number of consumers."* But is it not clear, that when all that is fertile has been cultivated to the highest pitch of industry, the progress must of necessity be stopped, and that when the human species shall have multiplied in proportion to this increase of food, it can proceed no further? Indeed, as we have remarked already of the savage state, should they establish a community of goods, their numbers for a time would certainly increase; but the quantity of food not being augmented in proportion, and that which had been sufficient only for a given number being now distributed to the increasing multitude, all would have too little, and the weakly would perish sooner than if he who tilled the soil had been left to reap the undivided fruits of his industry and labour. Nations may for a time increase their numbers beyond the due proportion of their food, but they will in the same proportion destroy the ease and comfort of the affluent, and, without any possible advantage, give universality to that misery and want, which had been only partial. The

25   course

---

* Sketches on Man, p. 56.

course of nature may be easily disturbed, but man will never be able to reverse its laws.

The earth is no where more fertile than it is in China, nor does any country abound so much in people ; yet the cries of deserted children prove, that even they have found limits to their population. Few countries have been more productive than the land of Canaan was ; a land described as flowing with milk and honey, fertile in corn, and rich in pastures : yet even in the land of Canaan they had many poor; and it was said to them, but not in the way of threatening, "the poor shall never cease from among you." * Indeed it was impossible they ever should, because whilst men have appetites and passions, what but distress and poverty can stop the progress of population? The inhabitants of Europe are said to have doubled their numbers every five hundred years : from which we may infer that their quantity of food has been doubled in these periods. Throughout America, for the same reason, they have been doubled every five-and-twenty years ; and in some colonies, in the space of fifteen years.

If a new and equal division of property were made in England, we cannot doubt that the same inequality which we now observe would soon take place again : the improvident, the lazy, and the vicious, would dissipate their substance; the prudent, the active, and the virtuous, would again increase their wealth. If the legislature were to make this distribution, the evil would not be equal to the injustice of the measure : things would soon return into their proper channel, order and subordination would be again restored, diligence would be encouraged, and the virtuous would be fed. But by establishing a permanent community of goods, and neither increasing the quantity of food, nor limiting the number of those who are to share

it,

---

* Deut. xv. 11.

it, they divert the occasional surplus of national wealth from the industrious to the lazy, they increase the number of unprofitable citizens, and sow the seeds of misery for the whole community; increasing the general distress, and causing more to die for want, than if poverty had been left to find its proper channel.

It is well known that our commons, without stint, starve all our cattle. Here we clearly see the natural effects of that community of goods, which the poor laws would render universal. In the infancy of the Christian church, this experiment was fairly tried; but even whilst the Apostles, blest with a perfect knowledge of the human heart, were yet alive, it was found to be intolerable. We have adopted it in England; and what has been the consequence? Are poverty and wretchedness unknown? or rather, are not poverty and wretchedness increasing daily, in exact proportion with our efforts to restrain them? One of the neatest writers of the English nation, who understood this subject, has well observed, "the sufferings of the poor are less known than their misdeeds: they starve, and freeze, and rot among themselves; but they beg, and steal, and rob among their betters. There is not a parish in the liberty of Westminster, which doth not raise thousands annually for the poor; and there is not a street in that liberty, which doth not swarm all day with beggars, and all night with thieves." His expression is nervous, his description animated; but even the simple truth, when divested of all its ornaments, must excite astonishment. The effect is striking; but the cause of this phænomenon will be evident to those only who can examine it with a fixed attention.

There is a parish in the West of England which has never wanted poor, and in which, excepting for one short period, the poor have never wanted work; yet their poverty and misery have uniformly advanced constantly, outstripping all efforts which have been made to provide

for

for their distress. The farmers at this time pay ten shillings in the pound on the improved rents; yet wretchedness seems to have taken up its residence in every cottage, and the most miserable are they whose gains have been the greatest.

SECT. IX.

ON the subject of population we have had warm disputes, whilst some have lamented that our numbers are decreasing, and others with confidence have boasted that our population has rapidly advanced; all seeming to be agreed, that the wealth of a country consists in the number of its inhabitants. When industry and frugality keep pace with population, or rather when population is only the consequence of these, the strength and riches of a nation will bear proportion to the number of its citizens: but when the increase of people is unnatural and forced, when it arises only from a community of goods, it tends to poverty and weakness. In respect to population, some countries will reach their ne plus ultra sooner, and some later, according as they surmount the obstacles which impede their progress. This period can be retarded by improvements in agriculture, by living harder or by working more, by extensive conquests or by increasing commerce.

The cultivation of rice in China enabled them to feed some millions of people, more than could have been maintained by any other grain; whereas in the highlands of Scotland, where neither rice nor yet wheat will grow, the inhabitants soon became a burthen to the soil. Their chief dependance for supporting the present population is on frugality, and constant, steady, unremitted labour, without any hope of being able to advance their numbers. Oatmeal and water, with a little milk, is their common

food,

food, and to procure this they work as long as they can see. They till the soil; they watch their cattle; and, at their leisure hours, they spin all the linen and the woollen which their families consume.

The Romans, even when they had lost their domestic industry and habits of œconomy, were able to feed their increasing citizens by tribute from the distant provinces, as the Spaniards do by purchasing provisions with the gold and silver of Peru. The Dutch have no other refuge but in good government, industry, and commerce, for which their situation is most favourable. Their pastures are rich, but not sufficient to maintain half the number of their inhabitants, who are employed and fed by every nation upon earth, but reside in Holland for the convenience of the water-carriage, the security of their persons, and the protection of their property.

When a country is so far advanced in population as to be distressed for food; and when the forementioned resources have been exhausted, it has then reached its utmost limits; and in such a case, against increasing want there can be two remedies only which are natural, and one unnatural: for either none must marry, but they who can maintain a family, or else all who are in distress must emigrate. If these natural remedies are rejected, it can remain only for the poor to expose their children the moment they are born, which is the horrid practice adopted in the richest country upon earth to preserve the community from famine. With regard to celibacy, we may observe, that where things are left to a course of nature, one passion regulates another, and the stronger appetite restrains the weaker. There is an appetite, which is and should be urgent, but which, if left to operate without restraint, would multiply the human species before provision could be made for their support. Some check, some balance is therefore absolutely needful, and hunger is the proper balance; hunger, not as directly felt, or

feared

feared by the individual for himself, but as foreseen and feared for his immediate offspring. Were it not for this the equilibrium would not be preserved so near as it is at present in the world, between the numbers of people and the quantity of food. Various are the circumstances to be observed in different nations, which tend to blunt the shafts of Cupid, or at least to quench the torch of Hymen. In many parts of Europe we see multitudes of both sexes, not from policy, but from superstition and religious prejudice, bound by irrevocable vows of chastity. In other parts we hear of numbers who are compelled to spend their days in a seraglio, where it is not to be expected that all should be prolific; whilst in consequence of this unjustifiable practice, a corresponding number must pass through the world without leaving a representative behind them. But in every country, at least on this side the Atlantic Ocean, we find a similar effect from prudence; and without the assistance of either a seraglio, or a convent, the younger branches of the best families have been left to wither. In every country multitudes would marry, if they had a comfortable prospect for themselves, and for their children; but if all should listen to this call of nature, deaf to a louder call, the whole world in a few years would be distressed with famine. Yet, even in such a case, when it is impolitic that all should marry, this should be wholly left to every man's discretion, and to that balance of the appetites which nature has established. But if, notwithstanding the restraints of distress and poverty, they who are not able to maintain a family will yet marry, there can be no resource but in emigration. In the highlands of Scotland, when the inhabitants became a burthen to the soil, they tried every possible expedient; and, when all others failed, their young men with reluctance turned their back upon a country which was not able to support them. It is well known that their emigrations are considerable. They do not issue

forth in assembled multitudes, like swarms from the northern hives of old ; nor do they, like a torrent, overflow
and desolate the adjacent countries ; but, like the silent
dew, they drop upon the richest pastures, and wandering
to the remotest corners of the earth in quest of food, with
the industry of bees they collect their honey from the
most luxuriant flowers. These active, hardy, and laborious people, are to be found in the temperate, in the
torrid, and in the frigid zones, in every island, and on
every habitable mountain of Europe, Asia, Africa, and
America. Yet in their native country the numbers never
fail : the supply is constant. Now, if, instead of collecting
for themselves wherever food is to be found, these wan-
derers had been equally supported on their barren mountains by contributions from the more fertile vallies of the
South, can we imagine that the births in Scotland would
be fewer than they are at present? The overflowings of
their population might have been accelerated, but could
not thereby have been retarded. Having no contributions
from the South, they have quitted their country, and
made room for others. We are told, upon the best authority,* that in the highlands of Scotland, a woman will
bring twenty children into the world, and rear only two.
Had she sufficient food for more, more would live. The
women there, like the women in all countries which are
come to their utmost height of population, are more
prolific than the soil. To provide more food on their
bleak and barren mountains, is beyond a question. But
if now, to rear these twenty children, a poor's rate were
to be collected in more fertile countries, yet in countries
which are fully peopled in proportion to their labour and
to the produce of the soil, is it not evident, that the scarcity
and distress would only be transferred, and that the

children

---

* Smith, Wealth of Nations.

children of the South must die, that the children of the North might live? But supposing these should live; yet at best they could only take the place of those that died, and more women in the North would increase and multiply, till they felt the same degree of pressure which they feel at present. Neither Switzerland nor the coast of Africa are depopulated by emigrations, because the quantity of food in each remains unaltered. It is with the human species as with all other articles of trade without a premium; the demand will regulate the market.

By establishing a community of goods, or rather by giving to the idle and to the vicious the *first* claim upon the produce of the earth, many of the more prudent, careful, and industrious citizens are straitened in their circumstances, and restrained from marriage. The farmer breeds only from the best of all his cattle; but our laws choose rather to preserve the worst, and seem to be anxious lest the breed should fail. The cry is, Population, population! population at all events! But is there any reasonable fear of depopulation? We have seen that corn upon an average has been considerably cheaper since the commencement of the present century, than it was for an equal term before; yet wages have been raised in the proportion of six to four, and the rent of land is doubled. May we not infer from hence, that the produce of the soil must have increased nearly in the same proportions. If we consider the improvements which have been made in agriculture, by clearing woods, inclosing wastes, draining morasses, laying the common fields in severalty, and making roads; by the introduction of clover, saintfoin, turnips, and potatoes; by the breaking up of extensive downs; and by the superior skill of the present race in the management of all sorts of land, with respect to stocking, manuring, cropping, not forgetting their superior weight of capital to work with; we shall cease to wonder at this vast increase of produce. But is it possible that

the

the produce should be thus increased, and not the people also who consume it? We need not desire any man to visit London, Norwich, Bath, Bristol, Hull, Liverpool, Leeds, Wakefield, Manchester, and Birmingham; we need not call upon him to view our mines of coal, copper, lead, iron, and tin, with all the new manufactures which depend on these: but let him at least count our flocks, and calculate the quantity of corn produced by recent improvements in our tillage; then let him ask himself if our population is increased.

Whilst food is to be had, there is no fear of wanting people. But should the population of a country get beyond the produce of the soil, and of the capital engaged in trade, how shall these people find employment? Whenever this shall be the case, the evil will increase, and the capital will go on constantly diminishing; like as in private life, when a gentleman breaks in upon his principal to pay the ordinary expences of his family. When a trading nation is obliged to spend more than the revenue which is derived from commerce, and not from accident, but as the effect of some abiding cause, exceeds continually the profit of its trade, without some substantial reformation, the ruin of that nation will be inevitable. Should the capital itself accumulate, the interest of money would be lowered, the demand for labour would increase, and the superlucration on this increase of trade would continue to enlarge the capital. Speculation apart, it is a fact, that in England we have more than we can feed, and many more than we can profitably employ under the present system of our laws.

SECT. X.

ALL the effects which I have been describing, have not been fully felt. Let it however be remembered, that a distinction must be made between those evils which have already been severely felt, and the greater evils which in the course of nature and due time may be expected. The tendency of a law may be most destructive; yet, by adventitious circumstances, the bad consequences may be checked and prevented for a season. It is not to be imagined that men, who by close application and watchful attention to their business, by rigid frugality and hard labour, have made a decent provision for their families, should freely part with a considerable proportion of their property, or suffer it to be taken from them without strong efforts to retain it. For more than a century the struggles have been obstinate and unremitted, yet for more than a century the poor's rates have been constantly increasing. From time to time, as men remarked the rapidity of this progress, their exertions were more than common, and some transient reformation was effected. When at last they found, that they had no other way remaining to protect the fruits of industry from the extravagant demands of indolence, and from the undistinguishing benevolence of power, they adopted, from necessity and not from choice, the miserable expedient of building work-houses. Till these are completely filled, and even after they are full, they serve a double purpose: they disarm the magistrate, they intimidate the poor.

As the law now stands, the parish officers, in certain cases, may build houses on the waste for the reception of the impotent and aged; but they have been hitherto so prudent as not to exercise a power, which would be destructive to themselves, without being beneficial to the poor. Happily the justices of peace have no legal authority to augment the number of our cottages. There can be no compulsion in this case. Some of them indeed have indirectly attempted this, but they have been resisted by the more provident and wary in most parishes. Hence the number of houses becomes a gage, at once to measure and to regulate the extent of population. In every

village

village will be found plenty of young men and women, who only wait for habitations to lay the foundation of new families, and who with joy would hasten to the altar, if they could be certain of a roof to shelter them at night. It has been chiefly from the want of houses that the poor have not more rapidly increased. If the most opulent parishes in the kingdom were obliged to find habitations, as they are to provide work, or food and raiment for the poor, they would be themselves reduced in a course of years to such extreme distress, that all moveable stock would be carried off, the land would be left uncultivated, the houses would go to ruin, and the poor would starve. As the rents have been advancing, new houses have been built; but hitherto the progress has been retarded by the superior value of money in the public funds. Should the present law subsist, the value of land will sink, and the rent of cottages will rise; each in proportion to the burthen of the poor, and the demand for houses. It is true, by a statute made in the thirty-first year of Queen Elizabeth, there is a penalty on every person who shall build a cottage without assigning four acres of land to be held for ever with it: but this statute, with which her famous poor law is in perfect harmony, and which, if observed, would have prevented the greatest evils felt and to be feared from that unlimited provision for the poor, has been long neglected, or perhaps was never regarded. The penalty is ten pounds for the first erection of the cottage, and forty shillings per month as long as it shall be occupied. Had this law remained in force, or had it been constantly observed, the poor would not have multiplied; but then the manufactures would not have flourished in the kingdom as they do at present. Under this law it is evident, that no poor man could marry till there was a cottage vacant to receive him; for no inmates were allowed.

The last circumstance which remains to be assigned,

as having checked and prevented for a season the evil consequences resulting from our poor laws, is the shame and reproach of being relieved by a parish: but these have long since ceased to operate. It is high time, therefore, that more effectual provision should be made for the protection of industry in affluence, and for the relief of industry in the seasons of distress.

SECT. XI.

THE best politicians in Europe have condemned the present system of our poor laws. Among these we may reckon two great and distinguished writers; one universally admired for his incomparable work on the spirit of laws; the other for his most elegant and judicious comment on the laws of England. A nobleman, who stands foremost among the literati in the north of Britain, has more freely and more fully delivered his opinion, and perfectly coincides in sentiment with those able lawyers. These respectable authors have condemned the principles, whilst others have blamed only the execution of our laws. But all who are even in the least degree acquainted with the subject have lamented, that two millions should be annually expended on the poor without relieving their distress.

SECT. XII.

IF it were possible to meet with proper persons to execute our laws, they would not be so hurtful to the community as they are at present. But where shall we find men qualified to be at once trustees and guardians for the public and for the poor? An overseer should be endued with more than common patience; willing to hear with calmness and composure the complaints of the most

untoward

untoward and perverse; blest with a command of temper such as few possess. He should be diligent and active, that he may visit the habitations of the poor, and examine with his own eyes the nature, the extent, and the cause of their distress. He should be a man of good understanding, sharp, sensible, and well-informed, that he may know what is the best, the cheapest, and the most effectual method, at once to relieve and to employ the poor. He should be a man of penetration, quick in discerning, and ready in detecting the false pretences of impostors. He should be a man of the most humane and compassionate disposition; not merely that he may shed the sympathizing tear, but that he may exert himself to the utmost to comfort and support the sick, and properly to sweeten the bitter cup for those who are drinking the dregs of life. He should be at the same time a man of firmness and resolution; not to be worn out and teazed into compliance, nor yet to be moved either by threats or by deceitful tears. He should be inexorably just, considering the public fund, out of which he is to relieve the poor, as a most sacred deposit committed to his care, in confidence that he will administer it to the best of his judgment and ability. He should be a man of a disinterested and honest disposition, that, in the discharge of this important trust, he may neither directly nor indirectly defraud the public, either to favour his friends or to promote his trade. In one word, if in him should centre all the excellencies, which are scattered with a sparing hand among the human race; if he had no other trade, occupation, or pursuit which required his attention; if, thus qualified, he were willing to give up his time for the benefit of the public, and for the comfort of the poor; if a succession of such were to be found, and if their power were supreme, subject to no controul from the interference of a magistrate; the burthen might yet be tolerable, and some of the evils, naturally attendant on the present system of our

poor

poor laws, instead of being severely felt, would for the present be seen only at a distance.

Many parishes have been sensible of this difficulty, more especially in the cloathing counties: but as if, whilst they severely felt it, they had only indistinctly seen it, they have made application to parliament, complaining that the business was too much for the attendance and attention of four overseers; and therefore praying, that one additional overseer might be appointed with absolute and sole authority to grant relief. Their argument appears to be absurd, but their meaning is precise and clear. They would be thus at liberty to choose the most proper person for the charge; and he, having little else to do, could pay more attention to the business. The event has in some measure answered their expectation; but, at best, this can be considered only as a good expedient to palliate one of those many bad effects which flow from a pernicious law.

SECT. XIII.

TO remedy these evils, various have been the schemes recommended to the public, by men who have been revered for the strength of their understandings, the extent of their knowledge, and the uprightness of their intentions. They have chiefly recommended palliatives; and such only have been tried, yet with little or with no effect. They have indeed checked the evil for a time, and only for a time, to return with accumulated force: for, notwithstanding all their efforts, the tax collected to relieve the poor is swelled in many places from ten or twelve pounds annually to five hundred pounds a year, where no manufactures have been established; and in the manufacturing parishes, from little or nothing to fifteen

hundred,

huudred, two thousand, and even three thousand pounds a year.

The legislature began with requiring the consent of two justices of peace, before the overseers could have power to relieve the poor.* They then insisted that none should be relieved, but those who were put upon the list by the parishioners assembled in their vestry, or by authority under the hand of a justice.† After this it was enacted, that no justice of peace should grant an order, without having examined upon oath the party making application to him for relief.‡ Upon all these occasions we hear the legislature constantly complaining that the evil still went on increasing.

The expedient which has been most often tried, has been to compel both the pauper and his family to wear the Roman P in scarlet cloth upon their shoulders;§ and from this much was expected, but in vain. It has operated, indeed, as a partial repeal of a bad law, repealing however all that could be considered as valuable, and leaving all that is noxious to the state; discouraging only the ingenuous, the modest, and the meek, that there may be the more for those who, lost to shame, have long since forgot to blush. Of all human inventions, none can be more cruel than this. You invite the poor, you offer him relief, but you will give it only upon this condition, that he shall receive it with a mark of infamy. The overseers are liable to a fine, if they do not impose this mark upon the indigent; but such is their humanity, that they risk the penalty rather than reproach the wretched with his poverty. Should they give this badge to some, they must impose it upon all. The worthless and the impudent would not regard it; the modest would sooner die than

39   wear

---

* 43 Eliz.   ‡ 9 Geo. I. c. 7.
† 3 and 4 W. and M.   § 8 and 9 W. c. 30. s. 2.

wear it. There is no doubt that time would reconcile them to it, more especially when they saw none or few without it; but then, what purpose would it answer? Whilst it took effect, it would be hurtful: when it ceased to operate, it would be useless.

Finding the futility of this device, the most common refuge has been to parochial and provincial workhouses; against which there appear insuperable objections. It was thought, that with watchful attention the poor would do more work under one roof, and be fed much cheaper, than when dispersed in their several cottages. An expectation, however, which experience has never yet confirmed. Even in parochial workhouses, and in those which are under the best regulation, the poor do so little work, that the produce of their labour almost escapes our notice, whilst they are maintained at a most enormous expence. In their cottages they might live comfortably on the average of four pounds each; whereas under the management of the public they cost from five to ten, and even twelve pounds each, per annum. It is not reasonable to imagine, that men, deprived of liberty, will work for others with the same chearful activity as when working for themselves; or that they will be contented with the hard and homely fare, which they could eat with thankfulness, whilst as freemen they were surrounded with their friends. It is hope that must sweeten all our labours. Let a man have no pursuit, no exercise for his hopes and fears, and you may as well take the marrow from his bones, which was designed by nature to supple all his joints. You may feed him well; but, without making him a more useful member in society, you will leave him to drag on a miserable existence, a burthen to himself and to the public. It is now a maxim universally received, that the service of a slave is the dearest service which can be had. Let a man consult his own feelings, and the reason will be obvious.

The

The terror of being sent to a workhouse acts like an abolition of the poor's tax on all who dread the loss of liberty. It is in effect a virtual repeal, as far as it extends, of those laws, which should long since have given place to better regulations. But unfortunately the most worthy objects suffer most by this repeal, and the advantage to the public is little more than negative. The quiet and the cleanly dread the noise and nastiness, even more than the confinement of a workhouse. They pant for the pure and wholesome air, which they can never hope to breathe where numbers are confined within narrow limits, and sigh for that serenity and peace, which they must despair to find where the most profligate of the human species are met together. By the fear of being sentenced to such society, many, who deserve a better fate, struggle with poverty till they sink under the burthen of their misery. Against county workhouses, improperly called houses of industry, the objections are much stronger. The buildings, the furniture, the salaries, the waste, and the imposition, every thing is upon a large and expensive scale, without its being possible to preserve, for any length of time, a system of œconomy. At first, indeed, there might be great exertion; but the novelty being over, few gentlemen would be found public spirited enough to continue their attendance and attention to a business in which, as individuals, they would be so little interested, and for which they must give up more important or more pleasant engagements and pursuits. By experience it is found, that without reckoning interest upon the prime cost of either furniture or buildings, the poor in these extensive establishments are not maintained for less than I have stated. But whilst the expence is so enormous, are they happy? Far from happy, they are wretched. With all the discomforts of a parochial workhouse, they feel themselves in a hopeless state of banishment from their relations and connections. It is true, they eat, they

41 drink,

drink, and they are miserable. This kind of banishment has the same effect in part as a repeal of the poor laws, because few are willing to be thus relieved. These houses of industry cannot be vindicated, either in point of comfort or œconomy : if they have therefore any merit, it can be only that kind of merit which I have stated ; and if it be wise to have recourse to them, it would be much wiser directly to repeal the laws, against the depredations of which these houses are to protect your property. A county workhouse, at best, may be considered as a colony to which a few of the superabundant members of the community have been transported to make room for others; or it may be considered as a new manufacture, beneficial in its progress to employ the idle hands : beneficial, if it were possible to make a profit on their labour ; yet like other manufactures, under the present system of our laws, increasing the number and the distresses of the poor.

That gentlemen of landed property should have taken the alarm, and that all who feel the burthen of the poor should wish to be relieved, is not to be wondered at. Yet surely we may be permitted to express astonishment, that when in the year 1775 the House of Commons were to provide a remedy for the growing evil, no expedient should present itself, but to erect county workhouses.

They resolved, 1°. That the laws relating to the poor are defective, and the good purposes intended by them in many respects prevented.

2°. That the money raised for the relief of the poor is a grievous, and, if no new regulations are made, will be an increasing burthen upon the public.

They then recommended county workhouses, leaving the parishes at liberty to draw at discretion on the county stock, for the relief of such as were not proper objects for a workhouse.

The counties, however, were not weak enough to

42   accept

accept an offer which must have entailed a tax of four shillings in the pound on their estates for ever, without procuring any benefit to the public, to the land-owner, to the farmer, or to the poor.

Another expedient, and the last which I shall mention, is the most abominable that ever was invented : it is to farm the poor. In some parishes they are farmed at so much a head, but in others the contract is for a given sum. In one parish in Gloucestershire a contractor has agreed to take all the expence of the poor upon himself for a very moderate consideration. Taking the present numbers in confinement, he has only two shillings a week for each; yet out of this he is to be at the charge of all litigations and removals, and to relieve all others who are not proper objects for a workhouse, and after all to make a profit for himself.

All these expedients have the same tendency. They are adopted with a professed intention to lower the poor rates ; and it is confessed, that many are thereby deterred from making application for relief, who would otherwise be a burthen to the public. But then is not this a partial, impolitic, oppressive repeal of a bad law, without reducing the tax; for it continues to increase, and without making a better provision for those among the poor who are most worthy of attention ?

Having thus endeavoured to display the imperfections which are most obvious in our management of the poor, let us now examine the provision made for their relief by other nations.

In the early ages of the world there could be no great difficulty in this matter, as the quantity of food was more than could be consumed. In process of time, when property had got footing in the world, they, who had neither flocks nor herds, became slaves, and, selling themselves for bread, together with their children, constituted the principal treasure of the rich. When the rich had so far

increased

increased their stock, that their cattle had not sufficient room to feed, they quitted their ancient habitations, and sought new settlements. Thus it is said, that Abraham was very rich in cattle, that he had sheep and oxen, and men servants and maid servants, and camels and asses, and silver and gold. The same nearly was the prosperity of Lot. But when the land was not able to bear them with their flocks and with their herds, they agreed to part, and Lot chose for himself the plains of Jordan. When the offspring of Abraham settled in the land of Canaan, they continued the same mode of relieving the distressed, only with this exception, that in the seventh year the poor, who had sold himself, was to go out free. This custom of exchanging their liberty for bread was followed by most of the nations upon earth, and was the general practice of the world, till Christianity prevailed, and became the established religion of the Roman empire. The milder genius of this religion, which proclaims liberty to the captive, and the opening of the prison doors to them that are bound, abhorrent to slavery in all its forms, has almost banished that cruel custom from our world; and in its stead has made the best possible provision for the poor, leaving them to be supported by the free bounty of the rich. It is true, the mistaken zeal of its first converts, inflamed by the expectation of that transcendent glory which the gospel had revealed to them, poured contempt upon their visible possessions of houses and of lands. These they sold, and being all of one heart, and of one soul, they agreed to have all things common.* But no such community of goods received the sanction of divine authority. When Peter reproached Ananias, it was for his falsehood only: "Whilst the land remained, was it not thine own; and after it was sold, was it not in thine own power?"†

44

The

---

* Acts iv. 32.   † Acts v. 4.

The positive injunctions of the gospel are clear and distinct, and should never have been forgot. "Every man according as he purposeth in his heart, so let him give; not grudgingly, or of necessity: for God loveth a chearful giver."* These voluntary contributions were collected on the first day of every week, when they assembled at their public worship. The Christian dispensation gives the highest encouragement to the overflowings of benevolence, but at the same time leaves every man at liberty to give or not to give, proceeding upon this maxim, that it should be lawful for a man to do what he will with his own. Whilst however the followers of this religion are left to their own judgment and discretion, they are under the strongest obligations to be liberal in their donations, and to relieve the distresses of their fellow creatures to the utmost of their ability. In the description of the great and final judgment of the world, it is said, "When the Son of man shall come in his glory, and all the holy angels with him, then shall he sit upon the throne of his glory. And before him shall be gathered all nations; and he shall separate them one from another, as a shepherd divideth his sheep from the goats: and he shall set the sheep on his right hand, but the goats on the left. Then shall the King say unto them on his right hand, Come, ye blessed of my Father, inherit the kingdom prepared for you from the foundation of the world. For I was an hungered, and ye gave me meat: I was thirsty, and ye gave me drink: I was a stranger, and ye took me in: naked, and ye clothed me: I was sick, and ye visited me: I was in prison, and ye came unto me. For inasmuch as ye did it unto one of the least of these my brethren, ye did it unto me,"† From this description we must not too hastily conclude that the charity of Christians is to be indiscriminate and blind. Among the various objects of

45   distress

---

* 2 Cor. ix. 7.   † Matt. xxv.

distress a choice is to be made, selecting first those which are most worthy, and reserving the residue for those who have nothing but their misery to excite compassion. Let the virtuous citizen be fed, then let the profligate and the prodigal share all that prudence and frugality shall have left behind them. To reverse this order is neither politic nor just : for surely nothing can be more inconsistent with equity, than to give the bread of industry to indolence and vice. Christian charity was never meant to discourage diligence and application, nor to promote among men a wanton dissipation of their substance. The Apostle of the Gentiles, both by example and by precept, teaches a lesson which too many among the poor have yet to learn. We hear him thus appealing to his converts : " We did not eat any man's bread for nought; but wrought with labour and travel night and day, that we might not be chargeable to any of you : not because we have not power, but to make ourselves an example unto you to follow us. For even when we were with you, this we commanded you, that if any would not work, neither should he eat."*

For many centuries the nations of Europe had no other way of providing for their increasing poor, when occasional benefactions became inadequate to their wants, but by driving them out, like swarms, to seek new settlements. It was not then difficult for warlike tribes, issuing forth in countless numbers, with their flocks and with their herds, to make an impression, when at any time they turned their arms against the peaceable inhabitants of more cultivated countries. But now that all have quitted the shepherd life and taken to agriculture ; now that each nation, although more numerous than formerly, is hemmed in by nations equal to itself in numbers,

wealth,

---

* 2 Thess. iii. 8—10.

wealth, and military ardour; it is become necessary to provide for their poor at home. This they have attempted by public hospitals and private benefactions. With regard to hospitals, they find that these only remove the evil for a time, and in the issue extend the bounds of extreme poverty and wretchedness. They at first pleased themselves with the idea, that they had put an end to human misery; but they soon found it returning back upon them, and the vacant places, which had been left by those provided for in their public hospitals, filled up again by objects of distress. When at Lyons they opened an hospital with forty beds for the reception of the poor, they could fill only half that number, but now eight hundred beds are not sufficient; and when they built the hospital of Saltpetriere, near Paris, it had few inhabitants, but now they lodge twelve thousand; and yet to their astonishment they find, that instead of having banished distress and poverty, they have increased the number of the poor. The effect has filled them with amazement; but they do not seem to have as yet discovered, that they have been attempting to stop a rapid river in its progress, and to push back the waters of the ocean.

In Holland their chief dependence is on voluntary contributions, and a rigid execution of the laws; and in Holland are to be seen more industry and fewer criminals, than are to be found in the best governed countries in Europe of the same extent.

SECT. XIV.

I AM now come to the most arduous part of my undertaking. Some remedy must be found for the growing evil, and those which have been hitherto proposed have been found inadequate. In laying down a plan, I

shall

shall begin with establishing the general principles on which we must proceed.

It is evident then, that no system can be good which does not, in the first place, encourage industry, œconomy, and subordination; and, in the second place, regulate population by the demand for labour.

To promote industry and œconomy, it is necessary that the relief which is given to the poor should be limited and precarious. "Languescet industria, intendetur socordia, si nullus ex se metus aut spes; et securi omnes aliena subsidia expectabunt, sibi ignavi, nobis graves." No man will be an œconomist of water, if he can go to the well or to the brook as often as he please; nor will he watch with solicitous attention to keep the balance even between his income and expenditure, if he is sure to be relieved in the time of need. The labouring poor at present are greatly defective, both in respect to industry and œconomy. Considering the numbers to be maintained, they work too little, they spend too much, and what they spend is seldom laid out to the best advantage. When they return from threshing or from plough, they might card, they might spin, or they might knit. We are told, that one thousand pair of Shetland stockings are annually imported into Leith, of which the price is from five to seven pence a pair: yet labour at Lerwick, the small capital of Shetland islands, is ten pence a day. These stockings are made at leisure hours. In these islands they have no dependance but upon their industry and frugality. They consume neither tea, nor sugar, nor spices, because they cannot afford to purchase these useless articles; neither do they wear stockings or shoes, till by their diligence they have acquired such affluence as to bear this expence. How different is theirs from the dress and diet of our common people, who have lost all ideas of œconomy! If by their industry they could procure these articles of luxury, or if their linen, their

48   cotton,

cotton, and their silk, were spun, and wove, and knit in their own houses, and at leisure hours, their desire to obtain these things would be advantageous to the state: but surely, if in the colder regions of the North these are not essential to their existence, or even to their happiness, they should be considered in the South only as the rewards of industry, and should never, from the common fund, be given promiscuously to all, as they will inevitably be, unless that fund shall have some other limits besides the wants and expectations of the poor. Unless the degree of pressure be increased, the labouring poor will never acquire habits of diligent application, and of severe frugality. To increase this pressure, the poor's tax must be gradually reduced in certain proportions annually, the sum to be raised in each parish being fixed and certain, not boundless, and obliged to answer unlimited demands. This enormous tax might easily in the space of nine years be reduced nine-tenths; and the remainder being reserved as a permanent supply, the poor might safely be left to the free bounty of the rich, without the interposition of any other law. But if the whole system of compulsive charity were abolished, it would be still better for the state. I am not singular in this opinion. Baron Montesquieu has given his opinion, " Que des secours passagers vaudroieut mieux que des établissemens perpetuels;"* and our own countryman, who had been long conversant with this business, has told us, " I am persuaded that to provide for the poor, who are unable to work, might be safely left to voluntary charity, unenforced by any compulsive law."†

To assist the industrious poor, who have neither tools nor materials, but more especially to train up the children of the dissolute in useful labour, there might be in each parish one or more work-shops, where they might be

certain

---

* L. xxiii. C. 29.   † Fielding on Robbers.

certain of employment, and of daily pay for the work performed. In these shops they should neither be lodged nor fed, being taught to depend each for himself on his own diligence and patient application to his business. The building, the tools, and the materials, would be all that required assistance from the public fund.

The grand resource however should be from the labouring poor themselves, previous to their being incumbered with families. They have throughout the kingdom a number of friendly societies established, which have been productive of good effects, and in some places have reduced the rates. But these societies have more than one defect. All their members contribute equally to the public fund, without respect to their ability, to the proportion of their gains, or to the number of their children. By this regulation some pay too little, others pay too much. The sum, which they deposit weekly, is insignificant and trifling when compared with what it ought to be. But the greatest misfortune is, that they are altogether left to their own option to join these societies or not; in consequence of which liberty, many of these associations for mutual assistance are going to decay. If this be indeed a good expedient, it should be pushed as far as it will go: it should be firmly established, made universal, and subjected to wholesome regulations. The unmarried man should pay one quarter of his wages weekly, and the father of four young children not more than one thirtieth of his income, which is nearly the sum which all contribute to their present clubs. To drive them into these societies, no man should be intitled to relief from the parochial fund who did not belong to one of these. Thus would sobriety, industry, and œconomy, take place of drunkenness, idleness, and prodigality, and due subordination would be again restored.

As long as it should be found expedient to retain a given proportion of the present poor tax, the disposal of

this

this should be wholly at the discretion of the minister, churchwardens, and overseers, or the majority of them, subject only to the orders of a vestry. By this provision the subordination of the poor would be more effectually secured, and the civil magistrate would be at liberty to bend his whole attention to the preservation of the peace, and to the good government of the people.

This plan would be aided and assisted much by laying a sufficient tax upon the alehouses to reduce their number, these being the principal nurseries for drunkenness, idleness, and vice.

Should things be left thus to flow in their proper channels, the consequence would be, that, as far as it is possible according to the present constitution of the world, our population would be no longer unnatural and forced, but would regulate itself by the demand for labour.

There remains one thing more for the legislature to do, which is to increase the quantity of food. This may be done with ease, by laying a tax upon all horses used in husbandry, gradually increasing this tax till the farmers have returned to the use of oxen. This change would enable England not only to maintain her present population, but greatly to increase it. The land which now supports one horse, in proper working order, would bear two oxen for draft and for the shambles, if not also one cow for the pail; or any two of these, with a man, his wife, and his three children. If we consider the number of horses at present used for husbandry in this island, should only half that number give place to oxen, it would not be easy to calculate, or even to conceive, all the benefits and advantages which the public would derive from this vast increase of food. In many parishes where they have no manufactures, but the cultivation of the soil, the horses consume the produce of more land than the inhabitants themselves require. Suppose a parish to

consist

consist of four thousand acres of arable and pasture land; let this be cultivated by one hundred and fifty horses, and let it feed one thousand souls: now if, for the present, we allow only two acres of oats and two of hay for each of the horses, the amount will be six hundred productive acres, which will be more than sufficient to feed the given number of inhabitants. But the fact is, that a horse, to be fully fed, requires five ton of hay, and from thirteen to three-and-twenty quarters of oats, per annum, according to his work. Some farmers allow the former, and the latter is given by the great carriers on the public roads, which would bring the computation to about eight acres each for horses used in husbandry; but then few farmers suffer their horses to be highly fed. If we allow three acres of pasture for each ox or cow, and consider, that in calculating the quantity of land sufficient to maintain a team of horses, the needful fallows must be carried to account, we shall not be at a loss for food, when we have substituted two oxen, and one family of five persons, in the place of every horse.

It must be confessed, that the tax on horses would be apparently a tax on husbandry, but in reality it would only be a tax on pride and prejudice. Neither would it be a tax for the purpose of revenue, which would certainly be most impolitic; but it would be a tax for the regulation of trade, beneficial to the public, and highly advantageous to the farmer. In China they use few cattle in the cultivation of the soil, and therefore they are able to support a more abundant population. By reverting to the antient practice of ploughing with oxen instead of horses, we should enjoy the same advantage; and till the population of our country had found its utmost limits, we should rejoice in affluence.

With the same intentions, the legislature should facilitate the laying common fields in severalty, leaving the inclosure of these lands to every man's discretion.

Wherever

Wherever these allotments have been carried into execution, the value of land has been nearly doubled. Yet, independent of the exertion, the time, and the fatigue, requisite to procure a private act of parliament for this purpose, the expence of the act itself, and of the consequent inclosure, is more than many are willing to incur. That the improvements of land should be subject to this expence is not just, and that men should be obliged to inclose these lands is neither just nor wise: because hedge-rows consume much land, stint the growth of corn, cause it to lodge, prevent its drying, and harbour birds. If men are left at liberty, without restraint, when they find it for their interest to inclose, they will inclose.

Should the House of Commons, agreeable to the resolutions of 1775, enter seriously into this business, and adopt such regulations as may effectually relieve the public from the grievous and still increasing burthen, which for more than half a century has been the subject of serious investigation and of loud complaints; it will be necessary for magistrates to pay more than common attention to the police, till industry and subordination shall be once more restored. The reins have been held with a loose hand, at a time when the idleness and extravagance, the drunkenness and dissipation, with the consequent crimes and vices of the lower classes of the people, called for the most strenuous exertions of the magistrate, and the most strict execution of the laws.

If the labouring poor, in health, previous to marriage, and whilst their families are small, are compelled to raise a fund for their own support, in case of sickness or old age; there can be no doubt, that when at any time, from peculiar circumstances, this fund shall prove inadequate, the most liberal contributions will be made to relieve any occasional distress. No one can doubt of this, who has witnessed the generous efforts which were lately made to assist the woollen manufacturers in Gloucestershire

during

during the stagnation of their trade. Money was collected for them from all the adjacent counties, and in the metropolis, to feed and to employ them. At Minchin Hampton in particular, when the poor's tax was seven shillings in the pound on the rack rents, and their poor were more than commonly distressed, two thousand two hundred persons were cloathed, fed, and set to work, by voluntary benefactions. It should be added, for the credit of these poor people, that they worked from six in the morning till eight at night. Had the manufacture fallen to rise no more, the manufacturers must in reason have retired, or must have turned their hands to something else; because no fund, no tax, no charitable contributions, can support such a multitude of people when their trade is gone. In cases of sudden emergency assistance will be loudly called for, and the affluent will not be tardy in sending a supply. The English have never yet been charged with want of charity. There need not many arguments to excite their pity and compassion: the only difficulty is to restrain the impetuosity of their benevolence, and to direct their bounty towards the most worthy objects.

Besides these sudden emergencies, affecting whole districts where extensive manufactures are established, individuals must be ever subject to occasional distress, from various accidents and from unexpected losses, which, without the kind assistance of a friend, they are not able to support. In such circumstances, where can the sufferer look for help? Not to the overseers of the poor; for their authority does not extend beyond food and raiment. To make good his losses, and to support him in his station, industry in distress can find no sufficient refuge but in the generous aid of his more affluent and charitable neighbours. This refuge will never fail him; nor will they ever suffer him to want, if they are able to relieve him, and if he has proved himself worthy of compassion.

To

To relieve the poor by voluntary donations is not only most wise, politic, and just; is not only most agreeable both to reason and to revelation; but it is most effectual in preventing misery, and most excellent in itself, as cherishing, instead of rancour, malice, and contention, the opposite and most amiable affections of the human breast, pity, compassion, and benevolence in the rich, love, reverence, and gratitude in the poor. Nothing in nature can be more disgusting than a parish pay-table, attendant upon which, in the same objects of misery, are too often found combined, snuff, gin, rags, vermin, insolence, and abusive language; nor in nature can any thing be more beautiful than the mild complacency of benevolence, hastening to the humble cottage to relieve the wants of industry and virtue, to feed the hungry, to cloath the naked, and to sooth the sorrows of the widow with her tender orphans; nothing can be more pleasing, unless it be their sparkling eyes, their bursting tears, and their uplifted hands, the artless expressions of unfeigned gratitude for unexpected favours. Such scenes will frequently occur whenever men shall have power to dispose of their own property. When the poor are obliged to cultivate the friendship of the rich, the rich will never want inclination to relieve the distresses of the poor.

F I N I S.

THOUGHTS AND DETAILS

ON

SCARCITY,

ORIGINALLY PRESENTED TO

THE RIGHT HON. WILLIAM PITT,

IN THE MONTH OF NOVEMBER,

1795.

———◆◆◆———

BY THE LATE

RIGHT HON. EDMUND BURKE

———

LONDON:

PRINTED FOR F. AND C. RIVINGTON,
AND J. HATCHARD.

1800.

PREFACE.

Beaconsfield, Nov. 1, 1800.

THE wisdom, which is canonized by death, is consulted with a sort of sacred veneration. A casual remark, or an incidental maxim in some ancient author, an interesting narrative, or a pointed anecdote from the history of past times, even though they bear but a remote and general application to the exigency of our own immediate situation, are caught up with eagerness, and remembered with delight. But how much more important is the instruction which we may derive from the posthumous opinions of those who, having been most eminent in our own times for superior talents and more extensive knowledge, have formed their observation on circumstances so similar to our own, as only not to be the same, yet who speak without influence from the little prejudices and passions, to which accident, folly or malevolence may have given birth in the present moment.

The late Mr. Burke, in the estimation of those who were most capable of judging, stood high, both as a scientific and a practical farmer. He carried into his fields the same penetrating, comprehensive, and vigorous mind, which shone forth so conspicuously in all his exertions on the stage of public life. Wherever he was, in whatever he was engaged, he was alike assiduous in collecting information, and happy in combining, what he acquired, into general principles. All that the ancients have left us upon husbandry was familiar to him, and he once encouraged and set on foot a new edition of those

3   valuable

valuable writers; but, though he might occasionally derive new hints even from those sources, he preferred the authority of his own mind to that of Hesiod or Virgil, of Cato or Columella. He thought for himself upon this, as upon other subjects; and not rejecting sound reforms of demonstrated errors, he was, however, principally guided by the traditionary skill and experience of that class of men, who, from father to son, have for generations laboured in calling forth the fertility of the English soil. He not only found in agriculture the most agreeable relaxation from his more serious cares, but he regarded the cultivation of the earth, and the improvement of all which it produces, as a sort of moral and religious duty. Towards the close of his life, when he had lost his son, in whom all his prospects had long centered, after lamenting, in an elegant allusion to Virgil, that the trees, which he had been nursing for many years, would now afford no shade to his posterity, he was heard to correct himself, by adding, " Yet be it so : I ought not therefore to bestow less attention upon them—they grow to God."

Agriculture, and the commerce connected with, and dependent upon it, form one of the most considerable branches of political economy; and as such, Mr. Burke diligently studied them. Indeed, when he began to qualify himself for the exalted rank which he afterwards held among statesmen, he laid a broad and deep foundation; and to an accurate research into the constitution, the laws, the civil and military history of these kingdoms, he joined an enlightened acquaintance with the whole circle of our commercial system. On his first introduction, when a young man, to the late Mr. Gerard Hamilton, who was then a Lord of Trade, the latter ingenuously confessed to a friend still living, how sensibly he felt his own inferiority, much as he had endeavoured to inform himself, and aided as he was by official documents, inaccessible to

4

any

any private person. He was also consulted, and the greatest deference was paid to his opinions by Dr. Adam Smith, in the progress of the celebrated work on the Wealth of Nations.

In parliament, Mr. Burke very soon distinguished himself on these topics. When the first great permanent law for regulating our foreign corn-trade was under the consideration of the House in 1772, he was one of its principal supporters, in a speech admired at the time for its excellence, and described as abounding with that knowledge in œconomics, which he was then universally allowed to possess, and illustrated with that philosophical discrimination, of which he was so peculiarly a master. About the same time, too, he zealously promoted the repeal of the statutes against *forestallers ;* a measure not lightly and hastily proposed or adopted in the liberal impulse of an unguarded moment, but the result of various investigations made by the House, or in different committees, during six years of scarcity and high prices; a measure which, although two Bills of a contrary tendency had formerly been introduced and lost, so approved itself, at length, to the reason of all, that it was ordered to be brought in, without a single dissentient voice. Yet, though such was his early pre-eminence in these pursuits, to the last hour of his life, as his fame spread wider and wider over Europe, he availed himself of the advantage which this afforded him, to enlarge the sphere of his enquiries into the state of other countries, that he might benefit his own. The consequence of all was, he every day became more firmly convinced, that the unrestrained freedom of buying and selling is the great animating principle of production and supply.

The present publication records Mr. Burke's most mature reflections on these interesting subjects ; the more valuable, because the sentiments which he delivered on the occasions already mentioned, have not been preserved

to

to us, either by himself or by others. He was alarmed
by the appearance of the crop in 1795, even before the
harvest. In the autumn of that year, when the produce
of the harvest began to be known, the alarm became
general. Various projects, as in such cases will always
happen, were offered to Government ; and, in his opinion,
seemed to be received with too much complaisance.
Under this impression, anxious as he ever was, even in
his retirement, and in the midst of his own private afflic-
tion, for the publick safety and prosperity, he immediately addressed to Mr. Pitt a memorial, which is the
ground work of the following tract. Afterwards, considering the importance of the matter, and fearing a long
cycle of scarcity to come, he intended to have dilated
the several branches of the argument, and to have
moulded his " Thoughts and Details" into a more popular shape. This he purposed to have done in a series of
letters on rural œconomics, inscribed to his friend
Mr. Arthur Young. It may be remembered, that he even
announced this design in an advertisement. But his
attention was irresistibly called another way. His whole
mind was engrossed by the change of policy which discovered itself in our councils at that period, when forgetting the manly arts, by which alone great nations have
ever extricated themselves from momentous and doubtful
conflicts, we descended, against the remonstrances of our
allies, to the voluntary and unnecessary humiliation of
soliciting a peace, which, in his judgment, the animosity
of our insolent enemy was not then disposed to grant,
and which, if offered, we could not then have accepted,
without the certainty of incurring dangers much more
formidable than any that threatened us from the protrac-
tion of the war. He hastened to raise and re-inspirit the
prostrate genius of his country. In a great measure he
succeeded, and was still employed in the pious office,
when Divine Providence took him to receive the reward

of

of those, who devote themselves to the cause of virtue and religion. After his decease, two or three detached fragments only of the first letter to Mr. Young were found among his papers. These could not be printed in that imperfect state, and they seemed too precious to be wholly thrown aside. They have been inserted, therefore, in the Memorial, where they seemed best to cohere.

The memorial had been fairly copied, but did not appear to have been examined or corrected, as some trifling errors of the transcriber were perceptible in it. The manuscript of the fragments was a rough draft from the author's own hand, much blotted and very confused. It has been followed with as much fidelity as was possible, after consulting those who were most accustomed to Mr. Burke's manner of writing. Two or three chasms in the grammar and sense, from the casual omission of two or three unimportant words at a distance, have been supplied by conjecture. The principal alteration has been the necessary change of the second for the third person, and the consequent suppression of the common form of affectionate address, where Mr. Young is named. That gentleman alone can have reason to complain of this liberty, inasmuch as it may seem to have deprived him of that, which in some sort was his property, and which no man would have known better how to value. But, it is hoped, he will pardon it, since in this manner alone these *golden fragments* (to borrow a favourite phrase of critics and commentators) could have been made, as they were designed to be, of general utility. To the reader no apology is due, if the disquisitions thus interwoven may seem a little disproportioned to the summary statements of the original Memorial. Their own intrinsic worth and beauty will be an ample compensation for that slight deformity; though perhaps in such a composition, as this professes to be (and the title is Mr. Burke's own) nothing of the kind could have been fairly regarded as an irregu-

lar

lar excrescence, had it been placed by himself, where it
now stands.

The Memorial, which was indeed communicated to
several members of the king's Government, was believed
at the time to have been not wholly unproductive of good.
The enquiry, which had been actually begun, into the
quantity of corn in hand, was silently dropped. The
scheme of public granaries, if it ever existed, was abandoned. In parliament the ministers maintained a prudent
and dignified forbearance; and repressed in others, or
where they could not entirely controul, interposed to
moderate and divert, that restless spirit of legislation,
which is an evil that seems to grow up, as the vehemence
of party-contention abates. The consistency and good
sense of the Commons defeated an attempt, which was
made towards the close of the sessions, to revive against
forestallers of one particular description, some portion of
the exploded laws.

Last year, on the approach of our present distresses,
the same excellent temper of mind seemed to prevail in
Government, in Parliament, and among the people. There
was no proposal of taking stock, no speculation of creat-
ing a new establishment of royal purveyors to provide us
with our daily dole of bread. The corn merchants were
early assured that they should not again have to contend
with the competition of the Treasury, in the foreign
market. A committee of the House of Commons ventured
to dissuade the stopping of the distilleries in a report,
very closely coinciding with the reasoning of Mr. Burke.
Little or no popular declamation was heard on the
miseries of "the labouring poor;" not a single petition
was presented, or motion made, against forestallers. The
least objectionable of the experiments suggested, to
encrease the supply or lessen the consumption, were
adopted. It is hardly worthy of mention, as an exception, that a parliamentary charter was granted to a

company

company of very worthy and well-meaning persons, who, on the notion of a combination (which, by the way, they totally failed in proving) among the trades that supply the capital with bread, opened a subscription for undertaking to furnish nearly one-tenth of the consumption. They were contented to do this with limited profits merely as humane badgers and jobbers, charitable millers, sentimental mealmen, and philanthropic bakers. But distrusting a little their own sufficiency for their new business, they naturally desired to be exempted from the operation of the bankrupt laws; and their bill was carried by a very small majority, consisting of partners in the firm. All this while, under trials much more severe than in the former dearth, the inferior classes displayed a patience and resignation, only to be equalled by the alacrity and zeal, which the higher and middle orders every where manifested, to relieve the necessities of their poorer neighbours in every practicable mode.

The present is a season of ferment and riot. The old cry against forestallers has been raised again with more violence than ever. It has been adjudged, for the first time, it is presumed, since the repealing act of 1772, that they are still liable to be punished by the common law, with fine and imprisonment at least, if not with whipping and the pillory, according to the notion which the judge may entertain of their crime. The interpreters of the law must expound it, according to their conscientious judgments, as it is, and the doctrine is not quite new; it has certainly been suggested in grave books since the repeal, yet men of sober minds have doubted, and will doubt, whether in the whole code of customs and usages, derived to us from our ancestors, there can be found any one part so radically inapplicable to the present state of the country, as their trade law; which, formed before commerce can be said to have existed, on mixed considerations, of police for the prevention of theft and rapine,

9   and

and of protection to the interest of the lord in the rights
of toll and stallage, permitted no transaction of bargain
and sale in any kind of commodity, but openly at a
market, or a fair, and more anciently still, with the
addition of witnesses also before the magistrate, or the
priest : which knew of no commercial principle, but that
of subjecting, in every instance, the grower, the maker,
or the importer, native and foreigner alike, to the consumer, and for that purpose prohibited every intermediate
profit, and every practice by act, by word, or by writing,
that could enhance the price ; by which, if the dragging
of the mouldering records into day be not a mere robbery
of the moths and worms, should a gentleman encourage
fishermen, brewers, and bakers to settle on his estate, it
may be pronounced a *forestallage* of the next town, and a
silk merchant, should he *ask* too much for his raw and
organzine (the unfortunate Lombard in the assize-book
only asked, he did not get it from the poor *silkewemen*)
may be punished by a heavy fine; which cannot now be
partially in force against one set of dealers, and abrogated
by disuse with regard to all others ; which, if generally
applied for a single term, without the interposition of
that wisdom of parliament, over which this resort to the
common law is by some regarded as a triumph, would
more effectually clog, distress, and ruin our foreign and
domestic commerce in all its branches, than a confederacy
of the whole world against us in many years. Be the
late convictions, however, what they may, in legal merits;
their practical effects have been much to be deplored.
Gross minds distorted them into authorities to prove, that
there was plenty in the land, and that the arts of greedy
and unfeeling men alone intercepted the bounty of Providence. Meetings were called ; non-consumption agreements were signed, and associations were formed, chiefly
in cities and great towns, to prosecute those, without
whom cities and great towns can never be regularly fed.

10 There

There is no weak, no wild, no violent project, which did not find countenance in some quarter or other. The fall of the market immediately after the harvest, and the subsequent rise, though the natural effects of obvious causes, encreased the public agitation; and the multitude began to pursue their usual course of providing in the shortest way for their instant wants, or of terrifying, or punishing those, whom they had been taught to consider as their oppressors; unconscious or unconcerned that they were thus only preparing for themselves a tenfold aggravation of their own future sufferings. The eyes of all were now turned towards parliament, not for a train of judicious measures, which, if it be possible, may hereafter again equalize the production with the consumption of the country, but for an immediate supply; as if the omnipotence of parliament could restore a single grain that has been injured by the most contemptible insect.

At such a juncture, however unfavourable it may be to the popularity of this little tract, the publication of it was felt to be a duty. He who wrote it, ever set that consideration before him as the first motive of all his actions. While he lived, he never ceased, publickly and privately, to warn his country and her rulers, against every danger which his wisdom foresaw. He now gives to her and them, this solemn warning from his grave.

THOUGHTS AND DETAILS

ON

SCARCITY.

O F all things, an indiscreet tampering with the trade of provisions is the most dangerous, and it is always worst in the time when men are most disposed to it :—that is, in the time of scarcity. Because there is nothing on which the passions of men are so violent, and their judgment so weak, and on which there exists such a multitude of ill-founded popular prejudices.

The great use of government is as a restraint; and there is no restraint which it ought to put upon others, and upon itself too, rather than on the fury of speculating under circumstances of irritation. The number of idle tales spread about by the industry of faction, and by the zeal of foolish good-intention, and greedily devoured by the malignant credulity of mankind, tends infinitely to aggravate prejudices, which, in themselves, are more than sufficiently strong. In that state of affairs, and of the publick with relation to them, the first thing that Government owes to us, the people, is *information* ; the next is timely coercion :—the one to guide our judgment; the other to regulate our tempers.

To provide for us in our necessities is not in the power of Government. It would be a vain presumption in statesmen to think they could do it. The people maintain them, and not they the people. It is in the power of

Government

Government to prevent much evil; it can do very little positive good in this, or perhaps in any thing else. It is not only so of the state and statesmen, but of all the classes and descriptions of the rich—they are the pensioners of the poor, and are maintained by their superfluity. They are under an absolute, hereditary, and indefeasible dependance on those who labour, and are miscalled the poor.

The labouring people are only poor, because they are numerous. Numbers in their nature imply poverty. In a fair distribution among a vast multitude, none can have much. That class of dependant pensioners called the rich, is so extremely small, that if all their throats were cut, and a distribution made of all they consume in a year, it would not give a bit of bread and cheese for one night's supper to those who labour, and who in reality feed both the pensioners and themselves.

But the throats of the rich ought not to be cut, nor their magazines plundered; because, in their persons they are trustees for those who labour, and their hoards are the banking-houses of these latter. Whether they mean it or not, they do, in effect, execute their trust—some with more, some with less fidelity and judgment. But on the whole, the duty is performed, and every thing returns, deducting some very trifling commission and discount, to the place from whence it arose. When the poor rise to destroy the rich, they act as wisely for their own purposes as when they burn mills, and throw corn into the river, to make bread cheap.

When I say, that we of the people ought to be informed, inclusively I say, we ought not to be flattered : flattery is the reverse of instruction. The *poor* in that case would be rendered as improvident as the rich, which would not be at all good for them.

Nothing can be so base and so wicked as the political canting language, " The labouring *poor*." Let compas-

sion

sion be shewn in action, the more the better, according to every man's ability, but let there be no lamentation of their condition. It is no relief to their miserable circumstances; it is only an insult to their miserable understandings. It arises from a total want of charity, or a total want of thought. Want of one kind was never relieved by want of any other kind. Patience, labour, sobriety, frugality, and religion, should be recommended to them; all the rest is downright *fraud*. It is horrible to call them "The *once happy* labourer."

Whether what may be called moral or philosophical happiness of the laborious classes is increased or not, I cannot say. The seat of that species of happiness is in the mind; and there are few data to ascertain the comparative state of the mind at any two periods. Philosophical happiness is to want little. Civil or vulgar happiness is to want much, and to enjoy much.

If the happiness of the animal man (which certainly goes somewhere towards the happiness of the rational man) be the object of our estimate, then I assert, without the least hesitation, that the condition of those who labour (in all descriptions of labour, and in all gradations of labour, from the highest to the lowest inclusively) is on the whole extremely meliorated, if more and better food is any standard of melioration. They work more, it is certain; but they have the advantage of their augmented labour; yet whether that increase of labour be on the whole a *good* or an *evil*, is a consideration that would lead us a great way, and is not for my present purpose. But as to the fact of the melioration of their diet, I shall enter into the detail of proof whenever I am called upon: in the mean time, the known difficulty of contenting them with any thing but bread made of the finest flour, and meat of the first quality, is proof sufficient.

I further assert, that even under all the hardships of the last year, the labouring people did, either out of their

direct

direct gains, or from charity, (which it seems is now an insult to them) in fact, fare better than they did, in seasons of common plenty, 50 or 60 years ago; or even at the period of my English observation, which is about 44 years. I even assert, that full as many in that class, as ever were known to do it before, continued to save money; and this I can prove, so far as my own information and experience extend.

It is not true that the rate of wages has not encreased with the nominal price of provisions. I allow it has not fluctuated with that price, nor ought it; and the squires of Norfolk had dined, when they gave it as their opinion, that it might or ought to rise and fall with the market-price of provisions. The rate of wages in truth has no *direct* relation to that price. Labour is a commodity like every other, and rises or falls according to the demand. This is in the nature of things; however, the nature of things has provided for their necessities. Wages have been twice raised in my time, and they bear a full proportion, or even a greater than formerly, to the medium of provision during the last bad cycle of twenty years. They bear a full proportion to the result of their labour. If we were wildly to attempt to force them beyond it, the stone which we had forced up the hill would only fall back upon them in a diminished demand, or, what indeed is the far lesser evil, an aggravated price of all the provisions, which are the result of their manual toil.

There is an implied contract, much stronger than any instrument or article of agreement, between the labourer in any occupation and his employer—that the labour, so far as that labour is concerned, shall be sufficient to pay to the employer a profit on his capital, and a compensation for his risk; in a word, that the labour shall produce an advantage equal to the payment. Whatever is above that, is a direct *tax;* and if the amount of that tax be left to the will and pleasure of another, it is an *arbitrary tax.*

If

If I understand it rightly, the tax proposed on the farming interest of this kingdom, is to be levied at what is called the discretion of justices of peace.

The questions arising on this scheme of arbitrary taxation are these—Whether it is better to leave all dealing, in which there is no force or fraud, collusion or combination, entirely to the persons mutually concerned in the matter contracted for; or to put the contract into the hands of those, who can have none, or a very remote interest in it, and little or no knowledge of the subject.

It might be imagined that there would be very little difficulty in solving this question; for what man, of any degree of reflection, can think, that a want of interest in any subject closely connected with a want of skill in it, qualifies a person to intermeddle in any the least affair; much less in affairs that vitally concern the agriculture of the kingdom, the first of all its concerns, and the foundation of all its prosperity in every other matter, by which that prosperity is produced?

The vulgar error on this subject arises from a total confusion in the very idea of things widely different in themselves;—those of convention, and those of judicature. When a contract is making, it is a matter of discretion and of interest between the parties. In that intercourse, and in what is to arise from it, the parties are the masters. If they are not completely so, they are not free, and therefore their contracts are void.

But this freedom has no farther extent, when the contract is made; then their discretionary powers expire, and a new order of things takes its origin. Then, and not till then, and on a difference between the parties, the office of the judge commences. He cannot dictate the contract. It is his business to see that it be *enforced*; provided that it is not contrary to pre-existing laws, or obtained by force or fraud. If he is in any way a maker or regulator of the contract, in so much he is disqualified

17 from

from being a judge. But this sort of confused distribution of administrative and judicial characters, (of which we have already as much as is sufficient, and a little more) is not the only perplexity of notions and passions which trouble us in the present hour.

What is doing, supposes or pretends that the farmer and the labourer have opposite interests;—that the farmer oppresses the labourer; and that a gentleman called a justice of peace, is the protector of the latter, and a controul and restraint on the former; and this is a point I wish to examine in a manner a good deal different from that in which gentlemen proceed, who confide more in their abilities than is fit, and suppose them capable of more than any natural abilities, fed with no other than the provender furnished by their own private speculations, can accomplish. Legislative acts, attempting to regulate this part of œconomy, do, at least, as much as any other, require the exactest detail of circumstances, guided by the surest general principles that are necessary to direct experiment and enquiry, in order again from those details to elicit principles, firm and luminous general principles, to direct a practical legislative proceeding.

First, then, I deny that it is in this case, as in any other of necessary implication, that contracting parties should originally have had different interests. By accident it may be so undoubtedly at the outset; but then the contract is of the nature of a compromise; and compromise is founded on circumstances that suppose it the interest of the parties to be reconciled in some medium. The principle of compromise adopted, of consequence the interests cease to be different.

But in the case of the farmer and the labourer; their interests are always the same, and it is absolutely impossible that their free contracts can be onerous to either party. It is the interest of the farmer, that his work should be done with effect and celerity; and that cannot

18   be,

be, unless the labourer is well fed, and otherwise found with such necessaries of animal life, according to its habitudes, as may keep the body in full force, and the mind gay and cheerful. For of all the instruments of his trade, the labour of man (what the ancient writers have called the *instrumentum vocale*) is that on which he is most to rely for the re-payment of his capital. The other two, the *semivocale* in the ancient classification, that is, the working stock of cattle, and the *instrumentum mutum*, such as carts, ploughs, spades, and so forth, though not all inconsiderable in themselves, are very much inferior in utility or in expence; and without a given portion of the first, are nothing at all. For in all things whatever, the mind is the most valuable and the most important; and in this scale the whole of agriculture is in a natural and just order; the beast is as an informing principle to the plough and cart; the labourer is as reason to the beast; and the farmer is as a thinking and presiding principle to the labourer. An attempt to break this chain of subordination in any part is equally absurd; but the absurdity is the most mischievous in practical operation, where it is the most easy, that is, where it is the most subject to an erroneous judgment.

It is plainly more the farmer's interest that his men should thrive, than that his horses should be well fed, sleek, plump, and fit for use, or than that his waggon and ploughs should be strong, in good repair, and fit for service.

On the other hand, if the farmer ceases to profit of the labourer, and that his capital is not continually manured and fructified, it is impossible that he should continue that abundant nutriment, and cloathing, and lodging, proper for the protection of the instruments he employs.

It is therefore the first and fundamental interest of the labourer, that the farmer should have a full incoming profit on the product of his labour. The proposition is

self-evident,

self-evident, and nothing but the malignity, perverseness, and ill-governed passions of mankind, and particularly the envy they bear to each other's prosperity, could prevent their seeing and acknowledging it, with thankfulness to the benign and wise disposer of all things, who obliges men, whether they will or not, in pursuing their own selfish interests, to connect the general good with their own individual success.

But who are to judge what that profit and advantage ought to be? certainly no authority on earth. It is a matter of convention dictated by the reciprocal conveniences of the parties, and indeed by their reciprocal necessities.—But, if the farmer is excessively avaricious? —why so much the better—the more he desires to increase his gains, the more interested is he in the good condition of those, upon whose labour his gains must principally depend.

I shall be told by the zealots of the sect of regulation, that this may be true, and may be safely committed to the convention of the farmer and the labourer, when the latter is in the prime of his youth, and at the time of his health and vigour, and in ordinary times of abundance. But in calamitous seasons, under accidental illness, in declining life, and with the pressure of a numerous offspring, the future nourishers of the community but the present drains and blood-suckers of those who produce them, what is to be done? When a man cannot live and maintain his family by the natural hire of his labour, ought it not to be raised by authority?

On this head I must be allowed to submit, what my opinions have ever been; and somewhat at large.

And, first, I premise that labour is, as I have already intimated, a commodity, and as such, an article of trade. If I am right in this notion, then labour must be subject to all the laws and principles of trade, and not to regulations foreign to them, and that may be totally inconsistent

20   with

with those principles and those laws. When any commodity is carried to market, it is not the necessity of the vender, but the necessity of the purchaser that raises the price. The extreme want of the seller has rather (by the nature of things with which we shall in vain contend) the direct contrary operation. If the goods at market are beyond the demand, they fall in their value; if below it, they rise. The impossibility of the subsistence of a man, who carries his labour to a market, is totally beside the question in this way of viewing it. The only question is, what is it worth to the buyer?

But if authority comes in and forces the buyer to a price, what is this in the case (say) of a farmer, who buys the labour of ten or twelve labouring men, and three or four handycrafts, what is it, but to make an arbitrary division of his property among them?

The whole of his gains, I say it with the most certain conviction, never do amount any thing like in value to what he pays to his labourers and artificers; so that a very small advance upon what *one* man pays to *many*, may absorb the whole of what he possesses, and amount to an actual partition of all his substance among them. A perfect equality will indeed be produced;—that is to say, equal want, equal wretchedness, equal beggary, and on the part of the partitioners, a woeful, helpless, and desperate disappointment. Such is the event of all compulsory equalizations. They pull down what is above. They never raise what is below: and they depress high and low together beneath the level of what was originally the lowest.

If a commodity is raised by authority above what it will yield with a profit to the buyer, that commodity will be the less dealt in. If a second blundering interposition be used to correct the blunder of the first, and an attempt is made to force the purchase of the commodity (of labour for instance), the one of these two things must happen,

21   either

either that the forced buyer is ruined, or the price of the product of the labour, in that proportion, is raised. Then the wheel turns round, and the evil complained of falls with aggravated weight on the complainant. The price of corn, which is the result of the expence of all the operations of husbandry, taken together, and for some time continued, will rise on the labourer, considered as a consumer. The very best will be, that he remains where he was. But if the price of the corn should not compensate the price of labour, what is far more to be feared, the most serious evil, the very destruction of agriculture itself, is to be apprehended.

Nothing is such an enemy to accuracy of judgment as a coarse discrimination; a want of such classification and distribution as the subject admits of. Encrease the rate of wages to the labourer, say the regulators—as if labour was but one thing and of one value. But this very broad generic term, *labour,* admits, at least, of two or three specific descriptions: and these will suffice, at least, to let gentlemen discern a little the necessity of proceeding with caution in their coercive guidance of those whose existence depends upon the observance of still nicer distinctions and sub-divisions, than commonly they resort to in forming their judgments on this very enlarged part of economy.

The labourers in husbandry may be divided : 1st, into those who are able to perform the full work of a man; that is, what can be done by a person from twenty-one years of age to fifty. I know no husbandry work (mowing hardly excepted) that is not equally within the power of all persons within those ages, the more advanced fully compensating by knack and habit what they lose in activity. Unquestionably, there is a good deal of difference between the value of one man's labour and that of another, from strength, dexterity, and honest application. But I am quite sure, from my best observation,

that

that any given five men will, in their total, afford a proportion of labour equal to any other five within the periods of life I have stated ; that is, that among such five men there will be one possessing all the qualifications of a good workman, one bad, and the other three middling, and approximating to the first and the last. So that in so small a platoon as that of even five, you will find the full complement of all that five men *can* earn. Taking five and five throughout the kingdom, they are equal : therefore, an error with regard to the equalization of their wages by those who employ five, as farmers do at the very least, cannot be considerable.

2dly. Those who are able to work, but not the complete task of a day-labourer. This class is infinitely diversified, but will aptly enough fall into principal divisions. *Men*, from the decline, which after fifty becomes every year more sensible, to the period of debility and decrepitude, and the maladies that precede a final dissolution. *Women*, whose employment on husbandry is but occasional, and who differ more in effective labour one from another than men do, on account of gestation, nursing, and domestic management, over and above the difference they have in common with men in advancing, in stationary, and in declining life. *Children*, who proceed on the reverse order, growing from less to greater utility, but with a still greater disproportion of nutriment to labour than is found in the second of these sub-divisions ; as is visible to those who will give themselves the trouble of examining into the interior economy of a poor-house.

This inferior classification is introduced to shew, that laws prescribing, or magistrates exercising, a very stiff, and often inapplicable rule, or a blind and rash discretion, never can provide the just proportions between earning and salary on the one hand, and nutriment on the other : whereas interest, habit, and the tacit convention, that

23 arise

arise from a thousand nameless circumstances, produce a *tact* that regulates without difficulty, what laws and magistrates cannot regulate at all. The first class of labour wants nothing to equalize it: it equalizes itself. The second and third are not capable of any equalization.

But what if the rate of hire to the labourer comes far short of his necessary subsistence, and the calamity of the time is so great as to threaten actual famine? Is the poor labourer to be abandoned to the flinty heart and griping hand of base self-interest, supported by the sword of law, especially when there is reason to suppose that the very avarice of farmers themselves has concurred with the errors of Government to bring famine on the land.

In that case, my opinion is this. Whenever it happens that a man can claim nothing according to the rules of commerce, and the principles of justice, he passes out of that department, and comes within the jurisdiction of mercy. In that province the magistrate has nothing at all to do: his interference is a violation of the property which it is his office to protect. Without all doubt, charity to the poor is a direct and obligatory duty upon all Christians, next in order after the payment of debts, full as strong, and by nature made infinitely more delightful to us. Puffendorf, and other casuists do not, I think, denominate it quite properly, when they call it a duty of imperfect obligation. But the manner, mode, time, choice of objects, and proportion, are left to private discretion; and perhaps, for that very reason it is performed with the greater satisfaction, because the discharge of it has more the appearance of freedom; recommending us besides very specially to the divine favour, as the exercise of a virtue most suitable to a being sensible of its own infirmity.

The cry of the people in cities and towns, though unfortunately (from a fear of their multitude and combination) the most regarded, ought, in *fact*, to be the *least*

attended

attended to upon this subject; for citizens are in a state of utter ignorance of the means by which they are to be fed, and they contribute little or nothing, except in an infinitely circuitous manner, to their own maintenance. They are truly " *Fruges consumere nati.*" They are to be heard with great respect and attention upon matters within their province, that is, on trades and manufactures; but on any thing that relates to agriculture, they are to be listened to with the same *reverence* which we pay to the dogmas of other ignorant and presumptuous men.

If any one were to tell them, that they were to give in an account of all the stock in their shops; that attempts would be made to limit their profits, or raise the price of the labouring manufacturers upon them, or recommend to Government, out of a capital from the publick revenues, to set up a shop of the same commodities, in order to rival them, and keep them to reasonable dealing, they would soon see the impudence, injustice, and oppression of such a course. They would not be mistaken; but they are of opinion, that agriculture is to be subject to other laws, and to be governed by other principles.

A greater and more ruinous mistake cannot be fallen into, than that the trades of agriculture and grazing can be conducted upon any other than the common principles of commerce; namely, that the producer should be permitted, and even expected, to look to all possible profit which, without fraud or violence, he can make; to turn plenty or scarcity to the best advantage he can; to keep back or to bring forward his commodities at his pleasure; to account to no one for his stock or for his gain. On any other terms he is the slave of the consumer; and that he should be so is of no benefit to the consumer. No slave was ever so beneficial to the master as a freeman that deals with him on an equal footing by convention, formed on the rules and principles of contending interests and compromised advantages. The consumer, if he were suffered, would in the end always be the dupe of his own tyranny and injustice. The landed gentleman is never to forget, that the farmer is his representative.

It is a perilous thing to try experiments on the farmer. The farmer's capital (except in a few persons, and in a very few places) is far more feeble than commonly is imagined. The trade is a very poor trade; it is subject to great risks and losses. The capital, such as it is, is turned but once in the year; in some branches it requires three years before the money is paid. I believe never less than three in the turnip and grass-land course, which is the prevalent course on the more or less fertile, sandy and gravelly loams, and these compose the soil in the south and south-east of England, the best adapted, and perhaps the only ones that are adapted, to the turnip husbandry.

It is very rare that the most prosperous farmer, counting the value of his quick and dead stock, the interest of the money he turns, together with his own wages as a bailiff or overseer, ever does make twelve or fifteen *per centum* by the year on his capital. I speak of the prosperous. In most of the parts of England which have fallen within my observation, I have rarely known a farmer, who to his own trade has not added some other employment or traffic, that, after a course of the most unremitting parsimony and labour (such for the greater part is theirs), and persevering in his business for a long course of years, died worth more than paid his debts, leaving his posterity to continue in nearly the same equal conflict between industry and want, in which the last predecessor, and a long line of predecessors before him, lived and died.

Observe that I speak of the generality of farmers who have not more than from one hundred and fifty to three or four hundred acres. There are few in this part of the

country

country within the former, or much beyond the latter, extent. Unquestionably in other places there are much larger. But, I am convinced, whatever part of England be the theatre of his operations, a farmer who cultivates twelve hundred acres, which I consider as a large farm, though I know there are larger, cannot proceed, with any degree of safety and effect, with a smaller capital than ten thousand pounds ; and that he cannot, in the ordinary course of culture, make more upon that great capital of ten thousand pounds, than twelve hundred a year.

As to the weaker capitals, an easy judgment may be formed by what very small errors they may be farther attenuated, enervated, rendered unproductive, and perhaps totally destroyed.

This constant precariousness and ultimate moderate limits of a farmer's fortune, on the strongest capital, I press, not only on account of the hazardous speculations of the times, but because the excellent and most useful works of my friend, Mr. Arthur Young, tend to propagate that error (such I am very certain it is), of the largeness of a farmer's profits. It is not that his account of the produce does often greatly exceed, but he by no means makes the proper allowance for accidents and losses. I might enter into a convincing detail, if other more troublesome and more necessary details were not before me.

This proposed discretionary tax on labour militates with the recommendations of the Board of Agriculture : they recommend a general use of the drill culture. I agree with the Board, that where the soil is not excessively heavy, or incumbered with large loose stones (which however is the case with much otherwise good land), that course is the best, and most productive, provided that the most accurate eye; the most vigilant superintendence; the most prompt activity, which has no such day as to-morrow in its calendar; the most steady foresight and pre-disposing order to have every body and every thing

27   ready

ready in its place, and prepared to take advantage of the fortunate fugitive moment in this coquetting climate of ours—provided, I say, all these combine to speed the plough, I admit its superiority over the old and general methods. But under procrastinating, improvident, ordinary husbandmen, who may neglect or let slip the few opportunities of sweetening and purifying their ground with perpetually renovated toil, and undissipated attention, nothing, when tried to any extent, can be worse, or more dangerous: the farm may be ruined, instead of having the soil enriched and sweetened by it.

But the excellence of the method on a proper soil, and conducted by an husbandman, of whom there are few, being readily granted, how, and on what conditions, is this culture obtained? Why, by a very great encrease of labour; by an augmentation of the third part, at least, of the hand-labour, to say nothing of the horses and machinery employed in ordinary tillage. Now, every man must be sensible how little becoming the gravity of legislature it is to encourage a board, which recommends to us, and upon very weighty reasons unquestionably, an enlargement of the capital we employ in the operations of the land, and then to pass an act which taxes that manual labour, already at a very high rate; thus compelling us to diminish the quantity of labour which in the vulgar course we actually employ.

What is true of the farmer is equally true of the middle man; whether the middle man acts as factor, jobber, salesman, or speculator, in the markets of grain. These traders are to be left to their free course; and the more they make, and the richer they are, and the more largely they deal, the better both for the farmer and consumer, between whom they form a natural and most useful link of connection: though, by the machinations of the old evil counsellor, *Envy*, they are hated and maligned by both parties.

I hear

1 hear that middle men are accused of monopoly. Without question, the monopoly of authority is, in every instance and in every degree, an evil; but the monopoly of capital is the contrary. It is a great benefit, and a benefit particularly to the poor. A tradesman who has but a hundred pound capital, which (say) he can turn but once a year, cannot live upon a *profit* of 10 *per cent.* because he cannot live upon ten pounds a year; but a man of ten thousand pounds capital can live and thrive upon 5 *per cent.* profit in the year, because he has five hundred pounds a year. The same proportion holds in turning it twice or thrice. These principles are plain and simple; and it is not our ignorance, so much as the levity, the envy, and the malignity of our nature, that hinders us from perceiving and yielding to them; but we are not to suffer our vices to usurp the place of our judgment.

The balance between consumption and production makes price. The market settles, and alone can settle, that price. Market is the meeting and conference of the *consumer* and *producer*, when they mutually discover each other's wants. Nobody, I believe, has observed with any reflection what market is, without being astonished at the truth, the correctness, the celerity, the general equity, with which the balance of wants is settled. They who wish the destruction of that balance, and would fain by arbitrary regulation decree, that defective production should not be compensated by encreased price, directly lay their *axe* to the root of production itself.

They may even in one year of such false policy, do mischiefs incalculable; because the trade of a farmer is, as I have before explained, one of the most precarious in its advantages, the most liable to losses, and the least profitable of any that is carried on. It requires ten times more of labour, of vigilance, of attention, of skill, and let me add, of good fortune also, to carry on the business of a farmer with success, than what belongs to any other trade. Seeing things in this light, I am far from presuming to censure the late circular instruction of Council to lord lieutenants—but I confess I do not clearly discern its object. I am greatly afraid that the enquiry will raise some alarm as a measure, leading to the French system of putting corn into requisition. For that was preceded by an inquisition somewhat similar in its principle, though, according to their mode, their principles are full of that violence, *which here* is not much to be feared. It goes on a principle directly opposite to mine : it presumes, that the market is no fair *test* of plenty or scarcity. It raises a suspicion, which may affect the tranquillity of the public mind, " that the farmer keeps back, and takes unfair advantages by delay ;" on the part of the dealer, it gives rise obviously to a thousand nefarious speculations.

In case the return should on the whole prove favourable, is it meant to ground a measure for encouraging exportation and checking the import of corn? If it is not, what end can it answer ? And, I believe, it is not.

This opinion may be fortified by a report gone abroad, that intentions are entertained of erecting public granaries, and that this enquiry is to give Government an advantage in its purchases.

I hear that such a measure has been proposed, and is under deliberation, that is, for Government to set up a granary in every market town, at the expence of the state, in order to extinguish the dealer, and to subject the farmer to the consumer, by securing corn to the latter at a certain and steady price.

If such a scheme is adopted, I should not like to answer for the safety of the granary, of the agents, or of the town itself, in which the granary was erected—the first storm of popular phrenzy would fall upon that granary.

So far in a political light.

In an economical light, I must observe, that the con-

struction

struction of such granaries throughout the kingdom, would be at an expence beyond all calculation. The keeping them up would be at a great charge. The management and attendance would require an army of agents, store-keepers, clerks, and servants. The capital to be employed in the purchase of grain would be enormous. The waste, decay, and corruption, would be a dreadful drawback on the whole dealing; and the dissatisfaction of the people, at having decayed, tainted, or corrupted corn sold to them, as must be the case, would be serious.

This climate (whatever others may be) is not favourable to granaries, where wheat is to be kept for any time. The best, and indeed the only good granary, is the rickyard of the farmer, where the corn is preserved in its own straw, sweet, clean, wholesome, free from vermin, and from insects, and comparatively at a trifle of expence. This, with the barn, enjoying many of the same advantages, have been the sole granaries of England from the foundation of its agriculture to this day. All this is done at the expence of the undertaker, and at his sole risk. He contributes to Government; he receives nothing from it but protection; and to this he has a *claim*.

The moment that Government appears at market, all the principles of market will be subverted. I don't know whether the farmer will suffer by it, as long as there is a tolerable market of competition; but I am sure that, in the first place, the trading Government will speedily become a bankrupt, and the consumer in the end will suffer. If Government makes all its purchases at once, it will instantly raise the market upon itself. If it makes them by degrees, it must follow the course of the market. If it follows the course of the market, it will produce no effect, and the consumer may as well buy as he wants—therefore all the expence is incurred gratis.

But if the object of this scheme should be, what I

31 suspect

suspect it is, to destroy the dealer, commonly called the middle man, and by incurring a voluntary loss to carry the baker to deal with Government, I am to tell them that they must set up another trade, that of a miller or a mealman, attended with a new train of expences and risks. If in both these trades they should succeed, so as to exclude those who trade on natural and private capitals, then they will have a monopoly in their hands, which, under the appearance of a monopoly of capital, will, in reality, be a monopoly of authority, and will ruin whatever it touches. The agriculture of the kingdom cannot stand before it.

A little place like Geneva, of not more than from twenty-five to thirty thousand inhabitants, which has no territory, or next to none; which depends for its existence on the good-will of three neighbouring powers, and is of course continually in the state of something like a *siege*, or in the speculation of it, might find some resource in state granaries, and some revenue from the monopoly of what was sold to the keepers of public-houses. This is a policy for a state too small for agriculture. It is not (for instance) fit for so great a country as the Pope possesses, where, however, it is adopted and pursued in a greater extent, and with more strictness. Certain of the Pope's territories, from whence the city of Rome is supplied, being obliged to furnish Rome and the granaries of his holiness with corn at a certain price, that part of the papal territories is utterly ruined. That ruin may be traced with certainty to this sole cause, and it appears indubitably by a comparison of their state and condition with that of the other part of the ecclesiastical dominions not subjected to the same regulations, which are in circumstances highly flourishing.

The reformation of this evil system is in a manner impracticable; for, first, it does keep bread and all other provisions equally subject to the chamber of supply, at a

pretty

pretty reasonable and regular price, in the city of Rome. This preserves quiet among the numerous poor, idle, and naturally mutinous people, of a very great capital. But the quiet of the town is purchased by the ruin of the country, and the ultimate wretchedness of both. The next cause which renders this evil incurable, is, the jobs which have grown out of it, and which, in spite of all precautions, would grow out of such things, even under Governments far more potent than the feeble authority of the Pope.

This example of Rome which has been derived from the most ancient times, and the most flourishing period of the Roman empire (but not of the Roman agriculture) may serve as a great caution to all Governments, not to attempt to feed the people out of the hands of the magistrates. If once they are habituated to it, though but for one half-year, they will never be satisfied to have it otherwise. And, having looked to Government for bread, on the very first scarcity they will turn and bite the hand that fed them. To avoid that *evil*, Government will redouble the causes of it; and then it will become inveterate and incurable.

I beseech the Government (which I take in the largest sense of the word, comprehending the two Houses of Parliament) seriously to consider that years of scarcity or plenty, do not come alternately or at short intervals, but in pretty long cycles and irregularly, and consequently that we cannot assure ourselves, if we take a wrong measure, from the temporary necessities of one season; but that the next, and probably more, will drive us to the continuance of it; so that in my opinion, there is no way of preventing this evil which goes to the destruction of all our agriculture, and of that part of our internal commerce which touches our agriculture the most nearly, as well as the safety and very being of Government, but

manfully

manfully to resist the very first idea, speculative or practical, that it is within the competence of Government,
taken as Government, or even of the rich, as rich, to
supply to the poor, those necessaries which it has pleased
the Divine Providence for a while to withhold from them.
We, the people, ought to be made sensible, that it is not
in breaking the laws of commerce, which are the laws of
nature, and consequently the laws of God, that we are to
place our hope of softening the divine displeasure to
remove any calamity under which we suffer, or which
hangs over us.

So far as to the principles of general policy.

As to the state of things which is urged as a reason to
deviate from them, these are the circumstances of the
harvest of 1795 and 1794. With regard to the harvest
of 1794, in relation to the noblest grain, wheat, it is
allowed to have been somewhat short, but not excessively;
and in quality, for the seven and twenty years, during
which I have been a farmer, I never remember wheat to
have been so good. The world were, however, deceived
in their speculations upon it—the farmer as well as the
dealer. Accordingly the price fluctuated beyond any
thing I can remember; for, at one time of the year, I
sold my wheat at 14*l.* a load, (I sold off all I had, as I
thought this was a reasonable price), when at the end of
the season, if I had then had any to sell, I might have
got thirty guineas for the same sort of grain. I sold all
that I had, as I said, at a comparatively low price, because
I thought it a good price, compared with what I thought
the general produce of the harvest; but when I came to
consider what my own *total* was, I found that the quantity
had not answered my expectation. It must be remembered, that this year of produce, (the year 1794) short,
but excellent, followed a year which was not extraordinary
in production, nor of a superior quality, and left but little

in

in store. At first this was not felt, because the harvest came in unusually early—earlier than common, by a full month.

The winter, at the end of 1794, and beginning of 1795, was more than usually unfavourable both to corn and grass, owing to the sudden relaxation of very rigorous frosts, followed by rains, which were again rapidly succeeded by frosts of still greater rigour than the first.

Much wheat was utterly destroyed. The clover grass suffered in many places. What I never observed before, the rye-grass, or coarse bent, suffered more than the clover. Even the meadow-grass in some places was killed to the very roots. In the spring, appearances were better than we expected. All the early sown grain recovered itself, and came up with great vigour; but that, which was late sown, was feeble, and did not promise to resist any blights, in the spring, which, however, with all its unpleasant vicissitudes passed off very well; and nothing looked better than the wheat at the time of blooming :— but at that most critical time of all, a cold dry east wind, attended with very sharp frosts, longer and stronger than I recollect at that time of year, destroyed the flowers, and withered up, in an astonishing manner, the whole side of the ear next to the wind. At that time I brought to town some of the ears, for the purpose of shewing to my friends the operation of those unnatural frosts, and according to their extent I predicted a great scarcity. But such is the pleasure of agreeable prospects, that my opinion was little regarded.

On threshing, I found things as I expected—the ears not filled, some of the capsules quite empty, and several others containing only withered hungry grain, inferior to the appearance of rye. My best ears and grains were not fine : never had I grain of so low a quality—yet I sold one load for 21*l.* At the same time I bought my seed wheat (it was excellent) at 23*l.* Since then the price has risen,

and

and I have sold about two load of the same sort at 23*l*. Such was the state of the market when I left home last Monday. Little remains in my barn. I hope some in the rick may be better: since it was earlier sown, as well as I can recollect. Some of my neighbours have better, some quite as bad, or even worse. I suspect it will be found, that wherever the blighting wind and those frosts at blooming time have prevailed, the produce of the wheat crop will turn out very indifferent. Those parts which have escaped, will, I can hardly doubt, have a reasonable produce.

As to the other grains, it is to be observed, as the wheat ripened very late, (on account, I conceive, of the blights) the barley got the start of it, and was ripe first. The crop was with me, and wherever my enquiry could reach, excellent; in some places far superior to mine.

The clover, which came up with the barley, was the finest I remember to have seen.

The turnips of this year are generally good.

The clover sown last year, where not totally destroyed, gave two good crops, or one crop and a plentiful seed; and, bating the loss of the rye-grass, I do not remember a better produce.

The meadow-grass yielded but a middling crop, and neither of the sown or natural grass was there in any farmer's possession any remainder from the year worth taking into account. In most places, there was none at all.

Oats with me were not in a quantity more considerable than in commonly good seasons; but I have never known them heavier, than they were in other places. The oat was not only an heavy, but an uncommonly abundant crop. My ground under pease did not exceed an acre, or thereabouts, but the crop was great indeed. I believe it is throughout the country exuberant.

It is however to be remarked, that as generally of all

the

the grains, so particularly of the pease, there was not the smallest quantity in reserve.

The demand of the year must depend solely on its own produce; and the price of the spring-corn is not to be expected to fall very soon, or at any time very low.

Uxbridge is a great corn market. As I came through that town, I found that at the last market-day, barley was at forty shillings a quarter; oats there were literally none; and the innkeeper was obliged to send for them to London. I forgot to ask about pease. Potatoes were 5s. the bushel.

In the debate on this subject in the House, I am told that a leading member of great ability, *little conversant in these matters,* observed, that the general uniform dearness of butcher's meat, butter, and cheese, could not be owing to a defective produce of wheat; and on this ground insinuated a suspicion of some unfair practice on the subject, that called for enquiry.

Unquestionably the mere deficiency of wheat could not cause the dearness of the other articles, which extends not only to the provisions he mentioned, but to every other without exception.

The cause is indeed so very plain and obvious, that the wonder is the other way. When a properly directed enquiry is made, the gentlemen who are amazed at the price of these commodities will find, that when hay is at six pound a load, as they must know it is, herbage, and for more than one year, must be scanty, and they will conclude, that if grass be scarce, beef, veal, mutton, butter, milk, and cheese, *must* be dear.

But to take up the matter somewhat more in detail— if the wheat harvest in 1794, excellent in quality, was defective in quantity, the barley harvest was in quality ordinary enough : and in quantity deficient. This was soon felt in the price of malt.

Another article of produce (beans) was not at all

37   plentiful.

plentiful. The crop of pease was wholly destroyed, so that several farmers pretty early gave up all hopes on that head, and cut the green haulm as fodder for the cattle, then perishing for want of food in that dry and burning summer. I myself came off better than most—I had about the fourth of a crop of pease.

It will be recollected, that, in a manner, all the bacon and pork consumed in this country, (the far largest consumption of meat out of towns) is, when growing, fed on grass, and on whey, or skimmed milk; and when fatting, partly on the latter. This is the case in the dairy countries, all of them great breeders and feeders of swine; but for the much greater part, and in all the corn countries, they are fattened on beans, barley meal, and pease. When the food of the animal is scarce, his flesh must be dear. This, one would suppose, would require no great penetration to discover.

This failure of so very large a supply of flesh in one species, naturally throws the whole demand of the consumer on the diminished supply of all kinds of flesh, and, indeed, on all the matters of human sustenance. Nor, in my opinion, are we to expect a greater cheapness in that article for this year, even though corn should grow cheaper, as it is to be hoped it will. The store swine, from the failure of subsistence last year, are now at an extravagant price. Pigs, at our fairs, have sold lately for fifty shillings, which, two years ago, would not have brought more than twenty.

As to sheep, none, I thought, were strangers to the general failure of the article of turnips last year; the early having been burned as they came up, by the great drought and heat; the late, and those of the early which had escaped, were destroyed by the chilling frosts of the winter, and the wet and severe weather of the spring. In many places a full fourth of the sheep or the lambs were lost, what remained of the lambs were poor and ill fed,

the

the ewes having had no milk. The calves came late, and they were generally an article, the want of which was as much to be dreaded as any other. So that article of food, formerly so abundant in the early part of the summer, particularly in London, and which in a great part supplied the place of mutton for near two months, did little less than totally fail.

All the productions of the earth link in with each other. All the sources of plenty, in all and every article, were dried or frozen up. The scarcity was not as gentlemen seem to suppose, in wheat only.

Another cause, and that not of inconsiderable operation, tended to produce a scarcity in flesh provision. It is one that on many accounts cannot be too much regretted, and, the rather, as it was the sole *cause* of scarcity in that article, which arose from the proceedings of men themselves. I mean the stop put to the distillery.

The hogs (and that would be sufficient) which were fed with the waste wash of that produce, did not demand the fourth part of the corn used by farmers in fattening them. The spirit was nearly so much clear gain to the nation. It is an odd way of making flesh cheap, to stop or check the distillery.

The distillery in itself produces an immense article of trade almost all over the world, to Africa, to North America, and to various parts of Europe. It is of great use, next to food itself, to our fisheries and to our whole navigation. A great part of the distillery was carried on by damaged corn, unfit for bread, and by barley and malt of the lowest quality. These things could not be more unexceptionably employed. The domestic consumption of spirits, produced, without complaints, a very great revenue, applicable, if we pleased, in bounties to the bringing corn from other places, far beyond the value of that consumed in making it, or to the encouragement of its encreased production at home.

As to what is said, in a physical and moral view, against the home consumption of spirits, experience has long since taught me very little to respect the declamations on that subject—whether the thunder of the laws, or the thunder of eloquence, " is hurled *on gin,*" always I am thunder-proof. The alembic, in my mind, has furnished to the world a far greater benefit and blessing, than if the *opus maximum* had been really found by chemistry, and, like Midas, we could turn every thing into gold.

Undoubtedly there may be a dangerous abuse in the excess of spirits ; and at one time I am ready to believe the abuse was great. When spirits are cheap, the business of drunkenness is achieved with little time or labour ; but that evil I consider to be wholly done away. Observation for the last forty years, and very particularly for the last thirty, has furnished me with ten instances of drunkenness from other causes, for one from this. Ardent spirit is a great medicine, often to remove distempers— much more frequently to prevent them, or to chase them away in their beginnings. It is not nutritive in *any great* degree. But, if not food, it greatly alleviates the want of it. It invigorates the stomach for the digestion of poor meagre diet, not easily alliable to the human constitution. Wine the poor cannot touch. Beer, as applied to many occasions, (as among seamen and fishermen for instance) will by no means do the business. Let me add, what wits inspired with champaign and claret, will turn into ridicule —it is a medicine for the mind. Under the pressure of the cares and sorrows of our mortal condition, men have at all times, and in all countries, called in some physical aid to their moral consolations,—wine, beer, opium, brandy, or tobacco.

I consider therefore the stopping of the distillery, œconomically, financially, commercially, medicinally, and in some degree morally too, as a measure rather well

meant

meant than well considered. It is too precious a sacrifice to prejudice.

Gentlemen well know whether there be a scarcity of partridges, and whether that be an effect of hoarding and combination. All the tame race of birds live and die as the wild do.

As to the lesser articles, they are like the greater. They have followed the fortune of the season. Why are fowls dear? was not this the farmer's or jobber's fault. I sold from my yard to a jobber, six young and lean fowls, for four and twenty shillings; fowls, for which, two years ago, the same man would not have given a shilling a-piece.—He sold them afterwards at Uxbridge, and they were taken to London to receive the last hand.

As to the operation of the war in causing the scarcity of provisions, I understand that Mr. Pitt has given a particular answer to it—but I do not think it worth powder and shot.

I do not wonder the papers are so full of this sort of matter, but I am a little surprised it should be mentioned in parliament. Like all great state questions, peace and war may be discussed, and different opinions fairly formed, on political grounds, but on a question of the present price of provisions, when peace with the regicides is always uppermost, I can only say, that great is the love of it.

After all, have we not reason to be thankful to the giver of all good? In our history, and when "The labourer of England is said to have been once happy," we find constantly, after certain intervals, a period of real famine; by which, a melancholy havock was made among the human race. The price of provisions fluctuated dreadfully, demonstrating a deficiency very different from the worst failures of the present moment. Never since I have known England, have I known more than a comparative scarcity. The price of wheat, taking a number

of

of years together, has had no very considerable fluctuation, nor has it risen exceedingly until within this twelvemonth. Even now, I do not know of one man, woman, or child, that has perished from famine; fewer, if any, I believe, than in years of plenty, when such a thing may happen by accident. This is owing to a care and superintendance of the poor, far greater than any I remember.

The consideration of this ought to bind us all, rich and poor together, against those wicked writers of the newspapers, who would inflame the poor against their friends, guardians, patrons, and protectors. Not only very few (I have observed, that I know of none, though I live in a place as poor as most) have actually died of want, but we have seen no traces of those dreadful exterminating epidemics, which, in consequence of scanty and unwholesome food, in former times, not unfrequently, wasted whole nations. Let us be saved from too much wisdom of our own, and we shall do tolerably well.

It is one of the finest problems in legislation, and what has often engaged my thoughts whilst I followed that profession, "What the state ought to take upon itself to direct by the public wisdom, and what it ought to leave, with as little interference as possible, to individual discretion." Nothing, certainly, can be laid down on the subject that will not admit of exceptions, many permanent, some occasional. But the clearest line of distinction which I could draw, whilst I had any chalk to draw my line, was this: That the state ought to confine itself to what regards the state, or the creatures of the state, namely, the exterior establishment of its religion; its magistracy; its revenue; its military force by sea and land; the corporations that owe their existence to its fiat; in a word, to every thing that is *truly and properly* public, to the public peace, to the public safety, to the public order, to the public prosperity. In its preventive police it ought to be sparing of its efforts, and to employ means

rather

rather few, unfrequent, and strong, than many, and frequent, and, of course, as they multiply their puny politic
race, and dwindle, small and feeble. Statesmen who
know themselves will, with the dignity which belongs to
wisdom, proceed only in this the superior orb and first
mover of their duty, steadily, vigilantly, severely, cour-
ageously: whatever remains will, in a manner, provide for
itself. But as they descend from the state to a province,
from a province to a parish, and from a parish to a private
house, they go on accelerated in their fall. They *cannot*
do the lower duty; and, in proportion as they try it, they
will certainly fail in the higher. They ought to know the
different departments of things; what belongs to laws,
and what manners alone can regulate. To these, great
politicians may give a leaning, but they cannot give a
law.

Our legislature has fallen into this fault as well as
other Governments; all have fallen into it more or less.
The once mighty state, which was nearest to us locally,
nearest to us in every way, and whose ruins threaten to
fall upon our heads, is a strong instance of this error. I
can never quote France without a foreboding sigh—
ΕΣΣΕΤΑΓ᾽ΗΜΑΡ! Scipio said it to his recording Greek
friend amidst the flames of the great rival of his country.
That state has fallen by the hands of the parricides of
their country, called the Revolutionists, and Constitu-
tionalists, of France, a species of traitors, of whose fury
and atrocious wickedness nothing in the annals of the
phrenzy and depravation of mankind had before furnished
an example, and of whom I can never think or speak
without a mixed sensation of disgust, of horrour, and of
detestation, not easy to be expressed. These nefarious
monsters destroyed their country for what was good in it:
for much good there was in the constitution of that noble
monarchy, which, in all kinds, formed and nourished great
men, and great patterns of virtue to the world. But

though

though its enemies were not enemies to its faults, its faults furnished them with means for its destruction. My dear departed friend, whose loss is even greater to the public than to me, had often remarked, that the leading vice of the French monarchy (which he had well studied) was in good intention ill-directed, and a restless desire of governing too much. The hand of authority was seen in every thing, and in every place. All, therefore, that happened amiss in the course even of domestic affairs, was attributed to the Government; and, as it always happens in this kind of officious universal interference, what began in odious power, ended always, I may say without an exception, in contemptible imbecility. For this reason, as far as I can approve of any novelty, I thought well of the provincial administrations. Those, if the superior power had been severe, and vigilant, and vigorous, might have been of much use politically in removing Government from many invidious details. But as every thing is good or bad, as it is related or combined, Government being relaxed above as it was relaxed below, and the brains of the people growing more and more addle with every sort of visionary speculation, the shiftings of the scene in the provincial theatres became only preparatives to a revolution in the kingdom, and the popular actings there only the rehearsals of the terrible drama of the republic.

Tyranny and cruelty may make men justly wish the downfall of abused powers, but I believe that no Government ever yet perished from any other direct cause than its own weakness. My opinion is against an over-doing of any sort of administration, and more especially against this most momentous of all meddling on the part of authority; the meddling with the subsistence of the people.

F I N I S.

AN
INQUIRY
INTO THE
POLICY AND JUSTICE
OF THE
PROHIBITION OF THE USE OF GRAIN
IN THE
DISTILLERIES :

INCLUDING

OBSERVATIONS ON THE NATURE AND USES OF A
VENT TO SUPERFLUOUS LAND-PRODUCE; AND A
PARTICULAR APPLICATION OF THE GENERAL
QUESTION TO THE PRESENT SITUATION OF THE
COLONIAL INTERESTS.

―――――――

BY ARCHIBALD BELL, ESQ. ADVOCATE.

―――――――

EDINBURGH:
PRINTED FOR AND SOLD BY ARCHIBALD CONSTABLE AND CO.

―――

1808.

CONTENTS.

CONTENTS.

ADVERTISEMENT

T O those who are familiar with the doctrines of
political economy, the minuteness of illustration
and detail, in the following remarks, may appear superfluous. But when we consider how important it is, in a
popular Government like ours, that the public be possessed
of just notions on schemes of national policy; and, when
we see such fundamental and exploded errors advanced on
a subject so interesting as the present, I am hopeful that
they who least require a detailed explanation, will be the
most sensible of its utility.

It will also be found, that the principles which I have
endeavoured to establish are of general application, and
may enable us to judge, not merely of the present
measure, but of all similar schemes of policy. They
indeed involve the most extensive and fundamental doctrines in the science of political economy.

I likewise hope that some of the facts and reasonings
which I have advanced, may tend to dissipate those
groundless alarms on the subject of scarcity, which some
persons seem at present to feel; a passion which, of all
others, is the most apt to bewilder the public opinion,
and to urge a headlong adoption of those measures which
are the most likely to create or aggravate such a calamity.

The present situation of our colonies I shall also touch
upon, as connected with the more general questions which

arise

arise on the present subject: though on this, as being less important in itself, and less within my opportunities of information, I shall be more brief.

The Report of the Committee of the House of Commons, relative to the distillation of sugar, and the very large and important mass of evidence contained in the Appendix, I have had the benefit of perusing. Any testimony of mine to the ability, patience, and candour with which that respectable body have conducted their researches, would be impertinent. I have taken the liberty of dissenting from their opinion; but I have stated the grounds of my dissent, and, I hope, with that becoming deference and moderation which should always accompany free inquiry. If any thing material in the evidence laid before the Committee should have escaped me, it will perhaps be excused, from the shortness of the time allowed for its perusal.

INQUIRY

INQUIRY

INTO THE

POLICY AND JUSTICE

OF THE

PROHIBITION OF THE USE OF GRAIN

IN THE

DISTILLERIES, &c.

THE distress of our West India Colonies has for some time excited the public attention; and as the persons chiefly interested in colonial produce, though a small, are not an unimportant class of the community, endowed with the spirit, and possessing the weight and activity of an affluent corporation, it is by no means surprising that their complaints have been heard. They have laid them before the public in various shapes; and, with the common propensity of human nature, in examining into the source of their distresses, they have found every one to blame but themselves. They have accounted for the present stagnation of their commodity in their hands by every cause but the true one,—their own imprudent speculation.

That the present glut of sugar has arisen from an

7   over

over cultivation of that produce, so as to overstock the market of the world; and that our planters must sooner or later diminish their cultivation, now that more fertile soils are reviving, and entering the competition; seem to me truths, which can hardly be doubted by any whose opinion is not in some degree biassed by their interest. The thing is probable in theory; and, were any confirmation of it wanted, it would be derived from the inadequate causes assigned for their present difficulties by the colonists themselves. It may perhaps be doubted, whether persons so suffering, are entitled to any relief from the public; or, whether they ought not to be left to that correction which the immutable laws of nature have provided for rash speculation. This is a question, however, on which I at present forbear to enter. My chief purpose is, to inquire how far, if any relief is to be granted, that which has been proposed, of confining the home distillation to sugar, be a proper one. I shall endeavour to shew, that it is improper in every view; impolitic in regard to the public interest; and unjust towards our home cultivators.

When the subject of prohibiting distillation from grain was so much agitated a few years ago, the complexion of the question differed materially from what it is at present. It was then debated entirely on general grounds. The only interests considered were those of the public, and of the home grower; the consumer and producer of our domestic supplies. The interests of the colonists were not at all insisted on. Indeed the idea of distilling from sugar does not then seem to have been generally entertained. The question was argued as if the stoppage of the distillery would altogether suspend the formation of ardent spirit; and hence two arguments were applied to it, on either side, which do not touch it in its present shape. The one was in favour of the distillery, on the score of its use to the revenue: the other against

it

it, on the effects of the consumption of distilled spirit on the health, morals, and happiness, of the people.

As an object of revenue, the distillery certainly has its advantages, chiefly in the view of easy collection. In any other light, it seems less important, as the grain used there, if consumed in the support of any other species of industry, would afford the same, or nearly the same revenue, levied on thé produce of that industry, whatever it might be.

The objection to distillation, on the score of its *moral effects*, has, I confess, always appeared to me by far the strongest counterpoise to the great benefits which it yields. When I consider the excessive indulgence in ardent spirits, which always attends their abundance; the destruction which it occasions to the health, morals, economy, and industry of the people ; the ruin of natural affection, and the general depravity and misery which it brings on the lower orders, and their families ; I am sometimes staggered in my prepossession of leaving all industry free, and inclined to prohibit a manufacture of poison, as I would any other public nuisance. I have need to recollect the other great benefits arising from the practice ; the general encouragement which it gives to agriculture, and the resources which it yields in occasional scarcity, before I can reconcile myself to its public toleration. In considering this objection, it is somewhat amusing to reflect on the different impression of arguments on different minds. This, which I look upon as so weighty, and indeed the only one of the smallest weight against distilleries, has, I suppose, never been a feather in the balance in determining the legal provisions on the subject. The minds of statesmen and legislators are swayed by far other considerations. Indeed I fear I shall risk any little credit my other notions might gain, by dwelling on so simple an objection.

But however this may be, the above objection is no otherwise important to the present inquiry, than as a

curious

curious speculation; for whether the measure now proposed be adopted or not, the quantity of distilled spirit will
probably not be diminished. The only question is, whether
it shall be manufactured from grain or from sugar? I
believe the spirit distilled from sugar is rather more
noxious than that distilled from grain; but this difference
is probably not so material as much to affect the argument. Neither, on the other hand, does the question of
revenue enter into consideration, for the quantity of
manufactured spirit, and consequently the duties, will
probably remain much the same.

The interest of the distillers seems likewise to be
pretty much unconnected with the present question. For
though it appears, by the evidence before the committee,
on the one hand, that corn is in general preferred for
distillation; and, on the other, that the suspension might
profit individuals who have speculated in the view of its
taking place; it would seem, that an arrangement of
duties may make the matter pretty nearly indifferent to
them as a body.*

A new and important interest, however, has made its
appearance on the present occasion, which was scarcely
thought of formerly,—that of our Colonial proprietors. They
have, some time ago, applied to Parliament for assistance
in their present distresses; have suggested the suspension
of the corn distillery as one mode of relief; and have had
sufficient influence with the Committee of the House of
Commons, appointed to inquire into their case, to induce
them to recommend it; after having failed in a like suggestion to a former Committee.†

10   Like

---

* See the evidence of Mr. T. Smith (of Brentford), and ¯Mr. T.
Smith (of the house of Stein, Smith, & Co.) in the Appendix to the
Report, particularly p. 34-81. Mr. D. Montgomerie, p. 126-8.

† "The result, therefore, of the inquiry of the Committee is,
" that however strongly they may feel the distresses and the diffi-

Like all bodies too who call for monopolies, they have not limited their argument, in suggesting the present measure, to their own necessities. They have endeavoured to persuade their countrymen, that the public interest is as much concerned in the suspension of the corn distillery as that of the colonists; and, as is usual, they have persuaded many uninterested persons that this is the case. We have been told so even from very high authority, and are daily told so in a mass of crude speculation on this subject, which now overflows the country. The Report of the Committee likewise, though, of course, it enlarges on ihe colonial difficulties, does, however, urge certain grounds for the adoption of the present measure, on public views, connected with the present state of our foreign relations. This makes it necessary to consider the question on general principles, as well as with a particular view to the present distresses of the colonists. Nor are such general principles confined in their application to the question now agitated, but will enable us to judge of the same, or similar proposals, at all times and seasons. It is useful to be set right in regard to first principles, even if we should occasionally depart from them. We shall thus be better able to estimate the grounds alleged for such departure, as well as to determine its nature and limits.

The present inquiry, therefore, divides itself into two branches. The *first* involves the question, Are there any

11 grounds,

" culties under which the West Indian trade at present labours ; " however anxious they may be to recommend the adoption of any " measure which may tend to afford, even a temporary relief, from a " pressure so heavy and alarming, they do not think the measure of " permitting the use of sugar and molasses, for a time to be limited, " in the breweries and distilleries, one that would give to the West " Indian trade any relief adequate to its distresses, *consistent with the* " *interests of other branches of the community,* or with the safety of " the revenue." Rep. from the Distillery Committee, Feb. 1807.

grounds, in the present circumstances of this country, independent of the distresses of the colonists, to justify the suspension of distillation from grain? The *second* involves the question, Supposing there are no such grounds, is the interest of the sugar colonists a sufficient reason for such a measure?

The *first* or general inquiry further subdivides itself into two branches. The present circumstances of this country, unconnected with the interest of the colonists, may be considered, in the *first* place more generally, as relative to a great nation producing its own supplies, and at amity with all the world. In the *second* place, under its present peculiar aspect, as importing a part of its supplies from foreign states; while there is a chance of these supplies being interrupted, from the violence of war, in the present extraordinary combination against us.

These two branches I shall consider in the two first sections, and I think they will exhaust all the views which have been taken of the subject unconnected with the interest of the colonists.

In the *second* place, supposing it to be made out, that, on all and each of these general grounds, the proposed suspension of the distillery would be unadvisable, I shall next enquire, Whether the present distresses of the colonists are a sufficient ground for granting them relief, by the suspension of the distillery of grain, either in the view of justice to the home cultivator, or policy towards the public? This will form the subject of a third section.

In all speculations regarding public measures, the great object of inquiry is the interest of the public. The interest of individuals, or classes of individuals, must be considered only as subordinate to this great interest. It is not to be inferred from this, that I maintain that

injustice

injustice is to be committed towards smaller classes, when the interest of the public requires it; because I believe it to be a rule without one exception, that it never can be for the public advantage, to prefer one class before another in the free direction of their industry. In the following observations, therefore, when I speak of the interest of the home grower, or of the colonist, I always speak of it, not in exclusive relation to either of those classes of individuals, but as subordinate to the interest of the public. When I speak of anything tending to the prosperity or discouragement of our farmers, I mean only in so far as the public interest is concerned in that prosperity or discouragement. When I speak of the propriety or impropriety of granting relief to the colonists, or of the mode of relief at present suggested, I speak of it, neither with favour nor dislike towards them as a body, but only in as far as it is for the public interest that any relief, or that such relief, should be granted.

It is further to be attended to, that the measure now in agitation is not merely the free permission of importing sugar, or, what is the same thing, an equalization of the duties on sugar, and on corn, used in distilleries. It will be seen that, according to all the principles on which the following argument is maintained, I not only approve of such free importation as a temporary measure, but as a permanent system. What is proposed in the Report of the Committee, and what I object to, is the monopoly of the distilleries granted to the colonist, and the forcible exclusion of the home grower from the competition.

S E C T. I.

Of the Operation of Distilleries in a Country which sup-
plies its own Consumption, or affords a Surplus beyond
it.

THE operation of distilleries on a country producing
its own supplies, or affording a surplus, may be
considered under two views : I. In years of average
home produce : and, II. In years of scarcity from deficient home produce.

I. To enlarge on the importance of a flourishing
agriculture, to the strength and prosperity of a state, does
not seem at present necessary ; for it is a truth which the
most erroneous systems of œconomical policy never could
entirely hide, and is one on which the public opinion
seems now to be pretty well awakened, although the
general views on this subject are still far from being
wholly just. The land produce of a state, though not the
only source of wealth (as some of its indiscreet favourers
have maintained) is at least the most important branch of
it, the foundation of all the rest, and the measure of their
extent and limits. In a large territory, the amount of
subsistence which can be imported, must necessarily be
small ;* and as the population of a state is regulated by
its means of subsistence, a large territory can only be
populous in proportion to the means of subsistence which
it raises within itself. It follows, that all other branches
of industry, which are carried on by that population, must
be regulated by the amount of the land produce. From
these plain premises I do not infer (as some very able men
have done) that agriculture should receive any peculiar
encouragement from the law, beyond other branches of

14   industry ;

---

* Smith's Wealth of Nations, B. 4. c. 2.

industry ; because I think such encouragement can do it no good. But I infer, that it should suffer no positive restraint or discouragement to the advantage of other branches of industry ; because, though some limited branch of industry may profit by such preference, the industry and prosperity of the country in general must suffer exactly in proportion as agriculture suffers.

Mr. Malthus (whose profound and original speculations have formed an æra in political science) has, however, shewn, that it is not merely the *gross* amount of land produce in a state, *in proportion to the extent of territory*, which is the cause of domestic prosperity, but the *relative* amount of that produce, *in proportion to the numbers of the people*. Thus, if two nations possess an equal extent of territory, and raise an equal produce, and one contain *ten millions* of inhabitants, the other *twelve millions* ; in the former, the food being divided in larger shares among the people than in the latter, the former people will enjoy greater comfort and happiness than the latter, in common and average years.

But although the *gross* amount of produce, in proportion to territory, and its *relative* amount, in proportion to population, be different things, and it be possible to conceive the gross produce, in proportion to territory, to be large, while the *relative* produce is small, and the people but moderately supplied (which I believe is the case in China) ; yet I imagine, in general, large *gross* produce and *relative* abundance uniformly go together, where no impolitic laws or usages encourage a superfluous population, or interrupt the commerce of grain.—Wherever these are left free to the operation of nature, a large *gross* produce is uniformly attended with a *relative* abundance among the people.

In regard, again, to the public strength of a country, as opposed to other states, it is needless to shew how much this depends on the amount of its land produce, in pro-

portion to the land produce of other states. If two
neighbouring nations are equal in extent of territory,
that which produces the largest supplies, will maintain
the largest population, and a given proportion of that
population will, of course, constitute a larger force than
the same proportion of the other population. On the
other hand, if two neighbouring nations are of unequal
size, the smaller may, by a superior agriculture, support
an equal population, and, of course, equal armies. In
the particular circumstances, therefore, of every state, its
force must be measured by the extent of its supplies. If
France be twice as large as Britain, or (what, in the
existing state of any two countries, is the same thing)
have twice as many acres in culture, and yet Britain raise
twice as much grain per acre, Britain will be as populous
as France, and will be able to support equal armies.—This
is supposing the gross produce of both countries to be the
same; their respective numbers to be the same; and the
proportion of these numbers which they maintain in war,
also the same.

But, strictly speaking, the power of a nation to maintain armies does not depend so much on the amount of
its population, compared with the population of other
states, as on the amount of its supplies, compared with
the supplies of other states. I have observed that, though
population always bears a *near* relation to supply, yet it
does not always bear *exactly the same* relation to it. In
one nation the supplies may be more abundant in proportion to the numbers, or, what is the same thing, the
people less numerous in proportion to the supplies than in
another nation. Now, in such circumstances, the nation
whose abundance is the greatest, though it use its whole
supplies in peace by the various modes of consumption,
may, in war, by a retrenchment of its consumption, yield
larger supplies than its poorer neighbour can do, to the
maintenance of an army, and of those arts necessary to

16

the

the supply of an army, and, of course, support a larger
army. Its population, though in numbers only equal to
that of its rival, yields in war a greater disposable proportion without diminishing the land produce, provided the
consumption in the richer nation be diminished in the
same proportion. The richer nation can support an army
of 120,000 men, *equally well* appointed and supplied, as
the poorer can support an army of 100,000 men.—Or,
the richer nation can support an army of 100,000 men
better appointed and supplied than the poorer nation can
support the same number.

It appears, therefore, that the public strength of a
state, as well as its domestic prosperity, is in proportion
to the amount of its supplies.

The encouragement of a great land produce, therefore,
becomes the first of all objects, towards both the domestic
happiness and the public security of a state; and while
on this subject, it is pleasing to reflect, that the example
of our own country is the best confirmation of the above
doctrines. No long settled community, of equal extent,
has, perhaps, ever yielded so large a produce as Great
Britain; has supported its population in such general
abundance; or possessed such prodigious resources for
offence and security. The average land produce of Great
Britain is as much superior to that of other nations, as
her manufactures and commerce.* This she has attained,
not from the perfect rectitude of her policy in regard to
agriculture, but because the errors she has committed
have been fewer than those committed by other nations;
17 and

---

* Mr. Ar. Young (the justness and importance of whose practical
observations in political economy shine through the uncertainty of
his general principles) has remarked, that England has always been
as much superior to France in agriculture as in other branches of
industry. By his calculation, the produce of this country was to
that of France when he travelled (1789-92) as 28 to 18

and the consequences of them have been more completely palliated. The first of these advantages she has derived from the influence of the public voice and interest over her public councils; the second from the freedom of individual exertion, overcoming the restraints of an injudicious policy.

Such, then, being the importance of increasing the actual land produce of a country, it may be laid down as an axiom, that every positive restriction, which limits the power of the farmer to augment the land produce, is immediately injurious to him, and consequentially injurious to the community. I say every *positive restriction*, which gives the preference to some other branch of industry over his; for, as far as respects a free competition, though that may sometimes diminish the farmer's profits in the mean time, it will be for the advantage of the community. It is only when the farmer asks some monopoly, that his interest and that of the public can ever be opposed.

It is the interest of the farmer to have an abundant produce, but yet somewhat under the demand of the market. It is the interest of the public that the produce should be abundant, and the market pretty fully supplied. In other words, the farmer wishes for plenty, and tolerably high prices; the public for plenty, and tolerably low prices. But while, on the one hand, it is not the interest of the farmer to have too high prices, which can only proceed from very deficient produce ; on the other hand, it is not the interest of the public to have too low prices, proceeding from over-abundance, which may discourage the farmer, and induce him to retrench his cultivation. Such retrenchment naturally leads back to scarcity, and a change of this kind, from plenty to scarcity, is a much greater evil than if the produce had never exceeded the lowest point of the vibration. Though it be the interest of the public, therefore, that grain should be cheap, it

18   never

never can be its interest that grain should be so cheap as to injure the cultivator. Such an over-cheapness may sometimes arise in the course of nature, by the farmer's improvident over-trading, and, in such a case, should be left to remedy itself by natural means. It will, however, scarcely ever amount to an evil, if things be left to their own course, and nothing obstruct the natural efforts of competition to relieve itself. But whenever the cheapness is produced artificially, or by forcible means, it may be pronounced pernicious, as injurious to the public in the long-run, as immediately to the grower.

Cheapness and dearness, it is to be observed, are variable terms, importing the relation between the demand and the actual supply. It is therefore impossible to fix them by any definite standard, or determine when either is excessive. When matters are left free each will accurately adapt itself to the actual amount of supplies. Corn will never be cheap but when it ought to be cheap, nor cheaper than it ought to be :—It will never be dear unless when it ought to be dear, nor dearer than it ought to be. The cultivator's complaints of low prices on the one hand, or, as it is usually termed, *the want of adequate returns to the grower*, are just as unreasonable as the public complaints of high prices on the other. The return in the market, when matters are left free, must be the *adequate* and proper return, in proportion to the amount of produce. If this last be too large, the farmer has overtraded, by advancing cultivation too rapidly, and must diminish it. This is the only sense in which I use the word *over-cheapness*, when arising from natural causes, and the only remedy I would propose, however low prices might fall.

There are two modes in which the farmer's profits may be lowered, and abundance created by forced expedients, which, in a course of average seasons, have nearly the same effect ; namely, the stoppage of his market, and the

increase

increase of produce;—the one professing to attain its end by restraint, the other by encouragement.

In the annals of legislation, we are no strangers to various schemes of policy which have professed to lower the price of grain by forced limitations of the market. The famous minister Colbert, wishing to encourage the manufactures of France, bethought himself of increasing the plenty, and lowering the price of grain, by prohibiting its export. In this way, no doubt, there was suddenly thrown back on the home market the whole quantity usually exported, and the consequence must have been an immediate plenty and cheapness. But all the effect of this was very soon over; for the farmers finding a glut of their commodity on their hands, and the prices so low as to yield them no adequate return, (an expression which in this case might be used with propriety,) were forced to retrench their cultivation, and thus reduce the produce to what it was formerly, exclusive of the export. The object desired, therefore, was almost immediately defeated. But this is by no means stating the full amount of the evil. For the discouragement to agriculture, from the closing up an indefinite vent to its produce, will always diminish that produce, or prevent its gradual increase, in a proportion far beyond the actual amount consumed by that vent at the time of the restriction. The policy of M. Colbert, therefore, not merely defeated its own end; not merely did not promote the cheapness, and advance the industry which he favoured; but was probably greatly injurious to it. He snatched at a hasty advantage by sacrificing the spring which was to prolong and augment it. The character of his policy (to use the illustration of Montesquieu on another subject) resembled the eagerness of the savage who, to get at the fruit, cuts down the tree.

The analogy between the above policy and that of prohibiting distillation from corn, is obvious and complete. The distillery affords the farmer a steady, con-

venient

venient, and profitable market for his produce, exactly in the same way as export. It is also indefinite in extent; and if the vent which it furnishes be in general more limited than that of export, it is nearer, more sure, and not dependent, like the other, on the demand of other states, or our connection with them. Like the former, it encourages a considerably larger produce than it actually consumes.* The effect of a stoppage of this vent, like that of the other, is to throw the whole grain used there into the common market, which, while it occasions a transitory cheapness, will lower the farmer's profits, and finally reduce his cultivation to the full amount of the grain usually distilled, and probably much further.

In short, the analogy, so remarkable in other instances, between produce and population applies perfectly here. A free emigration increases the numbers of the people in the same manner as a free export, or other vent, increases produce. All attempts to force either, by direct encouragements, are unavailing. All attempts to stop their natural vents lead to the very decrease that is feared.†

21

There

---

* This opinion is distinctly expressed by that very intelligent cultivator Mr. Wakefield, in his evidence before the Committee, App. to Rep. p. 109-111. The operation of even a very limited vent in encouraging produce is described by Mr. A. Young, in his evidence before the Committee. The quantity of grain used in the distilleries of the United Kingdom, is stated in the Report to amount to 781,000 qrs. 470,000 in Britain, and 311,000 in Ireland.

† They who doubt of the effects of a free and regular emigration in increasing numbers may, I think, be convinced by perusing Mr. Malthus's account of the irruption of the barbarous nations of the north of Europe. That author has completely solved the problem of their excessive numbers, which had puzzled so many of his predecessors. Dr. Ferguson has compared the attempts to increase population to the assisting a water-fall with an oar. The fears of its decay from emigration resemble the fears of the river running out, and leaving its channel dry. See this matter enlarged on, and

There are, however, certain reasoners who have denied that the home grower would sustain any loss from the stoppage of distillation. He would save as much, according to them, in the reduced wages of labour and poor rates, the easier maintenance of his family, &c. consequent on the cheapness, as he would lose by the fall of grain. If this be true, the price of grain is of no consequence to the farmer, and the fixation of a *maximum*, however low, would be to him a matter of indifference. By the same reasoning we may satisfy the woollen manufacturer, that a fall in the price of cloth is nothing against his interest, as he might then *clothe* his workmen, servants, and family cheaper than before. It is painful, at this time of day, to be obliged to reply seriously to such folly. Were the argument intended to convince those only whom it professes to address (the farmer or manufacturer), it would be idle, indeed, to take notice of it. Their interest and experience tell them its absurdity too plainly to allow them to be deceived. Let others be convinced, from what is observed of their conduct (if unable to see it themselves), that a forced decrease in the price of any commodity is never compensated to the dealer by the lower wages of his workmen, or any other consequences of the fall. If the farmers in this country consider the stoppage of the distillery as a matter of indifference to them, I have done with my objections.

Such, then, will be the consequence of stopping distillation, or any other natural vent to home produce, in a course of average years. The effect of taking away a vent to produce, in case of the occurrence of scarcity, I shall afterwards attend to.

But the forced limitation of the market is not the only device that has been fallen upon to increase abund-

ance,

practically applied, in Lord Selkirk's excellent treatise on the Highland Emigrations.

ance, and lower prices. Some persons expecting to attain the same end by encouragement, as in the former case was expected by restraint, have proposed a bounty on the improvement of wastes, or breaking up grass lands. But it seems evident, that, in as far as this is *forced* beyond the natural demand of the market, the former cultivation will just suffer in proportion as the new cultivation increases; and the supplies will merely be raised in different places, while their aggregate amount will remain the same. But, indeed, any encouragement of this kind must be so insignificant, that I rather think it will produce no effect at all. The effects of such a measure as to scarcity, and with the view of diminishing importation, I shall afterwards consider.

But while the direct encouragement of home produce is unavailing, or injurious to the farmer, and, in neither view, will lead to any increase of supplies, all obstacles to its free progress should be removed. This is indeed the whole length that the encouragement to improving wastes, or turning grass lands into tillage, should or can go; and, while thus free, the interest of the farmer and the public always go together.

The farmer, like the undertaker of every other branch of industry, must lay his account with the competition of every other person who pursues the same, or any other trade, in a lawful manner. If any other person pursue his trade in the way of breaking up waste lands, he does no more than he is entitled to, and has no preference over those who cultivate the more improved soils. The too rapid cultivation of wastes is a thing impossible, if left wholly to private interest and industry, because the inducement to that practice is only in proportion to the high price, or scarcity of land produce; and as the scarcity is relieved, or prices fall, the inducement to cultivate wastes must fall in proportion. The operation of improving wastes must therefore be gradual, and suited

to

to the public demands. The public demands, on the other hand, will adjust themselves to this natural and permanent increase of produce, and the community will receive a lasting benefit, while the class of cultivators will suffer no injury.

An analogy has been drawn from the plan of increasing supplies by the above means, to that of increasing them by the suspension of the distilleries; and although there be a difference between them in the view of scarcity, as shall afterwards be shewn, yet in the continuance of average supplies, I think the analogy may be admitted. The interference in regard to both is equally wrong; the farmer is injured by both; and the public will ultimately be so too; only, as the power of the legislature can operate much more surely in suspending the distillery than in forcing improvement, the injurious effects of the former will be more strongly felt. On the other hand, as the free competition of the culture of wastes can do no harm, neither can the free admission of the colonial produce into the distilleries.

Another mode of increasing the home supplies, from which an analogy has been drawn to the suspension of the distilleries, is the importation of corn. This case just resembles the last. If importation were promoted by a bounty, or other encouragement, while there was no call for it from scarcity, it would be equally wrong with the forced importation of sugars by the suspension of the distilleries. Did any of our colonists grow rice, and did we give it some exclusive encouragement in our market, the case would be just the same, at least in average seasons. Such encouragements, however, never have been given to foreign growers. They are never even allowed the fair competition of our market, (which I think both they and the colonial proprietors ought to be,) but all that they send in common years is loaded with heavy duties. Were the colonists at present asking no more

favour

favour than the utmost that has been ever extended to the foreign growers of corn, during average years, I should be far from objecting to their demands.

The discouragement of the British grower, therefore, from the improvement of wastes, or importation, can never bear any resemblance to his discouragement from the stoppage of his market, while the one is free, the other compulsive.

II. I have thus, I think, sufficiently shewn the beneficial effect of distilleries, and other vents, in encouraging cultivation in common and average years ; and the injurious consequence of a forced suspension of them, both to the home grower and the public. I now proceed to inquire into the nature of their operation in seasons of scarcity, and the consequence of their suspension in such an event. The scarcity to which I at present allude, is that which arises from deficient home produce, as I am now considering the question abstracted from the circumstance of importation.

They who have given the attention which it deserves to the excellent work of Mr. Malthus, must be aware of the uniform relation maintained between the population of any country and its means of support; of the constant tendency of the former to encroach upon the latter ; and of the inadequacy of the utmost assignable produce in any country to maintain the people in plenty and happiness, unless the natural tendency to increase be repressed by some forcible check, either directly or indirectly, a certain length below the means of subsistence.

Whenever the means of subsistence, however, are, from any cause, unusually abundant, and the people enjoy great comparative ease and comfort, the disposition to early marriage will speedily augment their numbers, which will rise till they begin to press against the limits of subsistence. This will bring a gradual decrease in the

comforts

comforts of the people, and again reduce their numbers, till they fall below the decreased means of support, and are then prepared to oscillate as before. This natural oscillation is far from being a light evil, as the periodical sufferings of scarcity greatly overbalance the additional comforts enjoyed in seasons of great abundance; so that, upon the whole, it would be far better for a people to have a steady supply, though not larger than the lowest amount in the scale of vibration just stated. Yet the evil, though far from light, would be trifling compared with what it really amounts to, were the products of the soil exposed to no other casualty than such a gradual periodical vibration as the above, only influenced by the increase or decrease of population. Were the products of the soil, like the products of other manufactures, wholly dependent on the exertions of man, they might suit themselves pretty accurately to the demand throughout every year, or series of years, and increase or diminish the supplies to a known and definite amount. But in determining the amount of land produce, another power must co-operate, over which man has no controul, namely, the influence of the seasons. This may occasion a sudden disproportion in the supplies, which can occur in no branch of industry wholly dependent on human exertion; while, at the same time, a deficiency of supply in this can much less be endured than in any other. It is not, therefore, a sufficient security against famine that a nation yields such a produce as to maintain all its people moderately in average years, if that produce really be all consumed as human food. It is necessary that a considerable surplus be raised for consumption in some other way than as human food, which may exist as a resource on a sudden deficiency, and may be thus turned from whatever other purpose it was destined for, to the use of man. To dispose of this surplus in average years, the following methods seem to be the chief :—1. Storing up

in

in granaries at the public expence, to be opened in times of scarcity. 2. Storing up by private individuals engaged in the commerce of grain. 3. A degree of waste in consumption and preparation, as the food of man, and the maintenance of inferior animals for luxury, which may be denominated *profuse consumption*. 4. Export to foreign countries; and, 5. The distillery and brewery. In the two first of these ways, superfluous produce is disposed of by *accumulation*, in the three last by *consumption*.

If the grain disposed of in any or all of these ways amount nearly to the utmost deficiency to be expected from an unfavourable season, the security against extreme want is as great as the nature of things will permit. They all serve the double purpose of an indefinite vent and encouragement to increased production in common years; and of a security against scarcity, both by repressing the over-increase of population in common years, and by yielding, in bad seasons, for the food of man, the supplies which were raised for their market.

1. The first of these methods of disposing of surplus produce, the storing up in public granaries, is by far the worst of the whole; and never need be resorted to in any country where impolitic restrictions do not impede the natural operation of the rest. When such a system of public storing is adopted, it can only be carried into effect by means of a tax on the people; and we may be sure that the fund so raised will be expended under the direction of Government, with much less judgment and economy, and the grain purchased will be much worse preserved, and more improperly applied, than if the same end were pursued by individuals engaged in the commerce of grain, under the free protection of the law. Their own interest will direct such men when and how far to purchase and store up, and when and how far to sell, in the manner best for the interest of the community. Accordingly, in most of the civilized nations of the world,

27   the

the duty of storing up has been pretty much relinquished by Government, and left to individual dealers. In the despotic and barbarous nations of the East, however, where agriculture labours under so many oppressions, the practice is still adhered to from necessity. In China, where an unwieldy government, and absurd prejudices among the people, combine to fetter internal industry, and forbid the export of corn, the practice of storing up grain for the public is carried to a considerable length; and, at the same time, we learn its inefficacy to relieve the frequent scarcities which occur in that country. We are told, that when a scarcity occurs, and the emperor's granaries are ordered to be opened, they are often found nearly empty, from the knavery of those having charge of them. Many difficulties are thrown in the way of transporting the grain, and the poor people are allowed to die in such numbers, as to reduce them within the limits of the subsistence which they can procure for themselves.* These evils, though, perhaps, aggravated from the bad government of China, are inherent in all such schemes of preserving a public supply. As already said, such schemes can never be needed where that matter is entirely committed to free individual exertion.

2. It has been the policy of all barbarous governments to discourage large dealers in corn, from the idea that their accumulation of grain might produce artificial scarcity; and this policy, with other prejudices of the same kind, has thrown the task, as already hinted, into much worse hands, that of the governments themselves. I need not mention the follies which have filled our statute-book on this subject, nor the disgraceful prejudices which appeared upon it during the last scarcity; even in those whose public station left no excuse for their igno-

28

rance.

---

* See Barrow's Account of China, and Life of Lord Macartney.

rance. It is only, indeed, because our laws have yielded to the general feeling of public interest, and are not enforced, that we are not all made sensible of their mischief. Were corn-dealers generally to be prevented from purchasing, or forced to sell, at the will of the legislature, or of judges, we should feel by experience the miseries of deficient supply. The interest of the corn-dealer, where he is left free, necessarily, in all respects, coincides with that of the public. It leads him to accumulate when corn is cheap, and thus takes an useless surplus out of the market; and to sell sparingly as scarcity increases, which diminishes consumption, and preserves the supplies from absolute failure before the ensuing crop. Any interference with this operation by the law must, as far as it goes, produce mischief to the public as well as to him.*

3. The vent of a luxurious home consumption in the food of man, and the inferior animals, is probably in all countries the most important resource in seasons of scarcity. It is both the greatest in extent, and has the singular advantage of being less liable to interruption than the rest from the interference of governments. The degree of waste in the preparation of food by the richer orders of society; the maintenance of a number of horses, and other animals, for luxury; as well as the over abundant feeding of those which are necessary; all occasion a vast consumption of corn, and of herbage, from land that may be turned to corn, which in common years disposes of a large surplus, beyond the necessary consumption of man; in so far represses the population in those years; and affords an important supply to be set free for the use of man in times of scarcity. Those well-meaning persons who lament the waste of luxury, and

29

the

---

* See Smith's Wealth of Nations, B. 4. c. 5.

the number of useless animals that consume the food of man in this country, may hence see how ill-founded are their regrets and apprehensions. Were every useless horse sent out of the kingdom, the number of those useful diminished as far as possible, and were all fed in the most frugal manner, the plenty of the people would no doubt be in the mean time increased; but the population quickly augmenting (as well as produce diminishing in various ways, from so absurd a measure,) the people would soon arrive at the same point of relation to the means of support, and their comforts would remain unaltered. All the advantage would be an actual increase of numbers even in common years. But if a scarcity were to occur, the situation of the people would be much worse. There would be no produce raised beyond what was annually consumed by man; any retrenchment from the usual moderate supply would occasion the severest suffering; and deficiency to any considerable amount would create absolute famine. Accordingly, it is in China, where the inferior animals are extremely few in proportion to man, that this dreadful calamity most frequently occurs. In Great Britain, where the number of the inferior animals in proportion to man is unusually large, scarcity has probably been less felt than in any country on the globe.*

30　　　　　　　　　It

---

* The consumption of the aggregate number of horses kept in Great Britain, has been calculated by a very competent judge, Dr. Coventry, Professor of Agriculture in the University of Edinburgh, in an estimate which he has favoured me with, at the produce of *sixteen millions of acres*, which, at the rate of *four* quarters per acre, might yield *sixty-four millions of quarters of grain*. In thus explaining, however, the use of a number of horses, or other inferior animals, I would not be understood to approve of that waste of labour which we often see, especially in England, in the employment of unnecessary horses for carriage or agriculture. These, in regard to labour, are absolutely useless, yielding neither profit nor pleasure;

It may be said, indeed, that the food wasted in luxurious preparation, or consumed by the lower animals, in common years, is a resource in time of scarcity, only on the supposition that the waste is then retrenched, and the consumption of the lower animals diminished or suspended at such a season; whereas, the rich, it may be said, will continue to pamper themselves and their useless horses, though the people should starve. But to this it may be replied, that the interests of the public are fortunately not left to depend on the feelings of moral duty on such occasions, but are enforced by the infallible provisions of nature. The rise of prices, which must happen on a scarcity, will force the rich, in spite of themselves, to retrench their superfluities; and it is in the admitting of this retrenchment that the habitual existence of a superfluity is so useful. The delicacies of the table must be retrenched, the maintenance of all inferior animals must be reduced, and the number of those merely kept for luxury or convenience must be lessened, through all classes of the community, (except, perhaps, among a small number of the most affluent) by the natural pressure of scarcity and high prices, however ill disposed individuals may be to such retrenchments; and the food raised to supply the luxurious consumption, will necessarily be turned to the use of man.*

31 4. The

---

and though the keeping of them we see has some advantage, it is paying too dear for it. We might as well throw the grain they consume into the sea. Besides, if dismissed, they would probably not altogether disappear, but be turned to more useful purposes.

* The above considerations (as already hinted) may relieve the fears of certain well-meaning people, as to the political evils at least (contradistinguished from the moral evils) of excessive luxury. The greater the general luxurious consumption of a country, the better is it secured against the risk of scarcity; nor can it go to a further extreme in this respect, than will be for its own advantage.

Neither can I help taking notice of the amusing inconsistency of

4. The export to foreign countries, when the state of our produce admits of it, affords no doubt a very useful vent. In as far, therefore, as perfect freedom of export goes, this vent ought to be encouraged; but, it is less to be relied on than those which exist within the country. For, in the *first* place, it depends for its continuance on the state of supplies in the foreign importing countries; and should their agricultural produce increase, so as to equal their demands, our market with them must gradually be closed. The plan of persisting to force a market by a bounty on export, has been recommended by very able men;* yet I cannot but think it a vain and frivolous attempt, useless, if our produce be so abundant as naturally to yield a surplus for export, and ineffectual, if it be not. *Secondly*, not only is the vent of export subject to this gradual stoppage, by the natural rise in the prosperity of the foreign countries; but if on a scarcity at home this exported surplus be retained for our own necessities, the importing nations whom we used to supply, on finding that we withdraw this supply occasionally for our own relief, will suffer so much that they will cease to depend on it, and use every exertion to increase their home growth, or seek for their supplies elsewhere. *Thirdly*, a year of plenty may occur, as well as of scarcity. In a year of plenty, the foreign market may not extend to admit of an enlarged export. It may even be interrupted by temporary causes. A glut then returns upon our own market, which discourages cultivation so as to reduce our produce to our own supply. The vent of export, there-

32

fore,

---

certain reasoners, who in one breath lament the luxury and corruption of the times, and the next exclaim against the load of taxes. Now it is very apparent, that the more we are relieved of taxes, the more luxurious, and (as far as it depends on luxury) the more corrupted we shall become.

* Malthus, Essay on Pop. B. 3. c. 7—10.

fore, depends on variable causes, and has not that principle of continuance, nor that power of suiting itself to circumstances, which the modes of home consumption possess.

While, therefore, for the above reasons, I think the vent of export less to be depended on than the other vents which we command at home; and that it is idle to attempt its encouragement by a positive bounty; I still consider it to be a very useful resource, when the state of our home produce, compared with that of other countries, naturally leads to it. It should be encouraged as far as perfect freedom of export goes; and while, on the one hand, I disapprove of its extension by a bounty; on the other hand, I think it should never be impeded, even in seasons of scarcity, but left to suit itself naturally to our home demand. The analogy between this and the other forms of disposing of superfluous produce, is complete. The interest of the corn dealer in exporting, is precisely similar to his interest in accumulating. He never will export when high prices make it his interest, and the interest of the public, that he should accumulate. He regulates the one and the other in the way most beneficial to himself and the public, when left wholly free. It is as inexpedient to impede or controul him in regard to the one, as in regard to the other.

5. The distillery and brewery afford a vent to the home produce, which resembles all the former, and, as far as it goes, is attended with the very same good effects. In average years, it takes out of the market a certain quantity of corn beyond what is necessary for human subsistence, thus encouraging increased produce, and repressing population; and when scarcity occurs, it yields this surplus to be turned to human food. As formerly hinted, too, this disposal of superfluous produce, like the three first mentioned, has an advantage over the vent of foreign export, as affording a market nearer, more certain,

more

more under the eye of the farmer, and less dependent on our relations to other states, or their internal regulation and prosperity. While always ready to give up its consumption naturally when necessity requires, and to yield the produce raised for that consumption to the use of man, it is a market equally ready to revive on the recurrence of plenty, to suit its consumption to the state of produce, and thus equalize the supplies throughout successive years. The operation of distilleries in this way is precisely analogous to that of the corn dealer and exporter, and the prejudices on the one subject exactly resemble those on the other.

The result of the above observations seems to be, that the four latter modes of superfluous consumption (which have a strong analogy to each other) are all eminently useful in common years, as affording an encouragement to land produce, while they somewhat repress the consequent increase of population; and, on the recurrence of scarcity, yield a sure and valuable resource. That while, on the one hand, it is absurd to encourage them for the interest of cultivation by positive bounties; on the other hand, it is wrong to repress them for the public supply, even in the greatest necessity, because they then naturally suit themselves to the public wants in the best possible manner, when left alone.

In applying the above general principles more particularly to the measure of suspending the corn distillery, now in agitation, it is natural to inquire, *First*, Whether there does at present exist any necessity for throwing the grain usually consumed there into the common market, from a scarcity of provisions? *Secondly*, If not, what will be the consequence of doing so prematurely, and before the necessity comes? and, *Thirdly*, Even in the case of actual pressure from scarcity, should such a compulsive measure ever be resorted to?

First, As to the existing state of our home supplies,

that

that there is at present any deficiency of these, the current rate of prices abundantly disproves. The wheat crop reaped last autumn in this country, it is generally allowed, was rather an abundant crop; and indeed this fact, as I take it, is proved in the best of all ways, by the rate of prices just alluded to. We are now nine months from the last harvest, and within three of the next, and the market price of wheat, which is our regulating standard, is as low, or rather lower, than it has been on an average of these several years past; a mere trifle above what it was immediately after the last harvest; and very nearly stationary since the month of November. The price in the London market, on the 16th of the present month of May, was from 50 to 78 shillings the quarter. The price for the preceding month of April, was from 64 to 74 shillings; that for October last, from 54 to 68; that of May last, from 64 to 80; that of May 1806, from 70 to 84; that of May 1805, from 80 to 100. Yet on none of those occasions was there any idea of stopping distillation, though the prices were often a good deal higher than at present. In short, the prices are at this moment lower than they have been, at an average, for some years past, and have not risen materially since last harvest. There is at present rather an abundance than a scarcity in the country.*

It is no doubt true, that oats and barley are comparatively at high prices, but this is obviously nothing to the purpose in view of scarcity; and is besides owing to temporary causes, which cannot be expected to influence another crop. In the view of scarcity, it is not the

35   relative

---

* The abundance of the last crop of wheat, the present moderate state of prices, the small import, and the sufficiency of this country to supply itself, are also stated by Mr. Wakefield, App. to Rep. p. 110. Mr. Claud Scott, p. 116-17. Mr. Kent, p. 121. Mr. Mackenzie, p. 122-3-4.

relative abundance or price of particular kinds of produce; still less of the smaller and less important; but the actual amount of the whole consumable produce in the country, or the standard price of bread-corn, that is the only matter of importance. The abundance of the people depends on the quantity of human subsistence; and it is idle to talk of the people suffering from the want of oats and barley, when wheat is plenty. The distillers have, it is said, in some places, tried to introduce wheat into their manufacture, yet even this has not sensibly affected the price of that article.

But further, the present relative scarcity and high prices of oats and barley, have arisen from temporary causes:—partly from both being comparatively an under crop last season, particularly in Scotland:—partly from the general failure of the pulse crop;—and partly from the sudden demand from the distilleries, which the prospect of the present measure has occasioned. None of these causes can be reckoned upon for another season.*

That there is no call for stopping the distillation from any *present* want of subsistence in the country, is therefore apparent. The people are at present eating bread as cheap as they have done for some years past, indeed rather cheaper; and no ground now exists for such a measure, that has not existed for all that time.

That there may be want in some particular districts at present, I will not deny. This may be a good reason for affording them relief from the abundance of other districts, but is none for a general measure like stopping distillation, when the state of prices shews that there is a general plenty in the country.

36

But,

---

* Notwithstanding these causes, (as to which all the agricultural gentlemen agree,) the price of barley, though certainly high, does not seem to be very extravagant. See Mr. Mackenzie's Evidence. App. to Rep. p. 125.

But, *secondly*, It is said, that although no scarcity now exists, the present or future crops may fail. It may then exist; and we must take precautions against that event.

To this I reply, that the present or future crops have as good a chance of being abundant as deficient. This is a contingency which no man can foresee; and there can be no reason for taking the precaution now, which will not always exist. This system of *perpetual precaution*, therefore, just amounts to a standing prohibition of the distillery of grain.

But in case the calamity of deficient produce should at some future time actually befall us, what will be the effect of this premature precaution? The grain raised for distillation being forced back on the grower, or dealer, and the general prices falling, he will cease to raise the same quantity by the whole amount of what was usually distilled, probably by a good deal more. This quantity will therefore disappear from the market. If it had been displaced by corn, even forcibly encouraged from waste lands, or imported by a bounty, as formerly mentioned, the same, or nearly the same, quantity of subsistence would still have been within the country; and that part of it consumed by the distillery, would still have remained to be set free for human use on the occurrence of scarcity. But, in the present case, the grain displaced, is replaced by sugar, a commodity which, in the utmost necessity, cannot be turned to human support. No resource will therefore remain from the suspension of distillation, when necessity shall call for that measure, if we now adopt it without any necessity.

But, *thirdly*, it may be said, that it is no longer time to betake ourselves to this resource, when the necessity has arrived, for then the corn will have been actually distilled. To this I reply, that there will be abundant time to take the precaution; and, indeed, the remedy will apply itself in the best way, without any such pre-

37   caution.

caution. The grain raised for distillation is not all distilled in one day or week; it is done gradually. As grain becomes scarce, and prices rise, it will be distilled more slowly every day, because the distiller can less afford to purchase it, or, if he has purchased, he will cease to distil it, as spirits fall in price, from the people giving up the consumption of them.* This will happen the sooner, if the importation of sugar be at the same time free. The distiller will thus either leave his stores to the corn-dealer, or become the corn-dealer himself. The evil thus necessarily cures itself, without any public interference. In the same manner, at such seasons the luxurious consumption of individuals will be retrenched; superfluous horses will be underfed, or dismissed; export will cease; the corn-dealer will be enabled to accumulate, as far as his capital will permit; and the more he accumulates, the greater is the public security, that the scarcity will not be increased to famine. No stoppage *can* be put to luxurious consumption, farther than what moral duty and interest enforce. None *should* be put to export or distillation, otherwise a part of the produce is forced on the market, which there is no capital to store up, and retrenchment is prevented from taking place among the people so soon as it ought to do. Corn will never be exported, when a good price can be got at home;—It will never be distilled, when it can be sold higher for food.

38

No

---

* This idea is very justly expressed by Mr. Ferguson, in his evidence before the Committee. " I cannot judge with regard to " the powers of merchants in importing grain ; but it has always " appeared to me, that one of the greatest and best founded securi- " ties against the effects of a famine, is to promote the flourishing of " the distilleries, the consequence of which would be, that when a " famine really occurred, people would give up the use of spirits, " which is not a necessary of life, and leave the grain for food, which " used in favourable years to be applied to the production of spirits." —App. to Rep. p. 158.

No stop *should* be put to the accumulation of the corn-dealer, whose storing up helps to enforce early re-trenchment, and whose stores come forth as scarcity increases, and prevent that extreme of misery which a rash over-consumption would have occasioned. The same rule of perfect freedom equally applies to all these modes of consumption. The arrangements of nature need no assistance from the feeble and presumptuous efforts of man, whose interference only disturbs what it cannot amend. In the system of human improvement, that knowledge, I believe, is as important and as slowly acquired, which informs us what we cannot do, as that which informs us what we can.

It may perhaps be prudent to prohibit export and distillation, when these vents are nearly closing of their own accord, to pacify the excusable prejudices of the people in times of severe scarcity. As to the corn-dealer, no interference with him should ever be attempted. The people may be assured, that any immediate relief received in that way will sooner or later lead to aggravated misery.*

It appears, on the whole, then, that the operation of distilleries is to lead to an augmentation of produce, beyond the amount which they consume; and that they should never be suspended, except in extreme necessity, which does not at present exist, nor is likely to exist, (from deficient home produce,) in this country.

The above doctrines seem to be just, with regard to a

39   country

---

* There is not a more irrational sentiment than one which we often see entertained, of indignation at the profits of farmers and corn-dealers. There is no class of the community in whose hands the accumulation of capital tends so directly to the public good.

country which produces the full supply of its inhabitants. But some persons conceive, that the circumstance of our importing a part of our subsistence from abroad, together with the present strange and gloomy aspect of our foreign relations, alters the application of the above principles, and justifies a departure from them now, which, at other times, might be wrong. This leads me to the second branch of my inquiry, in which I shall endeavour to shew, that our peculiar situation, as an importing country, makes no exception to the principles above laid down, but rather lends them additional weight.

SECT. II.

Of the Operation of Distilleries in a Country which imports a part of its Supplies.

THE operation of distilleries, with respect to importation, may be considered under two views, analogous to those taken in the last section.—I. In regard to average years of importation, that is, where our supplies from abroad are liable to no interruption.—II. In regard to years of interruption to our foreign supplies; which may proceed either from a bad season in the exporting country, or from war.

I. It is not material to the present question, that I should ascertain very accurately the amount of our importation, in proportion to our demand, for some years back. It has never, I believe, been determined with great certainty; and though my own suspicion is, that it is considerably smaller than has been supposed, I feel little concern in the inquiry, even in a general view, because I

think

think it a matter of very trifling moment.* I am disposed to agree with Dr. Smith, that the imported supplies of a large territory never can bear any considerable proportion to its consumption; still less in a country like this, where the agriculture is superior to that of any on the globe. I believe the importation does not now amount, nor is ever likely to amount, nearly to the supply which is carried off by the various modes of superfluous consumption in average years. I believe, therefore, we may regard, without much apprehension, the utmost possible limits to which importation can extend.

There have been very able heads, however, who have entertained different notions. Mr. Malthus, in particular, augurs, from the progressive increase of importation, the gradual decline of our own agriculture, and the final ruin of the country.† And this view, it is to be observed, is distinct from the advantages of an export, and the loss of subsisting by import, in case of a *sudden* deficiency of home produce: For this length I am not unwilling to go; though I think the danger, even here, less than is commonly apprehended. But the above author surely argues with an inconsistency very unusual with him, when he in one page prognosticates the progressive decline of our agriculture, from *the progressive increase of import to a great extent*; and, in the next, founds upon Dr. Smith's assumption, that in an extensive country, importation *never can be carried far*. This is not the time for exposing farther the above fallacy; nor is it indeed, any part of my business so to do: for the greater the amount of our importation;—the more likely it is to extend;—

41   and

---

* The average amount of corn imported into this country, for five years past, is stated in the Report at 770,000 quarters. But from this must be deducted our exports, to ascertain the balance of import.

† Essay on Pop. B. 3. c. 9, 10. 4to edit.

and the more ruinous the consequences to follow from it ;
—the more useful is the vent of distillation, and the more
inexpedient the stoppage of it.

I am fairly entitled to use the argument of the disadvantage of importation against the supporters of the
present measure, as they have enlarged on the danger of
that circumstance, and have, indeed, approved of the
stoppage of the distilleries, as the means of lessening it.
Many great authorities have agreed in the same notions
respecting importation; and although I cannot go their
length on general views, I certainly consider the opposite
state of produce, which yields an export, as more desirable, (when the natural circumstances of a country lead
to it,) chiefly as a resource against the occasional deficiency of home supplies. Assuming, therefore, that it
would be better for us were the balance of our corn trade
with foreign nations turned the other way; or, at least,
that we supplied ourselves; the question comes to be,—Is
the operation of distilleries favourable or unfavourable
towards diminishing importation, and attaining this end?

In the former section I endeavoured to shew, that the
effect of every indefinite vent for home produce was pro-
gressively to increase that produce, and that in a larger
proportion than the vent actually consumed; and, on the
other hand, that the forcible stoppage of any vent, not
merely diminished the produce to the amount thereby
consumed, but much further. The vent of free export,
when a country yields a surplus for that purpose, creates
an additional supply, much larger than the surplus
actually exported: and, on the other hand, when this vent
is shut up (as was done by Colbert) it will probably
diminish produce, not merely to the amount which had
been usually exported, but much further.

Exactly the same principle applies to distilleries, and
that whether the country where they are permitted possess
also a surplus to export, or whether, like this country, it

                                                        need

need imported supplies. The distilleries yield an indefinite vent to home produce, and probably create a much further production than they consume themselves; and, on the other hand, the stoppage of this vent will occasion a greater diminution of produce than they consume themselves. The vent of the distilleries is chiefly for our home produce, and, of course, is an encouragement to our home growers. It is stated in the Report of the Committee, and probably with truth, that little or no imported grain is used there. The more therefore this market is extended, the greater chance will our home growers have of increasing their produce, of gradually forcing the foreign importation out of the market, and finally turning the balance the other way. On the other hand, the stoppage of distillation in so far diminishes the capital of our home growers, lessens their produce to a greater amount than was consumed by that vent, and in so far gives a greater advantage in the competition to the grower of foreign corn.

The same causes, in short, which lead to an increase of home produce in a country which produces its own supplies, or exports a surplus, lead equally to such increase in a country that imports; and tend to diminish importation. The vent of the distillery is one of these causes; tends obviously to diminish importation; and, as far as that is an evil, is therefore more essential in a country where importation prevails, than in one which supplies itself.

Mr. Malthus accordingly, and others who join with him in the apprehension of an increased dependence on foreign supplies, have proposed as the means of preventing this evil, a bounty on the export of corn; thus endeavouring, for the encouragement of the farmer, to *force a vent* for his produce which did not exist of itself. That author must be a little surprised to see persons, professing the same opinion with him, endeavouring to attain the same

end

end by *stopping up a vent* for home produce in the suspension of distilleries. I am far from approving of the first of those measures, because I think it, as commonly applied, *ineffectual* toward either encouraging home produce, or diminishing importation ; and, if raised, so absurdly high as to produce a temporary effect that way, would be *pernicious.* The same objections stated in last section to the attempt of forcing *cultivation*, in the view of increasing produce, apply to the attempt to force *cultivation* or *export*, in the view of diminishing importation. I think the evil of importation is not such as to require any remedy, and, if it did, that the remedy proposed would not cure the evil. But, certainly, on the principles of those who hold the necessity of forcible means to diminish importation, the plan of a bounty on production or export, a direct encouragement to home produce, seems more feasible than the stoppage of the distillery, a direct discouragement to it. I believe the former will not do the good intended, but it will at least not increase the evil feared, which the latter assuredly will.

While on this subject, I cannot help adding one observation. The Legislature, influenced by the fears of a decreasing home produce, lately returned to the measure of granting a bounty on the export of corn, after having formerly virtually taken it away.* I do not inquire whether this was a wise measure or not ; but surely those by whom it was adopted considered it as an encouragement to the British farmer, and that the British farmer stood in need of such encouragement. But if the state of our home produce was such as to require this forcible enlargement of its market, and if it still continues to

44 need

---

* By the Corn Act of 1773. By this act, the bounty price was lowered from 48s. to 44s. the quarter. The same rate was continued by the Corn Act 1791. It was again raised by the late act in 1804.

need it, with what consistency can the same Legislature forcibly close another market to this produce, much more beneficial, I believe, than all the advantage it has reaped from the bounty? Both of these expedients may be wrong, as I believe they are; but it is quite impossible, I should think, that both can be right.

But it is said by some persons, that the corn displaced by the present measure from the distillery, and thrown on the market of general consumption, will not disappear from the country, but will only displace in its turn so much of the imported corn. To this, however, it is an obvious reply, that if our home growers cannot at the present prices compete with the foreign growers, and wholly prevent importation, they will still less be able to do so when prices are further reduced by the stoppage of the distillery. Nobody surely imagines that the small importation which we at present need arises from our having no spare land to produce it ourselves. It is because, in the present circumstances of the country, foreign growers can supply us with that small quantity cheaper than our home growers can supply us: And it is proper the foreign growers should do so, when the circumstances of the country naturally require it. It is clear, therefore, that if importation be no further burdened than at present, the foreign growers will quickly displace our home growers to the whole amount set free from distillation, probably somewhat farther.

Here, however, the advocates of a restrictive policy are at no loss; but, according to their usual mode, proceed to rectify one error by committing another. They have a beautiful scale of gradations regarding home and foreign prices, whereby they relieve nature of her cares for man, and take into their own skilful hands the adaptation of his wants and supplies.* As prices are *forced down* by the

---

* In arranging this scale our landed interest have too much

stoppage of the distillery, the duties on importation are *forced up*, and the discouragement of our home grower is compensated by the equal discouragement of the foreign grower. This plan, therefore, proceeds on the grand principle of the mercantile system, the advancing ourselves, not by a just protection of our own industry, but by repressing that of others. But, like all the feeble and meddling devices of that policy, it will produce the mischief without the good intended. The foreign grower will be injured, but the home grower will not be relieved in the same proportion. The free vent of distillation will not nearly be made up to him by all the rise of duties on the imported corn. He will raise less than he did; less will be imported than before, from the additional duty; the prices on both will rise, and the general supply of the country will be diminished.

But even supposing, what will not happen, that, by the rise of duty on importation, the whole corn set free from the distillery is forced on the common market, and displaces foreign produce to that extent, so that the home grower suffers nothing, and the general amount of subsistence raised in the country remains the same;—what happens in the case of a deficient season? There is no fund fit for human subsistence consumed in the distillery. The article used there is sugar, which cannot on any necessity be turned to such a purpose. In so far, therefore, as that fund goes, the public is deprived of the resource altogether.

The way in which the British farmer will be enabled (if ever) to displace the foreign grower in the home market, and, perhaps, to turn the scale of exportation the other way, is not by giving him the vain encouragement

46

of

interfered, and have set an ill example, which is now turned against themselves.

of a bounty : still less by forcibly closing any of the vents to his produce, even if, to make amends, the foreign grower is also repressed at the expence of the public ;— but by permitting him the free disposal of his produce, protecting him in the exercise of all his rights, removing obstructions in his way, avoiding all further interference in his concerns, and leaving him to the natural competition of the market.

I think it is then pretty clearly made out, that the effect of distilleries, in average years of importation, is to lead to a progressive increase of home produce, and consequently to a progressive diminution of import ; and that their suspension tends directly the other way. But it is said, that although this may be the case when there is no probability of the sudden interruption of supplies, yet, in the present strange and melancholy aspect of public affairs, when we must expect the certain suspension of supplies from abroad, it is advisable to throw the grain usually consumed in distillation, into the common market. This I shall now consider.

II. The sudden failure of supplies from abroad, may be occasioned either by a deficient season there, or by the shutting of their ports against us in war. With regard to both, I think it may be shewn in the *first* place, that there is no such probability of either taking place, at present, as to call for any change in our policy ; and *secondly*, if they should take place, at a future time, that the best way of preventing their bad consequences is to continue, not to suspend, the distillation from grain, as a general system. And even if the deficiency should happen during next season, that the forcible suspension of the distillery is unnecessary.

With regard to a bad season in the exporting countries, it is an accident which we cannot look forward to with certainty, any more than to a bad season at home. The

47 argument

argument formerly applied to the one equally applies to the other. If we are to abolish distillation at present, on such a contingency, we may abolish it always. If the contingency does not happen when expected, we have not only taken a needless step, but have deprived ourselves of the resource which would have relieved us when it did happen. When the pressure is felt it is time to apply the remedy; and even then, the less we interfere the better, as the remedy will apply itself.

The chance of a failure of supplies from the shutting up of the ports of Europe and America, is one which, being chiefly in view at present, will require a somewhat fuller consideration; although the very same principles apply to it as to the failure from a deficient season abroad or at home.

When we look with such apprehension to the failure of foreign supplies, as many persons do at present, it is natural to inquire, in the *first* place, into the probability of that event happening, so as to give us any material distress: and towards determining this point, the experience of the last nine months is peculiarly instructive. The whole ports of the Continent, from which we usually received supplies of grain, have been under the controul of our enemies, as far as such controul can be carried, ever since the last harvest was reaped. As far as the strictest embargo could prevent it, therefore, all supplies to this country have been stopped since that time. America, the only other country from which we receive supplies, has, more lately, adopted the same measure; and, (although I still hope the returning reason of both countries will prevent a rupture so injurious to both), the embargo there has been for some time enforced as strictly as the government could enforce it. Yet, what has been the consequence of all this? The price of bread-corn, as formerly mentioned, is at this moment rather lower than the average of some years past; has continued nearly

stationary

stationary since last harvest ; and we are now within three months of the next without any sensible rise.

The inference which I draw from this is, either that our importation is so small in proportion to our home supplies as to be absolutely insignificant ; or, that the utmost power of governments, stimulated by all the bitterness of human violence and folly, cannot obstruct those great provisions of nature, by which an over produce tends towards the place of demand, and thus equalizes supply, and relieves the mutual wants of mankind. Either of the above alternatives relieves us from any fear of material deficiency from the interruption of foreign supplies.*

As, in the last section, therefore, I concluded that it would be unreasonable to take the precaution of stopping the distilleries on the possibility of a scanty future produce ; so I may now conclude that it would be as unreasonable to take it on the possibility of a failure of imports ; from which, it appears, we have a greater security than we can have in regard to the season.

But in the *second* place, supposing that such deficiency of the usual importation should happen to a considerable amount, is the immediate suspension of distilleries a likely way of guarding us against its effects ? The arguments formerly applied to cases of sudden deficiency from other causes are precisely applicable here.

In as far as the chance of deficiency from abroad is increased by the present interruption, we have the more occasion for superfluous vents to extend our produce at
49 home.

---

* See evidence of Mr. Claude Scott, p. 116-17 ; Mr. Kent, p. 121 ; and Mr. Mackenzie, p. 122-3 4. From this statement it appears that, during the year 1807, we have received from foreign countries, notwithstanding the embargoes, pretty nearly the average supplies, which have reached us for some years past. From Holland 233,000 qrs. and even from France 27,000 qrs. It is probable we shall receive as much next year notwithstanding the restrictions. If we should not, we can do very well without it.

home. The failure of foreign supplies may not be felt the next year, but it may be felt the year after, or some future year. If it be felt the next year, we have gained little, for we might have resorted to the present measure when we saw the proof of the failure in the rise of prices; or rather, we might have permitted the rise of prices to produce the same effect naturally. But if the pressure be delayed till some after year, the resource will be lost, from our farmers having diminished their cultivation, distrusting a market so uncertain as the distillery becomes by such frequent interference.

Indeed, in a general review of this subject of our foreign supplies, I think we shall find it too insignificant materially to influence any branch of our policy. When we consider the proportion which the average importation of late years, of 700,000 quarters of all sorts of grain, bears to our demands, we need have little apprehension of material suffering, were the whole of this supply withdrawn for the next year. It appears that, by the distilleries alone, 470,000 quarters of barley are used in Britain, which is only calculated as *one-sixteenth* of the whole barley crop.* Of course the brewery must consume a vast deal more. A little retrenchment of these two modes of consumption, on the natural rise of prices, would supply the whole deficiency. But when we look to the vast amount of corn consumed by superfluous horses, and the over-abundant feeding of other animals, we must be satisfied, that a very slight diminution in this quarter would, in an addition to the above, much more than over-balance the whole foreign supplies withheld from us. The deficiency, I should think, would scarcely be felt in the

50

price

---

* This. together with the 311,000 qrs. used in the Irish distillery, amounts to 781,000 qrs. which is 81,000 qrs. beyond the average importation of all sorts of grain.

price of bread corn. It might, however, be slightly felt for one season; and this would stimulate the farmer to a production that would probably, in one season more, fully supply our home demand, and even turn the balance of export in our favour. On the other hand, this premature and unnecessary interference will give a shock to the agricultural products, otherwise advancing, and, we may be sure, will expose us to an increased importation at some future time.

But, indeed, I think there is little probability that we shall be exposed even to the above trial. I have no doubt, from what has appeared this year, that we shall receive our usual supply from foreign states next year, and every future year, as long as we want and can pay for it.

The above is no doubt on the supposition that the crop now growing proves equal to the average of the last few years, which may yet not be the case. There is an equal chance, however, that it will prove abundant as that it will fail. Its failure is a contingency which we have no more reason to reckon upon now than at any other time. If that misfortune should come, we must endeavour to palliate it, by retrenchment of every kind, the best way we can (for, as Dr. Smith observes, a real scarcity cannot be remedied, it can only be palliated); and the rise of prices will at once indicate the evil, and enforce the remedy. The difference made by all the foreign supplies which we ever did, or ever can receive, on a serious deficiency, is very trifling. It is known how little proportion the utmost importation of 1800 and 1801 bore to our demands. It is upon our domestic agriculture that we must mainly depend; and to tamper with it by closing its natural vents, and deranging its system, when called for by no visible need, is to stop its progressive increase, and lead to that real calamity which now only exists in the imagination.

Upon the state of produce in Ireland I have said nothing, as I have not the means of ascertaining accurately the prices there for some years back. It is, however, I believe, admitted, that no general scarcity exists there at present, such as to justify the suspension of the distillery. And, indeed, Ireland in this, as in other interests, ought never to be considered separately from Great Britain. If a free commerce of grain between the two countries be established, a partial deficiency there will be relieved by the abundance elsewhere; and should be no more a ground for legislative interference, than a partial deficiency in any district of this island.

It appears, indeed, from the report, that the Committee is in doubt whether to recommend the prohibition of the distillery in Ireland. Their doubts, however, are unconnected with the view of scarcity, and merely proceed on difficulties regarding the revenue. If the suspension be not extended to that country, a new host of restrictive expedients must be embodied, to prevent the passage of corn spirits from thence into this country.

As to the importation of corn needed by our colonies, which, in case of a rupture with America, must be supplied from elsewhere, I have added a state of its amount for the years 1804, 1805, and 1806. But in the first place, I think there is little fear of their being deprived of this supply; and secondly, it is stated by Mr. Blackburn to be his opinion, that Jamaica at least might supply itself.*

The whole argument treated in the two foregoing Sections may then be summed up in the following manner.

In

* App. to Rep. p. 23.

In a course of years of average supply, whether entirely drawn from home produce, or partly imported, the effect of distillation, like that of every other natural and indefinite vent, is to lead to a progressive increase of home produce, followed, in the one case, by the general extension of population and comfort, in the other, by the progressive diminution of import in the first place, and ultimately by the same extension of population and comfort. If the subsisting by importation, then, be considered as an evil, the distillery is still more indispensable in a country where that prevails, than in one which produces its own supplies; because the home cultivation has the more need of encouragement, to enable it to contend with the importation, and at length displace it.

But the benefit of the distillery, and other modes of superfluous consumption, though great in ordinary years, cannot be fully appreciated till the reccurrence of scarcity; whether proceeding from deficient home produce—deficient foreign produce—the interruption of war—or from all these taken together. At such a season, the superfluous produce raised for the consumption of the distilleries, affords a fund of subsistence, which will be set free for human food by the natural rise of prices; or, when the necessity becomes very high, may be set free by Legislative interference. This last, however, should, in general, be delayed till the whole effect had been nearly produced in the natural way. To encroach forcibly on this spare fund at any season of moderate plenty, or easy prices, is to deprive the country of it when the necessity arrives, by the discouragement of cultivation, which will probably be to a much greater amount than in proportion to the produce which the vent itself consumed. There is at present no such deficiency, or likelihood of deficiency, from any cause, as to induce us to risk such discouragement.

I have

I have thus endeavoured to shew, that on general and permanent principles, whether regarding this country as producing its own supplies, or importing a part of them, and whether during moderate years, or in the case of scarcity, the vent of the distillery to our home produce is a great public benefit; and it never can be for the public benefit that this vent should be forcibly interrupted.

We are told, however, that admitting the justice of all the above general principles, the present departure from them is too trifling and temporary, to be considered as an important exception. Admitting that the interest of the public, and of the home grower, will be injured by the stoppage of the distilleries, as far as their consumption goes, this consumption, it is said, is comparatively trifling. The wants of the colonists are urgent, and require immediate relief. The distilleries will afford them such relief; while the want of their vent will be little felt by the farmer. Whatever might be the effect of a permanent suspension, the present expedient will be but temporary; and even during its continuance; a power is proposed to be lodged with the King in Council, to open the distilleries again, in case the price of barley fall too low. This view then gives up the question on general grounds, and, admitting that the public and the British growers both suffer from the suspension of distilleries, only maintains, that they should voluntarily submit to this suffering, for the relief of the distressed colonists.

This leads me to the third branch of the subject, which I proposed to consider.

SECT. III.

How far the present Distresses of the Colonial Proprietors alone, afford a just Ground for the proposed Suspension of the Distillery.

THIS inquiry naturally divides itself into two branches: *First*, Whether the colonists should receive any relief? and, *Secondly*, Whether the relief proposed by the suspension of the distillery of corn be a proper one?

I. In the outset of these remarks, I intimated my opinion that the present distresses of our colonists had arisen from an over extension of the cultivation of sugar, during the temporary unproductiveness of other islands; that now, on the revival of more fertile soils, there is a quantity produced beyond the present demand of the world, and that our colonists never can be effectually relieved, till they reduce their cultivation.* The first

55

question,

---

* Notwithstanding the respectable authority of the Report of the Committee of the House of Commons, 24th July, 1807, to the contrary, I cannot help adhering to this opinion. The chief cause of the colonial distresses assigned there, is the import to the continent from the hostile islands, by neutral vessels. But this would never account for the difficulty, unless there were an over produce; for, during former years of peace, when the intercourse of the continent with its colonies must have been still more free and extensive, the present distresses were not complained of. It is further stated in the present Report, that the existing surplus of sugar from the *old British colonies*, of 1,312,419 cwts., is not equal to the continental demand of the last peace. But it is to be considered, that on a peace *all the other islands* would also find greater facility in sending their produce to the continent, so that, probably, very little of the above surplus would find a vent there. The fact of the rapid increase of colonial produce, is indeed distinctly admitted by Mr. Hibbert, a

question, then, that naturally occurs is, What right the colonists have to public relief of any kind, more than every other unsuccessful speculator, who is ruined by his own imprudence, or by unforeseen accidents? Whether or not it would be for the general advantage that relief were attempted in all such cases, is, I think, a question of little doubt. It would not only be impossible, but if possible would be wrong; as it would be an endeavour to anticipate the great corrective which nature has provided for human improvidence, in the sufferings which follow it. Even in the case of misfortunes produced by no imprudence, the same rule must hold; for it cannot be otherwise. How far the growers of sugar can shew any grounds for making their case an exception from the general rule, and extending that relief to them which cannot be extended to others, it is not my present business to inquire, even if I had the proper time and means of inquiry. Cases may occur, where, from motives of compassion to the sufferers, it may be excusable to extend such relief; but I doubt exceedingly, whether, in an enlarged view, it ever can be for the public advantage to infringe the general rule. I doubt if the public ever will suffer so much from the ruin of a few imprudent individuals, as it will from the cost of relieving them, and from the encouragement which such relief gives to further imprudence.

As already said, however, I do not wish to push general principles too far. Justice may sometimes relax from her rigid equality: And I have not the means of deciding, whether the case of the colonists may not be such as to justify some deviation in their favour. If their difficulties have been in part occasioned by the public measures of the country, their claim is no doubt the stronger.

At

---

member of the present Committee, who was examined. App. p. 166-7. The immense import of slaves, of late years, is also stated by other witnesses.

At the same time, it is not to be forgotten, that the present distresses of the colonists will never be removed by any temporary expedient. If they depend on a general cause, (the over culture of their commodity,) the only effectual remedy rests with themselves. If, by such forced enlargements of their market as this, they be encouraged to persevere in their present growth, the evil will receive but a slight palliation ; and at the end of any given period of suspension of the distillery, the colonists will require the continuance of the same violent expedient, as much as they do now, perhaps more.

We are further told in the Report, of the advantage derived from the colonies to the shipping and revenue. As to the shipping, it has probably partaken a little of the over-trade of its employers, and the allowing it again to find its own level, will do the country no serious injury. As to the revenue paid on sugars, it is equally plain, that if we force that commodity by encouragement, we tax ourselves to enable it to pay this revenue; or, in other words, pay it ourselves in the most expensive form. As already said, however, I am not now opposing the granting of assistance to the colonists as a general measure,

II. But if such assistance is to be granted, it should surely be in a way the least unjust towards any particular class of the community, and the least injurious to the whole. The projected mode of relief, by the suspension of distilleries, is objectionable on both these grounds. It is unjust towards the class of our home cultivators, and inexpedient in regard to the public interest.

It is unjust towards our home cultivators, in laying that burden on them, which, if borne, should be borne by the whole community. It is a positive restriction on their industry, in favour of the colonial industry. Nay, the injustice is not merely in laying the burden on the limited class of cultivators, (though the whole will suffer), but in

laying

laying its immediate weight on a small number of that class, the growers of barley. This hardship is great at any time, inasmuch as it forces into a different mode of culture, those soils which are best fitted for that produce;* and it is peculiarly aggravated in being imposed, without previous warning, at this season of the year, when the barley crop is already sown, or the land so prepared for it, as not to be conveniently turned to any other produce.

But it is said, the whole amount of grain used in distillation is small, and the loss to the British farmer will be trifling. It is further said, that the measure is temporary, and will be attended with no serious inconvenience.

With regard to this loss, I cannot correctly speak. The quantity of barley annually consumed in distillation in Britain is stated, in the Report, at 470,000 quarters, or about 1-16th of the whole. The loss to the farmer, even from an immediate want of sale to the above amount, is not inconsiderable. But it is to be observed that this argument cuts two ways. If the want of this vent be a trifling loss to him, it will be but a trifling advantage to the colonists; and the smaller the burden is, the less difficult will it be for the public to relieve it in some other way. However small it is, it must bear much harder when laid on one limited class of the community, than if equally imposed on all. I can see no reason why such a tax, if necessary, should be wholly borne by our home growers. Unequal taxes, even for the support of the state, are always to be regretted; but they become somewhat more intolerable, when imposed for the relief of a small class of individuals, whose distresses are at least a

presumption

---

* "I consider the cultivation of barley as almost necessary to the existence of Norfolk." Evid. of Mr. Nathaniel Kent, App. p. 118. The impossibility of turning barley land so well to any other culture, is also stated by Mr. Cox and Mr. Henning, p. 149, Mr. Elmar, p. 153, and Mr. Wakefield, p. 109.

presumption of their imprudence. However, this is a point which the British cultivators best know themselves. If they consider the stoppage of the distilleries as no hardship, I am satisfied. If they feel no grievance, they will not complain. If, on the other hand, as I rather suspect, it will be a very serious evil to the cultivators in general, and to the growers of barley in particular, they should, I think, take all legal means to oppose it.* I have endeavoured to shew, that in supporting their rights, and their interests, on the present occasion, they will promote the interests of the public.

But it is not the immediate loss that is the chief evil in the present measure. The future injury to agriculture, from the derangement of the system of cropping, and the want of a sure market, are far more important. Security in his market, is the great stimulus to the farmer's exertion; and if this be infringed, he must abandon his culture, in the prospect of that market, altogether. The mischiefs of a fluctuating policy towards any branch of industry, are perhaps more than can be easily calculated. This is the great objection to the present suspension, as a temporary measure. It is not so much the loss which the farmer will suffer for this one year; as the general loss to cultivation, from his never being sure, when, or for what reason, the measure may be repeated. In this particular view, it is even worse than if the stoppage were permanent; for in that case the farmer would change his system of culture, and endeavour to push a steady market some other way.†

Neither does the palliative of lodging a discretionary power with the King in Council, to permit the distillation

59   of

---

* On this point, the testimony of all the agricultural gentlemen, examined before the Committee, is uniform.

† "It is," says Mr. Wakefield, " the *bane* of a farmer to be " driven out of his natural course." App. to Rep. p. 113.

of grain, at all remedy this fundamental objection. It only introduces the principle of interference and fluctuation into that market still more completely than before.

Indeed, a moment's reflection must convince us that this argument, of the measure being but temporary, is one which must apply always when the same thing is in agitation. No civilized nation, I suppose, ever enacted that the distilling of corn should *always* be illegal. Even France, who has been so justly censured for her weak policy, in regard to the corn trade, did not prohibit export *at all times*. Her error only lay in resorting to that measure too lightly and frequently, and in listening to the vain alarms of future want, upon every trifling rise of prices. It was from this fluctuating system, rather than from permanent discouragement, that her agriculture suffered. But with all her folly, I doubt if she ever resorted to the prohibition of export, when not in force, as we are now called upon to suspend the distillery, at a time of *actual abundance*, and without any certain prospect of future deficiency. I doubt if she ever did so for the mere convenience of her colonial proprietors, without want being either felt or reasonably expected at home.

Within the last *forty* years, it appears, that the distilling of corn has been suspended only twice before this time :*—The suspensions, I am sorry to observe, are both lately. The relief obtained by the public, on those occasions, was probably trifling; but the discouragement to agriculture, from the frequency of the measure, may be both important and permanent. On those occasions, however, there was some apology for it, from the public necessities actually felt, and the market of the distillery naturally declining of itself. At present there is no such

excuse;

---

* From 10th July 1795 to 1st Feb. 1797, and from 8th Dec. 1800 to 1st Jan. 1802. App. to Rep. p. 205.

excuse : and the evils of the fluctuating system are continued and augmented.*

On the whole, when I consider the importance of a flourishing agriculture to the prosperity, and even existence of a state—the dependence of all other branches of industry upon it for their support or extension—its influence on our social happiness, as well as our public strength—the preference which our laws have so often given to less important branches of industry—the many obstructions which naturally or artificially retard its progress—and, I may add, the general character of that class of men who are peculiarly connected with it—when I consider these things, I am disposed to regard our agricultural industry with a sort of superstitious reverence ; to think it should not be lightly tampered with, to serve occasional views ; and to consider any unnecessary encroachment on it as loosening one of the foundations of our strength, which cannot be even slightly displaced, without a shock to the stability of the whole.

But if such superior estimation of agriculture be a prejudice in feeling, I carry it no such length in practice. I desire for agriculture no preference over other branches

61   of

---

* The following observations of Mr. Young, when speaking of the vine culture in France, are equally just and important : " There are " two reasons why vines are so often found in rich plains ; the first " is, the export of wheat being either prohibited or allowed with " such irregularity, that the farmer is never sure of a price ; but the " export of wine and brandy has never been stopped for a moment. " The effect of such a contrast in policy must have been considerable, " and I saw its influence in every part of France, by the new vine- " yards already planted, or begun to be planted, on corn lands, while " the people were starving for want of bread ; of such consequence " in agriculture, is *a steady unvarying policy*. The fact is the more " striking in France, because the vine culture is very much burdened " in taxation, but always possessing a free trade, it thrives." Trav. in France, Vol. I. p. 388.

of industry. It needs no such assistance; it can benefit by no such assistance. All that it requires is that equal protection which an enlightened legislature will extend to every branch of lawful industry; and to which it cannot surely be the least entitled, when the most valuable of the whole.

But so little am I disposed to carry its pretensions too far, and so little influenced in my present argument by any disregard of our colonial industry, that were the present measure designed to give the same exclusive advantage to our home growers over the colonists, as it gives to the colonists over them, I should equally dislike it. For this reason, were the intention only to give a free admission of sugar to the distillery, I should be far from objecting to it;—as far as I should be from objecting to a free export of our home produce to the colonies. Such mutual intercourse would not only be advisable as a present expedient, but as a permanent regulation. Let our colonists have constant free access to the market of distillation, and push it as far as they can.* Our home growers will never suffer materially from this in common years; and when prices rise, the natural competition of the sugar will, without violence, gradually displace the grain, and set it free for human consumption. The more deeply, and in the greater variety of lights, we view this great principle of competition, the more shall we be convinced that it adjusts all things best for the public advantage.

It is on this last ground, indeed, that I feel the chief objection

---

* The difficulties of equalizing the duties cannot, I should think, be insurmountable. If they should, however, I think matters must be allowed to remain as they are; partly because all changes of this kind are attended with some evil; and partly because, when we are driven to a choice between our home agriculture and our colonies, there can be no doubt which must yield. The relief of the colonists may be managed in some other way.

objection to the proposed measure, and am least disposed
to allow the particular reasons alleged as an excuse for it.
However minute in extent, or limited in time, its operation may be, it bears too strongly the marks of a departure from the great law of equal and steady protection,
and too much resembles the sacrifice of general interests
to the spirit of mercantile monopoly. It had better
appear (if it must appear) under any form than this. To
depart from the principles of a general policy on every
trifling occasion, and to substitute for it the petty resource
of temporary and shifting expedients, is a system of legislation the least becoming a great and civilized people. I
think I have sufficiently shewn the manner in which the
present *expedient* would operate unjustly towards a particular class of the community, and injuriously towards all.
But even in cases where this cannot be so clearly discovered,
we may rest assured, that every positive interference to
promote, retard, or direct the industry of individuals, is at
bottom prejudicial, and will be attended in its course with
more evil than can be foreseen at the time. This great
truth has been established in the inestimable work of
Dr. Smith, on grounds so sure, and by an induction so
patient and extensive, that since his time I do not think
one exception has been shewn to it, which can satisfy a
sound and impartial mind. The only exception which he
himself has made, (the approval of a fixed rate of interest
for money,) is one of the few great errors he has committed.* That we should ever see this principle carried

63   to

---

* The three great branches of our policy, wherein we have chiefly
attempted to regulate by positive institution the provisions of nature,
are our system of corn-laws, of poor-laws, and of laws respecting
usury. The consequence is, what might have been expected, in all
of these systems, inconsistent doctrine, ineffectual expedients, and a
constant desire to regulate by compulsive rules, which are silently
undone by the operations of nature. We leave the road which is

to its full extent in practice, I am not so sanguine as to imagine. As he has himself observed, the passions, the ignorance, and, what is worse, the narrow interests of men, unite to oppose it. But it is surely not too much to expect that we should keep the height we have gained. and not, in this enlightened age, fall back into the prejudices of barbarous times, and forge new fetters for ourselves, while we feel the weight of those already entailed upon us.

64

---

short, straight, and open before us, and exert our ingenuity to clear and level the circuitous by path which we have perversely chosen. People wonder, that the regulations daily multiplied in these systems do not render them perfect at last, and cry out for more amendments ; but they are not aware, that the only error is, that there should be a compulsive institution on any of them, in our statute-book.

The only new laws that will ever improve any of these branches of internal policy, will be such as abrogate the old, without putting any thing in their place. But this must be cautiously and gradually done. It is the great loss of artificial systems, that their very evils ensure their continuance.

On this subject, I beg leave to refer to the masterly Treatise on Usury, by Mr. Bentham. I wish that gentleman, in some of the late hints which he has given towards the improvement of our domestic policy, had preserved the same temperate and practical spirit which appears in that performance.

F I N I S.

INDEX.

PRINTED BY HARRISON AND SONS, ST. MARTIN'S LANE, W.C.

CL Press

A Fraser Institute Project

https://clpress.net/

Professor Daniel Klein (George Mason University, Economics and Mercatus Center) and Dr. Erik Matson (Mercatus Center), directors of the Adam Smith Program at George Mason University, are the editors and directors of CL Press. CL stands at once for classical liberal and conservative liberal.

CL Press is a project of the Fraser Institute (Vancouver, Canada).

CL Press includes a series called CL Reprints. CL Reprints was undertaken to make selected older works—no longer under copyright, chiefly—more available.

People:

Dan Klein and Erik Matson are the co-editors and executives of the imprint.

Jane Shaw Stroup is Editorial Advisor, doing especially copy-editing and text preparation.

Zachary Yost is Production Manager for CL Reprints.

An Advisory Board:

Jordan Ballor, *Center for Religion, Culture, and Democracy*

Caroline Breashears, *St. Lawrence Univ.*

Donald Boudreaux, *George Mason Univ.*

Ross Emmett, *Arizona State Univ.*

Knud Haakonssen, *Univ. of St. Andrews*

Björn Hasselgren, *Timbro, Uppsala Univ.*

Karen Horn, *Univ. of Erfurt*

Jimena Hurtado, *Univ. de los Andes*

Nelson Lund, *George Mason Univ.*

Why start CL Press?

CL Press publishes good, low-priced work in intellectual history, political theory, political economy, and moral philosophy. More specifically, CL Press explores and advance discourse in the following areas:

- The intellectual history and meaning of liberalism.
- The relationship between liberalism and conservatism.
- The role of religion in disseminating liberal understandings and institutions including: humankind's ethical universalism, the moral equality of souls, the rule of law, religious liberty, the meaning and virtues of economic life.
- The relationship between religion and economic philosophy.
- The political, social, and economic philosophy of the Scottish Enlightenment, especially Adam Smith.